Islam on the Street

Islam on the Street

Religion in Modern Arabic Literature

Muhsin J. Al-Musawi

ROWMAN & LITTLEFIELD PUBLISHERS, INC.
Lanham • Boulder • New York • Toronto • Plymouth, UK

ROWMAN & LITTLEFIELD PUBLISHERS, INC.

Published in the United States of America
by Rowman & Littlefield Publishers, Inc.
A wholly owned subsidiary of The Rowman & Littlefield Publishing Group, Inc.
4501 Forbes Boulevard, Suite 200, Lanham, Maryland 20706
www.rowmanlittlefield.com

Estover Road
Plymouth PL6 7PY
United Kingdom

British Library Cataloguing in Publication Information Available

Library of Congress Cataloging-in-Publication Data:

Musawi, Muhsin Jasim.
Islam in the street : religion in modern arabic literature / Muhsin Al-Musawi.
p. cm.
Includes bibliographical references and index.
ISBN 978-0-7425-6206-6 (cloth : alk. paper)—ISBN 978-0-7425-6633-0 (electronic)
1. Islam in literature. 2. Religion in literature. 3. Arabic literature—20th century—History and criticism. I. Title.
PJ7519.I84M87 2009
892.7'0938297—dc22

2008055420

Printed in the United States of America

The paper used in this publication meets the minimum requirements of American National Standard for Information Sciences—Permanence of Paper for Printed Library Materials, ANSI/NISO Z39.48-1992.

"We are all involved in an important joint enterprise, namely of bringing an awareness to the riches of the Arabic literary tradition to a much broader public, wherever it may be."—Roger Allen

To Roger Allen: Dear friend and great scholar whose contribution to Arabic literature is inspiring to many.

Contents

Acknowledgments

No book can be written in a coherent and argumentative manner without an actual audience, interlocutors, and at least implied readers. Especially in books of the nature and scope of *Islam on the Street*, with its focus on the religious dynamic in modern Arabic literary production, I had to argue its case with my students at Columbia University, especially the graduate seminar of fall 2008. The application of theoretical works to Arabic narratives proved to be very fruitful and engaged the attention of those highly dynamic students. The historical as well as the socio-political framework and context are given validity only through rigorous analysis from different theoretical perspectives. To Anne-Marie McManus (from Yale), Yasmine Khayyat, Asmi Rehenuma, Valentine Edgar, Zaki Amer Haider (from Univ. of Penn), Omar Khalifah, Elisabeth Nolte, Sara Anne Pekow, Casey Primel, Suzanne Lee Schneider and Ursula Lindsey (NYU) my great appreciation and gratitude for enriching a "differential" space with thoughtful discussions.

In the early stage of manuscript preparation my student assistant, Samantha Reitz was very helpful. A grant to support extra typesetting was kindly offered by the faculty of Arts and Sciences at the American University of Sharjah. I must mention the help of my students, Anne-Marie McManus, Yasmine Khayyat, and my former student Bouthaina Khaldi in proofreading the manuscript. I benefited from my colleagues, Professor Carl Ernst from the University of North Carolina, Professor Peter Heath, Chancellor of the American University of Sharjah, and Professor Roger Allen from the University of Pennsylvania who were the anonymous readers for the press. Their insights and comments made the book more coherently focused on its thesis. Professor Roger Allen offered help and support throughout my engagement with the project. In due recognition of his close friendship and solid scholarship in the field of Arabic literature, I dedicate this book to him. Due thanks are to my friend the great Iraqi painter and designer Ḍ iā al-ʿAzzāwī who was kind enough to provide the cover for this book. I must extend my gratitude to Rowman and Littlefield acquisitions editor Sarah Stanton and production editor Krista Sprecher for their attention and care.

Preface: Islam in Literary Production

The purpose of this monograph is to study Islam as viewed by the public and as it appears in modern Arabic literary production. It also tries to answer the thorny question regarding the traumatic and dramatic change in ideology among leftist intellectuals, especially novelists and poets, who switch to Sufism at a certain stage in their lives. Although theorists have already touched on the affinity between Sufism, existentialism, and Marxism, there is more to be investigated in literary production that problematizes this transformation, leading to a better understanding of this aspect of literature since the 1970s.[1] Such an emphasis on Arabic literary production is not intended to minimize the role of nonliterary writings by Arab and non-Arab writers since the mid-nineteenth century. However it is the contention of this monograph that literary production in the modern period goes beyond the limits of specific disciplines. It is better equipped to provide us with multiple perspectives and concrete situations which are badly needed to answer questions that are continually raised by readers regarding the so-called current resurgence of Islam in the street. Pierre Macherey's quotation from Lenin on Tolstoy is worth citing here, for if "the scholars trust the evidence of the surveys which are often partial and inadequate, which lack a sound theoretical basis, why should we not have faith in those observations gathered over eleven years by a man with a remarkable gift and an absolute sincerity, one who is intimate with his subject"?[2] Moreover, great novelists, Albert Camus contends, are philosophical novelists, not thesis writers, and their works of art are "the outcome of an often expressed philosophy, its illustration and its consummation." To this emphasis on literature he adds that "thought pauses to mimic it [the real]" because it is incapable of "refining" it.[3] Arab writers are more often concerned about ideas regarding their present life and situation. Their emulation of the novelistic tradition in Europe may have falsified some of this experience and marred the prospects of addressing concrete situations, but at a later stage there is much engagement with these realities. Both Arab intellectuals in the West and Arab writers at home have been trying for the last few decades to pose identical questions, usually without providing sufficient answers. Such questions pertain to the entire effort whereby the Arab elite endeavor to emulate Europe.

While it is taken for granted that this interest in Europe has enforced forms of simulation, mimicry, appropriation, and emulation, some Arab intellectuals consider it a faulty effort at base. In a provocative essay, "Islam and Modernization in the Arab World," the late Hisham Sharabi, a professor at Georgetown University, provides a neat reconsideration of the so-called Arab *nahḍah* (awakening) of the nineteenth and twentieth centuries, usually confused with such terms as enlightenment or renaissance.[4] Stipulating that it "did not constitute a renaissance," he further explains: it "was not an intellectual awakening but a *reaction* to the military and political threat of Europe. Even after the European impact had been transformed into a cultural challenge, response to it remained largely defensive and negative."[5] Instead of meeting the actual challenge of European modernization on its own grounds in order to become a driving force for an intelligentsia capable of wielding the meager but growing resources of the society and the emerging nation states, there was then an apologetic or, at best, compromising tone that proved too evasive to monopolize social and political resources to the full. The response sounds pertinent, but it obviously looks at the matter in political terms only, since the secularists among Arab intellectuals were more intent on engaging science, especially Darwinism and its applications to life and civilization. Their incentive obviously derives from the Enlightenment discourse, its emphasis on human reason and empirical evidence, with a concomitant neglect of metaphysics.

There is another sense in which Sharabi is right. The British and French colonial occupation that replaced an oppressive and autocratic Ottoman rule brought more pressure on a situation that was already in need of powerful engagement with social, economic, and cultural problems. More problems were created that diverted the intelligentsia from a purposeful effort aimed at achieving a full-scale mobilization of manpower and resources toward change. Insofar as the role of Islam is concerned, it needs to be emphasized that it cannot be described or labeled as a homogeneous creed. On the social level it includes common beliefs and practices that have a strong and tenacious hold in the street. Islam itself is not one, but its different sects and factions have often been overlooked in order to cater to an Orientalizing vision of a homogeneous entity called Islam. Practices and factions, each with its own gradations and relevant interests, have their political unconscious too, or a cultural underpinning that signifies identity and belonging regardless of the possibility of affiliation with secular-tracked political parties and organizations such as the Marxist and nationalist parties that began to appear, especially from the 1930s onward. For example, apart from the fact that the Qur'ān is the basic text for all Muslims, different sects and factions have had other priorities too, which continue to emerge whenever challenged or attacked. The undebatable presence of the Qur'ān does not preclude different applications or interpretations. On the other hand, its sonorous and rich Arabic language has exerted specific "moulds in which thought and evaluations are cast" (in Sharabi's words), leading to a specific Islamic approach.[6] Although Sharabi does not elaborate on this point, the Qur'ānic-rooted Arabic is not limited to either the Arabic-speaking regions themselves or to Arabic speakers all over the globe. Rather it signifies a status of belonging and affiliation to millions of people outside the Arab region. Both eloquence and message have exerted an enormous hold, one that has also been responsible for the valorization of the role of poetry and belles lettres among Arabs and Muslims. Conversely, poetry and belles lettres show a great deal of deviation from the text, not only in matter but especially in manner. The separation between the Qur'ānic language and belles lettres signifies an analogous separation between Islam and the nation-state, their divergence rather than convergence. The common ground is a standard language, but not the eloquence and message that are usually associated with Qur'ānic rhetoric. This is not an ordinary divergence, because secularism has created a discourse involving a basic Arabic that is divested of religious, metaphorical, or rhetorical aspects associated with the language of the Qur'ān. Secular language, especially in its national guise following the emergence of the nation-state and the subsequent rise of nationalism and its pan-Arabic rhetoric, retains its hold on professionals, educated publics, and middle-class audiences. However, its extension into the countryside has remained doubtful despite the spread of bookstores and the availability of newspapers and media communication concomitant with national revolutions. Through literature, the press, the media, and certainly the educational systems, there has been a consistent codification and formalization of a discourse that is communicative, pragmatic, and usable. Standardized as such through these channels, including schools and teachers, functionaries, grammarians, and editors of school texts, the emerging secular discourse moves far from a religious or classical one, not only in terms of rhetoric and metaphorical devices but primarily through a departure from a basic lexical norm. The so-called prose renaissance, applied to the Egyptian ʿAbdallāh Fikrī (d. 1890) by Muḥammad Mandūr, ʿAbbās M. al-ʿAqqād, and others after the attribute paid to him by Ḥusayn al-Marṣafīì (d. 1890) in his popular lectures on *Al-Wasīlah al-adabiyah*,[7] means two things: a standardization of prose away from classical rhetoric, and an effort to counter the degeneration of prose under the Ottoman neglect of Arabic. To grasp the divergence between two attitudes to prose in the practice of early twentieth-century writers, the reader has to check, for instance, on the debates between the renowned Egyptian scholar and man of letters Ṭāhā Ḥusayn (d. 1973) and his contemporary, the critic Shaykh Muḥammad Ṣādiq al-Rāfiʿī. Dailies, weeklies, and other journalistic forms made it easy for debates to reach this relatively wide reading public all over the Arab world. The press, schools, magazines, journals, and salons have been among the most effective means, however, of consolidating and fostering a discourse that is agnostic and neutral. Most of the material published from the mid-nineteenth century onward has appeared in journals and magazines before being published in book form. The tendency would continue, and by the 1950s onward we have Maḥfūẓ serializing his narratives in the popular daily *Al-Ahrām*, and al-Ghīṭānīì doing the same in magazines and, for *Zaynī Barakāt*, in the weekly *Rūz al-Yūsuf* (1970–1971). These channels are formative means in making and producing promising writers whose veiled autobiographical works or memoirs admit as much. Indeed, Ṭāhā Ḥusayn's autobiography *Al-Ayyām* (*The Stream of Days*), which has become since its early appearance the model and the source for narratives,[8] is no more than a journey from religious discourse, collapsed with traditions and outworn customs or practices, to another that combines in its formation Egyptian modernists, French scholars and philosophers, secular leaders, and well-known Orientalists.[9] Apart from this fact, there is more to it than we think, for it also conveys indebtedness to a genre that has been growing in Europe and Russia, namely the novel of education and autobiography. The author introduced Goethe's *Werther* in 1920, and the "awakening need" was in his mind then to acquaint his fellow litterateurs with a journey of education that demonstrates the prominence of one's individuality, striving, perseverance, and use of reason. A bourgeois drive is already there and a generation of writers would follow suit, though with more indebtedness, in the case of Ibrāhīm al-Māzinī, to the Russian Mikhail Artzybashev's *Sanin*, which, as he mentions in his autobiography, enabled him to be "better equipped for the struggle for life."[10] As Pierre Macherey argues, in the manner of T. S. Eliot and even more in keeping with the classical Arabic theory of plagiarism, "a book never arrives unaccompanied: it is a figure against a background of other formations, depending on them rather than contrasting with them."[11]

Language, with its symbolic power, is closely linked to issues of modernization and indigenous culture. It is especially so in respect to Arabic as the language of the Qur'ān and also as the repository of a rich tradition of poetry, poetics, proverbs, maxims, sciences, heritage of every cultural color, and narrative. The raging debates of the late nineteenth and early twentieth centuries in Egypt and Syria regarding mediums of expression and writing were soon to abate despite the involvement of many well-established writers in them, but these debates focused on expediency on the one hand and confrontation with colonial powers in view of what was taking place in Algeria on the other, but there is little to indicate that debates were elevated to an open discussion of religion and heritage. The question that may come to one's mind, do Arab intellectuals during the nation-state formation period, approximately 1919–1961, actually have anything to say in this respect? Readers are already aware of what learned scholars in Egypt and Syria have said on this matter, but let us instead consider an article written in 1912 by the renowned Iraqi poet Maʿrūf al-Rusāfī (d. 1945), whose popularity among both learned and common publics was remarkable. In the journal *Lisān al-ʿArab* (*The Arabic Language*),[12] he has this to say: "The language of each nation is irrefutably one of its historical glories. Hence: each language of a nation is part of its nationhood." But does this apply to religion? He explains, "For some nations like the Arabs, religion is the greatest factor in its glories; a great deal of its achievements rests on religion. Hence religion is included in its concept of nationhood." He concludes, "He who knows his homeland knows his God."

But, like Sharabi, intellectuals, whether in the Arab world or in the diaspora have searched in vain for an understanding of what Sharabi calls "the relaxing of Islam's grip on the Arab society," something that later in the essay he relates to "an inner collapse and withering away of its position and effective power in social and political life."[13] No actual reasons are offered to explain this "collapse." Was it caused by the dwindling role of the Islamic scholars, *ʿulamā'*, who were "reduced to a small ineffectual body dependent on the toleration of the state and on a meager income from the rapidly dwindling pious foundations?"[14] Isn't this an effect rather than a cause? Was it the result of the secularization of education? Was it due to the rise of nationalism and the alliance between seminationalist revolts (the Ḥijāzī[s] of Arabia for instance) and imperial powers, like the British, against the Ottoman caliphate in World War I? Could it be because this nationalism would soon espouse the cause of socialism in Egypt after 1952, followed by similar revolutions in Syria, Iraq, and Algeria? Were the foundations for this laid in the nineteenth century, due to the reluctance of the dominant clergy to consider the challenge in cultural and economic terms? Did the predilection of the Arab intelligentsia for Western positivism win over the educated segment of the society to the disadvantage of traditional beliefs and practices? Another issue that may pose a challenge to Sharabi's point is whether in fact such a thing as a loss of grip exists? Or have intellectuals fallen into an intentional fallacy that confuses personal visions with realities? No single answer can lead us to a comprehensive understanding of the Arabized European modernity project, its achievements and failures. Within the parameters of the *nahḍah* movement no single answer will ever venture beyond either a clerical dichotomous positioning—involving either an Islamic state and a return to a Qur'ānic-based rule, or else a compromise between traditional practices and European science; or alternatively the various projects of "secular-oriented intellectuals" who were equally incapable of achieving a critical system of analysis through a sincere belief in the masses, that is, people who are either debased by elitism as rabble or elevated by leftist ideology as leading social forces. To the angry and disillusioned masses of 1967 and thereafter, the nation-state as well as the intelligentsia were shown to be disastrously incapable of leadership. Ideological rhetoric collapsed as never before and along with it a system of thought that was once considered rich, although only in promises and tokens of achievement. Throughout the process, contestation occurs in the framework of language. Even reliance on the Qur'ān rises or falls in response to circumstances, though this basic frame of reference is always available as the symbolic system most effective in counteracting contending debates and shaking up positions and attitudes.

In this book I intend to provide readings and analyses of a number of poems and narratives that will take us beyond the interpretations commonly encountered within academe where attendants and disciples tend to conform to their teachers' visions. Narratives in translation are commonly focused on doubt, sarcasm, revisionist readings of the sacred text, and godlessness. Under the impact of European thought and certainly as a consequence of widespread disillusionment at the state of society, a sense of absurdity and nothingness invaded Arabic literature from the 1940s onward; all other preoccupations and obsessions seem no more than expressions of bad faith that prevent or complicate human free choice. Authors became more closely attached to existentialism; while faith sounds in their writings as little more than a hollow premise.

Of great relevance to Islam in the Arab region is the fact that existentialism, as valorized in translated narratives, was popular among Arab philosophical novelists in particular. It was no less in vogue, however, among other Arab writers of the 1950s and 1960s. In a postwar era, when the Palestinian debacle and the dismantling of a nation took place amid Arab disarray and colonial intrigues, absurdity was the most conspicuous sign of life among the elite that was not initiated in hard politics. An overview of existentialism's relevance is worthwhile in this context. Like such predecessors as Nietzsche and Kierkegaard, Camus's view of absurdity is very much a response to the collapse of philosophy and religion in Europe. Only through recognition of the absurdity of the universe and its godlessness can another philosophy of liberation emerge. Giving up hope in a life that is meaningless, the human can achieve a recognition of choice, a release from false and misplaced hopes and values. In *The Myth of Sisyphus* (1942), Camus lays emphasis on literature's ability to depict personal experience in concrete terms. Unlike philosophical reasoning, narrative is not bound by general or universal laws. Jean Paul Sartre urges that narrative and literature are necessary in order to maintain the contention that human freedom and choice can be thwarted by falling into bad faith, into "being-for-others," when the person resorts to self-absolution from responsibility, thus ending up by laying the blame for one's "existence on other people." More than metaphysics, narrative and literary criticism of major writers functions as a significant oppositional philosophy where there is, in Camus's words, "a confrontation of the irrational and the wild longing for clarity."[15] Both Sartre and Camus celebrate "a kind of reason pervaded by creativity and a kind of creativity characterized by critical self-consciousness."[16]

Arab writers were no less engaged in this discussion. The Egyptian writer of fiction Yūsuf Idrīs (d. 1991), in his short story "Lughat al-Ayy Ayy" ("The Language of Pain"), and the Iraqi writer Fu'ād al-Takarlī (d. 2008) in his short stories and his novel *Al-Raj' al-Ba'īd* (*The Long Way Back*), both argue for a choice that is free from social and moral imperatives and obsessions. In this world, religious faith has no place. Choice is first and foremost a secular affair, a perspective that ironically fits in well with Enlightenment discourse.

This emerging Arabic literature is unconcerned with the actual presence of Islam as part of a collective conscience that shows up in times of redress, distress, calamity, siege, war, and occupation. The presence of religion as solace in the face of inexplicable corruption or degeneration, especially in the Algerian novel, and its existence as integral to a collective consciousness, are factors that emerge relatively rarely in the Arab East. The Algerian novel, which became available to the Arab readership especially in the 1950s and 1960s, has many things to offer. Kāteb Yācīne's *Nedjma*, for instance, provides a new style that is in keeping with the French new novel, but significantly integral to Arabic narrative tradition. The anecdotal is mixed with the poetic; and anthems, songs, and slogans are interspersed through a narrative of struggle whose heroes are ordinary Algerians with mixed parenthood, hybrid origins, as befitting a nation under occupation for more than a century. They are like Rachid and his murdered father, the teacher, who has been accused of many things, but the real cause for his expulsion and subsequent murder is his support for the student committee held to constitute the Moslem Congress.[17] The novel distrusts muftis like its Arab East counterparts, but it does this through a specific context where lawyers and muftis are vested with a power that makes them part of a system whose discourse demands their acquiescence and participation. They are part of a bureaucracy that Bourdieu associates with an official discourse,[18] and whom Lefebvre finds necessarily complicit in managing the abstract space of power.[19] They are also Frantz Fanon's intellectual elite whose interests deter them at times from sacrificing these for the sake of their fighting nation. Thus, the lawyer asks the demonstrators to "have confidence in your leaders, we promise you. . . ." He cautions them "to be careful, we cannot fight against tanks." But he and the mufti "brought up the rear" in the end, as the masses moved on thundering, "No *more talk, no more leaders,* old rifles were spitting, *far away the donkeys and mules* were *loyally leading our young army,* there were women at our heels and dogs and children" (p. 75). The novel has another contribution: it does not confine itself to ideological positions or modernity paradigms. There is an Islam that is pure as the Prophet and there are institutions that manipulate it for their own benefit. These institutions are like their own officials who, "in their English gaiters," wear "the suspect uniforms evidently taken from the rejects of too many foreign armies." They remind Rachid in his pilgrimage to Mecca of their parents, "clowns glistening with vanity," and who "had banished the Prophet as they were banishing progress now, along with faith and all the rest, merely in order to choke the desert with their arrogant ignorance." "They" forced him to transplant his dream, to disseminate it wherever there was a "favorable wind" (pp. 157–58). It is only after the June War of 1967, for example, that Arabic literature in both East and West finds itself called upon to connect with the dynamics of the Francophone Algerian novel, a fictional genre that grew in response to occupation and depicted the colonial state as a brutal force, uncivilized and corrupt, whose proclamations of culture and civilization were seriously questioned. Especially after 1967 and with a whole series of narrative journeys to the heart of empires and in the wake of the scandalous exposure of colonial atrocity and heavy-handedness that had been depicted in the Algerian novel, no Arab elite could any longer claim to need any kind of cultural dependency on the colonial power. Indeed the subsequent disillusionment with the concept of the nation-state, its ideological apparatus and its claims and promises, has drawn writers more closely, not only to the postcolonial question as dissected in Fanon's works, but also to a mode of distrust in the nation-state. Its claims of resistance to foreign powers are exposed as no more than a camouflage to bureaucracy, absolutism, repression, and coercion. This does not necessarily bring writers closer to the street.

Until 1967 perhaps, with the total defeat of the nation-state and the bankruptcy of its rhetoric, Arab intellectuals, including those on the left, have relied for the most part on their middle-class familial and educational experience. Their family, office, readings, and acculturation inform their worldview. In the process of encountering the rise of secular thought ever since the *nahḍah* (during the last decades of the nineteenth century and the first half of the twentieth), they rarely speak of religion as a reality that also informs structures and currents of feeling. They consistently speak of it in a pejorative or condescending manner. Religion falls outside their immediate concerns. Its representations in narrative can serve to either debase or elevate it beyond its actual existence in the lives and practices of people.[20] Thus, Tawfīq al-Ḥakīm's protagonist, Muhsin, in *'Uṣfūr min al-Sharq* (*Bird of the East*),[21] is shocked to hear his French friend André speak of the café and church as "public spaces." For him, church and mosque both derive their representational power from an association with heaven. However, al-Ḥakīm's understanding of representational space cannot be taken out of context, and it needs to be noted that in Islam the mosque serves a different function. Traditionally, prayers and other practices are only part of its function. On the other hand, and in the colonial context of al-Ḥakīm's work, there is a deliberate colonial debasement of the mosque. Whenever speaking of this debasement of sacred space, writers usually draw attention to the number of mosques that were defiled, demolished, or destroyed. In the Algerian city of Constantine, for example, there were 106 mosques, but by 1961 the liberation movement could count only eight still in existence. Whenever Muslims were to use the mosque for shows of opposition, the colonial army would resort to brutal measures, including cutting off heads and destroying buildings. Egypt during Napoleon's expedition in 1798 and colonized Algeria can both offer many examples in this regard.[22] The mosque has been the center, core, and icon of the faith, its state and community. *Nahḍah* secular intellectuals showed no awareness of this historical role, since what worried them most was the Ottoman legacy and its burden.

No wonder therefore that writers like Najīb Maḥfūẓ speak of religion in conceptualized paradigms where there is a divide between upholders of faith on one hand and believers in science and material progress on the other. One may conclude that this great novelist believes in religion as a moral force, but he also considers it in opposition to science. Multiple perspectives complement each other, to be sure, but they also betray an unfortunate subscription to a dichotomous pattern that is disconnected from the dynamic forces to be found in Islamic thought. In his novel *al-Qāhirah al-Jadīdah* (1945, English translation *Cairo Modern*, 2008), there are three sets of characters: Ma'mūn

Raḍwān, the believer in the "principles laid down by God;" 'Alī Ṭāhā, the ardent advocate of knowledge and a perfect world whose intellectual itinerary is from Mecca to Moscow, or from faith to socialism and reason; and Maḥjūb ʿAbd al-Dāyim, a skeptic who sees religion as mere mythology. The divide between faith and skepticism, usually mediated through an intermediate character, is pursued in each of Maḥfūẓ's novels of this phase, including the *Trilogy* (1956–1957), before a narrative shift takes place based on the emergence of the nation-state, involving the forceful grip of its ideological state apparatuses and the assimilation of every public domain and proliferation into public life. In other words, and regardless of the application of linear time to depict these character types, the pre-1967 Maḥfūẓ is governed by a number of ideas that are conceived and applied in a manner that fits into *nahḍah* paradigms. The street is relegated to the background. While city life retains its usual attractions for intellectuals, the leaders of change, especially officers, are descended from rural roots. Their dissatisfaction with, and sense of abandonment by, the old regime (before 1952) in Egypt, for instance, makes their pronouncements echo the concerns of villagers, not those of political parties run by landlords and dignitaries. It is rare to find either these officers or villagers in bourgeois narratives by Maḥfūẓ and his generation. However, to quote John Badeau, who served a long term in Cairo as the president of the American University there: "Among the common people of the village and the bazaar there was usually a bitter resentment against the privileged position of the Pasha and Palace, whose lip service to social betterment did little to check either personal extravagance or rising living costs."[23]

The need to study literary production, especially its notable counternarrative since 1967, emanates from a number of cultural facts that constitute an epistemological terrain central to any discussion of Islam as faith. When we speak of the *nahḍah*, for example, there is an underlying premise suggesting that nineteenth-century contact with Europe led to a number of changes, transformations, and, also, problems. While distinguishing offers of modernity from colonial encroachments, Arab intellectuals felt more at ease to speak of cultural achievements as worthy of emulation, duplication, and transposition to the fullest extent. Even literary genres, the novel, the opera, and drama, are copied and transferred in order to satisfy the needs of a rising bourgeoisie. Of more significance and appeal to the emerging classes are translations, appropriations, imitations, and emulations that constitute a large portion of literary production. Significantly, since that time European novels and poetry have become household products that are more familiar than the traditional heritage and folklore.[24] In other words, the narrative structuration of material reality is heavily mediated through these lenses. What becomes a dominant trend in modern

Arabic literature, that is, from the mid-nineteenth century until the mid-1960s, is not only a secular worldview focused on the education of a group or a protagonist, but also a deliberate critique of whatever sounds different. Even when a novelist opts to strike a balance between these seemingly opposed positions, namely modernity and traditional faith, as in the conclusion to Yaḥyā Ḥaqqī's novel *Qindīl Umm Hāshim* (*The Lamp of Umm Hāshim*; English translation *The Saint's Lamp*), there is still an unwarranted conciliatory approach that treats the forged compromise in Ismā'īl's attitude as a faulty choice. Forged dichotomies and contrived compromises betray a strong dependency on European Enlightenment discourse and its subsequent bourgeois representations. Only after the shock attending major events, such as 1948 and 1967,[25] did some intellectuals decide to question this dependency.

However, cultural production since 1967 is not even. Dependency still shapes some practices. But, as a morally responsible agent, the writer has to question a legacy of dependency in order to understand the reasons behind failure. Though disparate and scattered, this literary production, and since 1967 in particular, provides a revisionist reading of the *nahḍah* project. It also draws attention to history and material reality as complex entities that demand engagement, scrutiny, analysis, and sharp critique. Now no sacred or profane borderlines and dichotomies are of paramount importance.

Issues relating to elite consciousness and evolving as master narratives demand their own formative space. Representational space, including opera houses and theaters, assumes another meaning which usually addresses the attitudes of the beholder and narrator. Language itself loses its innocence in this use, for its referentiality resides in sets of metaphors that do not exist on the street of customary practices and uses. The choice of the "street" as a location is not necessarily tied to its significantly lived sites (such as shops and cafés) as loci of action, as spaces of representation in Henri Lefebvre's terms, in spite of their obviously central role as meeting places and points of intersection. Its function, first and foremost, is as a producer of meaning. There, through the exercise of passion, deeds, and life, actions acquire power, and a materialization of concepts takes place. On the other hand, its relevance to an Islamic site resonates with multiple dimensionalities that have always been in keeping with a tradition of criers authorized by the state or other holders of power, including, until very recently, cinema halls and theaters, so as to reach a wider public and hence to claim, in the case of the state, the validity of a law or rule, a lack of knowledge of which does not negate or absolve responsibility. It emerges, as usual, as the symbolic space whereby the state or the sovereign proclaims and exercises power. We should remember, too, that the semantic and linguistic equivalent of a capital or metropolis, as the center where authority primarily resides and proliferates, is *al-ʿāṣimah*, cities like Baghdad, Cairo, Damascus, Beirut, Rabat, Tunis, Tripoli, Algiers, and so on.[26] While not excluding the commercial or social power of competing cities and centers, the Muslim *ʿāṣimah* is the recognized center of authority. It is the center, the abode, and the *ḥāḍirah* (which combines omniscience and civilization or urbanity). Its traditional referentiality emanates from its connectedness to the center of Islamic rule, like Baghdad before 1258. Even when after being weakened in the mid-tenth century, Baghdad continued to enjoy a symbolic role as the capital center. The competing Fatimid Cairo and, later, the Andalusian Cordoba remained peripheral within the context of that symbolic space with its actual or moral and religious obligations. More significant is the fact that the association between capital, as wealth channeled into a capitalist economic order, and space is differently assessed in Arabic historiography and tradition. The root *ʿaṣm* signifies power, control, guidance, and protection. Its Qur'ānic dimension is even more powerful, for it is only God who holds or confers such a power. Hence, the omnipresent Deity is the agent, the doer, the guide, the protector, the preserver, and so on. He is the *ʿāṣim*, and hence the *maʿṣūm*, the infallible. To confer this sacral power on a space implicates the modern nation-state in a deliberate act of power transposition that is derived from the model of European modernity and its predication on a total separation of the state from the church. The emerging homogeneous space is bound to combine its absolutism and differentiality in a dialectic of consensus and opposition which Lefebvre studies in *The Production of Space*.[27]

The term *ʿāṣimah*, capital, is a new coinage derived from a European legacy that has been appreciated and approved by Arab and Muslim travelers from the late eighteenth century onward. It situates itself plausibly and effectively in an emerging sense of nation-state during the fragmentary phase of Ottoman rule. No Muslim authority was strong enough to lay claim to supremacy in the Islamic world. World War I only added a colonial seal to a division of geographical spoils called nation-states under some mandatory imperial control. The nation-state needs a replica of the metropolis as its center. Only through partial duplication can it stand for a new order. Ironically, this replication also demands its own spatial divides, divides that are no longer based on caste or lineage. Apart from hotels, cafés, and clubs with names that echo the metropolis, there are streets and squares that recall history and tradition. The emerging entity is a mixture of Arabism and European legacy. The street as the locus and space for action assumes both historical and modernist connotations. It is space for a symbolic order and also an arena for other players and contenders. Its intersectional nature makes it rife with struggle among a number of contenders. Before defining the term "street," its maturation into an animated presence, an agent with a proper name of some significance or else another denoting a historical shift, we need to understand the street as indicative of all the properties of dialectics and, hence, dynamism. It includes process, gain, motion, stability, and contradiction. Islam in the street is neither unitary nor homogeneous. Depending on the contenders, Islam splits into ideological positions, beliefs, and practices that are embodied in different agents and platforms. The interchangeable transaction between human agency, space, and faith makes the street a narrative of paramount power which otherwise cannot be fully captured in news reports or anthropological surveys.

The duplication of the European metropolis was already being implemented through verbal constructions of sites and scenes, of landscapes that make up material space, as noticed and disseminated by travelers like Shaykh Rifāʿah Rāfiʿ al-Ṭahṭāwī (d. 1873) in 1838.[28] The verbal reconstruction of Paris was to become an incentive not only for more high-class ladies' sightseeing trips but also, and more significantly, for commissioned reports that would prepare the public for a new kind of urban setting. City planners and architects had a share of this enterprise as collaborators in Khedive Ismāʿīl's project to turn Cairo into a piece of Europe. In Baghdad and other centers that came under British rule after World War I, only certain portions of the city, like al-Rashīd's Street, would representationally duplicate some streets in London. The French did more to reshape Constantine and other Algerian cities into duplicates of Paris. Downtown should always duplicate the heart of empires. Emphasis was laid on functional spaces that were to be part of the colonial project, especially in the domain of communication and transportation. Railway stations and post office buildings were ironically designed as replicas of their British or French counterparts. The colonial mind was bent on seeing itself fitting well into a construct that was neither foreign nor alien. Thus, the railway station on the Karkh side of Baghdad was designed after Victoria Station in London, but without the size and grandeur of the latter. The metropolis has its representational monuments in its colonies, in signposts that remind the beholder of the remote but omniscient center, its supremacy and power. No mosque is nearby. It was only at a later stage in Baghdad, for instance, and with the growth of the Iraqi bourgeoisie, that the Bunniyyah family built a huge mosque on the other side of the street that leads to the Iraqi national museum.

The mosque is both an iconic site, one that carries the connotations of a symbolic Islamic power, and a virtual lived space. Its grandeur, however, could make it more of a bureaucratic or governmental enclave with an authority of its own. Important official rituals, memorials, and state-directed sermons can find no better location. On general or common symbolic and functional levels, the mosque holds the Islamic city together. At least in its early construction as the center of new cities, it has a functional role in holding life together. The urban center flows from it and toward it, and hence markets are designed to lead to it. Such are shrines, too, which have the double function of prayer and visitation. While the central mosque of the city may convey also the association with the symbolic power vested and instituted in the sovereign, shrines are more delegated by another consensus which is usually represented by the learned from among the religious society. Shrines as mosques, like Abū Ḥanīfah's in Baghdad, for example, have a different function from the central mosque. Nobody, regardless of rank or status, can manipulate a space that is claimed by a community. On the other side of Baghdad, Karkh, there is the Barāthā mosque, for example, which was established by the fourth Rightly-Guided caliph, the cousin of the prophet, 'Alī Ibn Abī Ṭālib (d. 660 CE).[29] Such a mosque site cannot be manipulated by the state, not only because of its status as a Muslim community property shared by all, but also because it was never taken to represent an official line of thought. Reserved for Shī'īs, it remains beyond the interest of the state, at least before the advent of so-called majority rule in 2005. On the other hand, the Sultan Ḥasan mosque in Cairo can be used by the state, for its name connects it to secular authority and hence divests it of public claims or sharp religious demarcations. Indeed, a study of mosques, old and new, may well indicate the parameters not only of public and official relations to Islam, but also the role of Islam in the fight against occupation and colonial or imperial encroachments.

The street as space fulfills both a real and symbolic function. The actual space, the representational space, where interaction and possible proliferation and dissemination of opinion occur is the marketplace. But, in the Arab-Islamic tradition, the marketplace is part of a symbolic and functional order usually associated with the street: its relative lawlessness, free interaction, transactional nature, gain, theft, exposition of tact, addressing an audience, and so on. The symbolic dimension lies elsewhere. To belong to the street does not resonate well in privileged or learned circles. When the jurist and preacher 'Abdullah Ibn Aḥmad Ibn al-Khashshāb (d. 1172) attended the gatherings around storytellers, he was reproached for leaving his sanctuary and mixing with the so-called rabble. Until very recently it has been considered derogatory to speak of somebody as *Ibn shāri'* (street scum, implying rootlessness or lack of refinement and education, a ruffian). On the other hand, the street, the square, the mosque, and the marketplace are the communal places in an urban center. They were so in tenth-century Islamic cities. In these places many of Badī' al-Zamān al-Hamadhānī's (d. 1008 CE) *Maqāmāt* were enacted as assemblies whereby the narrator tells his readers about his protagonist's foibles, activities, tricks, and achievements.

Space in Islamic cities is not innocent. It possesses an agency of its own whose origins relate in the first instance to its modes of production. By designing a place and giving it a function and a name, the state, the person, or the company have a mission, a goal, an interest, and an ideology. Indeed, whenever it loses its naturalness and gets mapped so as to fit into an ideology and repertoire of knowledge, it becomes a "conceptualized" space (to use Lefebvre's terms).[30] The moment when the street, the building, and the square appear, they have to be in keeping with their name and role; otherwise a gradual slippage takes place that entails a process of counter-naming chosen and used by its virtual manipulators. Whenever a correspondence between name, function, location, and history is retained, there is more loyalty to the place. Nobody has tried to change the name of al-Rashīd Street in Baghdad, for example, or Ṭalʿat Ḥarb Square in Cairo. Even when Baghdad was ravaged as a consequence of an ongoing occupation since 2003, and Muḥsin al-Saʿdūn's (d. 1929) statue was stolen, Saʿdūn Street retains its name. The name of the nationalist prime minister under the British mandate still retains respect for refusing to become a cog in the wheel of empire, even while suffering the blame of his compatriots for not being tough enough. When cities and places like Baghdad suffer under authoritarianism or the ravages of occupation, they are forced, at least for the new generations, to give up and forget locations and names that survive only in books of geography and history.

In such cases as these, history and its annals or recollections provide a reminder of a presence, a reminder that at times resonates in speeches and sermons as if it were still here, speaking and addressing all. Absence has an amazing agency of its own. It is remarkable how Islamic sermons use this absence to re-create not only an accumulating archive of traces, but also a dynamic image of Islam in its ups and downs through ages of turmoil or achievement. An effective preacher can be a scourge to the present. This is what a Cairene preacher in the nineteenth century, for example, has to say in his Friday sermon: "God teacheth by allegory. . . . The happy is the one who maketh amends for the time passed in the time to come; and miserable is he whose days pass away and is careless of his time."[31] Time and place interact, and continuity is sustained in order to convey the sense of meaningfulness and responsibility.

To speak of the street in spatial and symbolic terms implies a need to account for its many protean and permanent functions. Its symbolic role connects it to ideological state apparatuses, for it adopts as space monuments, mosques, stores, shops, cafés, schools, newspaper stalls, vendors, restaurants, police stations, banks, and so on. All these may have a coercive, ideological, and transactional function depending on use and manipulation. All respond to change and affect it. Even so, derogatory interpellation can still endow it with life as a subject nevertheless. To call it so also entails its subjection to the source of interpellation, that is, privileged discourse. Through the interpellation process it turns into a discursive body whose inscriber is no less than the privileged class or group. This derogatory status turns the street into an inventory of bruises and scars. There are bars, taverns, and merchants' shops. There are ruffians, carters, and also bullies. Everybody has God in mind. When referring to God, however, everybody means something different from the rest. Islam on the street speaks in many languages. Even when a God-fearing individual invokes the name of God, he or she means something that can be debated by another, as can be seen in the scene between ʿĀshūr al-Nājī (*the Saved*) in Maḥfūẓ's *Ḥarāfish* (*The Ḥārafish*), for example, and his first wife. He argues that it is God's will that draws him to the barmaid Fullah whom he plans to marry, an explanation that provokes his wife to describe the intention as no more than Satan's snares, not God's will. Interest colors ideological positions and informs them. Whence comes the dynamic presence, not only of invocations, supplications, benedictions, vows, and visitations, but also of group feelings, practices, decrees, speech acts, communiqués, sermons, heralds, rumors, and speeches. Taken together, these establish a discourse of one sort or another which cannot be studied in casual compartmentalized categories such as those that are regularly packaged for media use in a hegemonic discourse. In narrative, these differences, varieties, and variables take form in contestation or uniformity more than any that we meet in reporting or even in historical accounts. Narrative alone can provide enough space for these to be played out in all their variety. Its success depends on this availability where all agents participate in tossing out their products, vying for ascendancy in an arena where space and ideology interchange meaning, and where ideology is made to forego its limits to embrace its interlocutors in narrative.[32]

There are other reasons behind this monograph, however. There is first the need to explain the production of knowledge, not only as concomitant with the rise of humanism in Arabic-Islamic culture between the eighth and fifteenth centuries and the consequent growth of a solid body of prose writing that covers every field of knowledge, but also as an activity in tandem with modernity. Despite the implications of positivity and negativity in the latter, the herald of progress through scientific knowledge and the distrust of state coercive measures and constraints on individual freedom, modernity is avowedly conducive to knowledge and secular knowledge in particular. This secular knowledge is the space for rift, ambivalence, and indecision. As long as there is production, there is always a human agency whose certainty is doubtful and whose speech borders on silence. Its ostensible knowledge remains an incomplete product, leaving, in Macherey's terms, space for criticism, be it an ensemble of signs, annotation, explication, comment, or refutation.[33] In other words, this monograph finds even in texts that are not avowedly Islamist enough material to explain religious popular sentiments, not only as felt and practiced by the common people, but also in their proliferation in rituals, incantations, greetings, refrains, and songs.

The other side of the rationale behind this book lies in a deliberate valorization of literary works as necessarily more expressive or indicative of the real. Current theories of discourse are increasingly receptive to literary texts as significantly capable of conveying the sense of the real as no rational philosophy or metaphysics can ever do. Perhaps we need an explanation of this proposition as it evolves in theory, enforcing a paradigm shift in the social sciences that have recently begun to go beyond early limitations of reasoning or information gathering. A deliberate reliance on texts as carriers of problematic contexts is more conspicuous than ever. Needless to say, non-Western cultures have an older tradition regarding the nature of the real and its ghosts and shadows, but in Western philosophy the dawn of investigation outside the domain of positivist philosophy began with Nietzsche and Kierkegaard to reach a more consistent literary application in the critiques and narratives of Sartre and Camus.

The comparison between classical and modern narratives in Arabic literary production may lead us to significant conclusions, but within the limits of this reading we will be looking at literary production in terms of the quest for knowledge as an Islamic precept and slogan. Earlier travelers traversed the globe in search of experience and knowledge. The modernists have their commitment to study, too, and come back with enough knowledge to make them feel entitled to criticize their own cultures and social life. Previously the Muslim traveler had to start from the center of the universe, the center of power, where he was secure and powerful enough to notice, assess, and conclude. As late as the fourteenth century, such was the dominating feeling among Muslim travelers. Modernists are different. They go with a sense of desperate need for science and learning. The sense of cultural and social dependency overwhelms them. They are burdened by a feeling of limitation and inadequacy. Their writings convey a mixture of certainty and anger, hope and despair, appreciation and distrust. Arabic *Bildungsroman* narratives of the first half of the twentieth century that focus on the journey to Europe are not the usual journeys of old. This is the feeling that stays with the reader after putting down Ṭāḥā Ḥusayn's *Al-Ayyām*[34] (Vols. 1–2, 1929), Yaḥyā Ḥaqqī's *Qindīl Umm Hāshim (The Lamp of Umm Hāshim)*,[35] Tawfīq al-Ḥakīm's *'Uṣfūr min al-Sharq* (1937, *Bird of the East*),[36] Maḥmūd Aḥmad al-Sayyid's

(d. 1937) *Jalāl wa Khālid*,[37] Dhū al-Nūn Ayyūb's *Duktūr Ibrāhīm* (1936, 1938), and Ibrāhīm al-Māzinī's *Ibrāhīm al-Kātib* (*Ibrāhīm the Writer*).[38] Education becomes a process of acculturation. Especially in Egyptian narratives (and despite the relative absence of a clear educational purpose in *Bird of the East*, for example), there is some association between the acquisition of knowledge and an anxiety that keeps protagonists in suspense. As if driven to confront a frightening challenge, their sojourn in Paris, in Great Britain, or inside the sanctuary of European education back home is more focused on changing a mind-set whose ability to take full accountability of circumstance and responsibility is laid at the door of a person, usually a woman, who has to make decisions for them and, often, to push them out of her wished-for company and love. The experience may well betray some awe in the face of a Europe that obviously operates in their subconscious as knowledgeable and capable of either leading them to heaven or banishing them to hell. The *nahḍah* intellectual, the bearer of certain enlightenment, is also the internalizer of a colonial legacy as carefully nurtured and reproduced in literature since Macaulay laid the early foundations for a strong colonial control of the minds and souls of the colonized intelligentsia in India. Accordingly, a total cultural dependency becomes the norm for an assessment of a colonized selfhood. Only through this dependency can such selfhood ensure survival. Tradition is put aside as another source of nuisance and fear. All connotations that relate to family, community, and representational space (shrines for example) are looked upon with distrust. Sharabi is not far off the mark when he discerns such awe and ambiguity regarding knowledge:

> Knowledge (*'ilm*) came to be viewed with a kind of awe, and insistence upon its possession assumed a desperate urgency. For *'ilm* was seen not as the basis of truth and validity (in theological and philosophical contexts), but primarily as the source of power and strength in a concrete political and material sense. Europe came to be respected and feared in terms of its science and industry, the means of its fast power.[39]

This is what narratives before 1967 tell us. Not all narratives deal with this dependency, however, and particularly not after 1967 when writers have tended to become more disposed to taking responsibility.

In this context, it is time, perhaps, to ask another question of some relevance to Islam in a nation-state. Why do we have a number of novels that apart from narrative encounters with Europe focus primarily on a plagued quarter or town? Why do we have a plague in 'Abd al-Ḥakīm Qāsim's *Ayyām al-insān al sab'ah* (1969, *The Seven Days of Man*), and in Najīb Maḥfūẓ's *Malḥamat al-Ḥarāfīsh* (1977, *The Epic of the Ḥarāfīsh*)? We know that Qāsim's novel uses the plague as an occasion to portray the Sufi ʿAbd al-Karīm as being worthy of Sufism, someone who is ready to sacrifice everything, even working as "crow" to carry the sick, clean patients, and be always available to offer support and assistance. He is not the crow of late seventeenth-century Europe, of "little substance" and doing "many vile and abject offices," but a notable in a community that recognizes him as the most benevolent and charitable among them.[40] Even authority recognizes him as such. However, his entire community shows less of what Michel Foucault calls "the utopia of the perfectly governed city" where every person, district, action, and function is tightly registered, supervised, and watched by an anonymous power which, since the Napoleonic combination of monarchical ritual sovereignty and hierarchical exercise of power, has been associated with the state. In Qāsim's novel, the state is still far away from this tight control, whereas communal and religious ties still pertain on more than one level. Fear of contagious diseases does not as yet deprive the community of a certain carnivalistic and also organic wholeness that is more prioritized in a religious ethic and belief than in any procedural state exercise of power. Unless we take Qāsim's novel as a counter-critique, a reminder of beliefs, attitudes, and practices that compose a culture in danger of erosion, we may miss the significance of *Seven Days* as a text of cultural commitment that prepares us to debate and interrogate not only the state, its institutions, practices, and functionaries, including official preachers, but also the ever-present religious institution that shows up and appears in times of comfort and peace to furnish more benefits and privileges. This is the institution that Maḥfūẓ deliberately delineates in the aftermath of the devastating plague in *The Epic of Ḥarāfish*. To sap the virtual power of the protagonist, ʿĀshūr, and the religious fervor attending his anticipation of the plague and ultimate survival as the "Saved" one, the preacher or mufti visits him as the state representative, a herald not of good news but rather of forebodings that communicate to ʿĀshūr his transgression of state laws when residing in a deserted palace after the plague. The state has been absent during the plague, and most residents have perished. Only a few have fled. Now, ʿĀshūr wields a power granted to him by the public as the person endowed with a vision which allows him to see things that the state is too blind and careless to either realize or anticipate. The plague is used to illustrate this separation between the state and the public. Although a terminator of life, the plague ironically functions as a narrative catalyst to valorize a religious faith which mobilizes the masses that are as yet beyond the power of official propaganda and media reports. Only through dying to an old self can a new religion be reborn, innocent and sincere. Religion as popular faith operates in these narratives as never before in modern Arabic fiction. When Ṭāhā Ḥusayn wrote about his homecoming when he was not allowed to disembark in Alexandria in the 1940s because of a plague, his expressed aggravation was a product of frustration: "Is this the state we have exhausted our youth for," he wrote in *Al-Mu'aththabūn fī al-arḍ* (1947, *The Sufferers*).[41] Between this self-portrait as someone who can be responsible for the making of the new order, and the vision and dream that take ʿĀshūr away from the plagued city, there is a difference that can be our spatial metaphor to understand the role of the public and its "Islam in the street." The actor as the outsider in the first instance is unlike the insider, the visionary, and the activist of the second. Plague in the first instance unsettles positions and assumptions, but in the second it brings power back to people who now fill the streets with their clamor. The city in the first example ostracizes, for its absolute space is ruled by manipulators and thugs; but in the second its power lies in its legacy of visions and ultimate harboring of its people who pertain to the natural and historical forces that Lefebvre analyzes so cogently.[42] It is reborn through its newborn inhabitants, evolving as a social space lived and experienced and hence produced by its users before the encroachment of state power and other monopolies.

Notes

1. For a study of this in line with non-Arab scholarship, see Muhsin al-Musawi, *The Postcolonial Arabic Novel* (Leiden: Brill, 2003, 2005), 163–204.

2. Cited in Pierre Macherey, *A Theory of Literary Production*, trans. Geoffrey Wall (London: Routledge, 2006), 131.

3. Albert Camus, *The Myth of Sisyphus* (Hammondsworth: Penguin, 1942), 93.

4. The word *nahḍah* (from the verb *nahaḍa*, meaning to wake up or stand up) is usually used in reference to a movement in thought and consciousness that came in reaction to the Ottomans, but also in recognition of the need to import European achievements in science and secular thought. This usage occurred in the first half of the nineteenth century, in the writings of Rifāʿah R. al-Ṭahṭāwī (d. 1873) and others. Its burgeoning cannot be seen outside the context of the discourse of the European Enlightenment and modernity, and hence its epistemological underpinnings, as a way of connoting a break with the past. Although European Renaissance thinkers were more or less like Goethe in regarding modernity as a posture of opposition to the Middle Ages, there was nevertheless a revisionist reading of the ancient past as solely Greco-Latin, with enough logic and philosophy to consolidate the newfound lineage of modernity. Arabs themselves were no less focused on their comparable golden age of rational philosophy and science.

5. Hisham Sharabi, "Islam and Modernization in the Arab World," in *Modernization of the Arab World*, ed. J. H. Thompson and Robert D. Reischauer (Princeton, NJ: D. Van Nostrand, 1966), 26–36, at 32.

6. Sharabi, "Islam and Modernization in the Arab World," 27.

7. See J. Brugman, *An Introduction to the History of Modern Arabic Literature in Egypt* (Leiden: Brill, 1984), 78–79, 324–25; reference to al-Marṣafī's book (*The Literary Way to Arabic Sciences*, 1872–75).

8. See for example my references to Fu'ād al-Takarlī's protagonist in *Al-Masarrāt* (Gladnesses, 1998) in my book *The Postcolonial Arabic Novel*, p. 180.

9. Serialized in the 1920s; English translation: *An Egyptian Childhood*, 1932. See Ṭāḥā Ḥusayn, *The Days: His Autobiography in Three Parts*, trans. E. H. Paxton, Hilary Wayment, and Kenneth Cragg (Cairo: American University in Cairo Press, 1997).

10. See Brugman, *An Introduction to the History of Modern Arabic Literature in Egypt*, 143.

11. Macherey, *A Theory of Literary Production*, 53.

12. Maʿrūf al-Rusāfī, *Lisān al-ʿArab* (*The Arabic Language*, issued in Istanbul and established by the Iraqi Aḥmad ʿIzzah al-ʿAẓamī, 19 12), 7–9.

13. Sharabi, "Islam and Modernization in the Arab World," 26.

14. Sharabi, "Islam and Modernization in the Arab World," 29.

15. Camus, *The Myth of Sisyphus*, 26.

16. See Mark Currie's summary in "Jean-Paul Sartre, Albert Camus and Existentialism," in *The Continuum Encyclopedia of Modern Criticism and Theory*, ed. Julian Wolfreys et al. (New York: Continuum, 2002), 215.

17. Kāteb Yācīne, *Nedjma*, trans. Richard Howard (Charlottesville: University Press of Virginia, 1991), 208.

18. Pierre Bourdieu, *Language and Symbolic Power*, trans. Gino Raymond and Matthew Adamson (Cambridge, MA: Harvard University Press, 1991) , 57–60.

19. Henri Lefebvre, *The Production of Space*, trans. Donald Nicholson-Smith (Oxford: Basil Blackwell, 1991), 48.

20. In *Production of Space*, Lefebvre describes "representations of space" as pertaining to "conceptualized space, constructed by professionals, technocrats, urbanists, geographers: what is in the head. This is conceived space: ideology/power/knowledge lurks within its representation" (33). In this space there is "bureaucratic and political authoritarianism immanent to a repressive space" (49). This is not the "spaces of representation" or everyday experience space, like the café, the tavern, the post office, and so forth. It is alive; "it speaks. It has an effective kernel or center: Ego, bed, bedroom, dwelling, house; or square, church, graveyard. It embraces the loci of passion, of action and of lived situations, and thus immediately implies time" (42). As for the category of spatial practices, these include lived reality-like routes, networks, and patterns of interaction or manner of acting.

21. Tawfīq al-Ḥakīm, *'Uṣfūr min al-Sharq* (1938, *Bird of the East*, Beirut: Khayyat, 1966).

22. See Bassām ʿAslī, *'Abd al-Hāmid Bin Bādīs* (Beirut: Dār Al-Nafā'is, 1986), 45; see also ʿAbd al-Raḥmān al-Jabartī in S. Moreh, trans., *Al-Jabartī's Chronicle of the First Seven Months of the French Occupation of Egypt* (Leiden: Brill, 1975).

23. John S. Badeau, "A Role in Search of a Hero: A Brief Study of the Egyptian Revolution," *Middle East Journal* 9 (1955), 373–384 (at 374).

24. See Brugman, *An Introduction to the History of Modern Arabic Literature*, 1–14, 94–204, 215–18.

25. The division of Palestine and the establishment of the state of Israel confronted Arab intellectuals with what was referred to as *al-nakbah,* disaster. The idea of the nation-state was questioned and rejected in a number of countries. And 1967 was treated as *al-naksah,* setback or defeat, implying a temporary regression in an otherwise sustained advance. For relevance to literature, see Edward Said, *Reflections on Exile* (Cambridge, MA: Harvard University Press, 2000), 47–49.

26. For more on capitals, see Philip K. Hitti, *Cities of Arab Islam* (Minneapolis: University of Minnesota Press, 1973).

27. Lefebvre, *The Production of Space,* 48–52, 151–52.

28. Rifāʿah Rāfiʿ al-Ṭahṭāwī, *Takhlīṣ al-ibrīz fī talkhīṣ Barīz* (*Imam in Paris: an Account of a Stay in France by an Egyptian Cleric, 1826–31*; London: Al-Saqi, 2004).

29. Barāthā is one of the older sites in the Islamic history of Baghdad. According to common historical sources, it was built 108 years before the foundation of Baghdad in 756. In Assyrian it means "the son of the wonders" and in Arabic "soft and red ground." On his return from the Battle of the River against the Khārijītes, the Fourth Guided Caliph and Imam ʿAlī Ibn Abī Ṭālib saw a priest, Habab, in this monastery and held a discussion with him which the priest soon recognized as confirmation of his prediction that a caliph would pass by there and would also witness the conversion of the priest to Islam. The caliph then asked him to transform the monastery into a mosque. This priest built the mosque and joined ʿAlī in Kūfa where he remained until the latter's martyrdom in 40 A. H.

30. Lefebvre, *The Production of Space,* 33.

31. See Edward W. Lane, *An Account of the Manners and of the Customs of the Egyptians* (Cairo: American University Press in Cairo, 2003), 86–87.

32. Macherey, *A Theory of Literary Production,* draws definite lines between ideology and literary production (see pp. 144–47, 2006 ed.).

33. Machery, *A Theory of Literary Production,* 149.

34. Ṭāḥā Ḥusayn, *Al-Ayyām* (vols. 1–2, 1929; vol. 3, 1973; English translation: *The Days*). Trans. E. H. Paxton, Hilary Wayment, and Kenneth Cragg (Cairo: American University of Cairo Press, 1997).

35. Yaḥyā Ḥaqqī, *The Lamp of Umm Hāshim* (Cairo: American University in Cairo Press, 2004).

36. Tawfīq al-Ḥakīm, *ʿUṣfūr min al-Sharq.*

37. Maḥmūd Aḥmad al-Sayyid, *Jalāl wa Khālid* (1928).

38. Dhū al-Nūn Ayyūb, *Duktūr Ibrāhīm* (1936, 1938).

39. Sharabi, "Islam and Modernization in the Arab World," 34.

40. See Michel Foucault, *Discipline and Punish, A Critical Cultural Reader,* ed. Anthony Easthope and Kate McGowan (Toronto: University of Toronto Press, 2002), 81–89, at 81, 84.

41. Ṭāḥā Ḥusayn, *Al-Muʿaththabūn fī al-arḍ* (1947; English translation: *The Sufferers,* Cairo: American University in Cairo Press, 1993).

42. See Lefebvre, *The Production of Space,* 48–53.

CHAPTER ONE

Roads Not Taken: Arab Modernity and the Loose Ties with the Street

It may sound ironic to start this discussion of Islam in the public sphere with a short story by the superb Egyptian story writer Yūsuf Idrīs (d. 1991). The story, "Lughat al-Ayy Ayy" ("The Language of Pain"),[1] is among his best. The title's reference to language is deliberate, not only because of its conspicuous allusion to sounds, vocalizations, and shouts as languages of their own, languages that communicate, negate, and negotiate, but also because they go beyond the acclaimed and recognized levels of language to recesses that speak of the human search for expression. In other words, the usage is intended to draw attention to those same depths, an intention that serves the purpose of this discussion well before we embark on a critical assessment of language and legitimacy, especially in this reading of Islam on the street, or Islam as practiced by the general public. The story can also serve as a trope for the Arab version of European modernity, its mimicry and cultural dependency, and its discursive effort to comply with a model of the nation-state which has also suffered exposure for its lack of depth and substance. This effete offspring is made up of shreds and tatters for fear of disclosure in case its indigenous origins, now viewed as being lowly and uncouth, are exposed. As long as history contains all the reminders of old times, it becomes a challenge; those very reminders will surely reemerge one day to shatter placidity, complacency, hypocrisy, and sham appearance. In Idrīs's short story, a successful upper-class doctor, Mahmoud Hadidi, "the greatest authority on organic chemistry in the East, the chairman of the Board of Directors of a big organization" (p. 24), is once visited by a group of people from his own original village, Zinin. They are there to request that he treat one of them, Fahmy, who now suffers from an advanced cancer of the bladder that has changed him into a huddled human "bundle," torn by a spasmodic pain that is beyond human endurance. In his own life Hadidi is poised between, on the one hand, a comfortable home and a pleasant social quarter where everybody esteems him for his fame and current social status, and, on the other, a village memory now revived and materialized in this "bundle" that was once a brilliant classmate, one who had been behind the doctor's success, for it "was Fahmy who had been the voice that had echoed in his head for more than thirty years, driving him, filling him with the burning desire to be a success" (p. 24). Keeping him in the kitchen for one night, Hadidi, his wife Effat, and indeed the whole neighborhood are alarmed by Fahmy's piercing, uncontrollable screams of pain. These screams, cries, and noises have no equal in the usual language of pain. They come as a "strange eerie sound . . . sudden as a frantic stab, moaning with the agony of tearing apart" (p. 16). They are a "twisted tortured whistling cry, agonized, wronged, angry, wailing, godless, begging, helpless, hoping, and ascetic" (p. 19). Torn between his sensitivity toward his family feelings and the comfort and peace of the neighborhood, and his sympathy for his old classmate, coupled with an increasing sense of debt to Fahmy, he gradually gives up his social qualms and fears. He lies on the floor, "kissing Fahmy's hands and begging his forgiveness" (p. 45) for not being faithful enough, ending up crying while the sufferer switches positions with him, entreating Hadidi not to cry. The story culminates in the doctor's decision to pay back his debts in full: "Hadidi pushed them [the policemen who were asked by the neighbors to check on the matter] aside and carried Fahmy on his back" (p. 45). The process of gradual reversal from social and economic prerogatives to indigenous life and roots can serve as a trope and trajectory for the untaken road which Arab *nahḍah* (awakening) intellectuals might have taken in order to retain their identity after a long period of mimicry and duplication of Europe's model of modernity. Since the mid-nineteenth century they had been trying to copy Europe, but with few tools and a scanty belief in their own lifestyle and tradition. Even the shaykhs felt the need for this idol, Europe. Their efforts to revive the past, to regain the best of the bygone tradition in the form of new editions of classical texts like the *maqāmāt* (assemblies) of al-Hamadhānī, prepared by Shaykh Muḥammad 'Abdū, for example, remained insignificant in comparison with the longing for a Europe that posed a challenge on more than one level. Idrīs's professional intellectual, Hadidi, undergoes a transformation through pain that operates ironically as a release from bourgeois malaise and its social and professional shackles. In the same story, the connotations of a comfortable home life, a prosperous quarter, and great personal success sound as hollow as any other tokens of a fabricated identity: "He could not wait to leave the neighborhood. The stench had become unbearable" (p. 46). Unlike terms of regression that accompany economic or social failures, this reversal takes place within a context of reassessment, criticism, abandonment of mimicry, and an ultimate recognition of selfhood amid actual signs of human suffering and pain that Hadidi, like the nation-state, has been initially unable to cope with. His prior misgivings whenever visited by villagers are those of bourgeois irritation and repugnance: "No sooner did someone from that village start to shine than a thousand of its people rushed to clutch at him and drag him down with their problems" (p. 21). The scene that brings him to his senses is different. Fahmy reminds him of old days of community, sheer intelligence, and chivalry. For Hadidi each scream has a meaning, since he is well aware that this pain is "powerful enough to crush a creature as big and dull as an elephant" (p. 29). Hadidi is not as yet receptive to a full recognition of moral responsibility, for, like the whole process of revision, such a gesture demands confession and action; hence he "felt a heavy weight pressing down on him and was seized with a sudden desire to burst, and ranting and raving and hurling curses upon himself, his village and people" (p. 30). But Fahmy the villager is a reminder of a debt to be paid; without him Hadidi could not have achieved his current success. This explains why he has named his son after Fahmy. Each scream recalls that lurking sense of indebtedness from the deep recesses of the self: "slowly, gradually, the feeling began to creep over Hadidi that his ties with the bedroom and the wife, and the whole house . . . were becoming weaker" (p. 33). The screams begin to make their way into his soul, awaken it, and remind it of the buried self. Gradually, the cry becomes his, and what the *nahḍah* intellectuals avoid through the veneer of social and professional success is brought home to roost, alive and in waiting, since the scream "was not of the language of life, but rather the language of the depths, the language of pain. It was his, for it gave voice to his own pain. For years and years, he had wanted to stand in the middle of Tahrir Square [the main square in downtown Cairo], gather up his courage, and with all the strength he could muster, let loose this cry, loud, suffering . . . just as Fahmy was doing now" (p. 3). This cry would be taken over by others in the narratives of the next generation. Meanwhile this seminal narrative would soon be operating as the palimpsest for many subsequent narratives, such as *'Imārat Ya'qūbian* (*The Yacoubian Building*) by 'Alā' al-Aswānī. Every intellectual of the previous generation nurses a desire to defy the dominant regime of thought, the nation-state apparatus and the whole sham structure. The cry/scream is an inevitable culmination of repressed agony and pain. Through this scream Hadidi is led to a recollection of how rural life, despite its pain, has a different joy. There is a celebration of life to be found among people who all know each other, a community that deserves to be called such, not a mere amalgam of individuals brought together by profession, position, and social prosperity ("The Language of Pain," p. 37). Indeed, social climbing is meaningless: "getting to the top was worthless, if one got there alone" (p. 42). The act of communal identification and existentialist retention is what has been missing among many members of the Arab elite until, perhaps, 1967 (the massive Israeli attack during the June War and the occupation of still more territories) when the whole system of ideology, thought, and practice under the impact of the European modernist model seemed to collapse. Although many segments of this elite played no actual role in the formation of the political order or the failure in 1967 (usually associated with bureaucracy and political repression), there is nevertheless a complicity through unrestrained faith in a model that had become a given. The dividing moment, the decision to rescue one's own self from a veneer of status and achievement and instead to espouse the recreation of wholeness under pain, has been missed. Any movement of rigorous revisionism has been so lacking as to forestall the purgatorial journey, at least before 1967.

Idrīs's protagonist undergoes an existentialist choice. Unburdened by bad faith, he is in full control of his fate. He is free to act, undeterred by a premise of reputation and status. Although Arab intellectuals also had this choice, especially under the impact of existentialist thought, they were reluctant to make it. If Hadidi stands for the untaken road, the huddled bundle that was at one time a vibrant, chivalrous, and intelligent young man can stand for a nation whose history and culture speak of a great civilization which now suffers occupation and exploitation. The language of pain becomes the scream that should awaken the elite to assume responsibility. Failure to do so means an abandonment of a community, that is left with no alternative but to search for new representatives from among its own people to claim and practice a new ideology, one that combines religion and politics. Fundamentalism may be the most visible factor in the exploitation of this political and religious vacuum, but it does not cope with the whole life of a society whose needs require better accommodation. As Jürgen Habermas argues, "Fundamentalism is the false answer to an epistemological situation which demands insight into the inevitability of religious tolerance and imposes on the faithful the burden of having to endure the secularization of knowledge and the pluralism of world pictures regardless of the religious truths they hold."[2] Islam has been trying to accommodate this plurality in its centers, recognizing throughout the fact that its cultural growth took place whenever this plurality went into play. The growth of the bourgeoisie brought something new which Hadidi tries to cope with, for either he accepts his past, community, and affiliations or loses his inner soul, the poetry that sustains him with self-respect. The choice is not an easy one, but the outcome can be of enormous impact on literary production.

Yūsuf Idrīs's "Language of Pain" indeed serves as a trope as well as providing a trajectory to lead us into a discussion of Arabic literary production since 1967. "The Language of Pain" may not show any specific signs of Islam in the street, but its focus on "language" as the catalyst and locus for recognition, self-retention, and harmony against a value system that is upheld as the only viable road to salvation is important.

The "language of pain" is the translator's term for an agonized painful scream that erupts every now and then, uncontrollable and beyond human endurance. It may summon no symbolic power of its own, but its actual correspondence with Hadidi's sense of betrayal, indebtedness, and unfaithfulness to his buried self establishes a new rapport between the two, the sender and the receiver. It is therefore capable, we assume, of forging another link with the reader. It is a language nevertheless that disturbs, annoys, and shocks. It is a language that evokes fear and perhaps sympathy. Language operates and functions as a power of transformation in terms of social conditions. The short story may also have alerted us to a better mode of assessment for the resurgence of Islamism in the street, which also erupts in reaction to failure and pain. The Islamist reclamation of tradition, no matter how faulty it sounds, and its partial monopoly of the Qur'ānic expression in a new political discourse of religious overtones sounds very similar to the scream that awakens Hadidi and forces this retrieval of buried selfhood.

In a succinct analysis of the symbolic power of language, Pierre Bourdieu argues, "Religion and politics achieve their most successful ideological effects by exploiting the possibilities contained in the polysemy inherent in the social ubiquity of the legitimate language."[3] The language of pain is not legitimate, since it manages to annoy and disturb the house and the neighborhood, the realms of normalization and codification where formal language operates to sustain a new social and political order. The scream is deviant, relentless, and alien. It questions every other legitimacy and directs attention to what has been absent in the formal language: its emptiness of Islamic rhetoric and alternative reliance on contemporary Europeanized terms may sound normal nowadays. The formal Arabic language developed in tandem with modernity, but its fractured nature has something to do with early encroachments of colonialism and the subsequent student missions to Europe, along with the return to the region of those intellectuals who were to be in charge of education in the Arab world. Almost every scholar of renown participates in this language, and the differences among them relate to the degree of matter-of-factness.[4]

The nation-state, its early burgeoning in Egypt and Morocco in the nineteenth century, was deliberately engaged in a normalization process through a national language that should be as codified and formal as befits the state itself. This formal language does not appear only in state proceedings, the press, and official gatherings, but also and foremost in education and literature. Hence literary production has a significance of its own, especially as a substantial part of it consists of no more than veiled or ostensible autobiography.

For a number of reasons the issue of language is central to this discussion of Islam in the street. The elite, consisting of preachers, teachers, journalists, doctors, and professional intellectuals, has a vested interest in an official language, promoted and nurtured as the legitimate language of an emerging class. It is not the classical language, to be sure, but it has all the aspirations of a vibrant inheritor. The more effective the process of promotion to the level of a state national language is, the better it is for this class, which will gain the "de facto monopoly of politics."[5] The legitimacy accorded to this language through the state and the participation of these groups is a legitimacy of secular discourse, free from the sacral markers of the Qur'ānic language. While not entirely separate from the latter as the definitive yardstick, the official language is more adaptable to a situation that suits the nation-state based on the European model. Arabic phrases and expressions from this model were so many that a number of "scientific" societies were officially founded to fit these, through a schema of equivalence, into the Arabic lexicon.[6] The official practice, which has been continually open to the European model, is necessarily free from any perceptible Islamic register. Its discernible focus is communicative and is rarely interwoven with Islamic idioms and markers. Until the late 1970s the elite was so co-opted that its language displayed little similarity to, for instance, clerical discourse. Even *nahḍah 'ulamā'* (the learned clerics) tried to strike a balance between the sacral and the secular so as to ensure communication with their intellectual counterparts. Their attendance at ladies' salons, meetings with secular intellectuals, and use of the press, including the French, indicates an urgent sense of the need on their part to counter a European monopoly in the secular sphere. Their language is no longer a clerical one, rich with sacral connotations, proselytized and embellished. In the speeches and writings of Shaykh Jamāl al-Dīn al-Afghānī and his disciples, it flows with ease and shows a readiness to engage with an opposing and often hostile discourse. They realize that the encroachment of the European model is serious enough to require a confrontation on its own grounds.[7] Pierre Bourdieu explains the significance of gain and loss in this transactional activity: "the symbolic efficacy of religious language is threatened when the set of mechanisms capable of ensuring the reproduction of the relationship of recognition, which is the basis of its authority, ceases to function."[8] Certainly this association between the official language as the only legitimate one in a "unified linguistic market"[9] and the state applies in the same measure to the early Islamic practice of using the language of the prophet's tribe, Quraysh, as the distinguished "clear and eloquent Arabic tongue," to quote the text of the Qur'ān. Every other dialect or linguistic variant had to blend itself to the official language of the Islamic *'ummah* (community). The Qur'ān itself appropriated words and expressions from other cultures, but it sets itself apart as being supremely elevated in its clarity and distinguishable from every other dialect usually dubbed as being foreign.

Dialects gave way to the language of the Quraysh; in so doing, they agreed to be supplanted, but not necessarily obliterated and abolished from local use among the peasantry. The promotion of the Qurayshi language to a status as the "official" Arab-Islamic mode of discourse could not have happened without both the power of the language itself, the eloquence of its advocates, and the newly invested power of religion. Later it was to witness a sustained process of normalization and codification to prevent any relapse into dialects under the pressures of urban expansion and intercultural exchange. But no matter how we regard this process of normalization, we have to remember that basically the Qur'ān is the yardstick for linguistic assessment, before and after. Next to it in importance comes pre-Islamic poetry. Belles lettres also play an enormous role in this process, and yet even in times of political disintegration there is always a countereffort to prove subscription to the classical norm of Qur'ānic speech.

But before comparing further the official language of the nation-state with the reclaimed religious discourse, let us consider some issues of immediate relevance. What has been missing in scholarly discussions of the reason behind this breakup is twofold: they tend to be limited to Egyptian literature, understandably because of the centrality of Egypt in the colonial system, its actual hosting of Arab intellectuals since the fall of Baghdad in 1258, and especially during Muḥammad Alī's dynasty reign, 1805–1849 and 1849–1852, its emergence as the center of an intellectual and cultural "awakening," its relative political stability—something that has been conducive to a systematic growth of wide readership, genres, literary currents, names and celebrities, the availability of texts for Arabists and Orientalists, and its accessibility to an Arab readership. That said, however, the neglect of other Arab regions, including those under colonial control, has led to an obvious incompleteness in the assessment of wider attitudes, cultural exchanges, and also the rise of social and political powers in the anticolonial struggle. Moreover, the role of the Arabic language has tended to be marginalized in studies that have subsequently emerged, influenced by a concentrated Orientalist educational effort that had a great influence on Egyptian cultural life. Ever since the establishment of Cairo University, it has witnessed the emergence of this kind of Orientalist scholarship, which Ṭāhā Ḥusayn recollects with great appreciation in his *Al-Ayyām* (*Days*) autobiography. The magazine *Al-Risālah* (1933–1953), established and edited by a powerful littérateur, Aḥmad Ḥasan al-Zayyāt (d. 1968), published series of articles by these eminent Orientalists, including Sir Hamilton Gibb and Carlo Alfonso Nallino (d. 1938). However, the Orientalist coterie should not be held responsible for this neglect, since Arab intellectuals took it for granted that studies of Arab literature should follow the example already set by great minds. Overwhelmed by an enormous corpus, they found it useful to adopt the periodization approach to literary history, that being the great achievement of Carl Brocklemann, as a means of assembling the rich legacy of Arabic culture. Gibb established the pattern for neat surveys of ancient and modern trends, divided into gold and silver ages, and so on, and Schacht, Nallino, and the rest followed suit in studying *turāth* (heritage) in ways that had been popular in Europe. Every production harkens back to the European model, in state formation as well as in writing. In this process the Arabic language and the study of discourse in terms of power relations were relegated to the background. After all, the age is one of transition, in Ṭāhā Ḥusayn's words (in his introduction to al-Zayyāt's translation of Goethe's *Werther*, 1920), "an age bored with the old, searching for the new."[10] Indeed, whenever referred to, tradition is mentioned as a problem for the elite, a group that is more versed in foreign languages. Pierre Cacchia draws on Aḥmad Amīn (1878–1954), who tried to speculate on "why the same people discussing a problem in English put forward rigorous and concise arguments and counter-arguments, whereas if speaking Arabic they lost sight of the point at issue, strayed into verbosity and came to a conclusion of sorts only out of weariness."[11] The issue can be shrugged off as another sign of cultural dependency. Others may relate it to the discussion initiated under the colonial rule about the use of colloquial dialects, which found strong advocates in intellectuals such as Salāma Mūsā (d. 1947).

But this is not enough, in that the issue relates to the topic of this monograph: Islam on the street. Apart from the educated elite and emerging generations of readers throughout the Arab world, were the *nahḍah* intellectuals able to reach the common people? Could Ṭāhā Ḥusayn and Aḥmad Ḥasan al-Zayyāt in Egypt, or Maḥmūd Aḥmad al-Sayyid and Dhū al-Nūn Ayyūb in Iraq, or even Gibrān Khalīl Gibrān and later Tawfīq Yūsuf ʿAwwād in Lebanon, and Zakī al-Arsūzī in Syria, have ever considered how to reach such people? Important as the discussion is of standard and popular levels of the

Arabic language, there is always a need to study them in the contexts of use, social condition, class, occasion, disposition, sex, position, and ethnicity. Islam is inseparable from Arabic, especially in the Arabic-speaking region. The argument here is far from the separation of the elite from the rest. No. Have we thought of intellectuals as actual speakers, meaning public intellectuals with a sense of commitment to public platforms as equivalent to the Islamic pulpit? How and why did poets like Hāfiz Ibrāhim, Aḥmad Shawqī, Muḥammad Riḍā al-Shabībī (d. 1965), Muḥammad Mahdī al-Jawāhirī (d. 1997), and others in the neoclassical mode reach a wider public? The question targets the reasons behind something which is usually overlooked whenever we take for granted the viability of modernity in poetry and poetics. If we rephrase the question and ask why Ibrāhim ʿAbd al-Qādir al-Māzinī (d. 1949), for example, could not reach such a wide audience in his own time, we discover that he was one of a trio of poets (the others being ʿAbd al-Raḥmān Shukrī and ʿAbbās Maḥmūd al-ʿAqqād) who opposed the neoclassicists on the grounds that their style was far from the common man; very visible in the press, he wrote his autobiographical novel, *Ibrāhim al-Kātib* (*Ibrahim the Writer*, 1976), in conspicuous self-recognition and as being worthy of public attention.[12] And yet his invectives against the neoclassical poet Ḥāfiẓ Ibrāhīm, which he collected in book form, did not sell well, something that he himself admitted in a gesture of self-reproach and criticism.[13]

The colonial referent is of relevance because it leads us to the official language of the emerging nation-state. According to Pierre Bourdieu's neat premise, it is the goal of the upper class to gain monopoly through the dominating effect of an official language. In the case of Arabic, that is the one used by Shaykh Rifāʿah R. al-Ṭahṭāwī (d. 1873) as an official Egyptian emissary to Paris who was to become director of the Institute of Foreign Languages while remaining a religious shaykh who was already part of a system. In John B. Thompson's summary of Bourdieu, "the school [educational system] came to be seen as a principal means of access to the labor market."[14] The purpose is to promote "the official language to the status of the national language."[15] Whenever this promotion is seen as a process whereby a "unified labor market,"[16] with a systematic production of textbooks and dictionaries, takes hold, we can understand how significant was the role of the *nahḍah* intellectuals in a normalization process that inculcated an official language, one that was used, under pan-Arab agreements, all over the Arab world, reaching even postindependence Algeria where a pan-Arab effort came to the support of the national government in undertaking the enormous task of replacing French as the language of official use. This application answers one side of the question. The other pertains to the relation between the elite and the common people. Let us try to imagine Ṭāhā Ḥusayn, Zakī al-Arsūzī, or Dhū al-Nūn Ayyūb, addressing the common public, and then compare them to the Iraqi poet Muḥammad al-Jawāhirī reciting a poem, even though we may need to grant that some of his audience would not have grasped the full meaning of his words.

The same applies to such figures as Muṣṭafā Kāmil (d. 1908) in Egypt and Muḥammad Mahdī al-Baṣīr (1895–1974) in Iraq. The former was an eloquent speaker and orator who played a leading role in the preparation for the 1919 revolution against the British. The second was a renowned blind poet and scholar and one of the leaders of the 1920 popular revolution in Iraq. Both were capable of delivering effective speeches that reached large audiences. Their "institution"[17] was the cultural context of a rising bourgeoisie that had a vested interest in independence. Were they as effective in the long run (meaning the subsequent history of the state) as, let us say, Shaykh ʿAbd al-Ḥamīd Ibn Bādīs in Algeria (d. 1940), a figure who has remained beyond criticism as the epitome of religious sincerity and Arab-Islamic commitment in the fight for the liberation of Algeria? His power emanated from the Algerian context of identity: Islam and Arabism. He was the actual speaker per se who was spontaneously in control of the sacred discourse, peppering his speeches with expressions and quotes that managed to align listeners with a cause in which they had been brought up and which itself assumed an institutionalized form, empowering and accumulating through sets of social and cultural relations that were larger than any school system, family, factory, office, or party.

The difference lies in competence, but not in the sense that a chemical process limits it to the generation of sentences in grammatical sequence. In Bourdieu's terms, this competence is a "practical" one, intended to "produce utterances that are appropriate in the circumstances."[18] The "actual speakers are able to embed sentences or expressions in practical strategies which have numerous functions and which are tacitly adjusted to the relations of power between speakers and hearers."[19] The *nahḍah* intellectual, being significantly dominated by a Westernized mode of thinking, may have relished the privilege of being effectively embedded in state formation, its educational and media systems, and so on, but it is difficult to assume that each had the "capacity to make oneself heard, believed, obeyed," like Bourdieu's actual speakers or Austin's participants in acts of ritual.[20] The notion of Bourdieu's actual speakers applies well to potential and socially committed preachers, social advocates, and countryside notables whose reputation as speakers derives from their social institution "as any relatively durable set of social relations which endows individuals with power, status and resources of various kinds."[21] Indeed, some Arab elites enjoyed that privilege, like the Khūrīs and al-Bistānīs in Lebanon and Syria, al-Aḥmads in Syria, Aḥmad Luṭfī al-Sayyid in Egypt, and the Shabībīs in Iraq. They were known for their eloquence and knowledge of the cultural heritage, and yet they were less influential in nonelite communities. Unlike them was the poet Muḥammad Mahdī al-Jawāhirī (d. 1997), whose powerful impact rested on a rich rhetorical tradition that is appropriated within a current discourse against colonialism and its puppet regimes.

Political parties have their speakers. They will frequently court actual speakers to coalesce with their politics and henceforth become their speakers. Such processes function and can indeed be influential, and yet they are unable to answer the problematic and thorny questions with respect to the *nahḍah* elite and the subsequent debacle of the nation-state. Some narratives have addressed such issues, but criticism is often sidetracked to the obvious side of chronological and dramatic sequentiality, and the surface meaning of the protagonist's career. Let us take the example of the protagonist Ismāʿīl in the Egyptian Yaḥyā Ḥaqqī's *Qindīl Umm Hāshim* (English translation: *The Lamp of Umm Hāshim*). His childhood experience is rarely mentioned in critical writings, and, if it is, it is seen as no more than a prelude to his undistinguished secondary school career and a preparation for his father's plan to send him to London to study medicine. There he is involved in a love affair with Mary, a woman who is no more than a symbolic metropolis, able to offer comfort and affection to its future advocates. As soon as the protagonist is back on his feet and ready to return to his homeland, change Egyptian practices, and bring "light" to the "land of the blind" (as British people describe Egypt), she leaves him and chooses another lover. In Egypt, he tries to put what he has learned into practice, but finds that it runs up against the beliefs of his family and society, beliefs embedded even in their responses to medicine. Later in the narrative Ismāʿīl is forced to relent and accept the views of his society, a change usually summarized by critics as a fall into Egyptianness, a relapse into an Oriental primitivism which is "ironically viewed as a success; he is liked and respected and is successful in treating his abundance of patients."[22] The context of his success involves no more than his turning into a "womanizer" and "slovenly" individual with an "overlarge family."[23] Trevor Le Gassick is right in picking on the glaring conclusion to the narrative. Where does the author stand? What is he trying to show? Is the narrative representative of a traumatic contact with Europe at the turn of the century? The suggestion that follows makes use of Bourdieu's habitus as "a set of *dispositions* which incline agents to act and react in certain ways."[24] In his former paraphrase of Bourdieu, Thompson adds, "Dispositions are acquired through a gradual process of *inclination* in which early childhood experiences are particularly important,"[25] as they are inculcated, practiced, and turned into a second transposable nature.[26] If these ideas are applied to Ḥaqqī's protagonist, then a reversion to such dispositions of early childhood should not be surprising. Accumulated experience may add to a repository, but cannot dislodge it. Even when applying these principles to Dhū al-Nūn Ayyūb's protagonist, Doctor Ibrāhīm, in his novel *Duktūr Ibrāhīm* (1939; *Ibrāhīm the Doctor*), we find a childhood experience of distrust, suspicion, and social climbing that has left its imprint on a long career of opportunism and total cultural dependency on the British. He is meant to represent another segment of the Iraqi national elite of the 1930s whose education in England is mixed with a grossly malign disposition. Ṭāhā Ḥusayn's childhood, as portrayed in *Al-Ayyām*, disposes him not only to seek a replacement for a mother who is neither affectionate nor cautious, a brother who is unhelpful and inconsiderate, and an institution that is no less cruel or unsympathetic. Against these negative features there grows throughout the narrative a counterappreciation of French women, culture, and knowledge. Paris displaces Cairo as the celestial city. But are such protagonists capable of turning into actual speakers outside the limited domain of the elite? Although religion constitutes a culture for the leading elite, we need to remember that, on many occasions, learning religion was usually limited to recitations from the Qur'ān and the application of some rituals. Maḥfūẓ speaks of Islam as follows: "I was introduced to religion in the form of rituals (*shakliyyāt*); I need to hear things that you might call myths, until I finally chose the true essence of religion," which is no more than social justice and good conduct.[27] The confession, as represented in these interviews, can apply to *nahḍah* intellectuals whose knowledge of religion is scanty in comparison to their initiation in and reading of Western cultures. The outcome is evident in narratives that demonstrate an ordinary lexical knowledge, a casual Arabic register, and meager grasp of tradition. The Iraqis relegated religion to attitudes, conversations, and practices that, at best, depict tradition as a burden, cumbersome, and limiting. Until the late 1960s, Egyptians were more inclined to present religion in a symbolic space where the Prophet's granddaughter, Sayyidah Zainab, and the Prophet's grandson, al-Ḥusayn, are the focus of mixed attention and response albeit under a rubric of reverence. Al-Ḥakīm, Maḥfūẓ, Ḥaqqī, and Ṭāhā Ḥusayn were attuned to such an attitude. If we return to our question, we may again ask whether protagonists and, for that matter, the authors themselves could ever be actual speakers to a community? Can this meager and highly selective knowledge of one's culture lead to more than a rising petite bourgeois narrative of aspiration that is tied to a past but unable as yet to envision a future? If we accept Bourdieu's formulation of the body as the repository and inventory of whatever is ingrained in childhood, can we speak of *nahḍah* intellectuals as tied to this site, the body as the "incorporated history" whereby further processes of production or reproduction demand education? As noted earlier, for Bourdieu there exists a dialectic relation between dispositions and the habitus of institutions. These can be the fields or markets of action where economic, cultural, and symbolic (such as prestige) capital operates in terms that defy status. What is of significance here lies in the application of marketability, transaction, and profit or surplus to the entire cultural field which we consider here as basically discursive. Can we limit ourselves to a casual reading of change in styles or visions as a matter of fashion? Is it fetishism when a narrative becomes a commodity in a marketplace? Do we have novelists, dramatists, and poets whose symbolic capital has something to do with their emerging status? Are we speaking of outsiders to a private and highly secluded enclave who have made their way and fortune through writing? Was their writing only a rite of passage in order to assimilate into the bourgeois strata of society? None of them has gained renown on the basis of such symbolic capital. It is their cultural capital that participates in an ongoing transaction, one that is understandably losing ground nowadays. Their cultural products are no longer as powerful and popular as religious tracts of a very poor cultural content, such as the Saudi Shaykh Dr. 'Ā'iḍ in al-Qarnī's *Lā taḥzan* (*Don't Be Sad*). Dozens of works such as these rely on Qur'ānic verses or traditions of the Prophet to provide comfort to a young generation that is no longer receptive to Salāma Mūsā, for example—whose books were widely accessible all over the Arab world until the 1960s, or to his disciples, including Maḥfūẓ. In other words, the capital that dominated the market for a long period, being both lucrative and effective among the rising educated classes until the 1960s, is now rapidly losing ground. Competition has taken a new and different direction, and the traumas of individual childhood experience and, by extension, those of the elite, have receded into the background of a cultural scene which involves a complex mixture of individualism, identity, and national crisis. The new generation can and does wholeheartedly engage with any religious practice in order to fulfill a psychological and moral need, or to continue searching, while casting doubt on the past as a whole, especially its immediate predecessors and ancestors. Thus, the Saudi woman writer, Ṣabā al-Ḥirz (pseudonym), writes in her narrative *Al-ʿĀkharūn* (2006; *The Others*):

> I have never lasted even once on an Egyptian cultural production. In my childhood, I didn't watch the evening TV film series, nor the playful riddles of Nilly and Sharīhān, nor Būjī and Ṭamṭam. I was never infatuated by the handsome ʿOmar al-Sharīf, or drawn to the dream-like romanticism of ʿAbd al-Ḥalīm Ḥāfiẓ's songs. I was not spoiled by "The School of Troublemakers," or "The Kids are Growing Up." I have no clue about the famous Fīshāwī Café, or the Ḥilmiyah district. I never read Yūsuf al-Subā'ī, Yūsuf Idrīs, Najīb Maḥfūẓ, or Tawfīq al-

> Ḥakīm. Until later, I never heard about Arab nationalism, Sādāt, Nāṣir, Haykal, Sayyid Quṭb, the Muslim Brothers, the Arab Unity Project, or the Camp David Accords.[28]

Regardless of the veracity of this account, the denial is not merely a disclaimer, but rather a deliberate countererosion of a legacy of acculturation and intertextuality, whereby authors used to demonstrate to readers the extent of their readings and cultural engagements, especially in the journey narratives that make up a substantial portion of the *nahḍah* literature. The denial speaks also of a market that turns its back on an Egyptian legacy of secular writing, film production, the cinema industry, writers' meeting sites, and the once dominating issue of Arabism and Islamism. The quote also displays certain knowledge of that legacy, names of writers and sites of their meetings, comedies, and politics that were once so popular. The above quotation is addressed to a newly emerging generation of readers, readers who are totally unlike those of the Iraqi writer Kāẓim Makkī in his *Ṣafwān al-Adīb* (1939; *Ṣafwān the Litterateur*), for example, where the protagonist lists a number of Egyptian and international writers and thinkers who have played an important role in the formation of his mind. Until very recently, education all over the Arab world had certain elements in common. Run by educators like Ṣāṭi' al-Ḥuṣrī in Iraq until the 1940s and in Egypt by the enlightened minds of the early 1920s, state education spread though the Arab region in the form of common interests, curriculum, and instructors. After liberation in 1962, Algeria requested help in education, and the system soon found a strong base there where it struck roots and echoed the call of Shaykh Bin Bādīs and other national leaders. No Algerian or intellectual from the Arab West can ever deny this shared legacy. We need to investigate narratives in order to discern how strong this link is. As late as 1985, the Algerian novelist Aḥlām Mustaghānamī (b. 1953) writes in her *Dhākirat al-jasad* (*Memory of the Flesh*) of this strong bond that makes the protagonist unable to accept an opportunist postliberation state that turns its back on a legacy fought for with blood and costly sacrifice.

Every state in the Arab world made its start on the basis of a plan intended to create and normalize education in a way far removed from traditional *kuttāb* schools or *madrasas*. Indeed, such narratives as the celebrated Egyptian writer and thinker Ṭāhā Ḥusayn's (d. 1973) *Al-Ayyām* (3 vols: *An Egyptian Childhood*, *The Stream of Days*, and *A Passage to France*) detail this journey as one of departure from home rather than homecoming. It is an escape from traditional education toward another that is secular, passing on the way through Orientalist training at Cairo University before reaching the metropolitan center in Paris. The language of the author as well as the method of his argument, the frame of doubt and skepticism in respect to cherished traditions, and the desire to give up local and national identity and replace it with a geographical one spread over the Mediterranean—all these are basic to an educational effort spurred by normalization and codification that is able to impose uniformity on a national language and culture. Both the Iraqi Maḥmūd Aḥmad al-Sayyid in his semiautobiographical *Jalāl wa Khālid* (1928) and the protagonist of *Ṣafwān al-Adīb* (1939; *Ṣafwān the Litterateur*) by another Iraqi, Kāẓim Makkī, survey a similar journey from religiosity and traditional learning to a headlong engagement with secular ideology and thought.[29] It is perhaps worthwhile to look at some extracts from these narratives in order to understand both the gradual disavowal of tradition and its language and its replacement by a national one that may well sound standard enough, but with all the implications of a European jargon that at the time is new to Arabic. Concerning the disavowal of religion, there is the usual confusion in *Ṣafwān al-Adīb*, for example, between the misuse of religion and its message. The narrator asks the protagonist: "I remember you as one of the faithful who celebrate religion and perform its rituals, so how does it happen that skepticism invades your soul and uproots your faith?" The answer is devoid of any clerical or sacral reference: "I thought religion was the path of mercy, charity and justice, and I still believe so. I regarded clerics as messengers of benevolence, goodness and reform. When I came of age and started using my reason, I saw religion, alas, in the hands of such people as no more than a tool for evil, treachery and division. I saw those who claim to be its upholders as no more than exploiters of people who manipulate ignorance for the sake of their own interests."[30] But how does he change so radically? The protagonist mentions how various factors, his reading of Herbert Spencer, the latter's emphasis on the negation of anything that cannot be verified by the senses, and his acquaintance with the opinions of Lamarck and Darwin that emphasize the common origin of the human species all led him to change his attitude.[31] Ṣafwān is the precursor for Kamāl ʿAbd al-Jawād in the second volume of Maḥfūẓ's *Trilogy*, *Qaṣr al-Shawq* (*Palace of Desire*), whose studies "lead him to Darwinism, which he adopts with enthusiasm and advocates in published articles."[32] In the Egyptian context in particular, Arab intellectuals were gradually drawn to this understanding as inevitable in order to relinquish the Ottoman legacy and set themselves on an equal footing with Europe. Ṭāḥā Ḥusayn's autobiography represents a subdued effort to describe a trajectory taken and followed by most Arab intellectuals.

Like Salāma Mūsā, Ismāʿīl Maẓhar, Shiblī Shimayyil, Yaʿqūb Ṣarrūf, and Aḥmad Luṭfī al-Sayyid, Ḥusayn's approach needs to be placed within the framework of a dominating discourse among Arab intellectuals east of the

Mediterranean. These Egyptian voices that transported the legacy of European thought undoubtedly influenced education all over the Arab world, especially as many of them, including Ḥusayn, held important positions that were behind the implementation of an educational policy with deliberate secular curricula.[33] Again it is worth noting that even schoolmasters and instructors came under the impact of this group, especially Ṭāhā Ḥusayn's method and frame of thought, at an early stage in the first half of the twentieth century. The same Iraqi author of *Ṣafwān al-Adīb*, Kāẓim Makkī, has his protagonist explain how reading Ṭāhā Ḥusayn's *Fī al-adab al-jāhilī* (sic; 1926; *On Pre-Islamic Poetry*) led to a change in his approach to the traditional heritage, especially pre-Islamic literature: "I used to study pre-Islamic literature and find it difficult to understand, but I was accustomed to spending the night learning its prose and poetry by heart. I used to prefer it to anything else for its authenticity and excellence. Perhaps you can still remember the way I used to learn the pre-Islamic odes by heart." He continues, "But when I read Ṭāhā Ḥusayn—whom I used to venerate and admire and always aspire to emulate, I was struck by skepticism. I soon began to have doubts about this literature, and indeed to question its belonging to the poets who were supposed to be its authors."[34] Ṭāhā Ḥusayn's book provoked one of the fiercest literary controversies, but it was popular enough not only to become a major text in university curricula but also to promote a revived interest in classical texts, their annotation, and criticism. Writings in this vein generated enough publicity to ensure a powerful impact on younger generations. Since those days media, bookstore, press, and school have provided such competition for the pulpit that they have established a hegemonic national discourse that is basically secular.

These educational policies were no less focused on language, but the Arab educators' approach was different from that of the French colonial power, for example. The latter emphasized the need to limit the study of the Qur'ān to learning it by heart, not explicating it; to exclude the history of the Arabs to the extent possible; to avoid the study of Arabic literature and its associated disciplines; and last to avoid teaching the sciences.[35] Arab intellectuals are to be more interested in literature, history, and science, but to care less for the Qur'ān and its sciences. Arabic literature, however, is approached differently. Emphasis on historical periodization continues until the present day, but there is more interdisciplinarity that allows literature to be read within the context of other social-economic and political disciplines. Language itself is divested of Qur'ānic reference so as to fit into a functional national discourse that has been used and promoted by the state since its early burgeoning during the French occupation of Egypt, a process that has its own particular symbolic and utilitarian initiation in Muḥammad ʿAlī's request to have Jeremy Bentham as tutor for his son, ʿAbbās.[36]

In anticipating this process, but with a curious mind that was sensitive to difference and the hypocrisy of colonial discourse, the chronicler of the French occupation of Egypt (1798–1801), ʿAbd al-Raḥmān al-Jabartī (1754–1825/6), uses his *Tārīkh muddat al-Faransīs bī-Miṣr* (*The History of the Period of the French in Egypt*) to develop a narrative that is no less mixed than the ensuing *nahḍah* discourse. As a chronicler, he has to provide facts, but whenever the occasion warrants a comment, he comes up with a perspective that demonstrates an epistemological problem: should the chronicler speak on the basis of his own religious tenets? Shouldn't he apply national criteria against foreign occupation? Does he engage in a difficult choice, between the encroachment of the decaying Ottoman rule and the new invaders? Shmuel Moreh (otherwise known as Sāmī Murād) notes in the introduction to his translation: "Although he condemns cultural elements which are discordant with his own culture, he admires others, such as French justice, order, their great interest in learning and the sciences, their discipline and devotion to the cause of their nation, and their efficiency in getting things done. However, his first spontaneous description of the French arrival reveals his sensitivity to any behaviors which conflict with Islamic tenets and customs."[37]

The chronicler's analysis, stylistic corrections of the proclamation's written text, and sharp critique of the implications of its evasive language all display this mixed response despite the conspicuous tendency to see through its linguistic inversions that raise doubts regarding French intentions. More than once he comes to the conclusion that the French "have gone against the Christians . . . those people are opposed to both Christians and Muslims, and do not hold fast to any religion" (al-Jabartī, p. 47). Although the chronicler's style does not achieve the standards expected of good prose, he is sharp enough to detect deliberate or random problems in grammar and syntax that confuse and blur meanings. In other words, the language of the proclamation has the advantage of being composed in Arabic, a sign of condescension on the part of the empowered to win over the hearts of the populace through framing occupation in an Islamic discourse. However, its ungrammatical lapses undermine what Bourdieu calls "the social conditions of acceptability."[38] Al-Jabartī's inclusion of Napoleon's proclamation as the urtext of European colonialism in the Arab world is significant. Inclusion and appended critique serve our purpose well by tracing the forthcoming coalescence of both in a *nahḍah* discourse, usually described as the awakening discourse, which is so called for its association with the European model of modernity and its desire to court a possible retention of a glorious past. The inclusion of the proclamation signifies recognition; it confers legitimacy on a text that stands for French encroachment. Thereafter it has become a model for British, French, and American invasions of Arab lands. The pivotal purpose in such proclamations is to thwart resistance and ensure domination with minimum loss. Every bluffing strategy is habitually used, but without detracting in any way from an imperial arrogance which automatically comes with power and the availability of means of violence. A basic premise in this proclamation is to claim a respect for national cultures, but the very emphasis betrays a strategy of camouflage and deceit. Al-Jabartī shows how little the colonial power knows about Islam. As depicted in al-Jabartī's monograph, he and his shaykhs and dignitaries are able to demonstrate certain knowledge, but it is too meager to resist a conquest that manipulates isolated shards of Arabic and Islamic culture in order to win over or at least neutralize the street. The author tries to demonstrate the only power he can wield, that of language and theology, to refute and correct the French text in exegetical matters. His effort cannot match the proclamation's deliberate reliance on quotations from the Qur'ān and Ḥadith (the Prophet's sayings) that are used to support and consolidate its manipulation of the religious sphere. Like any defensive response, al-Jabartī leans on the French text throughout his analysis.

Al-Jabartī explores some expressions, explaining their obscurities and inexactitudes, all the while cursing the scribe and the French authority as the actual author. His reading and commentary are important, not only because they attempt to uncover the hidden message that lies in words and phrases and between lines, but also because they signify an attempt to question a colonial discourse that uses Arabic and appropriate Islamic terms in order to valorize a French position of conquest and mastery dressed up in the garb of the French Revolution and its banner of freedom, justice, and equality. This encounter with colonial discourse in 1798, over two centuries after the Ottoman conquest (1517), has Arabism and Islamism as its markers, and al-Jabartī is well aware that the French are desperate to isolate the Mamluk rulers of Egypt, expose their oppression, and highlight their backward administrative mechanisms.

The language of the proclamation is as faulty as the occasionally clumsy nonclassical style of Shaykh al-Jabartī himself. But thereafter a more functional language began to develop, to be used by professionals, administrators, jurists, and their like in order to meet the demands and responsibilities associated with the postexpedition regime of Muḥammad 'Alī as the new ruler of Egypt (1805–1849). This newly evolving prose deserves to be studied in detail, because it would soon become predominant as a result of the proliferation of the press and the imposition of an educational system. While unable to completely replace and dislodge the highly embellished style of neoclassical poetry, the ornate Mamluk epistolary school, and the Qur'ānic imprint on writing, it nevertheless became central to a journalistic style, *lughat al-Ṣiḥāfah*, which also became the official language of the state. To apply Bourdieu's significant insights once more, the struggle was "for symbolic power in which what was at stake was the formation and re-formation of mental structures." He adds, "it was not only a question of communicating but of gaining recognition for a new language of authority, with its new political vocabulary, its terms of address and reference, its metaphors, its euphemisms and the representation of the social world which it conveys."[39]

Both the journalist and the schoolmaster participate in this effort, not only to supplant competing dialects or languages, but primarily to normalize a language and through it to "build the consciousness of the nation"[40] toward a consensus which is central to Emile Durkheim's theory that was made available to Arab audiences, not only through Ṭāhā Ḥusayn's educational journey in *Al-Ayyām* and its popularity among national educators, but also through translations and authored works by the *nahḍah* intellectuals. While the battle in the Arab world was not focused on an encounter with the Qur'ānic language or regional dialects, the outcome was the same. The average Arab should have enjoyed the benefits of this language through a state-run education, free and available in cities first before expanding into rural areas. There would also grow a split between this codified and normalized language and an Islamist one that, in times of depression or disappointment, could provide a resort of rectitude and comfort.

The enormity of the symbolic power exercised through language to effect dispositions cannot be exaggerated. Intellectuals of a religious rural background often felt, with great discomfort, this encroaching symbolic power, the one held by the intelligentsia as subscribers to and participants in an official discourse. The Iraqi Shaykh Muḥammad Ḥasan al-Ṣaghīr, who was lecturing at the Iraqi Mustanṣiriyyah University, told me in 1987 that he started wearing a fashionable European suit instead of his traditional turban and robe because he began to hear students referring to him as Khomeinī, an appellation that could endanger his life during the war with Iran. The Egyptian shaykh and popular litterateur Muḥammad Ṣādiq al-Rāfi'ī (d. 1933) began to attend Mayy Ziyādah's (d. 1943) salon and once switched to wearing European dress.[41] In dozens of cases this act of switching dress indicates a tacit recognition of the obsolescence of what Bourdieu describes in a different context as "the earlier mode of production of the habitus and its products."[42] The religious and conservative segments of society felt dispossessed of their ownership, their language and identity, in a nation-state that had already crafted its symbols of modernity along Western lines. As its rulers, educators, and reporters compete in demonstrating their European modernity, especially against the religious institution and its traditional symbols and signs, clerics find themselves challenged in the arena of their symbolic power with its significations and icons.

This sense of dispossession is displayed in many ways, but markedly so in the orientation and subsequent accelerated growth of the nation-state, first under mandate but then through acquisition of partial, then full, independence. The intelligentsia, as narrated in fictional or autobiographical encounters with Europe, felt assured of its linguistic capital and its capacity to make it not only saleable but also lucrative in the educational and administrative fields. Almost every autobiography or narrative of education constructs a protagonist's intellectual supremacy and leadership against or in competition with other forces whereby one's primary means and potential are derived from an apprenticeship in a European institution. Whether we speak of Salāma Mūsā, Ṭāḥā Ḥusayn, Tawfiq al-Ḥakīm (d. 1987), Muḥammad Ḥusayn Haykal (d. 1956), or Maḥmūd Aḥmad al-Sayyid (d. 1963) and the protagonists of Dhū al-Nūn Ayyūb (d. 1988), their accounts of the 1920s and 1930s are narrative encounters whose achievement lies in their subscription to either a European modernity or also a Russian breakthrough resulting from the 1917 socialist revolution.[43] Although many choose to debate the colonial legacy and expose opportunism at home, there is nevertheless some residual faith in another culture that is cherished or called upon to mitigate a dire situation at home. Functional Arabic is impregnated with references to foreign names and phrases, along with quotes from poetry and prose. These postcolonial narratives take the European modernity model for granted in order to deprive competitors of every other kind of ownership. The educational and administrative markets are the arena where linguistic capital and its subscription to or participation in the making of the official discourse functions to the full.[44] To graduate from foreign, especially European, universities entails a legitimacy that is more effective than, but comparable to, the traditional *'ijāzah* (permission to act as a scholar), a tradition that continued in some Arab regions until the early half of the twentieth century. Significantly, the exception occurs only when the protagonist receives education in other regions: India, Russia, or Germany; it is only then that the narrative journey takes a different, mostly rebellious, turn against both colonialism and indigenous tradition. The critique of tradition nevertheless remains as the common denominator. We have to take into consideration narratives like Tawfiq al-Ḥakīm's *'Uṣfūr min al-Sharq* (*Bird of the East*), Yaḥyā Ḥaqqī's *Qindīl Umm Hāshim* (*The Lamp of Umm Hāshim*, or *The Saint's Lamp*), Ṭāḥā Ḥusayn's *Al-Ayyām* (3 vols.: *An Egyptian Childhood, The*

Stream of Days, and *A Passage to France*), and Suhayl Idrīs's *Al-Ḥayy al-Lātīnī* (*The Latin Quarter*), and then compare them with Maḥmūd Aḥmad al-Sayyid's *Jalāl wa Khālid*, for example, in order to see the difference in perspective and prospect in otherwise secular narratives of disavowal of faith.

Thus the rise of the Arabic novel in its bourgeois epic form cannot be studied outside the framework of this competitiveness. This takes place between, on the one hand, an official or formal Arabic language propagated and disseminated through a sustained educational and press effort until the American invasion of Iraq in 2003 and the coercive measures against any Arab regime that allows nonstate functionaries to preach in mosques, and on the other an emerging religious discourse that had been losing ground until perhaps the Iranian revolution of 1979. Whether produced as translations, imitations, or original reproductions of episodic conflict extended in their temporalities but substantiated in journeys between home and metropolis (Beirut, Cairo, Baghdad, Mosul, and Europe, for example), these narratives subscribe to the enactment of an official discourse legitimized through the concerns of the nation-state, its plans for reform, and its commitment to a national educational mission that was mostly informed and guided by nineteenth- and twentieth-century European theories. Whether under the impact of Matthew Arnold, Emile Durkheim, Humboldt, George Herbert Mead, Monroe, or others, education in Arab nation-states was informed by this faith in a consensus through codification and formalization, a process implemented by directors, schoolmasters, grammarians, and instructors. Every Arab intellectual participating in this effort has a narrative of one sort or another: Ismā'īl Maẓhar, Ṭāḥā Ḥusayn, Muḥammad H. Haykal; Aḥmad Amīn, Sāṭiʿ al-Ḥuṣrī, Sāmī Shawkat, Fāḍil al-Jamālī, and many others. Novelists who had the greatest impact on Arab consciousness, such as Maḥfūẓ, al-Ḥakīm, Maḥmūd Aḥmad al-Sayyid, and Dhū al-Nūn Ayyūb, for example, speak of their journeys in education as being guided by secularists like Salāma Mūsā[45] or through direct engagement with Darwin, Marx, Max Weber, Spencer, and other theorists and writers. Indeed, Maḥfūẓ was clear on this point, noting that Salāma Mūsā "directed me to two important things: science and socialism."[46] The Iraqi Kāẓim Makkī (b. 1912, Basrah) published his narrative *Ṣafwān al-Adīb* (Ṣafwān the Litterateur) in 1939, and it caused some controversy and opposition among religious groups, which led to his banishment from Basrah for one year, but the Iraqi Ministry of Education provided public libraries with copies of his novel. There Kāẓim Makkī also admits the influence of Darwin, Salāma Mūsā, and Shīblī Shimayyil, the Egyptian of Syrian origin.[47] This is not the only case in which the ministry sided with authors, for in Egypt Ṭāḥā Ḥusayn's *Qādat al-fikr* (*Leaders of Thought*, 1925), which accuses the Oriental mind of degeneration and backwardness in contrast to the Greek mind, received the support of the ministry, which prescribed it for reading in primary schools.[48] It is rare to come across a narrative that reveals different concerns, since the mode of production as perpetuated by the nation-state has also set the criteria of supply and demand. Even when narratives speak of generational conflict, priority is always given to secularists who participate in state legitimacy through the consecration and production of its distinctive markers of authority. Faithful to the bourgeois norm, narratives have to critique improper social practices, hypocrisies, pretensions, inadequacies, and failures. Literary criticism also participates to the full in this production. Usually siding with an independent voice in a novel, the critic takes upon himself or herself the task of setting right what may have otherwise gone wrong. As operating through "a semi-artificial language which has to be sustained by a permanent effort of correction," there is a task that "falls both to institutions especially designed for this purpose and to individual speakers"[49] to fix, codify, and inculcate discursive legitimacy. Indeed, complicity in literary production has left us, and readers for that matter, face to face with a glaring question in respect to other values and issues that relate to faith and culture. Narratives and poetry until very recently have been preoccupied with bourgeois practices and aspirations in a life that is divested of actual faith. This lack has the effect of presence, for its absence does not erase its demand for explanation.

Thus, in surveying the cultural scene and literary production in particular, one has to agree with Trevor Le Gassick: "One finds not only a striking absence of advocacy of Islamic values but even a consistent pattern of criticism of the role of faith in Arab society—a theme that occurs so frequently as to suggest that Arab intellectuals who write fiction have been out of touch with the current mood of their co-religionists."[50] This conclusion applies well to literary production until the late 1960s, but this literary production, usually made available through the press and publishing houses, is not one and the same. Publishing houses in certain places, like the Shīʿī center in Iraq, Najaf, for instance, have also produced works that have a religious flavor and, on the discursive level, a mixed register of traditional and standard lexica and themes, and an exploration of historicity and historical referentiality. Nevertheless, selection remains in the hands of the elite who have a vested interest in promoting the nation-state, its apparatus and needs. Production relates to the choice of literary editors and critics, their discriminating sense, control of major literary channels, and appeal to a specific class of readership, that is, the urban elite. There is some truth in Salih J. Altoma's conclusions, too, which Le Gassick accepts, that "the anti-religious attitude becomes more pronounced in the period following the Second World War."[51] When neoclassicists refer to Islam, they usually echo Aḥmad Shawqī, whose Islam is historic, as "repository of power."[52] Especially in the novel there is a tendency among the urban elite to follow their European model, where even God, and not only the protagonist, is in eclipse. As a relatively new outgrowth in its European garb, the novel, as made available through appropriation, adaptation, reproduction, and emulation, is not indigenous enough to warrant discussion under the rubric of Arabic and Islamic culture. Regardless of the religion of individual writers and translators, fiction as a bourgeois literary product has a specific consumer in mind whose religious sentiment may not be necessarily flouted or affronted if the work he or she is reading does not meet his or her parents' inclinations. The treatment of the bourgeoisie is never homogeneous, but bourgeois hypocrisy remains a primary focus of narrative. Its usual navigation between a secure well-disciplined home and an outside that becomes the arena for mapping and control reflects the most visible bourgeois double standards, a schizophrenic worldview, and lip service to God when necessary. Mammon is the habitual winner in bourgeois literary production, while God appears only metaphorically as a result of coincidence and those chance happenings with which fiction abounds, as if to leave just a token space for a forsaken God. Until the 1967 defeat of neighboring regimes, Arab intellectuals followed this model.

But are we sure that this is actually the case? Even when we reach the same conclusions, doesn't negativism suggest another hidden dimension? Doesn't this presence conceal an absence which Pierre Macherey, for one, asks us to explore?[53] Is literary criticism complicit like the novelist who is overwhelmed by this cultural dependency on the European model? What if we investigate other sites of acculturation where Arab writers respond to Thomas Carlyle's lectures and book, *On Heroes, Hero Worship, and the Heroic in History*, or Washington Irving's book on Islam and its Prophet, and see products by the elite as partially mediated through Europe? The writings of the Egyptians Muḥammad Ḥusayn Haykal, Ṭāhā Ḥusayn, Tawfīq al-Ḥakīm, and, later, ʿAbd al-Raḥmān al-Sharqāwī, on the Prophet or the Rightly Guided Caliphs and imams, have a different story to tell and cannot be seen as sacral contributions.[54] In its educational normalization, the nation-state has to impose an understanding of history that is episodic and historical, but usually lays little emphasis on its religious dimensions. The process of elite writing on Islamic subjects is part of a strategy of codification and normalization. Language itself has to be divested of its sacral markers and channeled into a national medium which looks upon history and Islam as no more than cultural identities in an otherwise nationally based culture in contact with others. Denying its historical contingency through systematic modeling on Western schools of thought, the nation state ends up rendering everything else, including religion, temporal and relatively contingent. Protagonists in narratives as well as poetic persona vacillate and falter whenever there are crucial confrontations with religious issues.

A better way of contextualizing these writings, not as signs of Islamic resurgence or intellectual concessions but rather as part of the national effort to codify and normalize, is to see these in light of, first, the appearance of organized Islamist discourse (as formally initiated by Ḥasan al-Bannā in Egypt through the organization of the Muslim Brotherhood in 1928); and, second, the element of condescension involved in the process of writing such works. The national elite had to cope then with a countereffort, openly initiated by Ḥasan al-Bannā and aimed at confronting a secularization process that had formerly been overlooked or accommodated by celebrated and privileged shaykhs. On the other hand, the involvement of the elite in the effort to revisit Islamic history betrays a deliberate stratagem. Muḥammad M. Badawī is touched, for example, by the amount of spirituality in Ṭāhā Ḥusayn's *'Alā Hāmish al-Sīra* (*On the Margin of the Life of the Prophet*). He thinks of it as the "most original of Islamic prose literature" produced in the 1930s. However he serves our purpose by continuing that the author "derives his inspiration from early Arabic literature and heritage in the same way as a modern European author might turn to Homer." The author, he comments, lays emphasis on "the unquestioning faith of the humble and pious souls" and on "depicting the doubts and anxieties of sophisticated and restless minds dissatisfied with the religious solutions offered to them." By focusing on these two elements, the author prepares the atmosphere for "some momentous event . . . to unfold itself" which, we are led to understand, is the birth of Islam.[55] In other words, the author is in tune with ideological writings and subsequent treatises by secular thinkers on the origination of the message as expressive of a need to terminate a period of placidity or anxiety. The author's return is reminiscent of a European literary mode of engaging with tradition. Ṭāhā Ḥusayn writes: "These pages were not written for scholars or historians . . . they constitute a picture that emerged in my mind in the course of my reading about the life of the Prophet, so I hastened to record it, and I saw no harm in publishing it." In order to depict this work as a sincere gesture, he adds: "As I read about the life of the Prophet, I found my soul swelling with it, my heart overflowing and my tongue set free."[56] While seemingly apologetic lest he be criticized by scholars and historians for overlooking facts and details, the author is fully engaged in a personal initiative, a romantic pursuit which establishes an affinity with the subject of the biography that provides him with freedom and love. Nobody will debate this or question his personal sincerity. More important, however, is the author's exclusion of historians and scholars as potential readers, for he would like us as readers to know that his target readership is the general reading public, that group that is also the focus of state education. The strategy of exclusion and inclusion is not all that innocent, as Badawī would like us to believe. If we invoke Bourdieu again regarding those who make use of public language, "whatever his intentions, it cannot fail to function as a strategy of condescension likely to create a situation no less artificial than the initial relationship."[57]

Other writers also appropriate Islamic themes into a context of thought that responds to current interests. This is especially so in ʿAbd al-Raḥmān al-Sharqāwī's (d. 1987) writing where language functions in its official capacity, the one made popular through state education and that allows him to provide something that substantiates the state's national endeavor. There he lays emphasis on a critique of preachers, a celebration of leftist commitment and martyrdom, and an interest in controversial characters of historic significance who are revisited on the basis of support from new centers of power that are in competition with the Iranian revolution (to be explored in chapter 2).

Although al-Sharqāwī was not alone among Egyptian and other Arab critics and writers in writing about Islamic life and culture, he left an impressive corpus of readings and studies that may illustrate and justify a compromise between the nexus of secularity and modernity on the one hand and Islamic culture and law on the other. While al-Sharqāwī would not have liked to be singled out as an Islamic thinker or historian, he may well fit more conveniently in the trend typical of many Arab intellectuals who tried to locate Islam and its leadership in the major currents of the humanistic tradition, but with more focus on the elevation of standards of living, freedom, and social equality. In line with his other books, novels, dramas, and long poems, his Islamic sketches of the Prophet Muḥammad, his cousin, the fourth caliph, Imam ʿAlī, and other caliphs, companions of the Prophet, and well-known and controversial *faqīh*s or jurists, like Ibn Taymiyyah (d. 1328), tend to underscore his primary humanistic and still somehow leftist concerns with the plight of the poor, dispossessed, and controversial. In 1962 he published *Muḥammad Rasūl al-Ḥuriyyah* (*Muḥammad the Messenger of Freedom*). The year of publication is not random, it being a starting point for the burgeoning of the bureaucratic nation-state, the unsettling disparity between great national claims and actual achievements on the ground, and the growth of a parasitic class not only in the public economic sector, the security apparatus, and power structures, but also among intellectuals. ʿAbd al-Nāṣir's significant social and political achievements, especially in land reform, socialization of the private sector, nationalization of the Suez Canal, and improvement of the status of the poor, confronted a serious challenge as a result of the increasingly coercive power of the nation-state. Co-opted into the ideological state apparatuses, a large number of professionals, functionaries, and intellectuals became not merely part of a state-run system, but also primarily involved in promoting its oppressive control. In his introduction to Jürgen Habermas's *Structural Transformation*, Thomas McCarthy sums up Habermas's thought on this matter as follows: "The press and broadcast media serve less as organs of public information and debate than as technologies for managing consensus and promoting consumer culture."[58] State-run systems were certainly looked upon with favor and great appreciation for the free medical service, free education, and almost every other service that they offered with no substantial charge. Even so, repressive measures carried out by the ideological state apparatus were a serious problem. Writings that appeared at the time were one aspect of the new outlook, but they may also have conveyed a subtle critique of the dwindling revolutionary honesty of the 1952 leadership. Al-Sharqāwī's Prophet emerges as a reflection on this matter, a mirror whereby the revolutionaries might see their image as reflected in the tarnished model of old times. His Prophet is not a duplication of the one delineated in established biographies, especially Ibn Isḥāq as reported and widely circulated in Ibn Hishām's recension. Al-Sharqāwī disclaims attempts at duplication, for "the biography of the Prophet needs no new book to speak of the age of Prophethood . . . to defend the authenticity and truthfulness of the Message, or to emphasize the Prophet's miracles."[59] This is not his purpose, nor to write a book that is to be read by "Muslims alone."[60] No, he would like to compose a book that can be read by "Muslims and non-Muslims," a book that can "depict the positive dimensions of our heritage and show what is humane in the life of the Messenger," a book "to be read by all people, whether they believe in Muḥammad's Prophethood or not."[61] The intention, in other words, is not to duplicate or propagate the Message, but to fit it into a new trend "to reassess our heritage . . . to resurrect what is humane in it and make it available to all . . . to represent the common aspect in the role of Messengers . . . to depict the human worldly aspect which has become a common civilizational heritage among all people regardless of their religions, philosophies, and opinions."[62] This work then represents an effort that belongs in the mainstream of Enlightenment discourse, with emphasis on the universal element in Islam. While echoing Sayyid Quṭb's famous explanation of Islam as the religion of the future, the writer divests Islam of a specific religiosity and re-lays it into a humanistic tradition without borders. This process fits into a tendency among Arab intellectuals to criticize the nation-state obliquely within a revisionist ideological process that questions the validity of some secular politics in the makeup of organized parties in the Arab world.[63] As usual with this discourse, language is divested of its classical rhetoric, and prose flows with ease as befitting journalism.

In other words, ʿAbd al-Raḥmān al-Sharqāwī spells out clearly the intentions that pertain to his primary concern with humanitarian values that are acceptable and common to all in a civilized cultural space. His language belongs within the mainstream as envisioned by the state and its educators and professionals. Subscribing to this education, he wishes to rewrite the Arab-Islamic heritage so as to make it accessible to all, highlighting meanwhile its common aspects as portrayed in the life and career of the Prophet. The method that he adopts toward this end is not simple, for there are groups and platforms that either disagree with the person or with the Message. Each position has to be addressed differently, he argues: "Let us confront those people who disagree with his person or his character, for in his life there is an endless wealth of pride, compassion, love, wisdom, simplicity, an enormous power to organize, and be creative, and a disposition to win over hearts."[64]

To deal with the man in the character of the Prophet is a challenge to those who choose to focus on something else. To ʿAbd al-Raḥmān al-Sharqāwī, this is "not merely a literary work; it is a nationalist duty, an artistic responsibility incumbent upon all who feel capable of undertaking it."[65] From here he declares his rewriting to be a national duty, not an Islamist one, for the emphasis is clearly placed on the humanization of the Prophet, divesting his biography of any clerical embellishment and making it part of a national heritage now favored by a secular nation-state. With this understanding the concept of "national" is prioritized, too, for it was an important factor in the early 1960s when nationalist feelings were at their highest and the Egyptian President Jamāl ʿAbd al-Nāṣir had already begun to fight leftist ideologies that were opposed to or competing with Nāṣirism. The wording chosen by al-Sharqāwī, "*wājib qawmī*" (nationalist duty) is thus of considerable significance. It justifies the project as being a concern that may not be receiving its due recognition from unnamed circles. We have no idea if they included Islamists, fellow leftists, or co-opted intellectuals; indeed it may well have included all of them, since at the time any investigation of Islamic issues was not enthusiastically welcomed by a secular intelligentsia, especially the nonacademic one. In a period of enormous translation projects, coexistence with third worldism and interest in softened (tempered) social realism, only a "nationalist" justification was able to silence critics. It certainly was to become a covert method for a religious tendency that needed an outlet amid many other preoccupations and obsessions. Al-Sharqāwī's book was dedicated to the author's father "who implanted the love for Muḥammad in me from childhood." The preface, with its equivocal navigation between piety and nationalism, was written on the fifteenth of Ramadan (1381 H.), February 20, 1962.[66]

More than historical annals, historicized narrative of this type has the power to reach a large reading public. On the artistic level it manages to blend sequentiality with explication, linearity with anecdote, and drama with theology. In other words, it concretizes the subject to make it accessible to its readers. Written in the very secular form of modern narratives, it has a sequential order based on reason and cause and effect, the secular concerns of characterization, and the trappings of dramatization. Indeed, fate has no role here, and the character of the Prophet is a dynamic one even in moments of extreme piety. While in line with standard biographies, ʿAbd al-Raḥmān al-Sharqāwī's narrative style, his emphasis on historical sequence, and his focus on personal details set the tone for his other historical narratives. The thematic focus always relates to issues of faith, social equality, political life, and the nature of pre-Islamic social structures, especially in Mecca. Developing an early attachment to other saints who resisted atheism and paganism and confronted exploitation and its practices, Muḥammad, we are told, replaced such epithets as "servant" or "slave" with "my boy" and "my girl."[67] Even his visions and dreams are recapitulated as anticipations of a better world.[68] But in order to make his narrative more dramatic, ʿAbd al-Raḥmān al-Sharqāwī devotes a substantial portion to battles, describing them with all their complications, polarizations, and varieties of human concern. Anything that involves the divides between masters and slaves, relatives and kinship, and heroic feats, find a place in this narrative.

In other words, the historical narrative is made available to the reading public without any concession that might contradict historical facts as mentioned in authoritative annalistic accounts. Yet there exists a different kind of patronization that Bourdieu describes as "symbolic power," whereby the speaker or writer condescends to audiences other than his own, especially if he or she descends to a lower class or less privileged social group, making them feel that he is doing so for their sake. By forsaking elevated intellectual discourse and using a mixed historical narrative, ʿAbd al-Raḥmān al-Sharqāwī is trying to reach these audiences who will accept him as such, approve his argument and purpose, and ally their own voices with his. The elite may criticize him, but his new audience accepts his new endeavor, applauds it, and endorses it even if it includes opinions or views that may not be entirely theirs. Albeit with a different target, ʿAbd al-Raḥmān al-Sharqāwī continues the endeavor of the 1930s when writers approached Islamic characters and issues with a greater sense of the literary, something that might have endeared them to the newly emergent reading public among the steadily growing middle class, while at the same time helping to dislodge traditional sites of power, including al-Azhar.

Is it possible, therefore, to accept these biographies, along with their authors' personal intimations, at face value, namely as mere reconstructions of history? Are they a continuation of Jurjī Zaydān's (d. 1914) historical narratives? We can be sympathetic enough to accept Jurjī Zaydān's influential historical novels as being connected more to an indigenous Arab tradition than to Walter Scott's significant contribution to the historical novel, a pioneering generic gesture that provided a threshold for romantic narrative in an age that had witnessed the eclipse of epic heroes and the rise of middle-class protagonists. Jurjī Zaydān's contributions are in line with a sense of national commitment and an intellectual and moral responsibility to participate in the education of the public. His own personal career as a hard-working, self-educated person with little means to provide for his higher education made him acutely aware of the need to serve as a provider of knowledge through his novels and the influential journal *Al-Hilāl*. M. M. Badawī has shown how poetry was more focused on this issue, celebrating the Prophet in the context of the fight against colonialism and the moral need to provide a boost to Islam in its confrontation with the colonial onslaught.[69] The focus on the person of the Prophet clearly has a particular function, for, as Badawī explains, "it is humanely easier to respond emotionally to a person than to an abstract idea."[70]

The question that remains unanswered is, why was there a need to secure such an emotional response? In the minds of poets and prose writers, who are the target readers? What has this engagement to do with the increasing interest in romanticism or the rise of the novel? These questions also demand further investigation of topics such as the emergence of the middle class, the spread of education, the emphasis on individualism, and the colonial context. The humanization of Islam and focus on events and characteristics both signify an attempt to create a new national discourse divested of clerical rhetoric but more attuned to a Western secular literature that had been invading the public sphere.

The Islamic faith is also revisited so as to become a chosen, not inherited, identity. Maḥmūd Taymūr's book on Muḥammad, "the prophet, the man" appeared after World War II, but it established the model for confessional journeys that remind one of Imam Abū Ḥāmid al-Ghazālī (d. 1111) and Thomas Carlyle's *Sartor Resartus*. Taymūr explains in prose his journey from denial to faith: "This outstanding personality took me by the hand and led me to the way of Truth and faith, with the result that I found myself loving this Religion, especially the message it has brought to provide guidance and compassion to mankind."[71] Muḥammad Ḥusayn Haykal wrote two books, one on the life of the Prophet, *Ḥayāt Muḥammad* (1935), and another titled *Fī manāzil al-waḥy* (*At the Site of Revelation*, 1937). Both are attestations of belief, a "return to the roots of Islamic faith," argues Badawī. The major critic, ʿAbbās Maḥmūd al-ʿAqqād, wrote his *'Abqariyyat Muḥammad* (*The Genius of Muḥammad*) as yet another contribution to this trend. These efforts combine faith and reason as if in continuation of a line of thought in Islam that is usually associated with the Muʿtazalites. They "represent a modern variety of the school of Muʿtazila," writes Badawī.[72] While many such responses respond to the metropolis against the way in which certain Orientalists depict Muḥammad, they accommodate many tenets of the humanist tradition and try to fit Islam into a national language as promoted and adopted by the state. Haykal, for one, wrote under the impact of Emile Dermenghem's *La vie de Mahomet* (Paris, 1929). Religion is not an esoteric pursuit, nor is it the private property of the preacher and the pulpit. Rather than a change of heart, these are deliberate contributions to intellectual writing that confront a counterdiscourse emanating from two opposite platforms: the Muslim Brotherhood, which has already combined nationalism and Islamism as being inseparable; and Orientalism, which has been prioritizing other faiths over Islam through a detractive or reductive humanization of the character of Muḥammad. On the other hand, these efforts are also part of a humanist gesture, in the sense that they build on Enlightenment discourse with its emphasis on reason and the relegation of religion to its literary core and its poetry, as Matthew Arnold had remarked regarding Christianity in his *Religion and Dogma*. In these Arabic biographies Islam is divested of dogma, stripped of its theological rhetoric, and reduced to personal faith. As participants in a movement of liberal thought, these writers had also to create a discourse of their own that could distinguish itself from other ideological discourses, especially the Marxist and nationalist. The nation-state found in liberalism a viable language that was in line with its aspirations as reflected in the hopes of the emerging bourgeoisie. Narratives of the 1960s onward look back with nostalgia on that earlier period in Egypt, Iraq, and Syria.

The situation in occupied Arab regions was different. Islamic discourse was powerfully combined with Arabism. Shaykh ʿAbd al-Ḥamīd Bin Bādīs (d. 1940) sums this up as follows: "If you say the Arabs, you mean a nation extending from the Indian Ocean to the east to the Atlantic Ocean on the West, with more than seventy million people, speaking Arabic, thinking in Arabic, and fed on its history . . . which history has invoked and melted together to become one nation."[73]

Pierre Cacchia is aware of some of these urgent questions. He bases his contentions on some premises: the traditional elite was replaced in the 1870s in Egypt in particular by one of "administrators and professionals who owed their worldly success and intellectual dominance to the mastery of some technique or science recently acquired from Europe"[74]; the foundation by Aḥmad Luṭfī al-Sayyid of the daily newspaper *Al-Jaridah* (1907) in Egypt signaled the domination of this elite, which confined the role of religion to the European example of separation between religion and the state and turned faith into a personal matter; if there were to be a controversy, as Ṭāhā Ḥusayn had argued in the 1920s, it was not with religion, but rather it "had been between modern liberalism and orthodox traditionalism";[75] there was a prevalence of national over religious loyalties, and a preference for what was national and democratic;[76] the occupation of Palestine and miserable conditions at home made writers question divine justice[77] or channel their anger at shaykhs and preachers; last, since the 1960s the modernists have no longer been the originators or articulators of ideas for political parties. The old alliance among religionists, believers, secularists, and others in the fight against colonialism no longer held.

The use of the June War of 1967 as the line of demarcation is not a random choice. It represents the bankruptcy of a discourse closely associated with the bombastic jargon of the nation-state and its exposure as hollow and sham. Indeed, another way of dealing with the issue of "Islam on the street" is to repeat G. E. Von Grunebaum's question: "at what period in modern literary development does the description by nations become more significant than that by cultures?"[78] It is easy to say that, with the fall of empires and the nadir of civilizations, disintegration takes the form of specific entities: dynasties, tribal federations, and regional alliances. City-states as well as nation-states emerge whenever the center loses its hold. In other words, the national emerges at the expense of the civilizational. The French expedition and occupation of Egypt in 1798 set the scene for further disintegration, which was also made possible by the enlightened elite, its discontent with the Ottomans, and its aspiration to a European modernity whose primary advocate and owner was the nation-state that virtually came into existence in the Middle East after World War I and its division among colonial powers in the wake of the collapse of the Ottoman Empire. As always, the choice between the seemingly lesser of two evils led to foreign encroachments and the creation of nation-states at the expense of an Arab-Islamic nation. This fact, the creation of a state against a background of an Islamic order, carries within it the seeds of a dichotomous struggle, but its bearing on the street varies according to power relations and use of the underlying symbolic capital and its availability for innocent use or deliberate manipulation.

Islam in the street is now influenced by a number of avenues of interpretation, involving the pulpit and its current media extensions such as the Internet, the satellite, and the newspaper. If religion tends to render philosophical truth into symbols in order to achieve a version of the ideal virtuous life, then symbolism itself also assumes a number of forms according to schools of law and their various factions and affiliates. For example, symbolism may only retain the rituals without questioning their purpose, as is the case with regard to Wahhabism. The ultimate goal in every rite is obedience to God and submission to his will. Other schools of symbolism combine the practices of antecedent authority with subsequent visitation, iconoclasm, and similar practices that are part of a cultural heritage.

The power of the nation-state in relation to contending concepts like the Islamic, *'ummah* or nation can also be gauged in terms of language. Any rich symbolic order that can have an impact on the masses in times of disintegration derives its complexity from the Qur'ān. Revered, studied, advocated, and designated as a miracle, the Qur'ān becomes the most pivotal referent as well as the ultimate crystallization of Islamic thought. According to a large number of classical scholars and rhetors, it resists closure, because its eloquence, clarity, and rhetorical and metaphorical richness elevate it to a level of inimitability beyond the reach of the most gifted poets. The Qur'ān speaks of this power in many places in its text, and the reference to itself as the Book sublimates the symbolic dimension. Even when there is a mention of monotheists as the "people of the Book," the believers in God, the Book itself, the Qur'ān, unfolds differently for a Muslim. Apart from its expressive or communicative skills, it is a repertoire of an endless interpretation, a mine of rhetoric and eloquence. Through recitation (the literal meaning of the word "Qur'ān") an emotive link, powerful and effective, holds the listener. The British Lord Cromer found in this response and attachment a solution to his plan for the introduction of British culture into the educational curriculum. The attachment to the Book, he notes, can be transposed to any other book as long as Muslims have this reverence for the written and recited word. Although more focused on their national mission to spread education and scientific knowledge, the *nahḍah* intellectuals were no less involved in the proliferation of a European legacy that was appropriated to fit into a national consciousness. In other words, they were no less enthusiastic than Lord Cromer in the implementation of a British legacy. It is no mere coincidence that the curriculum in the Teachers' College in Cairo and, later, in Baghdad was almost the same in certain departments, especially the department of English and foreign languages. When we read this in context and discover that a large number of the pioneers in modern poetry studied there and at the College of Arts, we can understand how Eurocentricism in culture also played a role in dissociating intellectuals from their native culture. Had intellectuals strived to combine acculturation and native tradition in a dialectical process, they could have helped lead the nation-state consistently and constitutionally and established more effective links with the masses (like preachers during the late Abbasid period, for example). Significant national happenings, such as the 'Urābī Pasha Revolt (1882), the 1919 revolution in Egypt, and the 1920 revolution in Iraq, could have become pivotal turning points in the intellectual leadership of the masses through sincere commitment to and respect for the common public and its culture. Instead, detachment and one-sided emulation of a European model widened the gap between them and the common people.

The revivalist movement of the late nineteenth century could not cope with the counteremulation of Europe under colonial rule. It is not enough, however, to speak of Islamic revivalism in the late nineteenth century as a compromise, especially in its reformist tendency under Shaykh Jamāl al-Dīn al-Afghānī (d. 1897) and, later, Shaykh Muḥammad 'Abdū (d. 1905) and the Iraqi Shī'ī clergy. The reformist tendency had this urge to indulge in such compromises, to be sure, to make use of new achievements in Europe that had not reached the Islamic world under a dying Ottoman order, while pointing out the failure of morals in Europe. In a large number of treatises and records there is emphasis on the respectability of Islamic moral ethics and the failure of Europe in fostering a sustained sense of morality. Shaykh al-Ṭahṭāwī (d. 1873) was more inclined to admire French achievements in statecraft, city planning, and efficient civil order. The secular elite that became more powerful after 1919, the relatively organized presence of the Wafd Party in Egypt, and the appearance of similar parties in Syria and Iraq had to devise a national ideology with more emphasis on economic and political independence. To displace competing ideologies, including Islamist discourse, there arose a deliberate process whereby the middle class forged a national frame of reference that regarded the state as an established entity with its own history and heritage of achievement. The language used by the revivalist movement and its successors adopted a compromise that involved openness to the emerging language of the nation-state taken over and promoted by its functionaries, including educators and journalists. However, compromises cannot hold for long in competition of this kind. By the 1930s it had already become difficult to detect any kind of religious discourse, pure and simple. On the contrary, narratives of the period until the 1960s depict preachers and clerics as opportunists, liars, and manipulators of faith. In Ṭayyib Ṣāliḥl's *The Wedding of Zein*, the Imam "was, in the opinion of the village, an importunate man, a talker and a grumbler, and in their heart of hearts they used to despise him because they reckoned him to be practically the only one among them who had no definite work to do: no field to cultivate and no business to occupy him. . . . In their minds he was connected with things they sometimes liked to forget: death, the afterlife, prayers."[79] But all this had to disappear after June 1967 and the stark exposure of a total bankruptcy in the discourse of the nation-state and its ideological apparatus and functionaries. We need to listen to the popular Syrian poet Nizār Qabbānī (d. 1997) as he disclaims any association with this nation-state in his: "Marginal Notes on the Book of Defeat":

> My poor country,
> You have changed in a moment
> from a poet who writes of love and longing
> to a poet who writes with a knife.
> It is not strange that we should lose a war:
> we enter them/ with all our Eastern arts of rhetoric
> and heroism which never killed a black fly.
> We entered
> with the logic of the drum and the rebab.[80]

Hence narratives thereafter leave behind Maḥfūẓ's middle-class narratives while continuing to invoke his scathing critiques of the nation-state. The emerging narrative after 1967 reveals another factor: it works with social fringes, juxtaposes their discourse with that of secular ideologues, and resorts to alternative narrative strategies to cope with new realities that have been overlooked under the previously compelling presence of the hybrid state.

In narrative proper, we come across works, like Tawfīq Yūsuf 'Awwād's *Ṭawāḥīn Beirut* (1972; *Death in Beirut*), that examine the issue of ethnicity and religious sects through its geographical and social dimension. The novel uses the predictable response of a young female who, as a young woman from southern Lebanon and a displaced villager, will suffer from a number of discriminatory measures because of the Israeli invasions in the 1970s. This novel attempts to deal with these issues by placing the aspiring female in Beirut among a number of intellectuals whose secular predilections and ideological rhetoric have long appealed to her. Unless this novel is viewed within the temporal context of its appearance, its anticipation of the Israeli occupation of the impoverished southern Lebanon, and the devastating consequences on the economy of the Shī'ī population of the south and the enormous number of human casualties among both them and the Palestinians living there, the reader may well overlook its significance as a narrative of nationhood, identity, and human suffering. Powerful as the novel may be, its decontextualization may produce a reading in which other dimension of identity crisis in times of dislocation and ideological confusion are overlooked. The novel can be regarded as a polyphonic reading of frustrations with the liberal tradition, its compromises and unsatisfactory modes of discourse, and the growing national momentum of the street. On the other hand, the conclusion of 'Awwād's narrative may be seen initially as the female protagonist's ultimate rejection of the whole experience of intellectual life, its superficial dealings, and its impotence in the face of grave circumstances. It may be seen as a radical turn, or even a reinitiation into a new life, but its ultimate significance lies in its foreshadowing of future events and its foretaste of a burgeoning discourse of action. As the Shī'ī female protagonist, Tamima Nassour, leaves her memoirs behind and mentions to her young colleague and lover, Hanī, that her old self is dead and survives only in the memoirs that she is leaving for him, she is actually relinquishing the secular experience, the one upon which the nation-state is erected. Passing through the turmoil of life in the city, imbibing the entire secular discourse of intellectual dilettantes, and in the process endangering her own life by "disgracing" the honor of her family (at least, in view of her brother Jabir and the street bystanders), Tamima's break with the past does not emerge out of the blue, at least not as a change of heart. It emanates from and grows out of enormous disappointment at the impotence of the state and its secular intellectuals. Both can do little against the invasion that has brought about death and destruction and caused havoc, especially in the south. Against this background a revolt develops on both individual and communal levels. It is to the credit of the novelist that he anticipates a power transposition to the street, to the people who now trust no one apart from themselves. Their leader is the guru who is one of them, pure and simple. This folk hero could well have been 'Awwād's protagonist had he decided to write a sequel to the novel. Tamima is joining the "man," who remains in an ambiguous position; like the little or street man, he has neither name nor identity. In the next few years this man will suffer still further. But out of this suffering inflicted by invaders and national opportunists, this little man, the little Ghandi of Ilyās Khūrī's novel,[81] does not seek an easy escape, migration, or surrender. Taking destiny in their hands, the common people have now forged an identity of their own. They soon find a legacy of martyrdom to consolidate their vision and strengthen their will. This is the ultimate power that has become known for inflicting so much damage on invaders and occupiers, something that no nation-state would ever have dreamed possible. Common people have no need to castigate the nation-state and its corrupt apparatus; it is enough simply to hold their destiny in their own hands. Their leaders speak of them as their heroes, not the kind of rabble that dictators and their ilk remind every now and then of their past misery, poverty, and hopelessness. These people by contrast make history, and hence are its creators. Now they are the ones who write it, and nobody can claim otherwise. Hence, Ḥasan Naṣrallah addresses them as the heroes whom he embraces, kissing their foreheads and feet. The claims of the secular state are shattered, for there is no national sanctity, no self-respect that demands admiration and appreciation. Its failures and downfalls are many, indeed too many to be excused. ʿAwwād's Tamima is the token and herald of this new birth, whose symbolic mushrooming is too conspicuous to pass unnoticed. It appears in the form of orphans in Maḥfūẓ's novel, *The Ḥarāfīsh*. It has other faces and genealogies too. Taken together, these are the surprising outcomes of past failures and the ultimate challenge posed by the undefiled new generation.

ʿAwwād's text problematizes the issue of the divide between the secular and the sacred. Focusing primarily on secular ideology, its discourses and practices, he deliberately lets the sacred recede into the background where it exists only as affirmation, mostly in relation to traditional values and family preferences. As his intellectuals and activists advocate secular discourse and participate in its making, his female protagonist is no less involved in such discourse, as would be expected from a young woman migrating to Beirut in the 1950s and 1960s. Her ultimate rejection of this kind of selfhood is made or formed through, and after, an uneasy balance between tradition and the growing secular discourse that is tipped toward Beirut of the 1960s.

ʿAwwād's text may well signify an important moment of trauma in Arabic literary production, not only in its young protagonist's itinerary and final break with the past, her own past history, and the secular tradition of the past, but also in the new initiation and apprenticeship that emerges. Everything in the text, its language, styles, paratexts, conversations, and narrator's comments, partakes of a foregone secular detachment from religion as a cultural dynamic. The compelling textual imperatives of desire, fulfillment, frustration, subservience, and resistance enforce their presence on every page as if preparing for a retreat from a narrative space that is compelled thereafter to host the emerging narrative practices, as found, for example, in ʿAbd al-Ḥakīm Qāsim's *Ayyām al-insān al-sabʿah* (1969; *Seven Days of Man*) and Jamāl al-Ghīṭānī's *Zaynī Barakāt* (1972; *Zaynī Barakāt*). In these and other narratives, writing assumes a polyphonic dimension, a space for multiple productions where users have their rights and privileges, and tradition no longer suffers under the burden of a monopoly. The space allocated to these ordinary individuals makes up more than 90 percent of the available sphere, whereas the state apparatus resides in the background, to emerge every now and then in iconic representations or repressive measures practiced by the state ideological apparatus and its forces. The heroine of *Death in Beirut* bids farewell to these intellectuals and instead joins some mysterious "man," whereas in Yūsuf Idrīs's story the knowledgeable specialist carries on his back the legacy of olden times, as he moves away from the state and the offers of status and privilege. No secular intellectuals return to the narrative sphere, the divide being between a failing state apparatus and a common people. The legacy of the nineteenth-century *nahḍah* is either far removed or else disappears once and for all. The narrative of education, the bildungsroman, a favorite of bourgeois intellectuals, disappears from the 1970s onward; its echoes are vague and far removed, something worth acknowledging only as a matter of history, worthy, before a final farewell, of comparison with a rejection of the recent past and its replications of modernity projects.

Notes

1. Yūsuf Idrīs, "The Language of Pain," trans. Nawal Nagib (Cairo: GEBO, 1990). Further references are incorporated with page number in the text. Proper names in the story are kept as they appear in the translation.

2. Jürgen Habermas, *Religion and Rationality*, ed. Eduardo Mendiete (Cambridge, MA: MIT Press, 2002), 151.

3. Pierre Bourdieu, *Language and Symbolic Power*, trans. Gino Raymond and Matthew Adamson; ed. and intro. John B. Thompson (Cambridge, MA: Harvard University Press, 1991), 39.

4. It is worth mentioning that the translator of Salāma Mūsā's autobiography, *Tarbiyat Salāma Mūsā*, L. O. Schuman, says as much: "to the translator's taste, the Arabic text is rather flat and monotonous; though Salāma Mūsā's journalistic language may be appreciated by Arab readers for clarity and matter-of-factness, it has not the elegance of some of his contemporary belletrists." Salāma Mūsā, *The Education of Salāma Mūsā*, trans. L. O. Schuman (Leiden: Brill, 1961), xi.

5. Mūsā, *The Education of Salāma Mūsā*, 47

6. See Yūsuf ʿIzz al-Dīn, *Al-Riwāyah fī al-ʿIrāq* (Cairo: Maʿhad al-Buḥūth wa-al-Dirāsāt al-Adabiyyah, 1973), 163, where he provides selections from Iraqi narratives of the 1920s and 1930s that demonstrate how phrases and idioms from current European or Russian thought invaded Arabic and Iraqi writings. On the other hand, the *nahḍah* Egyptian intellectual Ismāʿīl Maẓhar, professor at King Fu'ād Academia for Arabic Language issued *Qāmūs al-nahḍah* (*The Awakening Lexicon*) in the 1920s for the sole purpose of providing a compatible dictionary that could meet the needs of the age.

7. See Muḥsin al-Mūsawī, *Al-Istshrāq fī al-fikr al-ʿArabī* (*Orientalism in Arab Thought*), (Beirut: MADN, 1993).

8. Bourdieu, *Language and Symbolic Power*, 73.

9. Bourdieu, *Language and Symbolic Power*, 45.

10. Cited in Muhsin al-Musawi, *The Postcolonial Arabic Novel* (2003; Leiden: Brill, 2005), 92.

11. Cited from Aḥmad Amīn, *Fayḍ al-Khāṭir* (1942), 166–67, in Pierre Cacchia, *An Overview of Modern Arabic Literature* (Edinburgh: Edinburgh University Press, 1990), 203.

12. Ibrāhim ʿAbd al-Qādir al-Māzinī, *Ibrāhim al-Kātib*. 1931; *Ibrahim the Writer*, trans. Magdi Wahba (Cairo: GEBO, 1976).

13. See ʿAbd al-Laṭīf Sharārah, *Maʿārik Adabiyyah* (Beirut: Dār al-ʿIlm lil-Malāyīn, 1984), 237.

14. John B. Thompson, Editor's Introduction, in Bordieu, *Language and Symbolic Power*, 6.

15. Thompson, Editor's Introduction, 6.

16. Thompson, Editor's Introduction, 5.

17. In Pierre Bourdieu's specific use of the term as pertaining to context.

18. Thompson, Editor's Introduction, 7.

19. Thompson, Editor's Introduction, 7.

20. Reference to Austin, *How to Do Things with Words* (1962), in Thompson, Editor's Introduction, 8–9.

21. Austin, *How to Do Things with Words*, 8.

22. Trevor Le Gassick, "The Path of Islam in Modern Arabic Fiction," *Religion and Literature* 20:1 (Spring 1988), 10.

23. Le Gassick, "The Path of Islam in Modern Arabic Fiction", 10.

24. Bourdieu, *Language and Symbolic Power*, 12.

25. Thompson, Editor's Introduction, 12.

26. Thompson, Editor's Introduction, 13.

27. Cited by Fauzi M. Najjar, "Islamic Fundamentalism and the Intellectuals: The Case of Naguib Mahfouz," *British Journal of Middle Eastern Studies* 25:1 (1998), 139–68, at 162–63.

28. Ṣabā al-Ḥirz, *Al-Ākharūn* (Beirut: Al-Sāqī, 2006), 75–76.

29. See 'Izz al-Dīn, *Al-Riwāyah fī al-'Irāq*, 115–33, 151–66.

30. 'Izz al-Dīn, *Al-Riwāyah fī al-'Irāq*, 130.

31. 'Izz al-Dīn, *Al-Riwāyah fī al-'Irāq*, 130–31.

32. Le Gassick, "The Path of Islam in Modern Arabic Fiction," 104.

33. For extracts from Iraqi narratives and some critical insights, see 'Izz al-Dīn, *Al-Riwāyah fī al-'Irāq*, 130–32. See also Muhsin al-Musawi, *Reading Iraq* (London: I.B. Tauris, 2006).

34. 'Izz al-Dīn, *Al-Riwāyah fī al-'Irāq*, 132.

35. See Bassām 'Aslī, *'Abd al-Ḥamīd Bin Bādīs* (Beirut: Dār al-Nafā'is, 1986), 50–51.

36. See Muhsin J. al-Musawi, *Scheherazade in England* (Washington, DC: Three Continents Press, 1981), 136, 144.

37. S. Moreh, trans., *Al-Jabartī's Chronicle of the First Seven Months of the French Occupation of Egypt* (Leiden: Brill, 1975), 23.

38. Bourdieu, *Language and Symbolic Power*, 76.

39. Bourdieu, *Language and Symbolic Power*, 48.

40. Cited from G. Davy, in Bordieu, *Language and Symbolic Power*, 49.

41. Ḥāfiẓ Ibrāhīm asked him jokingly: "Are you in disguise, Ṣādiq? Where is the dust that used to cover your suit?" Kāmil Shinnāwī, *Alladhīna Aḥabbū Mayy wa Ubīrīt Jamīlah* [Those Who Loved Mayy and the Opera of Jamīlah] (Cairo: Dār al-Ma'ārif, 1972), 14–15. Cited and translated by Boutheina Khaldi, "Going Public: Mayy Ziyādah and Her Literary Salon in a Comparative Context," unpublished doctoral diss., Indiana University, Bloomington, 2008, chap. 2, p. 69.

42. Bourdieu, *Language and Symbolic Power*, 50.

43. For a detailed account of narrative encounters and counternarratives, see Muhsin al-Musawi, *The Postcolonial Arabic Novel.*

44. Bourdieu, *Language and Symbolic Power*, argues in this connection that threatened linguistic capital like classical languages cannot survive unless there is a counter-effort to save the market as a "whole set of political and social conditions of production of the producers/consumers." He adds that the value of linguistic competence that enables functioning as capital depends on the educational system, which in turn gets its politics from the state. See p. 57.

45. On Maḥfūẓ's indebtedness to Salāma Mūsā for his beliefs in socialism, see Fu'ād Dawwārah, *Najīb Maḥfūẓ* (Cairo: GEBO, 1989), 298–313.

46. Dawwārah, *Najīb Maḥfūẓ*. See also Najjar, "Islamic Fundamentalism and the Intellectuals," 142.

47. See his letter to Yūsuf ʿIzz al-Dīn, Al-Riwāyah fi al-ʿIrāq (Cairo: Ma ʿhad al Buḥūth, 1973) 307–8. See also the author's note, ibid. 116, n. 1.

48. Ṭāḥā Ḥusayn, *Qādat al-fikr* (Cairo: Al-Hilāl, 1925), 48–49. See Cacchia, *An Overview of Modern Arabic Literature*, 206.

49. Bourdieu, *Language and Symbolic Power*, 60.

50. Le Gassick, "The Path of Islam in Modern Arabic Fiction," 97.

51. S. J. Altoma, "Westernization and Islam in Modern Arabic Fiction," *Yearbook of Comparative and General Literature* 20 (1971), 81–88; cited in Le Gassick, "The Path of Islam in Modern Arabic Fiction," 98.

52. See Cacchia, *An Overview of Modern Arabic Literature*, 204.

53. Pierre Macherey, *A Theory of Literary Production*, trans. Geoffrey Wall (London: Routledge, 1978).

54. See M. M. Badawī's valuable reading of "Islam in Modern Egyptian Literature," in his *Modern Arabic Literature and the West* (London: Ithaca Press, 1985).

55. See M. M. Badawī, "Islam in Egyptian Literature," in *Modern Arabic Literature and the West*, 58–59.

56. Badawī, "Islam in Egyptian Literature," 58.

57. Bordieu, *Language and Symbolic Power*, 78.

58. Jürgen Habermas, *The Structural Transformation of the Public Sphere: Inquiry into a Category of Bourgeois Society* (London: Polity Press, 1989), xii.

59. ʿAbd al-Raḥmān al-Sharqāwī, *Muḥammad Rasūl al-Ḥuriyyah* [Muḥammad the Messenger of Freedom] (Cairo: ʿĀlam al-Kutub, 1962), 6.

60. al-Sharqāwī, *Muḥammad Rasūl al-Ḥuriyyah*, 6.

61. al-Sharqāwī, *Muḥammad Rasūl al-Ḥuriyyah*, 6.

62. al-Sharqāwī, *Muḥammad Rasūl al-Ḥuriyyah*, 6–7.

63. In a forthcoming book, *The Sacred Critique of the Nation State*, I have dealt with this issue.

64. al-Sharqāwī, *Muḥammad Rasūl al-Ḥuriyyah*, 7.

65. al-Sharqāwī, *Muḥammad Rasūl al-Ḥuriyyah*, 8.

66. al-Sharqāwī, *Muḥammad Rasūl al-Ḥuriyyah*, 8.

67. al-Sharqāwī, *Muḥammad Rasūl al-Ḥuriyyah*, 65.

68. al-Sharqāwī, *Muḥammad Rasūl al-Ḥuriyyah*, 68.

69. See Badawī, "Islam in Egyptian Literature," 45–61.

70. Badawī, "Islam in Egyptian Literature," 52.

71. Cited in Badawī, "Islam in Egyptian Literature," 51.

72. Badawī, "Islam in Egyptian Literature," 53.
73. Cited in ʿAslī, *'Abd al-Hamīd Bin Bādīs*, 12.
74. Cacchia, *An Overview of Modern Arabic Literature*, 201.
75. Cacchia, *an Overview of Modern Arabic Literature*, 207.
76. Cacchia, *an Overview of Modern Arabic Literature*, 206.
77. Cacchia, *an Overview of Modern Arabic Literature*, 209.
78. G. E. Von Grunebaum, "The Spirit of Islam as Shown in Its Literature," *Studia Islamica* no. 1 (1953), 101–19, at 113.
79. Ṭayyib Ṣaliḥl, *The Wedding of Zein* (Portsmouth, NH: Heinemann, 1968), 87.
80. Nizār Qabbānī, "Marginal Notes on the Book of Defeat," in *When Words Burn*: An Anthology of Modern Arabic Poetry, 1945–1987. (Dunregan, Ontario: Cormarant, 1988).
81. Ilyās Khūrī, *Riḥlat Ghandī al-Ṣaghīr* (1989; *The Journey of Little Ghandi*, Minn: University of Minnesota Press, 1994).

CHAPTER TWO

Before Bidding Farewell: What Do Narratives of Education Say?

The Arabic novel that modeled itself on the bourgeois epic is mostly concerned with education. With the exception of a few narratives that deal with the divides between tradition and modernity, the majority of narratives have a biographical, pseudo-autobiographical, or autobiographical drive that focuses on apprenticeship. The Western model does not necessarily involve a journey. At times, books, as readings with a formative impact on the impressionable, curious, or needy mind, can function in similar manners. Through contact there will be a change in one's thinking. Ṭāhā Ḥusayn has both in *Al-Ayyām* (serialized in the 1920s; English translation, *An Egyptian Childhood*, 1932) and *Adīb* (1935; *Man of Letters*). In *Ibrāhīm al-Kātib* (*Ibrāhīm the Writer*), Ibrāhīm al-Māzinī manages a transformation through readings and contacts, while Maḥmūd Aḥmad al-Sayyid's protagonists need to travel in order to meet Indian intellectuals and engage with the writings of Russian, Turkish, and Western ideologues and thinkers. Dhū al-Nūn Ayyūb has his Doctor Ibrāhīm, who acquires his doctoral degree in London and comes back with an English wife as part of the Iraqi elite which the British colonial powers need to secure their influence in Iraq. Salāma Mūsā (d. 1947) has his *Tarbiyat Salāma Mūsā* (*The Education of Salāma Mūsā*). Tawfīq al-Ḥakīm has his *'Awdat al-ruḥ* (1933; *The Return of the Spirit*, 1990). As late as 1980, Nawāl al-Saʿdāwī writes *Mudhakkirat Ṭabībah* (1980; *Memoirs of a Woman Doctor*, 1989).[1] It is rare to encounter a prominent writer without some autobiographical narrative or a biographical sketch of others. The novel of apprenticeship is the most dominant form in the first half of the twentieth century, and its presence should serve to draw our attention to a number of things. First, there is the perceived need for Europe to be the master who is needed by the novice in a cultural dependency transaction pure and simple. Second, there is a desire to have this recorded in writing so as to be effectively present in the minds of readers and thereby help initiate an educational process that will take form in educational missions and other procedures that have become part of the normalization and codification process of the nation-state. These narratives portray each protagonist's pride in being apprenticed to this European culture. There is, third, a faith in this endeavor as the only viable way to bid farewell to a past. In every narrative of biographical or autobiographical nature, past or present, there is a mention of writers and books that have helped in the education of the narrative's primary subject. In an ironic twist, the subject is subjected through writing to another informational order whereby books and influences shape and form the new character who is not the same as the one whom we met in the first pages. Indeed, Louis Althusser's statement in *Ideology and Ideological State Apparatuses* applies neatly to this transformation under the impact and readiness of the colonized subject: "ideology 'acts' or 'functions' in such a way that it 'recruits' subjects among the individuals . . . , or 'transforms' the individuals into subjects by . . . *interpellation* or hailing."[2] Chronology and historical boundaries create the frames within which a character, as conditioned by time, is detailed. The temporal element becomes more complicated, however, in the context of these readings and meetings that operate synchronically to retrieve the subject from a past which is usually taken to be one of loss and failure and to move that subjected being toward another where an active mind is still not necessarily free of the effects of mimicry or schizophrenia.

As many of these biographies and autobiographies have already received some attention in previous pages, I focus in what follows on an Iraqi writer, an Egyptian litterateur, and a historical figure, a *faqīh* or jurist, from Bilād al-Shām, greater Syria, who has reemerged through leftist writings that sound paradoxically like echoes of Wahhabi revivalism. In all these works it is biographical narrativity that functions as common denominator. Only in the last of the three does the encounter with another take place in past time; as a result, different paradigms of challenge and transformation are encountered. There it is the author who undergoes change.

Duktūr Ibrāhīm (1939)

The origin of this novel is personal. Its Iraqi author, Dhū al-Nūn Ayyūb (d. 1988), had published a short story titled "Naḥwa al-qimmah" ("Toward the Summit"), and it had led to a furious reaction from the Ministry of Education and the author's consequent banishment as secondary school teacher to Kwīsinjaq in northern Iraq. The ministry suspected that he was portraying one of its leading officials, Director General Fāḍil al-Jamālī, who had received his doctoral degree from the Teachers College at Columbia University in New York City (1932); the short story was read as a vituperative biographical sketch of this senior official. Years later, when the same senior official, who had since become the Iraqi premier in 1955 and minister of foreign affairs more than once, suffered imprisonment and was condemned to death after the 1958 revolution against the monarchy, Ayyūb denied that he had had al-Jamālī in mind.[3] The character sketched in this short story can fit any high-ranking intellectual with a Western education who ruthlessly pursues selfish ends against a specifically Iraqi context of integrity, solidarity, and deference in a communal climate of mutual understanding. The short story grew into a novel titled *Duktūr Ibrāhīm* (*Doctor Ibrāhīm*). It replicates the structure of an earlier narrative genre in Arabic, the *maqāmah* (assembly), in the sense that, as primary narrator, the novelist is the one selecting a character whom he listens to, hears about, and gives space and voice to so as to give full rein to a portrait of Iraq in the 1930s. He starts with a large and busy coffeehouse where people are busy playing dominoes, gossiping, and exchanging compliments or insults. Here is some material for a novel, he tells himself. He concludes that he has managed to collect some extremely abhorrent and disgusting images which are nevertheless worth listing since they belong to the reality that is his concern. The biographical sketch, or at least what the state believes to be so, portrays the protagonist as the son of a villager who migrates from Iran, settles in a village near Mosul, and comes to occupy a respectable position in the village as a descendant of the Prophet's family. The father gets married in the village, and it is there that he also discovers the tomb of a saint. He builds a shrine which becomes a sanctuary and a resort for people with vows, prayers, benedictions, and blessings, and hence a good source of income. The construction of the shrine also coincides with a good season of rain, something that enhances the belief of villagers and others in the blessings bestowed by the saint and his custodian. The village grows in prosperity, and many people settle there, including a *kuttāb* (traditional school) teacher who teaches Ibrāhīm, the son of the family, how to read and study the Qur'ān, all in preparation for sending him to Baghdad to attend state schools. His father then helps secure a government scholarship to send him to England. On his way to London, he stays for a few days in Damascus, where he sleeps with a prostitute and drinks wine. In London he begins attending church and meeting an Anglican priest, gets married to the priest's daughter, Jenny, and studies agriculture at London University. With a doctoral degree and a British wife he returns to Iraq, intent on securing the best positions by whatever ruthless means. Throughout he is portrayed as the epitome of selfishness, someone who alienates competitors and works with any group of opportunists to shake governments and help in their downfall, all in order to secure a better position for himself. One senior official tells him: "You are following a very thorny path, and I am afraid you'll be destroyed by your venom and desire to attack and destroy." His portrait is of an opportunist whom only the British trust and think of as their own protégé. He subscribes to clubs and secures membership in societies that claim to be nationalist or liberal. He usually does this through a negative assessment of competing societies and political parties. With the deterioration of the political situation, his participation in religious or political factionalism and partisan positions no longer helps: hence his decision to take his wealth and leave for England.

Regardless of this biographical sketch, one that was interpreted as a critical portrait of a senior official, the novel still retains its significance as a narrative of education. British education is not criticized, but there is a strongly negative view of the colonial system that looks upon the colonized nation as a factory for breeding weaklings in need of British care in order to best serve the interests of the empire. The opportunist is portrayed as a dangerous participant in factionalism, sectarianism, and both religious and political controversy. The native intelligentsia is shown as being divided between sincerely committed individuals who are marginalized and others who are opportunists and reprobates. Doctor Ibrāhīm's bildungsroman is an extremely negative version of Arab intellectuals who are implicated in an East-West nexus. This early negative portrayal serves to justify the reaction of the common public against this class, which had once enjoyed the privilege of leadership.[4] In one place, Ibrāhīm says:

> I found some notables in the Ministry of Education talking a lot about the great Arab cause and seemingly preferring to establish a society or a party whereby they can initiate procedures to establish the great Arab league on the basis of extreme nationalist principles. I found some of them to be influenced by Hitler's theory of purity of blood, and they established measures in order to distinguish between pure and impure Arabs. Thus the issue of lineage and filiations is raised. Some people suggested the need to examine blood samples to exclude intruders. Whenever I listened to more of these extreme views, I felt terrified because my father was Persian and my wife English. I was afraid too when the club was established and members began to formulate their plans. This was to be the weakest point, one for which I could be challenged. But my fears were soon dissipated when I noticed that senior officials were actually non-Arab descendants and that their parents had held important positions under the Ot-

> tomans. These then are the people who keep on talking about Arab purity more than genuine Arabs do. Thus, I asked for membership and began subscribing to the nationalist cause.[5]

Written at such an early stage in the development of modern Arabic fiction, this narrative conveys the understanding of nationalism based on pan-Arab ideas that are significantly different not only from the Egyptian regional understanding but also from that of the Muslim Brothers' call for a unified Islamic-Arab *'ummah.* It also conveys an understanding of the concerns of the intelligentsia who were either remnants of the Ottoman officer class, officials who had participated in the Arab cause of the Ḥijāzīs under the leadership of Sherif Ḥusayn, or new Western trainees. These people might offer leadership, but they were largely incapable of forging emotive links with the masses. Their presence is portrayed as a source of dangerous manipulation of the masses, whose reactions are identified through such disseminated appellations as "fascist, British, Arab nationalist, Nazi, communist, sectarian. . . . These appellations were heaped on dailies, magazines, even books, regardless of their specialization whether scientific or literary and novelistic. Personal interests were hidden behind these names which became strong weapons brandished by the powerful."[6] Official and formal discourses are henceforth laden with these to alienate and marginalize groups and individuals. It is rare to come across partisan political discourse or security offices' reports without these blunt adjectives and appellations. Whether referring to media and the press, or to social space at large, these activities mean a manipulation of an absolute space where the discourse of the powerful reigns supreme.

Iraqi writers seem to be more direct in dealing with the political scene as reflected in the education of the protagonist and his colleagues. The case is even more so in Maḥmūd Aḥmad al-Sayyid's *Jalāl wa Khālid* (1928; *Jalāl and Khālid*), which covers the period from 1919 to 1922. It assumes a number of forms since it is a journey, not to Europe, but rather to Bombay in the company of a Jewish family, the parents of a young woman with her fiancé. The main character is in love with the young woman, but in Bombay he loses track of the family, though he comes across the fiancé, who is distraught and mad after being jilted by the young woman. The protagonist thinks that it is his own love that lies behind this breakup and tries his best to discover the family's whereabouts. In a hotel in Calcutta he meets Swami, a revolutionary journalist, and the two of them discuss colonialism, socialism, Darwin, and many other issues. He attends lectures on Islamic thought and listens to others on Turkish, Russian, and German literature. In Bombay he asks a friend to trace the young Jewish woman with whom he is in love, but is disappointed to learn that despair and misery have caused her to work in a brothel. Back home again, he learns of the failure of the 1920 popular revolt in Iraq. This section is followed by an exchange of letters between him and his other friends who are ostensibly al-Sayyid's known comrades, especially the Communist Ḥusayn al-Raḥḥāl. The epistolary part of the novel illustrates the difficulty in continuing a narrative that is more concerned with ideas than events. Even so, the novel provides a good picture of Iraqi life and thought at the time, including detail about the newly emerging intelligentsia, its anxieties, and its quest for a new outlook in a world that is rapidly changing. Intellectuals are less involved in religion, and their attempts to find out about it constitute a small portion in comparison to other intellectual concerns.

In these narratives of intellectual formation it is the estrangement from the common public that constitutes the most conspicuous aspect. Islam recedes into the background. Years later, narratives of education are to gain more as the result of direct contacts with Russian and European narrative models of middle-class apprenticeships. Goethe has already offered his Werther, but Charles Dickens and others have their models too. The encounter with Europe has all the elements of an explosive contact whereby the novice has the chance to experience education differently and test the ups and downs of open communication, especially after World War I. Language as formed and informed by space in a specific time undergoes change and demonstrates the symptoms and scars of these encounters that narratives strive to engage under the peril of exactitude or suggestion that can be taken seriously by the newly empowered custodians of education and politics.

Yaḥyā Ḥaqqī's *Qindīl Umm Hāshim*

Yaḥyā Ḥaqqī's *Qindīl Umm Hāshim* (1944; *The Lamp of Umm Hāshim*, or *The Saint's Lamp*)[7] is like many novellas and long narratives that subscribe to the intellectual elite's depiction of their dilemma being positioned between the achievements of Western culture and their Arab-Islamic traditional background. Rather than demonstrating a rigorous engagement with traditions or even space as actually lived by Egyptians, the novella conveys the dilemma of a generation of writers who confuse their family upbringing and societal and familial strictures with Islam as a cultural space of representational symbols, practices, and class roots. This confusion is more conspicuous for being framed in a mind-set, a paradigm, of East-West dichotomy, which was popular in colonial discourse in general, but most notoriously signified and established in Rudyard Kipling's impossible convergence of the twain. More focused on this binary and dichotomous polarization than many other narratives, this novella reveals more about the author and the national bourgeoisie than about the popular Arab-Islamic tradition that is seemingly the focus of the novella and the reason behind the choice of this specific title. It portrays a national bourgeoisie, especially its petit segment from among the educated class, whose discontent with popular societal norms blinds them to the larger context of the Arab-Islamic tradition. The whole issue, the relation of popular belief and practices to the Arab-Islamic tradition, is summed up on the very first page in a few sweeping descriptive lines that juxtapose popular visitations to sacred shrines with the scholarly or fastidious religious tradition that upholds formal obligations and practices, as prescribed in the corpus of the *Sunna*. Thus, the boy, now the grandfather Shaykh Ragab ʿAbdullah, who joins the family in coming to Cairo and visiting the Mosque of Sayyida Zainab, "would drop down and cover the marble doorstep with kisses."[8] To problematize the difference between such practices and formal obligations, the narrator adds: "if their action was witnessed by one of the self-righteous men of religion, he would turn his face away in indignation at the times and would invoke God's aid against idolatry, ignorance, and such heresies."[9] There is not much choice between these two positions, adherence to popular beliefs of the downtrodden and the uneducated, or the astute religiosity of theologians.

This juxtaposition is not followed up, and the many ramifications of popular visitations and practices and the theological treatises for or against them are not the concerns of this narrative. No character will take over this role of contending with popular practices, shrine rituals, and the power of attachment to the family of the Prophet. The novella's focus is on something else; the upbringing of Ismaʿīl in preparation to and engagement with the subsequent polarization of action and belief under the impact of the Scottish woman, Mary, who functions as a dynamic influence that unsettles his early traditional background. When in Britain, Isma'īl looks upon Mary as his guide, teacher, and provider of love. Indeed, like many other intellectuals in Egypt, Yaḥyā Ḥaqqī endows Mary with enough logic, reason, composure, wit, and capacity to guide Ismaʿīl, along with a freedom from sentimentalism so that she is able to grow metaphorically into a trope for Europe. She is the epitome of science, progress, superiority, education, and resourcefulness. Her femininity is an endearing attribute that ensures her supremacy as befitting Great Britain. Her impact does not dwindle or recede. In terminating his apprenticeship, she duplicates the empire and its mandate rule. Her protectorate supervision is needed before granting full independence. Mary gives him up as a finished product, like the groomed national elite whose mission is to spread the white man's civilizational mission, one that, allegorically expressed, is no less than to bring light to a blind nation. As a specialist in eye disease, he is trained, says his instructor, to bring light to the "land of the blind." This is the rhetoric of empire that regards the national elite as the subjected national manpower put in place in order to control the ex-colony. The novella deals with the following stages in the career and life of the medical doctor Isma'īl: an understandable surrender to a traditional upbringing; a period of study, seven years, in England that changes and unsettles that upbringing; a return home to stand up to traditional practices; and an eventual recognition of popular tradition as so deeply involved in people's minds and emotions that an appropriation of knowledge through a return to traditional ways must take place.

Tradition is depicted in a number of sweeping descriptions that repeat common knowledge since classical times. Inside Isma'īl's house, "the reciting of the Qur'ān never stopped and . . . the canonical law of Islam represented the whole of truth and knowledge. This spirit had taken up residence in a small corner of the house, had covered its head and stretched out its body and had triumphantly fallen into a gratified slumber."[10] The comment is not random, for it recapitulates an understanding among the educated segment of the national bourgeoisie to the effect that stagnation is the image that emerges from a long period of immobility and slumber. The understanding is central to an Arab liberal tradition that was confronting and arguing with popular practices and the upholders of a conservative allegiance to the past.

The novella subscribes to the mind of common colonial discourse that these societies suffer from a cultural rather than social or political problem whose source and locus is Islam itself. Finding its basic tenets collapsed into a variety of popular practices, Islam becomes the butt of criticism throughout the nineteenth century. Compromising national identity in the process of catering to Western ideals of science and progress, intellectual elites repeat some of these criticisms without pause for thought, venturing thereby into a cultural terrain of great complicity and complexity.

This novella then underscores its critique of dormancy, as enshrined in the family house and its "canonical law of Islam," through another simulacrum of cultural disparity between the East and the West. We are told that the protagonist's mother's attitude and understanding are no less fettered by this tradition, to such an extent that she imagines her son's departure to foreign lands as being no more than "the end of a tall stairway that ended at a land covered in snow and inhabited by peoples who possessed the wiles and tricks of the djinn."[11] Predicated on the same dormant tradition of supernatural associations and superstitious practices and beliefs, such thoughts create yet another imaginary that is also intended to consolidate the disparity between a dormant local culture and a dynamic British one, between Islam and an enlightened Europe. This same imaginary receives a number of additional touches that allow for a consolidation of the contrast with a West exemplified by the character of Mary. Aside from the protagonist's father's advice to the son to be "scrupulous about . . . [his] religion and its duties,"[12] there is also a description of the shaykh's rituals, which are meant to balance formal obligations with common traditions. The shaykh is depicted as solemn looking, "standing with bowed head, as though exhausted or overcome by awesome fear."[13] In compliance with this solemn performance, the protagonist "Ismail walked round the shrine until he came to the wall separating the place for the women from the men."[14] As if that is not enough, the narrator proceeds to further disturb this moment of serenity by means of an irreverent act of deviation that leads him to stare at a "dark-skinned girl" whose image will remain with him. This young girl is a supplicant for mercy. As she herself says, "Here is my soul at your threshold, felled to the ground, twisting and writhing and wanting to recover."[15] The protagonist's secular concerns and meditations may well be preparing him for his trip, but they are present nevertheless as a perspective on his other self, the one that is not totally numbed. "The girl placed her lips against the railing of the shrine. The kiss was not part of her trade, it came from the heart," says Ismā'īl to himself, adding: "Who is there who should assert for certain that Umm Hāshim had not herself come to the railing, her lips ready to exchange kiss for kiss?"[16] Speaking for a bourgeois mind-set that marked the national elite during a specific interwar period, the protagonist has already confiscated the sacral and turned the shrine into another space where a different discourse reigns. Indeed, this early confiscation foreshadows a homecoming that is replete with power to subdue the natural and the sacral through violent means. His destruction of the lamp attests to what Lefebvre describes as the dominant form of space, "that of centers of wealth and power, [that] endeavors to mould the spaces it dominates . . . and it seeks, often by violent means, to reduce the obstacles and resistance it encounters there."[17] The protagonist cannot achieve this goal and his impassioned action shows infantilism that reflects badly on the empire and its trainees, but the conflict is set in blunt terms against rituals and practices which are still dear to the common public. The act speaks for a tendency, a trend, that state education disseminates and consolidates in keeping with the interest of a rising class whose aspirations also coincide with the interests of the empire.

The journey to the heart of empire tells us much. Although the fear of the unknown is no less pivotal in the protagonist's experience, it is given less space and hence less narrative power than the civilizational gap as he perceives it. The unknown is more personal, for it means "loneliness and the unknown living in a strange land."[18] The things that he is asked to take with him amount to no more than slippers, baggy underpants, and "peasant cakes and pastries" that he will perhaps recall later as evidence of backwardness.[19] The rural attitude is not depicted as any less parochial than rural life in England at the time. But the people who present him with these gifts have a different intention. As the narrator notes, the protagonist's father insists that his son take a "pair of wooden slippers" because "making one's ablutions before prayers in Europe was rendered difficult by the fact that people had the habit of wearing their shoes indoors."[20]

The seven years he spends in England bring about his transformation, but that process is summarized in a few sentences that are meant to consolidate the difference between the two cultures. The personal record is one of juxtaposition, for he "had been chaste and had been led astray, had been sober and had got drunk, had danced with young girls and had misbehaved."[21] In his evaluation of such activities, these are negative developments, but they are balanced by his new bent, which is able "to appreciate nature's beauty, to enjoy sunsets . . . and how to find pleasure in the sting of the cold of the north" (p. 126). These personal impressions operate differently within the binary structure that holds the narrative together, subscribing as they do to an image of an Orient, Egypt in this case, that is conservative, communal, unused to worldly pleasure, and incapable of enjoying nature as it is. By extension, this may imply that such people do not deserve what they have, for they are incapable of experiencing joy or are reluctant to do so. Certainly, Yaḥyā Ḥaqqī's approach in this novella cannot be regarded as representative of a tendency among the elite to see their life as being devoid of joy and love of nature, for writers like Salāma Mūsā provide a different perspective. In his *Education* the latter says that country life "imparted to me so much practical knowledge and wisdom that I certainly consider it a true part of my education. . . . I acquired above all that love for nature which caused me to feel throughout my life that the Earth is our Mother."[22] Directing this love into his Darwinist evolutionary perspective, Mūsā speaks for another segment of the intelligentsia that was focused on science and economic development, whereas Yaḥyā Ḥaqqī's worldview is tied to popular practices as barriers to scientific growth. Everything else in local life dwindles to nothingness. Negativism is the dominating marker of this outlook, whereas positivism distinguishes Mūsā's thought.

But the list of differences does not end here in that Ḥaqqi's protagonist Ismā'īl looks forward to establishing "a program for . . . [his] life," while Mary tells him how mistaken he is, as "life is no fixed program, but an ever renewed debate."[23] Based on the paradigm of absolute difference, the contrast represented by these two characters clearly subscribes to the dormancy-progress binary. The West connotes motion and mobility: whereas Ismā'īl suggests that they "sit down," Mary tells him to "walk" (p. 65). When he expresses his desire to get married, Mary talks to him of love. Marriage becomes another trope for settlement and immobility. It becomes associated with an unwarranted convenience in an age of experimentation and exchange where commodity gives way to larger transactions and capital overrules all, involving the whole society in mobility and competition. His idea of marriage contrasts with a dynamic love that makes use of the "present moment," not the "future."[24] These comparisons and contrasts sustain the paradigmatic structure of the novella, its dichotomous composition and polarized characterization. These distinct traits and tendencies also build on a specific depiction of the protagonist as lacking individuality, brought up to look "outside himself for something to cling to, to lean on: his religion and his faith, his upbringing and his roots."[25] While this reliance on an outside power may well represent the Sartrean idea of bad faith, there is something more here that predates any possibility of choice: Ismāʿīl is a product of a system of beliefs and attitudes that are restrictive; it is only under the impact of a symbolic representative of the empire, Mary in this case, that Ismāʿīl can release himself from the shackles of faith and only through this kind of guidance that he can be freed from normative ethics or values that emerge in the text as if they existed for one person, one society, and one culture. Mary is the educator, and Yaḥyā Ḥaqqī's protagonist is the disciple in a process of apprenticeship, like the nation in Lord Cromer's terms. As long as he searches for succor and power outside himself and his religion and tradition, he will remain in need of Mary. Thus, she tells him, as if speaking in the author's own voice, "he who resorts to a hook will remain his whole life a prisoner alongside it, guarding his only coat. Your hook must be inside yourself."[26] But the contrast between the two is endless: she is afraid of "fetters," while he is afraid of "freedom." These are not depicted as passing traits or characteristics, but rather each of them is intended to demonstrate differences that cannot disappear without a full apprenticeship. He is afraid of socialization; for him life unfolds as a "clash between personalities," an attitude that she castigates as lacking any incentive to engage with people.[27] Her teaching does not come to an end, since Ismāʿīl becomes yet another blank page, just like the Orient in colonial records. If there is any kind of inscription, it must be erased so as to allow enough space for the new teaching. The native intellectual returns home to celebrate the civilizational mission and subscribe to it. Even when he eventually succumbs to his innate disposition to care for the weak and forlorn among his patients, Mary is still at the back of his mind, since she has already ridiculed such a move as no more than an invitation to defeat, something that will inevitably lead in the end to a "circle of the sick and the defeated closing in on him and clinging to him." Considering such an attitude as mere sentimentalism, she advises him not to let himself drown along with the other drowning people. "These Oriental sentiments of yours are despicable and disgusting because they are not practical or productive."[28] Indeed, the last pages of the novella speak of Ismā'īl as a complacent doctor, self-satisfied, inclined to food and sex, and completely subsumed in a society of lazy, shabby, and untidy people. Mary's stigmatization of this attitude as an "Oriental" one relies heavily on a colonial discourse that has been unwavering in its binaries and rejection of others. To forge a character that is "productive" enough to dislodge the "Oriental" one becomes the mission of empire which the novella pursues as an interpellation process whereby subjects accept subjection to the empire as subject.

In this novella, the apprenticeship represented by the relationship with Mary is accepted despite a feeling of unease and discomfort, "under the blows of her axe."[29] The blows symbolically reiterate the colonial rhetoric of debasement of the native and celebration of the colonial. Based on both Darwin's determinism and deeply implicated in a racist inferiorization of the native, this rhetoric survives by aggrandizement, something that is so repeatedly affirmed that it infects the native intellectual, forcing him or her to repeat the very same jargon as a given. We should keep in mind that Darwin's thought had already penetrated liberal discourse and left quite an impression on the intellectual sphere as well, not only through its primary perpetrator, the intellectual, Shīblī Shumayyil, but also through the liberal media, which were receptive to any scientific critique of tradition. This celebration was not limited to Egypt; Iraqi and Syrian intellectuals were no less inclined to Darwinism in its stand against religion, which at that time they associated with Ottomans as the ultimate outgrowth of Islam.[30] Hence, Ismā'īl—the native intellectual whose grounding in his native tradition is very superficial and thin—easily succumbs to hearsay and surrenders the little learning with which he is familiar from his own culture. Thus says Yaḥyā Ḥaqqī's narrator: "Religion became for him [Ismā'īl] a fable that had been invented in order to keep the masses in control, while the human spirit could find no strength, and thus no happiness, unless it detached itself from crowds and from confronting them; to immerse oneself in them was a weakness spelling disaster."[31] In other words, the agents and material in support of Islam in the street are left on the sidelines in the context of a colonial discourse that many *nahḍah* intellectuals absorbed while fighting military and political encroachment.

Although lightly touched on by the narrative, Mary's choice of another "fellow student of her own race and color" is no ordinary matter within this verbal construct of dependency and subordination. The native elite, groomed and prepared by the colonizing culture, is meant to outgrow this dependency as cultural apprenticeship, not as economic or political sovereignty. The author is more implicated than at first appears in cultural dependency as part of a narrative journey through backwardness to enlightenment and ultimate compromise between the two. Although at times the narrative is given enough multiplicity, there is nevertheless a framing voice that puts everything into shape so as to fit into a compromise that is no less damaging than the *nahḍah* discourse itself, which applies the premises of modernity without any serious effort to subsume it within a local or national knowledge that has a corpus and inventory of its own. Yaḥyā Ḥaqqī's narrative is content to portray an eventual apprenticeship that signals the birth of a pro-Western elite: Ismā'īl "no longer did . . . sit before his master, but as a colleague."[32] Armed with this coming of age, the native elite should be sufficiently equipped to duplicate the culture and knowledge of the metropolis. Now that Ismā'īl has been stripped of the little religion in which he has been brought up, he can participate in implementation and further cultivation of the seeds of Western enlightenment, just like hundreds of other members of the newly emerging national bourgeoisie. As instructor, the bearer of the metropolitan legacy, Mary is like "every artist" who has grown bored "with her work of art, and it had been completed."[33] The next sentence is no less problematic, however, in that it shows us how implicated this narrative is in the colonial rhetoric. The native is progressing, under imperial gaze and touch, from a primitive to a civilized stage. "Once cured, Ismā'īl for her lost all his magic, becoming just like the other people she knew."[34] There is no exoticism or charm anymore. The body that is addressed, talked to, guided, and taken care of is now resuscitated. Hence, it loses its attraction. The Lacanian love is now replaced by a love-hate relationship, not one involving a parity of equals, but instead as an inevitable matter of an almost clinical procedure. The patient is now well enough to leave, but still not good enough to assume total independence.

This explanation should not detract from subsequent recapitulations that focus on European women, seen through Ismā'īl's newly awakened desire for them and Mary's "keen appetite."[35] These awakenings of desire are regularly emphasized in narratives of cultural and geographical encounters, not because they do not exist back home, but because to some degree such indigenous encounters are somewhat more subdued and for a number of reasons, including religious tradition, availability of public space for meetings, and sensitivity to social codes and ethics. Yaḥyā Ḥaqqī's Mary is, like al-Ḥakīm's Suzy, an invention that betrays the impact of an Orientalization process within the construction of Arab *nahḍah* (awakening) discourse. The choice of the female is not random. The British romantics, Byron in particular, have their dark and attractive females who also sometimes have Greek origins. They are waiting for a hero from Europe to ensure their rescue and provide them with love rather than servitude. The Arab intellectual borrows the female trope and uses it in the context of a colonial binary where Europe is the empowered female while the Eastern male is the powerless and dying patient. Their native female is not applicable to such a context, since she belongs to a long tradition of association between woman and nation. The male must also be used to fit the narrator's voice, conveying all the weaknesses that are already internalized in native intellectual discourse through apprenticeship and subordination.

More significant, however, is what the narrative recounts as national awakening. Soon after Mary's initiation of Ismā'īl into European, specifically British, life and culture, he develops a different sense of nationalness,[36] a sense that is assumed to be a duplication of the European nation-state. "Ismail used to have only the vaguest of feelings for Egypt. He was like a grain of sand that has been merged into other sands and has become so assimilated among them that he could not be distinguished from them even when separated from all other grains."[37] The wording here needs to be closely examined: everything is dehumanized to fit into a paradigm of conformity that is leveled against the Orient in nineteenth-century European sociology—as a region of conformity, communal imposition, and hence lack of individualism. That is the way in which Walter Bagehot used to collapse European neoclassicalism into the discussion, using the developing methods of sociological analysis that blend well with colonial and Orientalist discourse.[38] The underlying assumption is that Islam is an equalizer in everything, but especially in customs and ways of life that, according to Bagehot, leave the individual with no will, and hence no "tragic" sense of life. This combination of classical literary generic principles with a vague knowledge of Islam as faith creeps into Yaḥyā Ḥaqqī's narrative in much the same way as it infiltrates the very heart of the so-called awakening discourse, thus involving it in a series of contradictions, presumptions, and ethics of dependency. This awakening discourse has thus come to play an enormously important role in the education of the national bourgeoisie, but with little profundity in covering those areas that might serve to redirect attention toward tradition and religion as objects of thoughtful analysis, discussion, and much-needed dissection. Long left to languish on the shelf and removed from the common public and its usual practices of faith, Islam and tradition have now returned with greater power and force, a force that neither the nation-state nor the elite are prepared to handle.

Yaḥyā Ḥaqqī's apprentice now joins the national bourgeoisie in the cultivation of "nationalness," which is very much an echo of the so-called Egyptian nationalism that Salāma Mūsā, among others, associates with Aḥmad Luṭfī al-Sayyid's role early in the twentieth century.[39] "Now, however, he felt himself to be a ring in a long chain that tightly bound him to his mother country."[40] It is the role of the national elite to pursue its educational message after returning to the homeland armed with enlightenment discourse and its paradigms of progress to be placed in opposition to fixity, rationalism versus emotionalism, and individualism versus conformity, all of them confrontations exemplified in Ismāʿīl's rehearsal of Mary's teachings.[41] The national elite are now expected to assume responsibility for the duplication of the nation-state, not only through statements but other methods as well, and with little or no regard to one's area of specialization resulting from seven years spent in Europe. Thinking of his enlightenment mission and in line with Aḥmad Luṭfī al-Sayyid and others, Ismāʿīl "let his mind wander and saw himself as a journalist writing in the newspapers or as an orator at a meeting expounding his views and beliefs to the masses."[42] The other thought that occupies his mind upon his return to Egypt is one of satisfaction or even complacency: "He was returning home equipped with the very weapon his father wanted for him"; moreover, "he was determined that with this weapon he would carve for himself a path to the front ranks."[43] In this aspiration and the accompanying complacency he is no different from members of other national elites who, in a number of narratives, take pride in being educated in Europe. They too return home with a definite intention of copying their European experience back home, implanting European ways of life and culture, and building a nation-state that is no different from the European model. "First of all, he would astonish the Cairenes, then the Egyptians in their entirety, with his skill and the breadth of his experience."[44]

Instead of studying his society back home, the actual conditions, and the standard of living, his newly adopted metropolitan lenses only provide him with a dim picture. The scenes of poverty, misery, and devastation make him angry rather than involve him in a rational comparison that might lead to a more fruitful approach to life, material conditions, and culture in Egypt. His shock and anger accumulate, a natural consequence of his failure to appreciate that the society and the economy of his homeland have been drained for many years as the result of occupation and exploitation. "The flame of revolt grew stronger within him, and he became more determined than ever to gird himself for action."[45]

While any homecoming will rarely burgeon into an experience of enormous satisfaction, its realization within a national bourgeois consciousness only serves to exacerbate its associations with despair and frustration. Ismāʿīl aspires to implement an imaginary topos of codes, ethics, and realities upon his family's home, which "looked as though . . . [it] had been dumped in some land of exile."[46] Finding everything around him disagreeable, he ends up aligning himself with another discourse that is arrogant, superior, and dismissive of the Orient.

While his prescriptions for his fiancée, Fatima, who is in the process of losing her sight are right, his approach to the situation he discovers upon his return is as emotional, angry, and naive as his responses to other situations. The words he uses, the anger he directs at his parents, and the heedlessness with which he acts all portray him as an awkward misfit, a mimic who has not yet achieved a full selfhood. He conforms to the image held by colonial officers and administrators who will compare any display of difference or resistance to adolescence; in colonial rhetoric, these colonized nations are in need of more time in order to mature.

Away from Mary's influence and also from the metropolis or the colonizer, Ḥaqqī's protagonist is given to these convulsions and outbursts of anger. Had she been around, Mary would have told him to recognize such situations as facts and symptoms that might, to use Cromer's discourse, take longer to manage. On the other hand, there was also a deliberate colonial stratagem to let issues be prolonged and to procrastinate. In Salāma Mūsā's *Tarbiyat Salāma Mūsā* (*The Education of Salāma Mūsā*), the writer emphasizes Cromer's tendency to sustain Egypt's dependency on the colonizer by resisting any displays of selfhood, especially in matters pertaining to the education of women.

The protagonist's outburst against the very saint whom his family and the common public venerate comes as a tremendous shock, unsettling beliefs and attitudes that have been upheld for long. The naive intellectual shouts, "So this is your Umm Hāshim, the one that will make the girl blind."[47] With this kind of dismissal, loaded as it is with disrespect and unbelief, the protagonist Ismā'īl cuts through traditional beliefs and their penetration into the fabric and nerves of the social order. "A grave-like silence of despondency descended on the house inhabited by readings from the Qur'ān and the echo of calls to prayer."[48] Rather than emerging as a new member of their educated elite, the son whom they have cherished now shows himself in this dichotomous situation to be a "strange spirit [that] had come to it from across the seas." In this sense the protagonist metamorphoses into another creature, a jinni perhaps, which the family regards with both shock and surprise. The writer is obviously intent on problematizing the encounter between tradition and modernity, faith and science, and Europe and Egypt. The saint, Sayyida Zainab, also known as Umm Hāshim, epitomizes faith and belief. She stands for a public that finds its satisfaction in worship at her shrine in the absence of other means of improvement and change. Living in poverty, the society has no other alternative but this reciprocity that is built on love and veneration. Its communal base and spiritual liaison help establish a concordance that stands as the only available succor. Assuming unwittingly the will and power of England, its systems of thought and domination, the son thinks in terms of enforcement and domination. He thinks he can also control a seemingly abstract space, empty and inviting, in order to eradicate its historical and natural aspects and replace all with the relics of a new power, with its symbols and practices. He goes so far as to think that the shrine and all its connotations can be vanquished and eradicated, to be experienced from now on "as nostalgia," as Henri Lefebvre explains in respect to abstract and social spaces.[49] Hence the father is disturbed by his son's outburst. "What are you saying? Is this what you learned abroad? Is all we have gained to have you return to us an infidel?"[50] The implications of this "coup de grâce," as the author terms it,[51] emanate from the self-assurance that the returning national elite have under the influence of the metropolitan center or "the advantageous position of education in the London metropolis," as Salāma Mūsā calls it.[52] Rather than accommodating its own new role to the nature of the society in some reasonable proportion, the elite imagine that they have returned home with the right prescription to cure the entire society once and for all. It is no mere coincidence that the author assigns this function to the protagonist, an eye doctor; prescription is to serve as the methodology of the elite that emanates from a sense of superiority over the rest of society. His status as an eye specialist also stands symbolically for the feeling that these elite are able to "see" on behalf of the whole nation, act in its best interests, and accordingly address its problems. Hence, the author allows us to listen to the protagonist as he keeps telling himself that he "would not flinch from delivering a coup de grâce to the very heart of ignorance and superstition, be it the last thing he did."[53] Although he will change his means of recourse and yield under the impact of the enormous amount of affection and veneration shown by the masses toward the shrine of the saint, anger and revolt remain firmly fixed in the minds of a large segment of the national bourgeoisie who believe that they must move beyond this stage toward a Western model that the elite conceive as being not necessarily identical with colonial intentions and designs for Egypt. Indeed, Salāma Mūsā accuses Cromer of a deliberate preservation of "tradition," implying veiling for women and the turban and *quftān* for men.[54] However, as a social class the bourgeoisie in general are more accommodating and intelligent than their educated elite. Within their own pragmatic program and the extent of achievements and gains, they are ready to accept all signs of veneration and respect for Islamic shrines as long as the process does not prevent them from the accumulation of wealth and the education of their members to fit into a new secular order. Ismā'īl himself will pursue that direction, return to his family, and gain acceptance in society as a son worthy of recognition and admiration. Though lessening his expectations and appropriating them into the social order as it actually is, his role is essentially and finally one of resignation. The writer's perspective is no less so, like many other authors in his time who come to realize that some form of compromise must be reached. Reform as such should take place in areas that demand it, like education, social welfare, and health, but not in opposition to people's beliefs. The echoes of this attitude can be traced in the programs of many political parties that at the time recognized the power of faith and belief.

The problem with this narrative, and with many others like it that deal with similar encounters, lies in its paradigmatic structuration, its application of facile dichotomies, binary classifications, and similar presumptions and premises that are out of touch with their own societies, their inner life, and preoccupations and concerns in the face of exploitation, poverty, and discord. To make such use of Ismā'īl to represent the national elite under the impact of enlightenment discourse, Mary as the embodiment of this discourse, and the saint Umm Hāshim as the symbol of backwardness, is naive and lacking in genuine appreciation of both metropolitan and national centers. No wonder that the elite, which have been given the power to lead these nations for more than ninety years, found itself in an awkward situation and unable to continue its leadership role. The grip on the common public held by the clergy and their like, albeit under the encouragement and grooming of the New World Order, can help explain the widening gap that separates the elite and the masses. Like the policies of the colonizer before, the neocapitalist order needs to return these societies to a premodern condition, though with the trappings of modern cyberspace achievements and technologies. In the end, these societies, without their potential structures, institutions, and research and library centers and museums, are returned to their premodern state. The direction is toward another infantile condition, one of adolescence that generates endless chaos but nevertheless one that allows monopolies to continue under the local leadership of a new apparatus, one that has already lost touch with the masses but has flooded its representatives with enough wealth to continue the state of chaos, as the endgame for not only the nation-state but also the nation as a whole.

Writing Ibn Taymiyyah: Sharqāwī's Difficult Choice in Literary Biography

Writing Ibn Taymiyyah (d. 1328) is no trivial matter, especially if it is undertaken by a writer like the Egyptian novelist, dramatist, and critic 'Abd al-Raḥmān al-Sharqāwī, whose intellectual life and career testify to a lifelong commitment to leftist positions. Published in 1983, a few years before the author's death, this book should be seen as a controversial contribution and intellectual risk in its own right. The title, *Ibn Taymiyyah al-faqīh al-mu'adhdhab* (Ibn

Taymiyyah: *The Suffering Jurist*), attempts to plunge headlong into the controversy while providing some justification for the project. The plan is to study the Muslim theologian and jurist, perhaps vindicate his career, and also sympathize with his sufferings. The title also reveals an intention to study the man, his career, and his controversial life. On the other hand, the publication of the book (Cairo: Dār al-Mawqif al-ʿArabī, 1983) occurred at a moment when the Iraq-Iran war involved Arabs and Muslims in heated controversy and raging differences concerning the legitimacy of war among Muslims and the justification of such wars in religious or nationalist terms. Those who claimed a one-sided nationalist agenda were supportive of Saddam Ḥusayn's rhetoric, while Islamists outside the Gulf region were opposed to the whole nationalist discourse and its subject. Even when not supportive of Iranian Islamist ideology, they regarded the war as no more than an "international" trick intended to divide the Islamic *'ummah* (nation or community) and drive it into warring factions. Iraq, Saudi Arabia, Kuwait, and the Gulf countries were more or less in agreement on curbing the Iranian Islamic revolution and preventing it from reaching their territories. Part of the struggle was implemented through a waged war, another through espionage and media, while the rest involved a Wahhābī endeavor to limit the ideology of the revolution, forestall its impact, and preempt its potential for ideological expansion. A major part of this campaign focused also on the resurrection of the life and career of primary theologians, jurists, and Islamist polemicists who had fought Shīʿism or some of its extravagant factions. Ibn Taymiyyah had certainly been a pioneer in the ideological and polemical war against Shīʿism in the thirteenth century CE, especially certain factions which he designated as extravagant and fanatical, *ghulāt*, who deserved to be annihilated, whose rituals needed to be stopped once and for all, and whose shrines should be demolished. For him, such rituals and shrines were signs of paganism. Such was also the pattern of ideas espoused by his ardent follower in the last decades of the eighteenth century, Muḥammad Ibn ʿAbd al-Wahhāb, who became the organizer of the desert-like militant Wahhābī movement. Thus the timing of the publication of al-Sharqāwī's book was not incidental and must be considered outside the context of Saddam Ḥusayn's statements against what was then seen as an instance of religious fervor in confrontation with the secular ideas of a large number of intellectuals. Rather it implies an attitude that is supported and perhaps financed by interested groups. Written by an intellectual, novelist, and dramatist, this biography sits well among other literary products as required by circumstance, need, and other motivations.

Many writers published articles and books in this historical context, but nobody made a breakthrough that managed to win public favor. Indeed, Iraqi conservatives and their bureaucratic apparatus were so sensitive to this issue that even books devoted to the study of the House of the Prophet, and authored with caution and moderation, were regarded with suspicion; indeed some were banned and their authors persecuted, imprisoned, and subsequently executed. Such was the fate of the late Iraqi thinker 'Azīz al-Sayyid Jāsim, whose book *'Alī Ibn Abī Ṭālib: Sulṭat Āl-Ḥaqq* ('Alī Ibn Abī Ṭālib: *The Authority of Righteousness*; Beirut: Dār al-Ādāb, 1988) led directly to his imprisonment in 1988 and subsequent imprisonment and execution in 1991.

Al-Sharqāwī perhaps knew how difficult it was going to be to approach his subject, even though the learned theologian and jurist deserves a good deal of attention for his valor, involvement in wars against invaders, and scholarly effort to curb many signs of failure in practice and belief. Al-Sharqāwī does not present a one-sided case, although his jurist is a man of many aspirations, whims, and firm beliefs that invite unitary interpretations. To account for this, al-Sharqāwī has to use a narrative of multiple perspectives that can try to explain contending opinions and also present other Islamic jurists whose viewpoints are worth reading and discussing. In other words, al-Sharqāwī uses biographical material to explain Ibn Taymiyyah's upbringing, his father's impact on him, and his mother's effort to cool his ardor so that he will not regard himself as the only one in the right while others are at least faulty or even infidels.

Al-Sharqāwī tries to provide a psychological dimension for the case. The child grew up in difficult circumstances: when he was just seven years old, the Mongols invaded Syria and devastated his home town, Ḥarrān, in 1261 CE (660 AH) (p. 5). While this was bound to impact his political outlook, his mother's concern that he should always be seen in the best attire can serve to direct attention toward a similar Wahhābī streak that demands tidiness and elegant dress (p. 7). This amount of detail serves to illustrate the development of a whole attitude: his father allowed him to use his private collection of books that he inherited from his own father, with its rich collection of works on law, philosophy, language, Qur'ānic studies, and pure sciences (p. 7). To prepare the reader to encounter a controversial life and career, al-Sharqāwī also adds that "his father noticed a cantankerous streak in his son and urged him to calm down, as such behavior might well lead to animosity and provoke intolerance" (p. 8). Along with these details, the narrative tells us that the son learns many kinds of sports and takes a lot of physical exercise (p. 11). Looking around him, the young man, we are told, is also appalled by a corrupt political order in which even religious leaders participate, unlike such learned shaykhs as al-'Izz Ibn 'Abd al-Salām or al-Nawawī, who enforce the "awe-inspiring power of religion" (p. 12). The protagonist is presented as aspiring to emulate the position of Shaykh al-Nawawī under the strong Mamluk Sultan Baybars, who at the time was a valiant warrior fighting on behalf of Islam, and who forbade whatever was thought of as contrary to Islamic morals (p. 25). Yet his weakness stemmed from his insistence on collecting money from people in order to provide for his military expeditions. The sultan asked the shaykh to issue a *fatwā* justifying money-collecting, but the shaykh objected: "I heard that you had a thousand slaves dressed in gold and two hundred women slaves with precious stones. When you have spent all that wealth . . . and made use of whatever is available in the treasury, then I'll justify collecting money from the people" (p. 26). The sultan ordered him to be deported, but the shaykh continued to object to any practice that might smack of injustice. The sultan called on him when he was in Syria, asking him why he had not shown the same courage against the Tartars. The shaykh reportedly answered: "The Tartars were invaders who confiscated property, and the Muslims were fighting against them. But you are the Sultan, the legitimate ruler who should enforce justice" (p. 27). Al-Sharqāwī goes on to report how Shaykh Taqī al-Dīn Ibn Taymiyyah follows the same line, acting with no less daring when meeting the Tartar ruler. Noticing Shīʿīs in his company (p. 44), he quotes Imam ʿAlī's sayings in which he justifies making war on those who have seceded (meaning ʿAlī's supporters who objected to any arbitration in the battle of Ṣiffīn). Al-Sharqāwī emphasizes the shaykh's presence and address, impressive enough to make the sultan listen to him with respect (pp. 44–45). When the sultan asks him for a word of supplication to God, he responds: "O God if You know him to be fighting in order to have Your word be supreme, then support him; but if it is only for power, the concerns of this world, and prosperity in this life, then destroy him" (p. 46). To make this image of a pious shaykh conform to his other image as a fighter for the victory of Islam, al-Sharqāwī describes his sermons in every mosque, which are intended to mobilize the public to fight the Tartars (pp. 50–51). Al-Sharqāwī also reports how Ibn Taymiyyah dresses in military uniform during the campaign against the Tartars. It is at the same time that he warns against rumors that describe the Tartars as Muslims. "They are like those who seceded from ʿAlī's army and Muʿāwiyah," he says, "people who claimed they had a better right to lead than either of them. But the Commander of the Faithful fought them. . . . If you see me in their company with the Qur'ān on my head, then murder me too" (p. 74). At that time Shaykh Taqī al-Dīn Ibn Taymiyyah decides to focus his attention on the esoteric practices of *Ahl al-bāṭin* (the people of inward interpretations of the Qur'ān), using the term in more general ways to include all Shīʿīs. Al-Sharqāwī quotes him: "When the Tartars came to the land, they were happy about their progress and committed major atrocities against Muslims. They corresponded with the people of Cyprus who are Crusaders, invaded the coast, carried Crusader banners, and transported an unlimited number of Muslim horses, weapons, and prisoners to Cyprus. For twenty days they established a market on the coast, selling Muslims, horses, weapons, to the people of Cyprus" (p. 82). The shaykh, reports al-Sharqāwī, issues a *fatwā* authorizing their killing. "Since they are aggressors, fighting back against them is a duty" (p. 83). But al-Sharqāwī hastens to explain that the shaykh does not include the Zaydis or twelvers in his condemnation; they have a better faith and their own particular beliefs. The shaykh defends the twelver Shi'īs as followers of Imam Ja'far al-Ṣādiq (the sixth imam for Shi'īs, d. 763) who of all the imams was the most knowledgeable about *al-Sunnah*. He adds, "When Imam Mālik used to see Imam al-Ṣādiq entering the mosque and sitting at the back, he would stop his lesson, call him over, surrender his seat to him and have him sit next to him" (p. 84). Ibn Taymiyyah's attack is focused on *Ahl al-bāṭin*, who consider Islamic law as one with "covert and overt dimensions: the extrinsic is what is known to Ahl al-Sunnah, but the intrinsic is their own property" (p. 85).[55]

The other target of Ibn Taymiyyah's attack is Sufism. Both these targets are still the focus of Wahhābī opprobrium and opposition. To the Wahhābīs, Sufism and the process of reading and interpreting texts beyond their literal meaning (esotericism) implies paganism, or at best a deviational undertaking that brings about division. According to the biographical material that al-Sharqāwī relies on, Ibn Taymiyyah aimed his onslaught primarily at *al-Bāṭiniyyah* (esotericists) and Sufism, based on his impression of popular belief in his own time. He refers, for example, to the former *Ahl al-jabal* (People of the Mount) who were Nuṣayrīs or Alawaites, and heaps many accusations on their heads, including some that are nonsensical. They are the people, he claims, who interpret the Qur'ānic verse "And your God inspired bees to have the mount as home, and from the trees, and the evergreen" in their own particular way; to *Ahl al-Bāṭin* (esotericists), he argues, bees are the imam's missionaries, mountains are the messengers, and trees are the evidence. He goes on to argue that they deny that God can be described in affirmation, in terms of existence or nothingness, in ability or inability, or in knowledge and lack thereof. He concludes that they negate his blessed attributes (p. 85). It is difficult to determine whether al-Sharqāwī is intentionally filling this documentary record with interpretations and rumors in order to debate Ibn Taymiyyah and leave him unprotected, alone with his own rhetoric in the face of his exteriorization of details and religious and eschatological references. To all this he adds more details concerning Ibn Taymiyyah's dicta, including the use of hashish and drugs and the celebration of a night called *laylat al-had'ah* (the night of certitude—so called after the site of Muzdalifa on the pilgrimage trail near Mecca).[56] Ibn Taymiyyah accuses them of condoning the free mingling of sexes in total darkness, so nobody knows who is who (p. 86). With these notions and rumors, Ibn Taymiyyah campaigned widely in Syria against the Nuṣayrīs until the sultan led an army against them, a campaign in which he was joined by Ibn Taymiyyah and another Shīʿī leader from the twelvers (p. 86). Ibn Taymiyyah justifies cutting down trees and destroying houses, as he compares them to tribes which the Prophet fought using similar procedures and means (p. 87). In other words, al-Sharqāwī, basing himself on Ibn Taymiyyah's biographies, justifies his campaigns in terms of an Islamic context. Certainly the same set of accusations—dubious arrangements with enemies, denial of *Sunnah*, and immoral behavior—will all be used later by groups that invoke Ibn Taymiyyah's ideas and popularize his Islamicist self-righteousness among the masses.

The same ideology was invoked to oppose the Sufis, especially those belonging to the community of Sayyid Aḥmad al-Rifāʿī (499–577 H./1106–1182 CE). Al-Rifāʿī, who sojourned in the marshes of southern Iraq, had a large number of followers, some of whom indulged in unusual practices such as eating snakes or swallowing fire. With their iron neck rings, they have also been called the "poor to God." He describes them as innovators, a charge of which Sayyid al-Rifāʿī was innocent. Ibn Taymiyyah campaigned vigorously against them, delivering sermons and raising a hue and cry, especially since the deputy sultan appears to have believed in their miracles. The shaykh asked him "to order them to stop innovations and atrocities! Everybody must abide, in speech and practice, by the Holy Book and the Sunnah; otherwise he will be denied" (p. 88). But Ibn Taymiyyah also talks about other concerns, including a rock on a certain mountain where the populace apparently circumambulates as though seeking blessings as if it were the Kaʿbah itself in Mecca. This caused him to issue a *fatwā* in which he denounced all such practices and even included the Dome of the Rock of al-Masjid al-Aqṣā in his condemnation (reflected in the antagonistic attitude of Wahhābīs to shrines all over the Muslim world, especially in neighboring Shīʿī areas) (p. 89).

Biographical material enables al-Sharqāwī to delineate Ibn Taymiyyah as a character of great vigilance, valor, and pragmatic commitment to a specific understanding of religion. Al-Sharqāwī tries to provide a narrative of multiple perspectives, making extensive use of conversations, dialogues, discussions, and debates with a strong bearing on the burgeoning discourse of Islamicist essentialism that claimed to rely on the doctrinal statements of Imam al-Shafiʿī and Aḥmad Ibn Ḥanbal, while actually steering a different course in keeping with the essence and direction of life and faith at that stage in the history of Islam. Even when al-Sharqāwī shows a definite sympathy for Ibn Taymiyyah, something that is still noticeable in the predilections of certain Arab intellectuals who are as distant in ideas from each other as Āʾishah ʿAbd al-Raḥmān (Bint al-Shāṭiʾ) in her study of Muḥammad Ibn ʿAbd al-Wahhāb, and the modernist exemplary, the poet Adūnīs (the pseudonym of ʿAlī Aḥhmad Saʿīd) in his similar publication.

Some of these debates are left open-ended, since al-Sharqāwī is inclined to favor an Islamicist "purism," an originary discourse, that may not be overshadowed by practices which he, like many intellectuals who grew up in the awakening tradition, accused of dormancy, backwardness, and failure.

Hence, when it comes to the issue of authority, al-Sharqāwī has no choice but to refer the reader to the debates conducted by Ibn Taymiyyah. How was it possible, a student avowedly asked, that the imam who used to ask his followers to remedy things on the spot, including destroying and looting pubs, invading brothels, shaving people with long hair, and beating reprobates, had now changed course and was asking the sultan or his deputy to take action? (pp. 89–90). The question is not discussed or analyzed by al-Sharqāwī as being central to the application by the community of the principle of *al-Amr bi-al-Maʿrūf wa-al-Nahy ʿan al-Munkar* (*Commanding the Good and Forbidding Evil*), which, though originally a key principle in Muʿtazilī thought based on a Qurʾānic verse (Surat āl-ʿUmrān), had become a core aspect of practice under the Wahhābīs. But there is also another difference to be observed, in that Ibn Taymiyyah is said to be against further application of the practice as long as there is a ruler: "We used to fight evil ourselves twenty years ago without the permission of the ruler in charge, but, after God opened our eyes and increased our knowledge of His benevolence, it became clear to us that what we used to practice is illegitimate. So, be aware as of today that to enforce the limits, punish sinners by beating, imprisonment, whipping lightly, etc., and destroy unlawful wealth—all this is the right of the ruler in charge, who is solely responsible for the enforcement of retribution and punishment. Nobody from among the *ʾummah* has this right unless authorized to do so" (p. 90). The seemingly relaxed tone is loaded with a number of meanings that should direct our attention not only to the role of the sovereign as the subject in charge, the one vested with Divine authority as long as he is safe, sound, and acting as the leader of the community, but also to the manipulation of space where "spatial consensus" is enforced. No deviation is allowed to enforce laws as long as there is a ruler. In other words, the ruler owns the space and dictates consensus.[57]

While this is seemingly a shift in Ibn Taymiyyah's discourse and practice, its actual application in the context of an acceptance of authority whenever a rapprochement is required is to become central to the followers of this scholar's thinking on the political level. It helps to explain many apparently bewildering positions regarding the reluctance of his adherents to challenge authority even when it is avowedly misdirected. Ibn Taymiyyah, in al-Sharqāwī's extensive quotes from his debates, asks his followers to abide by the dictates of the ruler in charge: "The proper governance of people is the most important religious duty; and religion is incomplete without it" (p. 91). He adds: "It is said that the Sultan is the Vicar of God on earth. It is said: Sixty years of an unjust ruler is better than one night without a sultan." He also adds, quoting other predecessors, "if we have one acceptable intercession, we'll reserve it for the Sultan," a saying that means, in his words, "any sultan whether he is good or bad, but it is better for the *'ummah* to have good ones" (p. 91).

In al-Sharqāwī's narrative record, Ibn Taymiyyah is ready to accommodate religious tenets to circumstances when followers of a specific *madhhab* exaggerate a practice. The followers of Imam Ibn Ḥanbal, for example, began to veer away from his restrictive applications. They had no "right to attack houses, spill wine, or beat a woman singer" (p. 92); nor did they have the right to interrogate people on the streets. According to al-Sharqāwī's version, Ibn Taymiyyah criticized such practices and argued for the sovereign authority of the state and the sultan (pp. 92–93).

In this version Ibn Taymiyyah appears as a jurist who is more concerned with "the matters of this life, and politics, than with the Islamic law," quoting the words of a Sufi shaykh in an assembly presided over by the sultan's deputy in Damascus. Ibn Taymiyyah reportedly answers: "What is the purpose of Sharī'ah other than to reform people, cultivate the lands, and foster good treatment and management of people?" (p. 96).

In this same narrative account, it is the reported statement to the effect that a shaykh should occupy himself with "truth" that leads to Ibn Taymiyyah's study of Sufism, but in order to be able to counteract its shaykhs and followers (pp. 96–97). Hence another round of controversial debates occurs. In those debates it is Ibn Taymiyyah, the subject of al-Sharqāwī's narrative, who is the primary player and provocateur. His debating points rely on a specific interpretation of the Qur'ān in its surface meaning, but in "a manner understood only by God" (p. 98). Following his pronouncement, he is reported to have descended from the pulpit, saying, "God descends like my descent now" (p. 98). This is the literal interpretation he espouses.

The lifetime of Ibn Taymiyyah was one of political disturbance during the reign of the Mamluk Sultan al-Nāṣir Ibn Qalāwūn, especially following the death of his mother and the consequent vacuum that was created by the absence of a rigorous authority, leading in turn to the increasing power of both the minister Baybars and Prince Salar (p. 104). It was at this point that the sultan summoned Ibn Taymiyyah to submit to an inquisition organized by a number of jurists with the purpose of assessing the validity of complaints against the content of his theological debates and sermons. Al-Sharqāwī's narrative dramatizes the event, although he does also allow sufficient space to offer descriptions of his jurist as he takes full advantage of visitations to tombs and shrines, of scenes of people bringing their supplications and invocations of the dead as support for intercessions on their behalf, and of others with long hair and drums who dance in delirious rhythmic patterns as other people on both sides of the street stand and watch (p. 109). This is the way in which the author establishes his setting, all of it in preparation for his protagonist's response in opposition to Sufism and its principal shaykhs, especially the followers of al-Ḥallāj, Ibn ʿArabī, and Ibn al-Fāriḍ (p. 111). While excluding such prominent Sufi figures as al-Junayd, Abū al-Ḥasan al-Shādhilī, Aḥmad al-Badawī, al-Gīlānī, and al-Miṣrī from his condemnation, Ibn Taymiyyah argues that the rest are to be viewed as performers of pagan practices (p. 111). But this description is not enough to dramatize the narrative and make Ibn Taymiyyah appear in a complete and effectual way as a jurist of great caliber, someone who had many preoccupations and endured enormous suffering in uncongenial circumstances. His own authority emanated from the common public, and yet, by attacking Sufism, he was bound to lose since the Sufis held the most power over the common public (p. 112). At this point the "trial" had already been ordered to convene. At the outset, Ibn Taymiyyah is reported to have said: "How can I remain silent when I see the common people asking the intercession of the dead, rubbing shrines, praying and performing their invocations for them in such places? If it were any part of Islamic law, the Prophet would have ordered us to do so. He commands us to do every good and avoid every evil, not omitting anything that can bring us closer to Heaven while warning us too how to avoid Hell" (p. 112). But Shaykh Ibn Makhlūf, who was in charge of the court, ordered Ibn Taymiyyah's detention (p. 115), a decree that also led to the persecution of all other Ḥanbalites. In spite of a series of intercessions on Ibn Taymiyyah's behalf, most notably a forceful one from the deputy sultan of Damascus (p. 115), it was to no avail, and he spent a year in prison in the most unpleasant conditions (p. 116).

Al-Sharqāwī's narrative also focuses on Ibn Taymiyyah's predicament as being one of a collision between forces that cannot be reconciled without some kind of intervention. In this conflict the Cairo jurists are portrayed as more adamant and arrogant than those of Damascus. Without the intercession of the Bedouin knight Ḥusām and his group, who traveled to Cairo to convince Salar to release the Damascene jurist, Ibn Taymiyyah might have stayed in prison even longer. Ibn Taymiyyah advised the jurists to note how cautious Imam Jaʿfar al-Ṣādiq was in not accepting the either/or dichotomies whenever asked about God and the Qurʾān. The same is true of Ibn Ḥanbal, whose doctrines Ibn Taymiyyah was following. Ibn Taymiyyah accused the Egyptian jurists of the four official Islamic law schools of an excessively strict and literal application of the views of Abū al-Ḥasan al-Ash'arī (873/4–935/6) of Basra. For, while the latter may indeed have renounced the rationalist theology usually associated with his own early affiliation with the Mu'tazalites, he continued, at least according to Ibn Taymiyyah, to use their logic, which differs from that of *Ahl al-Sunnah*, "for he prioritized reason, and interpreted some texts in order to take reason into account" (p. 123). To Ibn Taymiyyah, only paraphrase, not hermeneutics, should be applied.

But in this version, Ibn Taymiyyah managed to communicate and debate cases with many jurists. The only group that he could not accept or tolerate was the Sufis, especially the followers of Ibn ʿArabī. "Didn't Ibn ʿArabī speak of the Sufi," he asked, "as a lover annihilated in the love of God and hence as one who passes into a seeming insanity that removes him from the provisions of right and wrong?" (p. 131). He made fun of the Sufis and composed poems to denigrate them. This led the grand Sufis, Ibn 'Aṭā' al-Sakandarī and al-Shaykh Nāṣir al-Munbijī, to complain to Prince Salar. Ibn Taymiyyah ended up yet again in prison, this time that of the Department of Justice, which was better accommodated to meet followers and disciples (p. 136). It was more like a hostel, a location that only increased the size of his circle and made him more accessible to scholars and disciples. Released from detention, he was allowed to move to Alexandria, only to be recalled to Cairo where he was given audience by a number of jurists including Ibn ʿAṭā' al-Sakandarī, who debated his views on popular beliefs and Sufis. Ibn 'Aṭā' explained that Ibn ʿArabī should not be read in a superficial literalist fashion; Sufis have their own discourse and signs, their own secrets and codes. The meaning is a soul hidden in a body which is the word. Shaykh 'Izz al-Dīn Ibn ʿAbd al-Salām, a scholar revered by Ibn Taymiyyah, changed his mind and asked for God's forgiveness when he realized the sheer depth of thought contained in Ibn ʿArabī's texts (p. 141). In other words, al-Sharqāwī undergoes a change of heart while reading Sufism, siding with the Sufis and wishing that his primary subject might be won over to their side. Islam in the street seems to emerge the winner in this account, but the effort to depict Ibn Taymiyyah as an acceptable public figure is also successful, in that the subject is shown to be a normal human being with many obsessions, weaknesses, and strengths, a subject suitable enough to demonstrate multiplicity in Islam, which may run at times against his views and perspectives.

Notes

1. For a brief survey, see Muhsin al-Musawi, *The Postcolonial Arabic Novel* (2003; Leiden: Brill, 2005), 38–39.

2. Cited from an extract from Louis Althusser, in *A Critical and Cultural Theory Reader*, ed. Antony Easthope and Kate McGowan (Toronto: University of Toronto Press, 2002), 55.

3. For a brief survey of the controversy, see Muhsin al-Musawi, *Reading Iraq: Culture and Power in Conflict* (London: I.B. Tauris, 2006).

4. For an assessment, see Muhsin al-Musawi, *The Postcolonial Arabic Novel*, 64–67, 340–41. See also Yūsuf ʿIzz al-Dīn, *Al-Riwāyah fī al-'Irāq* (Cairo: Maʿhad al-Buḥūth wa-al-Dirāsāt al-Adabiyyah, 1973), 210–22.

5. ʿIzz al-Dīn, *Al-Riwāyah fī al-'Irāq*, 216.

6. ʿIzz al-Dīn, *Al-Riwāyah fī al-'Irāq*, 218.

7. Yaḥyā Ḥaqqī, *Qindīl Umm Hāshim* (1944; English translation: *The Lamp of Umm Hāshim*, Cairo: American University in Cairo Press, 2004). It appeared also as *The Saint's Lamp and Other Stories*. Trans. M. M. Badawī. (Leiden: Brill, 1973).

8. Ḥaqqī, *The Lamp of Umm Hāshim*, 47.

9. Ḥaqqī, *The Lamp of Umm Hāshim*, 47.

10. Ḥaqqī, *The Lamp of Umm Hāshim*, 57.

11. Ḥaqqī, *The Lamp of Umm Hāshim*, 57.

12. Ḥaqqī, *The Lamp of Umm Hāshim*, 58.

13. Ḥaqqī, *The Lamp of Umm Hāshim*, 59.

14. Ḥaqqī, *The Lamp of Umm Hāshim*, 59.

15. Ḥaqqī, *The Lamp of Umm Hāshim*, 60.

16. Ḥaqqī, *The Lamp of Umm Hāshim*, 60.

17. Henri Lefebvre, *The Production of Space*, trans. Donald Nicholson-Smith (Oxford: Basil Blackwell, 1991), 49.

18. Ḥaqqī, *The Lamp of Umm Hāshim*, 60.

19. Ḥaqqī, *The Lamp of Umm Hāshim*, 61.

20. Ḥaqqī, *The Lamp of Umm Hāshim*, 61.

21. Ḥaqqī, *The Lamp of Umm Hāshim*, 64.

22. Salāma Mūsā, *The Education of Salama Musa*, trans. L. O. Schuman (Leiden: Brill, 1961), 13.

23. Ḥaqqī, *The Lamp of Umm Hāshim*, 65.

24. Ḥaqqī, *The Lamp of Umm Hāshim*, 65.

25. Ḥaqqī, *The Lamp of Umm Hāshim*, 65.

26. Ḥaqqī, *The Lamp of Umm Hāshim*, 68.

27. Ḥaqqī, *The Lamp of Umm Hāshim*, 66.

28. Ḥaqqī, *The Lamp of Umm Hāshim*, 66.

29. Ḥaqqī, *The Lamp of Umm Hāshim*, 66.

30. See Muhsin al-Musawi, *Reading Iraq*.

31. Ḥaqqī, *The Lamp of Umm Hāshim*, 67.

32. Ḥaqqī, *The Lamp of Umm Hāshim*, 67.

33. Ḥaqqī, *The Lamp of Umm Hāshim*, 67.

34. Ḥaqqī, *The Lamp of Umm Hāshim*, 67–68.

35. Ḥaqqī, *The Lamp of Umm Hāshim*, 68.

36. *Nationalness* is used in reference to a bourgeois national commitment to a nation-state. *Nationalism*, however, is used alternately with pan-Arabism.

37. Ḥaqqī, *The Lamp of Umm Hāshim*, 68.

38. See Muhsin J. al-Musawi, *Scheherazade in England*, (Washington, DC: Three Continent press 1981)102–10; 134–36.

39. Mūsā, *The Education of Salāma Mūsā*, 29. There in his daily newspaper, *Al-Jarīda*, he "called for a purely Egyptian policy without any bias towards Turkish or Arabic or Islamic preponderance."

40. Ḥaqqī, *The Lamp of Umm Hāshim*, 68.

41. Ḥaqqī, *The Lamp of Umm Hāshim*, 65–67.

42. Ḥaqqī, *The Lamp of Umm Hāshim*, 69.

43. Ḥaqqī, *The Lamp of Umm Hāshim*, 70.

44. Ḥaqqī, *The Lamp of Umm Hāshim*, 70.

45. Ḥaqqī, *The Lamp of Umm Hāshim*, 71.

46. Ḥaqqī, *The Lamp of Umm Hāshim*, 72.

47. Ḥaqqī, *The Lamp of Umm Hāshim*, 74.

48. Ḥaqqī, *The Lamp of Umm Hāshim*, 74.

49. Lefebvre, *The Production of Space*, 51.

50. Lefebvre, *The Production of Space*, 51.

51. Lefebvre, *The Production of Space*, 175.

52. Mūsā, *The Education of Salāma Mūsā*, 23.

53. Mūsā, *The Education of Salāma Mūsā*, 75.

54. Mūsā, *The Education of Salāma Mūsā*, 27.

55. ʿAbd al-Raḥmān al-Sharqawī, *Ibn Taymiyyah Al-Faqīh al-Muʿadhdhab (Ibn Taymiyyah: The Suffering Jurist)* Cairo: Dār al-mawqif al-ʿArabī, 1983). The term connotes inwardness in reading the Qur'ān in its symbolical or allegorical dimensions beyond the literal meaning. Its use in reference to nonmainstream groups means dissent, deliberate deviation, and heresy.

56. A place included in the rituals of the Ḥājj (pilgrimage). It lies between Minā and ʿMount Arafāt and is the place where pilgrims spend the night after returning from ʿArafāt.

57. On spatial consensus, see Lefebvre, *The Production of Space*, 57.

CHAPTER THREE

The Religious Dynamic

While the nation-state claims at times to be sacral, its intent and power relations tend toward desacralization, not only because, as Paul Ricoeur argues, this is the general tendency of the human race but also because any would-be modernity impulse entails such a process. Like its individual prototype, the nation-state adopts a demythologizing direction even while claiming otherwise. "In a certain way," argues Ricoeur, "it is the destiny of man to dominate all things and perhaps even his own life; this great enterprise seeking to desacralize, to profane the universe, in its cosmic, biological, psychic, aspects is in line with a certain destiny proclaimed in the Old Testament."[1] Islamic religious leaders are no less aware of this tendency, for, according to Shaykh Yūsuf al-Qaraḍāwī (b. 1926): "We claim we follow Islam but fail to put Islam into practice. . . . We write in our constitution that the state's religion is Islam, but fail to give it the place it merits in government, legislation and orientation."[2]

Modern and postcolonial narratives cannot confine their concerns to middle-class politics for long. Arabic poetry has proved to be in the lead when it comes to capturing the other forceful power that serves to balance and at times to tip the scales to the benefit of idealization in the face of reality in all its sordidness. On many occasions it has been successful in reaching to the mythopoetic core of existence in order to stimulate the "generation of possibility in the heart of our language," as Ricoeur proposes.[3] The more horrible wars and their consequences are, the greater the tendencies to search for ways to remedy the situation, to retain heaven on earth, if not to associate earthly paradise with the heavenly. Poetry can solve this dilemma through the study of language where horizons are wide enough to accommodate visions, but narrative is different. It assumes the role of philosophy, not only in order to explain the phenomenon but also to set out the directions for an outcome. The more urgent the outstanding questions, the greater the involvement of the writer as philosopher, in that philosophy is in both method and vision, method and outlook, able to provide alternatives to reality through allegory or mythology. Such is the case with Maḥfūẓ's *Layālī Alf Laylah* (1982; English translation: *Arabian Nights and Days*, 1995).

Recruitments in a Political Vacuum: Maḥfūẓ's *Layālī Alf Laylah: Arabian Nights and Days*

The significance of this text is not limited to its postcolonial use of indigenous tradition, its intertextualization of antecedent narrative, and its resurrection of the *Nights* from oblivion and misuse. On this occasion Maḥfūẓ uses it as the subtext for a test of his worldview as sustained throughout his earlier narratives. That subtext distances its author's critique of the nation-state while testing his primary belief in moderate change through the underlying articles of faith. The *Arabian Nights* is extensively combined with trajectories of transformation, challenge, and love, all of which are reducible to a scenario that was once Maḥfūẓ's primary focus: the emerging bourgeoisie and its nation-state apparatus. Maḥfūẓ had been pondering this sensitive issue even before writing *The Thief and the Dogs* (1961), where the shaykh's ambiguous utterances keep the protagonist suspended between militancy and inaction. Now, in *Arabian Nights and Days*, he is more at ease, for there is no longer any obvious need to assess the concepts of rebellion or individual action against the status quo. Even when seen in terms of disappointment and frustration at the failing or fallen ideals of equality, freedom, and social welfare, *The Thief and the Dogs* looks at Sufism as the unchallenged source of comfort and faith, a force that runs counter to materialist ideologies and mundane middle-class arrangements of convenience. No matter how confused the protagonist Saʿīd Mahrān may be by the shaykh's riddles, the mere search for comfort and religious solace speaks to the author's subtle piety, a gesture that does not necessarily have to be viewed as in conflict with his ideal of science and modernization.

Arabian Nights and Days transfers the dichotomous and binary hiatus that lies between state and people onto a past, making use of a text that was once an Arab-Islamic repository of marginal cultures. The tales rarely bother listeners despite their potential to generate social and political criticism of one sort or another. The collection of *The Arabian Nights* tales as it stands raises no serious questions and is sufficiently persuasive and appealing to numb the critical faculties. And yet Maḥfūẓ revives it in order to critique the nation-state. Distancing his outlook and locating it in the distant past, he is able to give his Islamic Sufism free rein to assume its role as the primary force that will claim the attention of the majority of society. For Maḥfūẓ Sufism has no concern other than repose and comfort in the divine presence. By choosing a popular subtext that also commands an archetypal presence in collective consciousness, he brings to the common reader the truth of Islam as it is lived in the street. In order to allow his narrative to flow as Arabian Nightism, he also retains the major structural patterns of the original: there is a patriarchal order that assumes absolute power but suffers subversion and challenge; there is a state apparatus that coordinates efforts to preserve its control and power; there is also an inescapable process of change in power relations that reflects on the nation and its constituents; there are groups and organizations that work in secret to destabilize the political status quo and enforce change; there exists the usual state propaganda aimed against enemies of its own creation in order to justify its coercion and repression. Last and no less significant is the urban setting: facing the palace and its governmental apparatus is the Amīr (prince) Café where almost everybody gathers and takes a seat according to a tacit hierarchical order where all are complicit in this symbolic power, its class attributes, and moral and social obligations. The upper class sits separately from the lower. It is only when someone from the underprivileged category assumes a degree of power in a murky situation that things start to change, forcing the privileged to offer unconditional invitations to the newly empowered to join them. In other words, Maḥfūẓ borrows recurrent thematic dichotomies, poverty versus riches, love versus sordidness, unlimited power versus restraint, so as to highlight two significant patterns that serve our purpose here, that is, Islam in the street.

First he focuses on the underlying piety, a theme that is usually subsumed under the recurrent reminder of human frailty and weakness in the face of death, the destroyer of happiness and the disperser of communities, that being a recurrent leitmotif in the antecedent text, *The Arabian Nights*. Then he brings the supernatural down to earth to fit into a common understanding and imaging of good versus evil and Satan versus the *quṭb* (pole) of piety: the Shaykh al-Balkhī. As Maḥfūẓ's representative of symbolic spiritual and unworldly power the shaykh evolves, not only by drawing the underlying critique of neopatriarchy, but also by summarizing the undefined incomprehensible power of the Divine whose mention is on the lips of everyone on the Arab-Islamic street. Everybody repeats "If God wills," and the wording gathers momentum as a powerful embodiment of the Divine on earth where evil temptations seem to threaten the whole order. It is only when the temptress female jinn, Zirmbaha, metamorphoses into the most ravishing woman whom even the Ruler Shahrayar cannot resist that the divine power comes to rescue the falling order. Satan, personified as a red-faced Persian with blue eyes, will have his say in tempting all who are lured by luxury or power, the magic ring or the magic cap, but temptation can be corrected or halted by the use of human ingenuity, reason, and solid unshakeable faith, a pattern that also sustains the original narrative, the ghost text which Maḥfūẓ condenses and collates in his own text. Aladdin is executed when Satan becomes annoyed by his decision to stop working according to the pact between them. Now exposed as a human with a criminal record, Aladdin is left unprotected, undefended, and naked. Conversely the figure Ma'rūf the cobbler is aware of his limits. The moment temptation is offered in order to challenge his faith, he rejects it. Left with no support from the centers of power, it is the street that comes to his rescue as being a devout believer who has used his temporary power for the sake of his fellow people, the poor and the underprivileged. Here Maḥfūẓ is obviously expressing his belief in the power of the street as a harmless source, and yet powerful enough to make itself recognized and reckoned with. This is the power that stands for Islam in the street, which in this case is not a "passive receptacle," but dynamic users who emerge from the abstract space that is monopolized by power to a differential one where homogeneity no longer obtains. Here is a site of difference, opposition, and dissent.[4]

To suggest that Maḥfūẓ's *Arabian Nights and Days* is an exceptionally dense narrative in which he focuses on Islam in the street cannot be fully understood without a careful reading of this text of re-creation. The basic premise relates to the author's sustained emphasis on Shaykh al-Balkhī as being someone who is not only a distinguished personality—a person who belongs to the divine presence rather than the worldliness of this life—but also with regard to Maḥfūẓ's own interpretation of Islamic Sufism, his learned references, and sustained characterization of the *quṭb* (pole) whose disciples and followers take his word for granted as being the word of God. The novelist perhaps mutters the same statements as someone who is a deeply rooted devotee of God on earth.[5] In terms of delegation of symbolic power, the shaykh holds no actual power, and hence he cannot stop the state from invading his private space and searching for evidence to incriminate his son-in-law. On the other hand he summons his symbolic power from the street as people have faith in him. This faith evolves into a symbolic power, like the very power of religion. His riddles and explications have something of the ontological, the sacred, against the ontic, anthropological, and profane language of the state and its functionaries.[6] But the shaykh as a Sufi, with no ritual symbolism of his own, cannot expect unconditional support from the populace as long as there is no liturgical code to constitute effective delegation.[7] In a constantly polarized order where power relations change and social mobility is murky, there remains the usual conflict of faith versus power; Sufism versus Sunni theologians, muftis, and state functionaries in Islamic law; and of faith and belief versus sheer bluff and corruption. His critique of these functionaries is similar to one voiced by al-Qaraḍāwī, who states that the "priority of the contemporary mufti should be to take people out of the narrow prison of the [four orthodox] legal schools into the wide open space of the sharī'ā."[8] The newly initiated believer in that open space is in danger of temptation, whereas the steadfast adherent cannot be deluded or led astray. In the novel Faḍil Ṣan'ān is not well initiated in Sufism,[9] and the shaykh is well aware of the limits of his efforts as a political activist. He is also aware of his good intentions. Maḥfūẓ is not keen to provide us with such a model of the old dichotomy of shaykh and novice in terms similar to the ones he employs in his earlier portrait of the two to be found in *The Thief and the Dogs*. The Islamic fervor of the 1970s gained President al-Sādāt's support as a ready means of quelling and subduing Nāṣirītes and leftists in the Arab Socialist Union, Nāṣir's melting pot for the political left in Egypt. Islamic sentiment was running high, and both the Muslim Brotherhood and other opposition groups became seriously engaged in organized politics as a way of filling the vacuum left behind by Nāṣir and his charismatic leadership. This vacuum had already been felt in the entire region, especially after the growth of a series of scathing critiques of nationalist platforms that had totally failed to foresee the 1967 defeat and other political failures of the nation-state. Maḥfūẓ had all this in mind, and he was perhaps even more concerned to question the parameters of his earlier worldview. The rise of Islam on the street was a reality at that time, as it is now, and he anticipated its growing influence while at the same time imposing his own discursive restrictions on the militant Islamists whom he equated with other militant groups, whence comes his sketch of the militant indoctrination process involving Fāḍil Ṣan'ān, something that is deliberately distanced through an association between him and both Shī'īs and Khārijītes as part of his premodern context. The other process of indoctrination, the one he favors, is Sufi teaching. In other words, Maḥfūẓ transposes his early secular preferences into Islamic trends that were actively displacing those same secular ideologies.

In order to provide an occasion for this latter process of indoctrination, Maḥfūẓ follows 'Abd al-Ḥakīm Qāsim's *Seven Days* (1969) in choosing a festival for Sufi gatherings and popular jubilation. The occasion involved is the birthday (*mawlid*) of Abū Bakr al-Warrāq (a tenth-century Sufi), when his shrine becomes the site of celebrations. The occasion reminds his followers of the need for faith and piety. Al-Warrāq, we are told, "was seen wearing a long coat on which he had written *kh* on one side, the letter *m* on the other side, so that he could always remember the *kh* for *ikhlās* (sincerity) and the *m* of *muruwwah* (virtue).[10] The occasion is appropriate for an overview of the whole social and political panorama, and for understanding the broader prospects for political organization and contact. Here Islamic activism and devotion take separate directions, as is to be expected in Maḥfūẓ's secular work until the 1970s. This particular scene covers pages 158–161, introducing the reader to Islam in the street as a phenomenon that is increasingly displacing secular ideologies. The focus of the scene is the Islamic militant Fāḍil Ṣan'ān and the hesitant believer Aladdin. Fāḍil has him "sit beside him" (p. 158). The scene thus provokes their comments on the state, rulers, and questions involving opposition and revolt. Fāḍil says: set out

> "If al-Warraq were to be resurrected, he would draw his sword!" and adds: "Since the good do not draw their swords, then I shall do so."
>
> "But what if state propaganda is right, namely that Shahrayar is changing his mind and repenting for past mistakes and atrocities? If so, should he raise his sword? They speak a great deal about the repentance of His Majesty the Sultan," says Aladdin innocently (p. 159).

We should take this response neither lightly nor at face value. It relates to questions that have long been the business of the learned and jurists. Who should be targeted by rebels? The believer or the infidel? What if the ruler is despotic but still powerful in the face of enemies? Is the just despot a preferable choice? These questions have long divided the learned *'ulamā'*, and every possible answer justifies a specific position against another. Hence, Fāḍil's answer is equivocal: " 'Sometimes,' says Fāḍil sarcastically, 'he repents of his repentance. For sure he is not the most deserving of Muslims to possess sovereign power' " (p. 159). For Aladdin now comes the test when he needs to align himself with militancy or detach himself from his companion. On the street indoctrination is the driving and dynamic force; the youth is faced with such a choice, one that was once in the hands of secular ideologists. Islamist activism is now the force on the street, and Maḥfūẓ has foreseen its growing momentum. Fāḍil expresses great faith in Shaykh Abdullah al-Balkhi, whose eyes have been inviting Aladdin to join with him rather than devote himself to militancy: "Shaykh Abdullah al-Balkhi is the principal holy man," he says (p. 159). The language evolving here partakes of the legitimate one used on such occasions as distinctive from the one used, for example, at the café. The popular is excluded here, but there is an opposition that survives in it now in keeping with the growing tension between Sufism and militancy. Although not exactly pertaining to this kind of distinction,

Bourdieu's "bodily hexis," where dualistic taxonomies emerge and are used by custodians of legitimacy to prioritize or degrade other qualities, may be used here to designate the change in power relations and politics of discourse among groups that are supposed to have a common cause.[11]

The meeting between Aladdin, the young barber, and the shaykh illustrates the other side of Islamic indoctrination: the rejection of corruption through Sufism. The first stage in this indoctrination involves touching the heart of the novice, winning it over, and orienting it toward esoteric (Gnostic) knowledge. The shaykh repeats to him al-Warrāq's training of Sufis, a process whose first step requires adherence to the shaykh's commands to throw "small scraps of paper" into the river (p. 160). The novice's own sense of reason tells him not to throw away such precious scraps handwritten by the master himself. Returning with the false assertion that he has done what he was asked to, he is asked to explain what he has seen. Nothing, he says. "In which case, you didn't do as I ordered. Go back and throw them into the river" (p. 160). Now doing as the master ordains, he "throws them into the river. The water parts and a box appears. Its lid opens so that the pieces of paper fell into it, at which point it closes, and the waters flow over it" (p. 160). The master explains: "I wrote a book about Sufism to which only the perfect can aspire. My brother, Al-Khidr [the stranger in the story of Moses in the Qur'ān] demanded it of me, and God ordered that the waters should take it to him" (p. 161). This story is one of thousands in Sufi hagiography that has become part of the inventory of Sufism, its antecedent authority since its early emergence as the ultimate source of repose in the divine presence. But Shaykh al-Balkhi is also true to Maḥfūẓ's model of the pious critique of power. He quotes the Prophet: "The corruption of scholars is through heedlessness, that of princes through injustice; that of Sufis through hypocrisy" (p. 161). The shaykh feels a need to advise the uninitiated youth: "So be not one of the associates of devils" (p. 161). But who are they? The shaykh goes on: "A prince without learning, a scholar without virtue, a Sufi without trust in God, and the corruption of the world, all lay in their corruption" (p. 163). The shaykh's position wins the youth over. The shaykh knows that there is a sincere side to Islamism that is ignited and provoked by corruption. It strives therefore to curb it or struggle to the limit against it. Even so the shaykh's outlook is very close to Maḥfūẓ's own preferences, as seen from the time of their earlier manifestation in *The Thief and the Dogs*. In *Arabian Nights and Days* he explains it through his mouthpiece, Shaykh al-Balkhi, who tells Aladdin that his Islam is not yet the true Islam. "You should accept Islam anew so as to become a true believer. When belief is effected in you, you can start off, if you so wish, on the path from its very beginning" (p. 164). Does this mean that others like the militant Fāḍil are not following the path? Doesn't Fāḍil justify his rebellious attitude as necessitated by need and legitimized by faith against the forces of corruption and tyranny? The shaykh does not negate this route, and yet it is not the one to which he adheres. "The path is one at first, then inevitably it splits into two. One of these leads to love and obliteration of self; the other to holy war" (p. 165). The followers of the latter path, we are told, "dedicate themselves to God's servants" (p. 165). Although not aiming at social integration, such discourse moves beyond riddles to benefit from the linguistic capital,[12] its distinctive clarity and purposefulness, to apprentice a novice, not in preparation for a profession or a job, but to receive due indoctrination in the true Islam, not the one of official discourse or the counter one of militancy. This indoctrination has logic and its drive is to ensure social and moral integration, which the shaykh calls Islam.

Through his characterization of the shaykh, Maḥfūẓ is unequivocal in his expression of distrust of Islamic militancy. This distrust is only an extension of his earlier feelings regarding radical ideology. True to his quietism, with its focus on reform and obliteration first of corruption through self-reform, he makes Shaykh Abdullah al-Balkhi describe Fāḍil as follows: "A noble youth who knew what suited him and was satisfied with it" (p. 167), and then adds, "He is waging war against error as much as he can" (p. 167). He further explains, "One creed for the sword, and another for love" (p. 167). The shaykh doesn't fault him, but the creed of the sword is not his path. In other words, Maḥfūẓ would like to have the street won over to the creed of love: "Before receiving the wine, you have to clean the container, removing all elements of dirt" (p. 167). Maḥfūẓ is not oblivious to the fact that the shaykh's devotion to the divine is not a guarantee of protection against the challenges of the corrupt world. His house is raided by the police, and his uninitiated innocent follower, Aladdin, is executed as the result of a plan that has already set the trap for him as an associate with the Khārijītes (p. 169). The term Khārijītes is deliberately invoked here by the author, alone or in its association with Shīʿism, the latter being a group with which there is no correspondence either historically, theologically, or politically. The Egyptian judge and jurist Muḥammad Saʿīd al-ʿAshmāwī, who in the 1980s and 1990s became an outspoken critic of the Islamists and what he calls "political Islam," used the term not in the Maḥfūẓian sense: that is, as a pejorative term used by the state to discredit opponents. He compares the Muslim Brotherhood and similar groups to the Kharijītes and Shīʿīs as "negative symbols."[13] He draws the comparison as a way of alienating the Brotherhood since, in his view, they share with both groups either Bedouin tribalism seen in a willingness to indulge in conflict, or a desire to fuse religion and politics, especially through clandestine organizations, prudent dissimulation, and martyrdom.

Maḥfūẓ's use is different. He does not find religious extremism reprehensible, something to be shunned. Instead he lets his shaykh speak of its limits and ties to this world and its mundane politics. His counterdiscourse, one that nobody can dispute, emanates from a personal liking for Sufism as an exemplary path of effective piety and affection that obliquely offsets authoritarianism.

Sufism evolves in the novel as a delicate power that permeates society through disciples. It works as a language that operates through space, which itself amounts to one of codes and rituals that entail transformation and change in the recipient. The sovereign power suffers subtle replacement or conversion. Another legitimate discourse digs deep into the abstract space of sovereignty.[14] Most important, it works on Shahrayar through the tales. Here the idea culled by the author from primary sources receives still more validation in his *Layālī*. We are introduced to the concluding tale of *The Thousand and One Nights* when festivities, celebrations, and jubilations are taking place all over the kingdom in appreciation of the ruler's decision to relent regarding his treatment of women and his consequent acceptance of Scheherazade as his wife. We are told that he is to be a family man now, a point that Maḥfūẓ accepts and exploits with due faithfulness to the original text and also in keeping with his own thematic pattern of social conviviality, replenishment, and fruition. No less is his belief in authority as the guarantee of order. Shahrayar with a son sustains a dynasty that will survive troubles and turmoil.

What balances this basic premise is a two-way dramatization. There is first the intervention of the supernatural, in its good and evil facets, not only as a reminder of the Divine, but also as a strategic narrative tool that invokes imagination and fancy. It serves as his deliberate interventionist scheme, one that finds its self-justification in the primary ghost text of the *The Thousand and One Nights*. On the other hand, it also functions as a distant trope for hope and aspiration, representing the yearnings of the forlorn, downcast, and helpless, the refuge for the underprivileged and the deserted. Imagination acts on reality, transforms it, and offers its own soothing cues that reality only negates or denies. The supernatural intrudes into the most unexpected places and moments, announcing its presence in a bite or embodiment, like the Persian notable who is the owner of the cap of invisibility. It metamorphoses into souls and persons, depending on the seeds of goodness or evil to be found with them. It manifests itself in madmen and strange occurrences that keep everything else in suspense. Only the Sufi shaykh has his repose, repeating to complainers and protesters his enigmatic pronouncements on an alternative order of things.

Sufism permeates the madman's language and operates an inventory that defuses ordinary seductive discourse, the language of desire. Every word that has proved successfully ravishing and enchanting, and has overwhelmed every human being without exception, dwindles into nothingness. The language of desire along with its locations falls apart when confronted with the impenetrable madman who has passed beyond states and stations to become an embodiment of divine order which the female jinn can never dream of affecting (p. 143).

But Maḥfūẓ does not let this narrative of divinity occupy the entire stage. While he allows the real and supernatural to disperse into his reconstructed narrative fabric, he creates his own Sufi power of gravity that distances the allegorical dimension of the new text and also solves the problematic politic which he needs to consider as worthy of a serious reconsideration in view of the new political transformations that have taken place in Egypt and the Arab world. Sufism exposes corruption and indirectly suggests ways to curb or limit it. It does not provoke rebellion but may prompt disillusionment and dissatisfaction. Beyond that, its interpretations of worldly affairs may work in dubious ways that allow a broad scope for misinterpretation. On the other hand, they establish other tracks or horizons for new understandings of both Islam and life in general. Every journey in this palimpsest becomes viably open to allegorical interpretation. Even Sinbad's tales, for example, can be turned into readings of Sufi literature concerning the soul's journey from desire to bliss, as in Ibn Sīnā's (Avicenna's) many pieces that form the basis for Ibn Ṭufayl's (d. 1185) *Ḥayy Ibn Yaqẓān*.[15] Other variations include Yaḥyā al-Suhrawardī's cities in *Haykal al-Nūr* (*The Shape of Light*). Curbed or quelled desires may not be part of Maḥfūẓ's intentions, and yet, when they are viewed in a context of gain and power, as the dynamic motivation for possession, we can better understand the recourse to Sufism as a means of countering corruption and infatuation with power.

Power relations function forcefully in the tales in keeping with the author's awareness of the political realities of eras of contraction, when repression becomes a method, perhaps the only one, of quelling opposition and protecting and preserving a crumbling order. In Maḥfūẓ's terms, opposition by itself is not enough. As long as it is human, it partakes of the same frailties, especially the love of power. Even Fāḍil Ṣan'ān, the "living epitome of work" who "spoils" the "intuitions and plans" of the evil jinn, is susceptible to the seductive lure of unlimited power, as the author intimates through his supernatural agent. If al-Ḥallāj follows the Qur'ānic model by depicting Iblīs or Satan as the deserted lover who, because of unalienable love of God, becomes stained with arrogance, disobedience, and total trust in reason, then Maḥfūẓ depicts his agents as being no less bent on exposing the most committed and ideal youth to human frailties. Fāḍil Ṣan'ān, as their "target [is] truly worthy . . . [of our] skill and . . . wiles" (p. 179) and thus in the same vein as Satan, may trap the most incorrigible elements in his snares. Apart from this unleashing of the power of temptation, the supernatural thus becomes the agency for unlimited power and seduction. Like the lure of postcapitalism, this agency has an almost total monopoly on other sources of power that incorporate the double bind of great promise and dreadful fall. Working on the human psyche with all its fragility and weakness under stress (such as Fāḍil's mourning of his innocent friend and companion, Aladdin), such an agency exploits this human emotion so as to further obliterate his noble traits. "When will release from suffering come?" asks Fāḍil with a "wounded heart" (p. 180). The man with the "radiant appearance and smiling countenance" is Maḥfūẓ's image of Satan. Although meant to be the jinn's own creation, it is the embodiment of Satan with all the attributes of temptation: the cap of invisibility and its like. The terms require the use of the cap for everything "except what your conscience dictates" (p. 181). Maḥfūẓ is here repeating the dictates to the second mendicant in the original *Arabian Nights*, which oblige him to abstain from the mention of God during every hazardous trip.

Unleashed power knows no limits. The process of behaving as he is supposed to in order to thwart evil is sidetracked by the dictates of the radiant man, the tempter, or Iblīs as the source of power. Thus, Fāḍil "wondered how he could save his brothers and comrades. He was shocked by the steel grip which enveloped him. He was both the slave of the cap and its owner, as well as the prisoner of darkness and nothingness" (p. 191).

While authority is eager to sustain an order that will not disrupt its plans and privileges, the institutionalized religious segment or Sunni authority represented in the person of the mufti (the spokesman for the religious institution) is ready to lay the blame on dissenters: "the Shīʿītes and the Khārijītes" (p. 190). Instead of searching for the reasons behind the disorder, the mufti is concerned with the preservation of power as a shared monopoly with the state. His attitude is in stark contrast with the Sufi position, which sees disorder as being already there, regardless of its present manifestations in the street. The shaykh sums it up as follows: "we lack true faith." Responding to the governor's statement that "the people are believers," he elaborates: "True faith is rarer than the unicorn" (p. 190).

In other words, the author is keen to explore the faith of the institution, its representatives, and people. Lack of faith becomes synonymous with lack of aim or purpose. In a vacuum that ultimately emerges from a corrupt power center there is room enough for new players. Maḥfūẓ is no less loyal to his intertext, that is, *The Arabian Nights*, than to his politics of moderation in the face of a corrupt center. The narrative subtext, with its many cycles and tales, builds on pairing and opposition in compliance with a popular narrative technique in Abbasid narratology, as noticed earlier by Nabia Abbott in her 1949 analysis of an early ninth-century fragment of the *Nights*.[16] The tendency is in keeping with an urban mood that caters to the demands for stability in the face of a history of warfare and political disorder. Hence Maḥfūẓ repeats the Fāḍil/cap pact in its opposition to institutionalized religion and the state apparatus. But instead of letting the Ma'rūf/Solomon's ring axis overpower the state and shake it up, he portrays it as being no less frightening and destabilizing to the state and its muftis than Fāḍil's cap of invisibility. The other difference lies in its wholesale devotion to the service of the poor. Exceptional power in the service of the underprivileged aligns itself with faith as upheld by the pious, who, in Maḥfūẓ's paradigms, are by no means synonymous with the muftis and their religion—as a co-opted state tributary established through official jurisconsults and theologians. Although leaning heavily on the muftis to calm down the populace and intimidate the rest, the state finds itself driven to new pacts with other forces. The muftis' authority is no longer as binding. Looked upon as opportunist and self-serving, this official religious authority loses in this competitive space. In Bourdieu's words, "the symbolic efficacy of religious language is threatened when the set of mechanisms capable of ensuring the reproduction of the relationship of recognition, which is the basis of its authority, ceases to function."[17]

The exchange between the mufti and Ma'rūf the cobbler is worth noting here, since it illustrates Maḥfūẓ's schema for an institutionalized religion represented by the mufti versus a popular and sincere faith as represented by Ma'rūf the cobbler. The mufti has the power of an institution, while Ma'rūf makes use of the whole precarious situation to feign that he is still in possession of King Solomon's ring. The mufti says:

> I have a word for you, Ma'rūf, that I hope you will accept from a man who fears none but God. God puts His servants to the test in good times and bad, and He is always and ever the most powerful. He brings the strong person to trial through his strength, just as He brings the weak to trial through his weakness. Others have come into possession of Solomon's ring before you, and it was a curse for them. May your possession of it be an example to the believers and a warning to the polytheists. (p. 201)

Maḥfūẓ lets the mufti speak in terms of social and political divides of strength and weakness. In this discourse the contrast of believers and polytheists, the strong versus the poor, and good times versus bad, is taken for granted. Only a counterdiscourse that points to the implication of power without intention to use it, a defused kind of force, can serve Maḥfūẓ's strategy as a means of warning against upheaval. Ma'rūf speaks to those in authority as follows:

> Listen, you men of eminence—it is indeed fortunate that Solomon's ring should fall to the lot of a believing man who has the name of God on his lips morning and evening. It is a power against which yours cannot prevail, but I have kept it for times of necessity. It is within my ability to order the ring to construct palaces, to fit out armies, and to gain control over the sultanate, but I have resolved to follow another path. (pp. 200–201)

This response can be read on a number of levels. It partakes first of what Bourdieu calls on other occasions a "compromise formation" where a transaction takes place "between expressed interest" and "a censorship which is imposed on a speaker or writer" with some symbolic power.[18] In this instance the feigned posture adopted by Maʿrūf helps in this compromise, but his defiant note is much in keeping with this posture too. The ring has all the accumulation of this symbolic power as a provider of material and spiritual potency and wealth. Maʿrūf's discourse can be seen also as the author's expressed variation on the role of the imaginative faculty, the one that has already spoken through Scheherazade of such things and happenings. Maʿrūf puts his ruse to the service of his comrades. The poor are to enjoy a certain degree of luxury from the gifts and money which he has secured from the state and the wealthy class. This is obviously what the author dreams of as a possible social order. When ordered by the satanic power to use his power to eradicate the center of faith and love, namely the shaykh and the madman, he is unequivocally against the idea. Like the author, Maʿrūf never lets himself be carried away by power or dreams of luxury and success. "Imagination pulled him this way and that, but he always held firm to the ground at the edge of the abyss" (p. 205).

This is Maḥfūẓ's narratological premise. The whole idea of narrative rests on a locus, a worldview that makes use of facts to devise a world to be known and cherished. "Knowledge is not gained by numerous narratives, but through pursuing knowledge and making use of it," says Shaykh al-Balkhi to Sinbad the sailor (p. 210). Although meant as gnosis, the knowledge of the Divine, its recurrence in Maḥfūẓ's *Arabian Nights and Days* is meant to debate the equation of adventure and narrative, of quantity and value. A purposeful narrative that imbibes knowledge of the Divine through a balanced use of imagination and realism is what he believes in as a way of ultimately enforcing faith, the Islam on the street, and not the one advocated by the muftis or waged through holy wars, no matter how justified they may be.

On the other hand, al-Balkhi's premise or Sufi maxim challenges the idea of travel merely for gain and endorses the alternative notion of travel for wisdom. The ambiguity of this maxim provides an excellent occasion for the author's exploitation of his palimpsest, *A Thousand and One Nights*. Both the realistic narrative of adventure and sociopolitical life are shaken every now and then by a happening that partakes of the supernatural. This incursion of the supernatural, including satanic manifestations, becomes Maḥfūẓ's trope for imaginative re-creation. In this vacillation between imagination and fancy and the "ground" of the real, the author resorts to Sufism as a way of providing an outlet for his reading of Islam in the street. In this Islam, as he sees it in cafés and quarters, Sufi belief operates as a sieve to be used to select articles and rituals that reshape the understanding of Islam beyond the claims of jurists and official functionaries or the calls of zealous advocates of essentialist Islam. The shaykh may perhaps be willing to accept advocacy of holy war, but it is not part of his own faith or that of his disciples. It amounts to no more than the limited endeavor of people like Fāḍil Ṣan'ān, but not the comprehensive Sufi view of the universe.

In Maḥfūẓ's hands narrative becomes the path and knowledge base that lead to change. Through it and under its impact the ruler becomes a reformed person. The wanderer of the frame tale in the underlying text continues his wanderings, just like the mendicants. As an act of renunciation of this world, he decides to roam the globe, but not to forsake the throne without an heir. Maḥfūẓ is tied to his source, but the issue of governance and rule bothers him, and he cannot go beyond his belief in the validity of a dynastic stable order run by a just ruler. It is enough for him to investigate the change of heart in Shahrayar and make him speak for a desired understanding of corruption as an associate of unguarded or absolute authority and power:

> The falseness of specious glory was made clear to him, like a mask of tattered paper that does not conceal the snakes of cruelty, tyranny, pillage, and the blood that lie behind it. He cursed his father and his mother, givers of pernicious legal judgments, and poets, the cavaliers of deception, robbers of the treasury, the whores from noble families, and the gold that was plundered and squandered on glasses of wine, elaborate turbans, fancy walls and furniture, empty hearts and the suicidal soul, and the derisive laughter of the universe. (p. 216)

Meant as a critique of power, this reading into the ruler's stream of consciousness may represent a position that the author is reluctant to approach differently. Loyal to bourgeois politics of reform and aware of the typical official discourse among dominant schools of Islamic law, the author is ready to acknowledge corruption and injustice as sources of evil and incentives for rebellion. His version of the underlying text is nevertheless as cautious as that of the storytellers of Abbasid times: the ruler is the commander of the faithful, whose power is needed more than his justice.

To understand Maḥfūẓ's method in dealing with the issue of the leader of the Muslim community, we need to study his particular references to the Khārijīs and Shī'īs that occur a number of times in the text. (pp. 38, 46, 137,

190). There is no such mention in the underlying text, and the only reference to *Rāfiḍīs* occurs once in the *Būlāq* edition of *A Thousand and One Nights.*[19] In keeping with his understanding of Islamic law and siding with his own Sufis, including al-Warrāq, Maḥfūẓ clearly criticizes injustice and corrupt authority as he does in his other narratives. However, he is now at some pains to cope with the increasing Islamism of the street. As the state ideological apparatus proceeds to defame opposition under a variety of names (such as calling communists traitors or infidels), Maḥfūẓ finds identical pejorative terms used by centers of power to quell opposition. Khārijīs and Shīʿīs fit his palimpsest as they also conform to the historicity of the underlying primary text.

The central issue of his narrative is the ruler and opposition. No such polarization exists in the primary text. In the themes of patriarchy and despotism Maḥfūẓ traces the seeds of failure, which he singles out as worthy of dramatization in a number of collated tales, including "The Porter and the Three Ladies of Baghdad," "The Fisherman," "Nūr al-Dīn Ḥasān," "Maʿrūf the Cobbler," "The Barber of Baghdad," and many others. These are rewritten to fit into a postcolonial dramatization that seeks to resurrect narrative tradition as cycles of progressive dramatic acceleration. All echo the new fervor of the street, while the question of Islamic polity and leadership assumes primary significance.

The author's mention of marginalized positions in religion does not imply a process of siding with them. Maḥfūẓ does not subscribe to the Imāmite notion of executive power, for example, something that they regard as both a birthright privilege confined to the Prophet's ancestry through his daughter Fāṭima the Glorious and as a prior investiture of the person endowed with "impeccability" and infallibility. On the other hand, the Khārijīs believe it to be the duty of believers to kill the unjust or disqualified commander. The choice should settle on the most qualified believer or the next most qualified. On the other hand, the Muʿtazilites believe that any believer from Quraysh is eligible for rule.[20]

Thus mainstream Sunni theology and orthodoxy are not smoothly and unobtrusively upheld throughout this narrative. His two supernatural beings are reluctant to create total chaos, even after tempting the ruler to the house of enchantment where the female jinni Zirmbaha acts as a ravishing temptress. The Sunnis stress the need to obey the nonapostate Muslim leader, the only condition being that the leader honors Islamic rites and duties. Since 36H./656CE, the murder of the third of "the rightly guided caliphs," Uthmān, jurisconsults and Islamic lawyer divines and imams have repeated the same premise.[21] Specifically, they do not confuse "a call to order" or *amr bi' l-maʿrūf-wa'l-nahy 'an al-munkar* with either "holy war" or "repression of sins."[22] Nor do they consider injustice and tyranny to be reasons for revolt, rejection, temporary silence, or "methodical dissimulation" (*taqīya*).[23] Maḥfūẓ is well aware of these details; in keeping with this underlying understanding he is obliged to allow his characters to voice their disagreement and offer advice. In this particular matter Maḥfūẓ's shaykh and Sufi model is no different from mainstream Sufism. Even al-Ḥallāj (d. 922) addresses the Caliph al-Muqtadir (r. 908–932) as follows:

> As for you (Caliph), you are this middle term that executes the sentences of God, the decree of God, on whichever of his servants he pleases, in that which pleases Him. As for me, I am a servant among the servants of God, ready to accept [*mustaslim*] His decree [*qaḍā'*] to endure [*Ṣābir*] His sentence, and to accept [*rāḍ*]. Therefore, do that thing for which you have been constituted.[24]

This reliance on antecedent Sunnite authority need not be assumed to be the writer's undisputed position. It serves to sustain an underlying narrative structure so as to bring about a change and transformation in Shahrayar's character, one that renders him unfit for rule and instead leads him to solitude as the only desirable domain for meditation. On the other hand, this same superimposition of a change of heart is dramatized through narrative and representation. Ugr, the "spinner of tales" (p. 106), passes through both domains in an interchangeable transaction which suits the purposes of the author himself. Imagination carries Ugr beyond representational reality and the wonderful or fantastic creeps its way in order to open more windows on this reality. He also shares apprehensions and fears with other characters. They all seem to agree that the instrument, government and state, is ungodly (pp. 42–43); whence the increasing religious fervor that makes the shaykh and his disciples the center of gravity (pp. 44–45, 57–58). The underlying premise that keeps this fervor under control and almost subdues the spirit of rebelliousness is the underlying factor that aims to turn the ruler into someone who will be powerful and just (pp. 129–30). To facilitate the narrative's task of coping with this political and theological complexity, the author resorts to the device of having supernatural agents intervene in times of upheaval. Any resort to human agency implies an endorsement of revolt and rebellion. When even the Sultan and his vizier fall into the trap set by Zirmbaha, Abdullah the madman, the metamorphosed character with many faces, appears on the scene. When asked why he is not punishing all these rulers and notables for their transgressions, his answer affirms the underlying premise: his purpose is to sustain rule and order (p. 145).

Dramatization of politics and state maneuvers aimed at avoiding revolt is revealed in a number of ways. Every exemplary tale in the primary text offers Maḥfūẓ some help and direction. The story of Nūr al-Dīn and Anīs al-Jalīs, as well as that of Qamar al-Zamān (pp. 78, 137–38) and the Damascene governor's daughters (p. 110), become parts of this dramatization as examples of tests of authority, examinations of corruption, and provision of solutions. Some characters, such as the police prefect, tend to display instincts of self-preservation through the misuse of power and an ultimate resort to the framing of innocent people. For example, the police prefect implicates the innocent porter, Rajab, in order to demonstrate his vigilance to the sultan (p. 149). Other methods of dramatization have as their goal the distribution of narrative dynamics and refocalization, shifting the interest from the center to the margin, for example. The repressed may be given power for a time, not to install a new order but rather to preserve authority and power (pp. 137–38). Maḥfūẓ has 1967 in mind: specifically Nāṣir's announced resignation from the presidency of Egypt and the resultant demonstrations that demanded that he stay in control. Maḥfūẓ may also have another shift in power politics in mind, involving the way in which the new President al-Sādāt pampered the Muslim Brotherhood against Nāṣirītes and leftists.

As a sacred critique of the nation-state, Maḥfūẓ's *Arabian Nights and Days* tends to prefer oblique exposition rather than any subscription to an ideology of rebellion. Like Maḥfūẓ's other narratives, it finds enough justification in antecedent authority for his cautious navigation between justice and power.

ʿAlā' al-Aswānī: *'Imārat Yaʿqūbian (The Yacoubian Building)*

Since its appearance in Arabic in 2002, *'Imārat Ya'qūbiān* (*The Yacoubian Building*)[25] has been gaining in popularity and reputation among readers, especially university students. This type of interest is not homogeneous. In my own course, Islam in Modern Arabic Literature at Columbia University, students' interests vary. While they choose to focus on space as productive of a narrative of confluence and separation, of solidarity and rift, more attention is usually paid to the theme of homoeroticism, especially the graphic description of encounters and love scenes. The Islamic element recedes into the background despite its centrality to the narrative of change and corruption. They argue that these love scenes are too graphic to come from an outsider. These students' arguments testify to the power of this narrative, especially its focus on homosexuality. The narrative is too implicated in street talk, a phenomenon that it duplicates without any of the saving touch of an artist. But this narrative vigor cannot take place outside the bounds of other issues that complement each other and create something integral to the seemingly disparate thematic elements. The character of Hatim is presented as the product of loneliness that is affected by the concerns and preoccupations of an effete bourgeoisie weakened by hybridity. His homosexuality is depicted as a consequence of failures that will also end in failure. His agony culminates in a condemnation of *nahḍah* politics that is represented by the ideals and practices that constitute the legacy of his parents' generation. The faint or nonexistent knowledge of same-sex literature in Arabic that might serve to redirect his incrimination of the *nahḍah* legacy reveals a serious gap in the grounding of Arab intellectuals in their own cultural traditions, leading, on the representational level, to the internalization of transposed concepts and methods of analysis. The father is thus presented as the ultimate failure of the national bourgeoisie and the incomplete *nahḍah* project. His wife evolves as a symbolic partnership with these *nahḍah* intellectuals. Unrepresented and vaguely touched on, her character seems like some European ghost or shadow, something to be searched for without any genuine engagement with the complex interaction with France or Europe. Under the impact and attention of the Nubian servant Idrīs, Hatim ends up as the outcome of circumstance rather than a human being with needs and desires. Placed in this particular building, he grows to become one of the many other types who make up a society with an ironic pyramidal structure, one in which the roofs of buildings serve to bring together villagers, functionaries, workers, and ruffians. The margin is now the generator of activity within a society where a dying bourgeoisie and remnants of an aristocracy are in imminent danger of extinction, usually represented by actual death or spatial displacement. The building becomes a broad-scaled site for an investigation of public life in Egypt after the 1952 revolution and the gradual demise of its ideals. Time is captured in space in order to determine a rapprochement, even alliance, between a dying bourgeoisie and an emerging *lumpen proletariat*, between Zaki and Bouthaina, amid scenes of corruption.

Although meant to bring together an Egyptian society in a murky urban space, the ultimate representation in this work is culturally based, one in which Islam provides the actual frame of reference even for the most intimate conversations, debates, petitions, and encounters. The Copts are there, for example, dynamically involved in a contemporary vision of Egyptian society. Abaskharon and his brother Malak are no less implicated than others in subservience and manipulation. The Nubian Idris is not given a sufficient voice, and yet his presence through Hatim's imagination and incessant enactment of his love maintains an active role for the Nubian, one that also smacks of a vengeful and vindictive attitude, a punishment leveled at aristocracy or elite societies that is often concealed under the false experience of consummation and joy. Within the Islamic domain of this public space, religion has a number of challenges to face. No encounter or debate can escape its presence, and it permeates even the most passionate love tiffs or scenes between Ṭāḥā and Bouthaina and between Hatim and his partner, the married police officer, `Abd Rabbuh. Within the framework of this narrative, then, religion is present, in discourse and action. It occupies the space used by the porter and his son Ṭaḥa, downstairs where Ṭāḥā cleans cars, or on the roof where he resides with others. It is behind the irritating sense of guilt after each love scene between the officer and Hatim Rasheed. It dictates Ṭāḥā's discourse on love and defines his perspective of how married life should be. It permeates Bouthaina's experience as a worker at a clothing shop before she attaches herself to the aging remnant of the old national bourgeoisie, Zaki Bey el-Dessouki. It fills her conscience with scruples, qualms, and irritations. Not only this, but the Islamic factor also defines the social, economic, and political order. The very efforts made by characters to elude its prescriptions, redefine them, twist them, and sell them anew in order to fit more conveniently with personal whims and passions indicate how powerful that grip actually is. Ḥājj Muḥammad Azzam needs the services of a shaykh like al-Samman (p. 52) to vindicate his aspirations and twist religion to fit into his plans to have the enjoyment of a new wife without any marital commitments other than financial provisions and privileges. The shaykh is certainly able to offer such support, since he is part of the regime, its spokesman and advocate, not merely in family matters but also in political affairs. Al-Aswāny (al-Aswānī) is outspoken in this matter to an extent replicated by very few other novelists, relating the phenomenon directly to a Saudi-led institutionalization of Islam that manages to justify the American-led invasion of Iraq (pp. 171–72) and the correctness of Arab rulers' policies in inviting American troops to liberate Kuwait from the "Iraqi invasion" (p. 171). The whole attitude, as presented in sermons, seminars, and TV speeches, gets support and guidance from no less than the Saudi religious institution that spends a good deal of money in order to validate this reading of religion. Al-Aswāny has his shaykh say the following:

> It was Shaykh el-Ghamidi, an outstanding scholar—we give precedence over God to none—who contacted me. I shall participate with my brother scholars there in issuing a legal ruling that will silence the arguments of the strife-makers and demonstrate to everyone the incoherence of their arguments. We shall mention in the ruling, God willing, the legal reasons for the possibility of seeking the help of the western Christian armies to save the Muslims from the criminal unbeliever Saddam Hussein. (p. 172)

This seemingly personal response places itself within the cultural context of an institution, a group of shaykhs, who are spoken of in the plural and see themselves as making up the majority, the consensus of all Muslims, against other shaykhs who are now shoved aside as strife seekers, dissenters, and outlaws. Speech, now elevated to a distinctive absolutist discourse, is validated by reference to Ibn Taymiyyah as the definite antecedent source for Saudi Wahhābism. His position against invasions by foreign armies is well known, but now the emerging institution needs to rewrite it so as to fit it into the new discourse of justification and subordination. Being tied to the American version, the institution realizes that it is only through money and satellite media that it can purchase its own way.

In other words, the author is adding his voice to a plethora of others by providing a polyphonic narrative that seeks to justify the convergence of disparities which find no place better than a building at the center of Cairo that was once the pride of its planners and architects (going all the way back to the days of Khedive Ismā'īl [1862–1879], who was bent on changing Cairo into a piece of Europe). These voices take Islam as a frame of reference, not only in arguments and patterns of conduct central to narrative focalization, but also in ordinary matters and communication that reveal a general Islamic climate.

In order to study Islamic parameters as dynamic narrative strategies, we need to examine specific narrative cycles that fit into a structural pattern. As I explain below, these relate to, first, the nation-state and its "Islam"; second, Ṭāḥā and the social-political order, or organized religion versus the police state; and third, Islam in the street and its internalized versions. All these need to be fitted into a larger frame of social order where corruption is rampant. Throughout, the narrative develops in the way that all these elements play out within the building in its social, political, religious, and spatial dimensions. The building emerges as the catalyst that gathers and generates further concerns. Fourth, there is the context of change downtown, from "a piece of Europe" to a miniature nation, whose own *nahḍah* discourse disintegrates like the building itself (pp. 33, 73, 92–94, 94–99, 115–25).

First, the "Islam" of the nation-state: Al-Aswāny is not completely absent from his narrative. Despite the fact that it is a polyphonic narrative that can leave only little space for authorial intrusions or digressions, the focused emphasis on misrepresentations of Islam in official and elitist discourse is so conspicuous as to leave the reader with multiple Islams. The official version is one of greed, corruption, and injustice. By allowing women characters to speak up against misuse or deliberate misreading of the Qur'ān, the text establishes the existence of a political and economic alliance between authority and its official jurists, shaykhs, and other functionaries. Shaykh El Samman is depicted, for instance, as both the gateway for individual appropriations of Islamic law and the representative of authority nationally and regionally. For the opportunist and rising millionaire, Ḥājj Azzam, the shaykh is "the celebrated man of religion and president of the Islamic Charitable Association, whom Azzam considers his spiritual leader and guide in all matters pertaining to this world and the next" (p. 52). The same shaykh "organized lectures and seminars and wrote lengthy articles in the press to explain the legal justification for the war to liberate Kuwait" (p. 171). This association underlines a frame of reference in the narrative which, despite its polyphonic aspect, resorts to explanatory and informational commentaries to make its point. Thus, we are told how Ḥājj Azzam "spoke of how he loved the people and of his desire to serve them, quoting more than one of the Prophet's noble hadiths concerning the rewards waiting for those who strive to meet the needs of the Muslims" (p. 83). The irony that pervades this ideological commentary and liberates it from its closed environment turns into a counterdiscourse, defusing and deflating the seeming solemnity of Azzam, exposing both its advocates as beneficiaries of a corrupt system. As part of this system, the mediator between the state and the opportunist Ḥājj, El Fouli is fully cognizant of this manipulation of religious discourse; far from being fooled by this jargon, he responds with a "drawing" that "represents a large rabbit," meaning, in their language, a million as a bribe for support to win the parliamentary election (pp. 83–84).

In such a discourse with its subjects well-entrenched in power, religion is the loser, and yet its burgeoning counternarrative gains momentum through opposition. Perhaps Henri Lefebvre's "differential space," the one that emerges as conflictual and subversive, applies here, versus the space of state power or the abstract space. Abstract space, says Lefebvre, "carries within it the seeds of a new kind of space," the "differential space," which "accentuates differences" against homogeneity.[26] The narrative picks its voices in hotels, stores, mosques, a university campus, streets, and primarily the building itself. Each opportunist's move is exposed, laid bare, and widely invoked among newly organized Islamic youth groups in order to reveal the scandal of a completely corrupt system. It needs to be realized that the system depends on a sustained internalization of certain essentialist value judgments made concerning Egyptians as being docile, submissive, and subservient to authority. The political operative and corrupt mediator, El Fouli, is so sure of this that he takes the whole thing for granted. As he explains to Ḥājj Azzam: "Our Lord created the Egyptians to accept government authority. No Egyptian can go against his government . . . It says so in history books," and he continues, "It's just the way God made him" (pp. 84–85). In his renowned work of historiography, *Al-Muqaddimah*, Ibn Khaldūn wrote: "Royal authority in Egypt is most peaceful and firmly rooted, because Egypt has few dissidents or people who represent tribal groups."[27]

The entire premise is debated through narrative polyvalence. The overall growth of Islam on the street belies it, and emerging social voices challenge it using a number of strategies, actions, and organizations. If official discourse can claim such representatives as El Samman, El Fouli, and Ḥājj Azzam, Islamic discourse takes as its point of departure the recruitment of Ṭāḥā al-Shadhli into the students' Islamic movement. The personalization of apprenticeship and focus on individual recruits enables the narrative canvas to go beyond romantic heroics. Poor recruits from among university students are the material for the new Islamist movement. Throughout the work it is Qur'ānic language that has the most effective symbolic power; users contend with each other to manipulate it to the utmost extent possible. It becomes the domain for contestation, between the state, its platforms, and satellites on the one hand and the small mosques or secret meeting places on the other. Throughout the narrative, we come across stylistically marked discourses that are "idiolects." Fashioned from the common language of the street, these discourses are bent on securing the approval and support of the recipient, who is another participant in producing the message conceived as he "perceives and appreciates it by bringing to it everything that makes up his singular and collective experience."[28] What Shaykh Shakir conceives may not be in keeping with the bent of a recipient like Ṭāḥā who has his own experience, but there is a common faith that holds the two together and endows the message of the former with meaning, especially if it fits his own thirst for revenge. This is why one has to discriminate between the particular and the common, for religion has its own codes, messages, and layers of meaning and appeal. It is only when there are appropriate senders and receivers, argues Bourdieu, that there is efficacy. Otherwise, as in the scene between Azzam and El-Fouli, "when the set of mechanisms capable of ensuring the reproduction of the relationship of recognition, which is the basis of authority, ceases to function," the symbolic power or efficacy of the religious language no longer holds.[29] Throughout, there is a shared symbolic system which is the condition for any form of integration.

Among the alternating tableaus that enable the narrative to assemble its disparate units in linear and dramatic movements, there is space for the omniscient narrator to act like a reporter. Ṭaḥa and the Islamic movement have to appear in a milieu that is surging with Islamic sentiment. In the 1970s, an "inexorable wave of religiosity swept Egyptian society; it was no longer socially acceptable to drink alcohol" (p. 33). Furthermore, the narrator-reporter informs us, "successive Egyptian governments bowed to religious pressure (and perhaps attempted to outflank the opposition Islamist current politically) by restricting the sale of alcohol to major hotels and restaurants, and stopping the issue of licenses for new bars" (p. 33).

This narrative report reproduces facts about a specific period and certainly helps the reader understand the Islamic movement that is able to convert such fervor into an organized body. There has to be a mentor, a shaykh with a number of close disciples and advocates as ardent as any missionary. In addition to the fervent participants, activists, and enthusiasts, there must also be a continuous process of enlisting the dispossessed and frustrated. Ṭāḥā is portrayed as an intelligent young man of poor social origins who believes in Islamic justice, pure love, and the nation-state. Gradually he discovers other realities that dismay and radicalize his outlook. A romantic love for Bouthaina cannot be sustained in the face of the needs that she explains to him in unequivocal terms. The nation-state has built its own corrupt system of nepotism, elitism, and injustice, and so, despite all the national discourse on equality and justice, a doorkeeper's son cannot be allowed to become a police officer. In other words, Ṭāḥā's mood changes from one of aspiration to disappointment, and as a direct result, he throws himself into the Islamic movement with passion and faith. The author obviously subscribes to the premise that Islamic fervor is the ultimate reaction to the 1967 defeat, Nāṣirism's failure to establish an effective nation-state, with a transparent rather than totalitarian discourse, and with a belief in constitutional democratic processes. Ṭāḥā, as the embodiment of the individuation of an entire movement, moves from political faith to denial and thereafter to an alternative religious commitment. In this narrative the Islamic movement emerges out of widespread feelings of disappointment, resentment, and anger. While these are significant dynamics in both life and narrative, they cannot operate without the existence of a cultural and social milieu that has Islam as its informing and decisive factor. The narrative falls into a trap of its own making, one that suggests an adherence to quasi-secular justifications of nation-state failures as the result of a rise-and-fall paradigm. Still the narrative is on firmer ground in its focus on Islamic fervor, organization, and recruitment of potential militants.

The ultimate outcome of this state of corruption is devastating, not only in relation to individuals and communities, but also on a more general level to urban life and the forceful birth of official gangsters as the unfortunate production of police states. Although primarily associated with the figures involved in a revolutionary military junta (namely the one that carried out the 1952 revolution against the Egyptian monarchy of King Farouk), this particular group inherited the privileges and gains of the old aristocracy, but without also possessing its caution, refined manners, and taste. It may be worthwhile to draw on Lefebvre's interpretation of this phenomenon, for in France the "bourgeoisie smashed the aristocratic space of the Marais district in the centre of Paris, pressing it into the service of material production and installing workshops, shops in the luxurious mansions of the area." He concludes, "This space was thus uglified and enlivened, in characteristically bourgeois fashion, through a process of 'popularization.' "[30] But certainly the process of turning the building into a petit bourgeois entity shows two sides of the 1952 revolution: its effort to extend socialism to the masses, and its failure to curb corruption and opportunism among its own officers and technocrats who turn into the new owners of the social space. Hence the question set by Lefebvre, "Has state socialism produced a space of its own?" is worth asking here too. The 1952 revolution, like many experiments in third world countries and Russia, "has failed in that it has not changed life itself, but has merely changed ideological superstructures, institutions of political apparatuses." He adds, "A social transformation, to be truly revolutionary in character, must manifest a creative capacity in its effects on daily life, on language and on space."[31] This "failed transition," as Lefebvre calls it,[32] dynamizes this narrative and endows Zaki's anger with meaning. Although Zaki Bey cannot be taken as typical of the old aristocracy, his perspective is more in line with the Wafd nationalist ideals of pre-1952 times. His view may help explain the change that took place in the years after 1952 without there being any clear vision or mechanism for a new order. "I lived through beautiful times," he tells his young girlfriend. "It was a different age. Cairo was like Europe. It was clean and smart, people were well-mannered and respectable, and everyone knew his place exactly" (p. 162). To know one's place is, needless to say, another way of describing a stable hierarchical social fabric, demarcated by privilege. While leveling the blame at the leader of the uprising, Jamāl 'Abd al-Nāṣir, Zaki cannot see the change that occurred in the social structure, as rural workers are brought into urban centers and young officers who were part of a once petit bourgeoisie now come to power with enormous ambitions and little discipline. The damage to the social fabric was so severe and widespread only because of a radical shift in a social order without sufficient forethought, preparation, and training. "Abd al-Nasser was the worst ruler in the whole history of Egypt. He ruined the country and brought us defeat and poverty. The damage he did to the Egyptian character will take years to repair" (p. 162). Certainly this criticism can be directed at the junta that conducted the 1952 revolution, one that, along with sheer greed, inherited the brutality of the colonial order and its mechanisms of punishment. On the other hand, the ideals of freedom, justice, and nationhood were soon converted into mere words and slogans within a strictly secular system of domination and coercion. Driven by an overwhelming sense of power and dismissing a gnawing feeling of guilt for having betrayed proclaimed ideals, the junta and its associates entrenched themselves in opposition to the street. The latter's sense of frustration and shame, especially after the 1967 defeat of the police state, accumulated and changed into a convulsive feeling of betrayal that secular politics were unable to exploit. It was in this climate of disappointment and national shame that organized religious groups were to find the right ground to strike roots and thereafter begin to take the initiative. Within such a social and political context the character of Ṭaḥa in this narrative becomes a recognizable player. While the focus on his disappointment in love and his failure to enter the police academy partake of stock-in-trade images and motifs in Maḥfūẓ's novels, for example, al-Aswāny has carefully set them within a scenario of religious fervor that provides both solace and comfort. The author cannot wait to inform his readers about this religious fervor, rushing therefore to insert authorial intrusions to illustrate: "An inexorable wave of religiosity swept Egyptian society, and it became no longer socially acceptable to drink alcohol. Successive Egyptian governments bowed to the religious pressure (and perhaps attempted to outbid politically the opposition Islamist current" (p. 33).

The emergence of organized religious cells is certainly a probable outcome from such a political environment. Indeed, al-Aswāny follows Najīb Maḥfūẓ and Jamāl al-Ghīṭānī in considering national politics since 1967 as being centered on a collision between a nation-state with a mixed agenda, blurred vision, confused procedures, and rampant corruption, and a countering religious movement that builds its essentialist ideas on a total rejection of Europeanized modernity. In Ṭāḥā's countermovement, which takes spatial form as a change of direction toward Cairo University as the alternative to the Police Academy, he creates a divide between nation-state and the nation itself, between the corrupt arm of a corrupt state and an institution that stands for a civil society with conflicts and trends of its own. In this civil society there are different nations and communities: country boys are "good-hearted, pious, and poor" (p. 92), but they are as far distant from wealthy students as "oil separates from water" (p. 91). "These poor students clung to one another like terrified mice, whispering to one another in an embarrassed way" (p. 91). The rich "made up numerous closed coteries formed of graduates from foreign language schools," and it "was to these that the most beautiful and best-dressed girls gravitated" (p. 91). The spatial shift from police academy to university has both metaphorical and realistic dimensions. The metaphorical lies in a shift toward ideology, ideals, and ideas, as befitting an academic center. Ṭāḥā will gradually conceptualize Islam. Under the guidance of Islamist mentors, he will no longer speak of absolute faith in nationalness. On the level of material reality, universities produce students as effectively as factories employ and create a labor force with a gradual awareness of alienation, exploitation, and misuse. This shift then, one that shatters his faith in proclaimed social equality, is symbolic of a radical change in power politics, from force, subservience, and supplication (as demanded by the job) to opposition and conflict.

The divide takes a cultural turn, too, one that the author employs to trash Islamists as less experienced in other aspects of knowledge. The poor find their solace, unlike the rich students, "With their own cars, foreign clothes, and imported cigarettes" (p. 91). Ṭaḥa has recourse to a prayer book, *The Book of Answered Prayer*, where he asks for support and "unalloyed forgiveness and generosity" (p. 16). Although he firmly believes that his prayers will be answered, ultimate failure does not divert him from his new religious path. Performing his prayers and rituals in a righteous manner, he is convinced that everything will come to pass in accordance with God's words: "I am according to my slaves' expectations of me: if good, then good, and if bad, then bad" (p. 20). Although he cannot hide his anxieties before the crucial interview at the police academy, his faith in God remains solid: "I have placed myself in the hands of God," he tells the girl (p. 22). His mounting fears and worries after submitting his application to the police academy cannot be assuaged without some form of solace that has one single source of assurance, the Qur'ān. "His exam nerves came back, and he started reciting the Throne Verse in a whisper as he approached the gate" of the academy (p. 23). In other words, the author is trying to distance himself from elite intellectual discourse and its condescending manner in speaking of and for the masses. Instead he focuses on Islam in the street, as it is ostensibly performed and expressed.

Although al-Aswāny's protagonist belongs to a long line of failed heroes and thwarted ideals (ever since Dhū al-Nūn Ayyūb's *Duktūr Ibrāhīm* [1938], and especially Maḥfūẓ's Sa'īd Mahrān in *The Thief and the Dogs* [1964]), the author nevertheless makes an effort to depict the purported quests for justice and equality by whatever means possible, as duly proclaimed by political leaders. Thus, even though Ṭāḥā's fiancé tells him that this "country doesn't belong to us . . . It belongs to the people who have money" (p. 59), he reenacts in the confines of his own room the role of someone in authority punishing the members of the police academy committee in order to establish a semblance of justice. Then he writes a petition to his "Excellency the President of the Republic" (p. 61), the outcome of which only confirms his fiancé's conclusion that the country belongs to the wealthy and the privileged. The petition (p. 68) simply rehearses the kind of thing usually addressed to authorities in most nation-states where people feel so utterly powerless and deprived of any means of communication that they decide to write messages to presidents just in case the president happens to engage with one or two every month as a way of claiming a closeness to the masses and dispelling accusations of elitism (p. 68). Such letters had already appeared in different forms in Arabic novels, but especially in Salwā Bakr's *Al-'Arabah al-dhahabiyyah* (*The Golden Chariot*).

With the failure of this last effort, Ṭaḥa, like many young idealists, is almost bound to switch to the other side of belief: organized religion. Like many writers who try to explain Islamism as another form of ideology, promoted and consolidated through scholars, mentors, and ideologues, al-Aswāny makes his protagonist join his brothers in reading the words of "Abu al Awla al Mawdudī, Sayyid Quṭb, Yūsuf al Qaradāwi, and Abu Hamid el Ghazali" (p. 92), a tendency that can also be observed in the works of Arab and non-Arab writers, including the Nobel Prize–winning Turkish novelist Orhan Pamuk in his work, *Snow*.[33] First come the articles of faith that lay the groundwork for his understanding of Islam as advocated by the Brotherhood. Although there are earlier writings that discuss this initiation, especially ʿAbd al-Ḥakīm Qāsim's *Al-Mahdī* (1977), al-Aswāny treats it as part of a process that leads to action. In other words, Qāsim's narrator stops short of depicting military training, focusing instead on organized parades of Muslim youths. Protagonists in both narratives share essentialist beliefs that reject the religion of the nation-state as no more than a sign of ignorance, of the pre-Islamic era. Thus, Ṭāḥā "learned for the first time that Egyptian society was at the same stage that had prevailed before Islam and it was not an Islamic society because the ruler stood in the way of the application of God's Law" (p. 92). Repeating the usual markers and ideological premises of the Muslim Brotherhood's discourse, the initial stage fuses Nāṣir's nationalism with communism, depicting both as flouting Islam and opposing the Brotherhood. Nāṣir is especially singled out as being the force behind crimes against the Brotherhood (p. 92).

The second stage depicts Islamic fervor itself: specifically sermons by shaykhs from the leadership who purport to influence disciples. Shaykh Muḥammad Shakir is the model in line with Hasan al-Bannā and Sayyid Quṭb. Following the example of Qāsim, rather than Maḥfūẓ or al-Ghīṭānī, the author carefully describes the shaykh and his devotees: their dress, appearance, rituals, and general clamor. True to the fraternity of the Brotherhood, Muḥammad Shakir knew most of "the students" and "shook their hands and embraced them," as if to prove Islamic intimacy and warmth in contrast with the arrogance displayed by state officials and bureaucrats. In a word, the "atmosphere was fabulous, authentic, and pure; the ascetic, homespun, primitive scene bringing to mind the first days of Islam" (p. 93).

The third stage is the crucial one: the shaykh's sermon is intended to encapsulate Islamist discourse at a certain point in the history of Arabs and Muslims, namely the American-led attack on Iraq in 1991 and the destruction of its basic industries and infrastructure. Its significance also lies in the stark contrast that it draws with state politics and muftis like al-Shaykh al-Samman (p. 171) and his associates in "Saudi Arabia" such as Shaykh al-Ghamdi (p. 172). While the latter are recruited by states to defend the invasion of Iraq (pp. 171–73), Shaykh Shakir is made to speak on behalf of Islam for Muslims. This sermon, with its deliberate and well-wrought structure, has a poetics that responds to similar sermons in 1991 before the encroachment of Arab governments on mosques under threat from the United States, and it is to the author's credit that he manages to reproduce the markers of a typical 1991 sermon. (As a point of contrast, by 2002 it had become almost impossible to find such sermons in many parts of the Arab world that are bound by a treaty or arrangement with Israel or the United States.) The sermon needs careful study, since it evolves as an integral piece of narrative that both promotes action in the novel and spells out the politics of the Islamist movement as represented by the Muslim Brotherhood, Ḥizballāh, and Ḥamās, they being the movements that are mentioned by name in the sermon (p. 96). Shown in contrast with Arab regimes with all their miserable failures and defeats, these movements are cited by the shaykh to illustrate his main argument based on a Qur'ānic verse. Advocating *jihād* (religious struggle) as the only way to show Muslims the viability of fighting for God and not this world, he concludes that Nāṣir (and hence the nation-state) has failed; his "huge armies were routed because they fought for this world and forgot their religion" (p. 96). Against these failed regimes, he argues that a "handful of warriors from Ḥizballah and Ḥamas were able to defeat almighty America and invincible Israel" (p. 96). Again, he relies on the Qur'ān, suggesting that, if God so wills, a small but sincere and faithful group can defeat a big one. Contrary to what is usually regarded as a significant component of sermons, the shaykh draws on known Qur'ānic verses that are popular among fighters. And, while the author is not one to introduce a sermon for superfluous reasons, it is clear that this particular one has a narrative purpose built on ideological polarization as pivotal to dramatic effect.[34]

Like Friday sermons, Shaykh Shakir's starts with "praise and thanks to God," before setting the stage for its main thrust, namely the advocacy of sacrifice and martyrdom in the cause of God. His main analogy builds on a Qur'ānic division between dreams in an ephemeral world and immortality secured by God for his sincere servants. The division between materialists and believers is clearly delineated: the first aspire to lives of luxury while believers realize that death "is the transition of the soul from the ephemeral body to everlasting life." He concludes that "this sincere faith . . . allowed a few thousands of the first Muslims to be victorious over the armies of the great empires of that time, such as Persia and Byzantium" (p. 94).

This careful preparation and use of prosified Qur'ānic verses serves to open up the space of the sermon to further discussion which can only occur if and when countersermons by muftis of the state and its other "hypocritical men of religion" (p. 95) are dislodged from their positions. The latter, we are told, are behind the effort to rob Islam of its "real meaning," transforming it "into a collection of meaningless rituals that the Muslims performed like athletic exercises, mere physical movements without spiritual significance" (p. 95). As is usual in such sermons, military defeats are explained as signs of God's wrath and disregard for those people who forsake Him. "When the Muslims abandoned jihad, they became slaves to this world, clinging to it, shy of death, cowards. Thus their enemies prevailed over them and God condemned them to defeat, backwardness, and poverty, because they had broken their trust with Him, the Almighty and Glorious" (p. 95).

The sermon acquires its power from its contentious thrust, since other competing discourses exist that need to be dislodged or displaced in order for the sermon to command total mastery of space. If muftis, fake shaykhs, and hypocrites are easily dispensed with, the discourse of democracy fostered by the nation-state demands a different approach, a comparison that links it to European commodities. This presents an opportunity for an attack on Europeanized modernity and for ridiculing the nation-state's claim of democracy (p. 95). That nation-state is said to be no less vain and arrogant than one "who wants to build himself a luxurious, elegant house but makes it of sand, on the seashore, so that the house is exposed to the possibility that at any moment a wave may come and knock it down" (p. 94). The Qur'ānic verse that he renders in prose here interweaves images on the vanity of human wishes and on the loss that is the inevitable consequence of pleasure and greed.

The author makes his selections with a view to Islamist politics on the eve of the invasion of Iraq in 1991. Since some Arab regimes claim Islam while others claim democracy, the sermon has to cope with both; and its political message is geared to expose both. Islamist discourse has to forge its own poetics and politics with due regard to its pioneer advocates, notably Ḥasan al-Bannā and Sayyid Quṭb. If both men tried hard to debate the tenets of liberal intellectual discourse, both the secular socialist version and the mediatory approach of certain religious shaykhs, then now is seen to be the time when the vacuum created by a series of failures, defeats, and unholy alliances with neocolonialist powers needs to be filled. In this particular example Islamist discourse questions the status of all other discourses. As Shaykh Muḥammad Shakir puts it: "our rulers claim that they are applying the Law of Islam and assert at the same time that they are governing us by democracy" (p. 95). Capturing the powerful rhetoric that is habitually manipulated so as to ensure the widest acceptance, the shaykh debates it on similar lexical and semantic grounds. Are the advocates of secular democracy right? Is there such a concept? The author allows his shaykh to recapitulate: "God knows they are liars in both" (p. 95). With such a rebuttal the shaykh prepares to expose both claims. "Islamic law is ignored in our unhappy country," not only because the state benefits "from gambling and the sale of alcohol," but also because "we are governed according to French secular law, which permits drunkenness, fornication, and perversion so long as it is by mutual consent" (p. 95). The state is even less equipped to implement a French-style democracy, since this "supposedly democratic state is based on the rigging of elections and the detention and torture of innocent people so that the ruling clique can remain on their thrones forever" (pp. 95–96). This reference to the French in particular is not random, in that not only does it form a textual and ideological connection with other critiques of Hatim's French mother and father as vestiges of the *nahḍah*, but also, and more important, it primarily critiques the whole advocacy of the principles of democracy as being a French commodity, sold and processed ever since the French expedition of 1798. The author may well be inserting more of his personal voice into this sacred critique of the nation-state, but the sermon definitely possesses all the markers, poetics, and politics of a sample of Islamist discourse. Hence its major surmise, namely that "Islam and democracy are opposites and never meet" (p. 96), will only sound startling to the uninitiated reader. Even so, it repeats what has already been said in Islamist discourse that equates democracy with a European model of modernity. The shaykh explains that a people's assembly can never replace "God's Law." Quoting the Qur'ān, the shaykh is shown concluding his earlier accusation of rulers as liars thus: "A monstrous word it is, issuing from their mouths; they say nothing but a lie" (p. 96). By reclaiming Islamic law, *sharī'ah*, the shaykh emerges as the spokesman for the Islamist movement. Islamic law ordains resistance, not collaboration; that is the basic premise that official discourse has tried hard to quell. The Saudis, for one, have found themselves in trouble because many Islamic groups have stood in opposition to this alliance with foreign powers, and the same applies to many Arab states. The call to *jihād* was voiced then, and ever since it has become a recurrent incentive in the fostering of political organizations. It has also been manipulated, diverted, and redirected in an attempt to preempt the competing power of both Ḥamās and Ḥizballāh.

The author's loyalty to his own semileftist discourse has to find a way to negotiate with the narrative requirements of Islamist discourse and his own knowledge of the political polarization involved in the power struggles around oil, markets, and Israel. He is aware of the rising Islamic fervor, which has been on the increase ever since 1967, something that Maḥfūẓ realized long ago. Now the shaykh has to acknowledge this as a fact, a reality that his audience has to internalize in full in order to meet the demands of the next stage in the struggle for Islam as represented in the sermon. It is now the task of Muslims, says the shaykh, to bring *jihād* "back to the minds and hearts of the Muslims" (p. 96). America and Israel, he argues, are terrified, along with "our traitorous rulers." The reason is "the great Islamic Awakening that gains greater momentum and whose power becomes more exigent in our country day by day" (p. 96). In the context of other sermons written in times of trouble, conquest, and war, this sermon can point to the meaning of "Islamic Awakening."

This sermon is a deliberately paradigmatic and semantic shift that turns away from a history of ideas, nation-state rule, secular ideology, and even literary production. The phrase "Islamic Awakening" is intended to counter the other awakening, the Arab *nahḍah*, which since the 1960s has completely lost its old glitter. In a deft transposition of compound lexical association, the shaykh replaces the term "Arab" with "Islamic" and thereby sets the tone for an Islamic discourse that is gradually dislodging the Arab *nahḍah* as usually discussed, historicized, and more generally established as the landmark of Arab modernity. The emphasis on this awakening is also a retrospective reminder that is founded on a lengthy history of Friday speeches and sermons, going back perhaps as far as Ibn Zakī al-Dimashqī's famous sermon in celebration of Ṣalāḥ al-Dīn's (Saladin's, d. March 4, 1193 CE) recapture of the city of Jerusalem from the Franks (which he entered on March 4, 1187 CE; Friday 27 Rajab 583 AH, after eighty years of occupation). However, the difference between the two lies elsewhere. Ibn Zakī had no reason to call for an Islamic state which was already supposedly there, with a caliph centered in Baghdad (at least until 1258, the year of the Mongol invasion and destruction of the caliphal capital city). Now, however, the shaykh has to proclaim its possible rebirth: "By God, I see that the Islamic state lies in your hands and that it has been reborn mighty and proud!" (p. 97). The rebirth will be as thunderous as any great achievement, he argues. It means a new era in the history of the region and of Islam: "Our time-serving, traitorous rulers, servants of the Crusader West, will meet their just fates at your pure hands" (p. 97). Dispensing with Nāṣir as the symbolic instigator of nationalist ideology and implicating the nation-state apparatus in corruption and its ideology of coercion, the author now manipulates the sermon to the full in order to place the whole phenomenon in a regional and global context. Drawing on examples from Islamic history and reclaiming rhetorical devices from the Qur'ān, Shaykh Muhammad Shakir can now be sure that his listeners associate the nation-state's coercive authority with regional systems that serve imperialists. The sermon speaks for Arab nationalness only as part of an

Islamic revival and not the other way round as has normally been the case in *nahḍah* or nationalist rhetoric.

As usual with Islamist discourse, it does not minimize the enormous sacrifices needed for the cause. The author is careful to relate this to the starting point whereby this life is described as transitory, fleeting, and brief. He adds God's words on martyrdom: "Count not those who were slain in God's way as dead, but rather living with their Lord" (qtd. 98). In these heated gatherings, the possibility of provoking immediate demonstrations and violence is also present in the minds of Islamist preachers who ask for caution and patience (pp. 98–100) in order not to fall in the trap of the police state until "the right time" (p. 100). On the other hand, this atmosphere is certainly conducive to the cause of enlisting and recruiting new members of the Brotherhood. Ṭāḥā is introduced to the shaykh and henceforth becomes involved in Islamist cells.

What this sermon leads to is a deliberate involvement in incipient political action. It begins with demonstrations (pp. 140–42), but, as usual, the police state begins its campaign of terror against participants, throwing them all, including Ṭāḥā, into prison, torturing them to obtain confessions, or forcing some to fabricate confessions in order to escape torture, or humiliating others through sexual abuse, a practice already seen in al-Ghīṭānī's *Zaynī Barakāt* and, particularly, in the Jordanian Ghālib Halasā's *Al-Su'āl* (*The Question*). This humiliation is worse than any physical torture, as it touches the sensitive chord of honor and drives political prisoners either to give up further political organization, as is the case with Rajab in ʿAbd al-Raḥmān Munīf's (d. late January 2004) *Sharq al-Mutawassiṭ* (*East of the Mediterranean*) before he meets up with European exiles and resumes his activities, or else to rush headlong into action in a desperate attempt to avenge one's honor under an Islamist banner. This is Ṭāḥā's ultimate choice: "They humiliated me, master," he tells Shaykh Shakir. "They humiliated me till I felt the dogs in the street had more self-respect than me" (p. 168). He adds what many political prisoners repeat in their memoirs and confessions: "They blindfolded me so that I wouldn't know who they were. But I have made an oath and committed myself before God to hunt them down. I will find out who they were and take revenge on them one by one" (p. 168). The author puts all this into the context of Islamist organization: "You must direct your anger against the whole regime and not particular individuals," and carry this out in the same fashion as the Prophet did against infidels (pp. 68–69). On the other hand, the shaykh, as the head of this organization, needs to explain the reasons behind this humiliation. The author knows the history of political prisons in Egypt, a situation that has also existed in every other Arab country since the emergence of the postcolonial state. History maintains a long record of such abuses, but nation-states have a notorious reputation for abuse. "What they want is to destroy them [Muslim youths] psychologically so that they lose their capacity to struggle. If you surrender to melancholy, you will have realized the objectives of these unbelievers" (p. 169). This is what generates Ṭāḥā's anger even at the training camp where the "rhythm was exhaustingly rapid" (p. 204). When he is made to speak in "a dead voice" of himself as a woman, he is rehearsing the torture scenes (p. 204). But channeled into the program for a revolutionary and retaliatory struggle, this recollection only increases his anger and hatred, feelings that "would not abate until he thought of the voices of the officers, categorizing, distinguishing, and storing them away carefully in his memory" (p. 205). Now he is ready to take revenge.

However there is something else to the credit of the author, in that he does not allow this initiation and involvement in political action to become stereotypical. His protagonist has first to lead the life of a brother in a camp where there are also sisters, who have been bereaved and are now waiting to become politically active. Ṭāḥā is married to a woman who also supports the idea of martyrdom. From now on, Ṭāḥā is a typical brother who has gained enough experience, suffered through turmoil and trouble, finished his training, and is equipped to act (pp. 237–44). Although this has been the procedure of Egyptian militant groups since Sayyid Quṭb's days, accounts of it in fiction have thus far been rare. In other words, this organization does not merely exist within the context of a religion of the oppressed which Ṭāḥā and others internalize (pp. 16, 20–22, 61), nor does it indicate the "powers of the weak" (to cite Victor Turner's terms, p. 161) as a means of turning events in an opposite direction. No, recruitment is here a deliberate manipulation of a sense of exploitation and humiliation that builds on one's piety to reverse material reality. Islam's initial appeal was as a religion of the oppressed; it is rich in piety, a feature that Ṭāḥā notices in the prayers of his colleague at the university, Khālid 'Abd al-Raḥīm (p. 91): Khālid "was deeply religious and when praying would stand and invoke God's presence in the full meaning of the words . . . in total submission." But organization goes several steps further to include reading manuals, attending discussions, participating in Friday congregations, and perhaps getting involved in demonstrations. The intervention of the police state is presented as the most decisive factor in turning a devotee toward political action, the initial ideological point being the belief that occupation and the secularization of a society are contrary to Islam: "Egyptian society was at the same stage that had prevailed before Islam," says Khālid, "and it was not an Islamic society because the ruler stood in the way of application of God's Law" (p. 92).

The author diversifies perspectives among his primary characters, and the multiple voicing that results broadens the novel's polyphonic scope, something that the narrative badly needs as a way of balancing its extensive reliance on factual detail and newspaper reports. It enables it to traverse wider textual terrains that include a number of conflicting discourses. The official religious discourse of Shaykh al-Samman and Ḥājj Azzam is rife with contradictions that are a natural consequence whenever associated with warring interests. Money becomes a major motivator and instigator of action. The democracy that Shaykh Shakir ridicules deserves to be jeered at, not only because of the police abuse of political prisoners, but in large part because of the corrupt core represented by Kamal el Fouli and his ilk. "I hope that the Patriotic Party [the government's] will agree to nominate me," says the Ḥājj, "and I'm yours to command, Kamal Bey" (p. 83). Kamal el Fouli is carefully described as a typical opportunist, a middle man, unrelated either to the *nahḍah* elite or to the dying aristocracy, a person with "a plebian manner" and "vicious, impertinent looks" (p. 83).

While religion constitutes a divide here, one between Islamists and the state and its opportunists, national identity is no less so. This identity is at the very heart of the lives of ordinary women like Bouthaina and others. It is in Zaki Bey's heart, too, for "[a] person has to love his country because his country is his mother," as Zaki says to Bouthaina in response to her feelings of hatred toward Egypt because of her poverty (p. 138). For Zaki, "Being poor doesn't mean you can't be patriotic" and he continues: "Most of Egypt's nationalist leaders were poor" (p. 138).

While this represents still another narrative divide in the novel, not a binary one in this case but instead one that gets blurred whenever it is swept away by the machinery of the nation-state or thunderous Islamist discourse, the line of demarcation between Islamism and secularism also exists in the other tales of downtown Cairo as found within the novel. In these tales desire, temptation, and space work together to change Abduh, the police officer, from a "shaykh" who is a person of piety and unblemished reputation to someone who is swept away by material temptation and latent homosexual desires (p. 133): "In the village they used to call me 'Sheikh Abdū': I always prayed the appropriate prayers at the proper time in the mosque, and I fasted in Ramadan," he tells Hatim, "till I met you and changed." Hatim is a *nahḍah* product, we are told. A refined intellectual, he becomes gay because of his background and his parents' preoccupation with bourgeois habits and jobs. Leaving him in the care of the Nubian Idrīs, he ends up in Idrīs's lap: "The latter was so aroused by the sight of his smooth, white body that during the encounter he sobbed with pleasure and whispered incomprehensible Nubian words" (p. 75). Both Abdū and Idrīs end up in the same role, making love to Hatim. In allegorical terms, the building witnesses a shift in roles, attitudes, positions, and discourse. It is no longer the one dreamt of as "part of

Europe," but a normal site of social and ideological diversity supervised by a brutal political system. The 1952 revolution has led to a radical change that has turned downtown Cairo into another arena of mixed societies, roles, and genders. The center, the *nahḍah* model, no longer holds. Everything trembles and quivers, just like Idrīs in one of his moments of sexual anxiety and satisfaction. Hatim's father is now no better than Idrīs, and the latter is as much of an actor as Dr. Hassan Rasheed, "the leading figure in the law in Egypt and the Arab world" (p. 73). Idris's Nubian race may have suffered dislocation and discrimination, but now he compensates for it with moments of joy and pleasure. Hatim's father returns from abroad with Western values, "democracy, freedom, justice, hard work, and equality" (p. 73), but he fails to offer his son enough love and attention. Is this applicable to all great intellectuals of the 1940s whom the author puts together in one definitional compartment? Did they have "the same ignorance of the nation's heritage and contempt for its customs and traditions which they considered shackles pulling us towards backwardness?" (p. 73). Hatim's father never prayed or fasted. His mother's job as a translator at the French embassy "occupied all her time" (p. 74). The *nahḍah* outcome suggests deprivation and psychological loss, implying a complete failure to grasp material reality and cope with its demands and a total divorce from tradition and culture; in brief, a one-sided application of a one-sided perspective on Western culture. In other words, the novel resorts to the authorial voice in order to critique the *nahḍah* and its state as freaks whose eventual outcome was and is bound to lead to Islamist fervor. The transposition of the term "awakening" from its Arab-oriented formulation in the mid-nineteenth century to a current Islamic one in a Friday sermon strongly supports Lefebvre's suggestion that "violence of power [imposed and promoted by the state] is answered by the violence of subversion."[35] Hence the emergence of these new forces: "These seething forces are still capable of rattling the lid of the cauldron of the state and its space, for difference can never be totally quieted."[36] In this way the author is clearly succumbing to a revisionist critique that has been gaining in momentum since the late 1960s, one that regards with suspicion everything that has been involved in the making of the nation-state, including literary production and its leading figures like Maḥfūẓ. But, no less dependent on Maḥfūẓ than his contemporaries, the writer takes his lead from Maḥfūẓ's narrative of recruitment. He is more outspoken than Maḥfūẓ, and certainly more challenging in his depiction of Islamist organizations. Although written at a later stage in Maḥfūẓ's own career, his *Arabian Nights and Days* makes use of allegories created from a popular text. His narrative style remains faithful to his middle-class tableaus where Qur'ānic phrases and expressions creep in every now and then without disturbing the overall bourgeois sentimentalism. Everybody undergoes adjustments to fit into this climate. Al-Aswāny allows the Qur'ān and Ḥadith to flood his narrative and become the domains of manipulation or application so that they can represent various perspectives and positions. The symbolic power of the sacred text is called on to cover or expose ideological and economic situations. Maḥfūẓ hints at these, but his narrative is able to elude closer scrutiny. While he allegorizes the whole issue of the nation-state, al-Aswāny puts allegories aside and lets his narrative unfold as table talk, or perhaps more like a witness to daily reports on corruption, change, and an Islamist takeover of the street that was once mobilized by Nāṣirism. The street has its own languages, and earlier writings by Qāsim or more historicized accounts by Maḥfūẓ deal with this in more elaborate detail. In writings since 1969, that being the date of publication of Qāsim's *Ayyām al-insān al-sab'ah* (*The Seven Days of Man*), religion operates on people's feelings and consciousness as a power in its own right, one that relates to authority only in terms of temporary deals or open conflict. In this text as well as in Maḥfūẓ's *Ḥarāfīsh*, mass culture occupies the whole narrative, leaving only a small portion to the state apparatus, a topic to be taken up in the next chapter.

Notes

1. Paul Ricoeur, *The Critique of Religion and the Language of Faith*, trans. R. Bradley DeFord (New York: Union Theological Seminary, 1971), 14.

2. Cited by Ana Belén Soage, "Shaykh Yūsuf al-Qaradawi: Portrait of a Leading Islamic Cleric," *MERIA* 12, no. 1 (March 2008), 1–26, at 7.

3. Soage, "Shaykh Yūsuf al-Qaradawi," 23.

4. See Henri Lefebvre, *The Production of Space*, trans. Donald Nicholson-Smith (Oxford: Basil Blackwell, 1991), 52, 90.

5. See Najīb Maḥfūẓ, *Layālī Alf Layla* (1982; English translation: *Arabian Nights and Days*, 1995), 106.

6. See Pierre Bourdieu, *Language and Symbolic Power*, trans. Gino Raymond and Matthew Adamson; ed. and introd. John B. Thompson (Cambridge, MA: Harvard University Press, 1991), 144, 192.

7. Bourdieu, *Language and Symbolic Power*, 115.

8. Cited in Soage, "Shaykh Yūsuf al-Qaradawi," 8.

9. Spelling and transliteration should be as above, but I use the proper names as they appear in the translation thereafter.

10. Annmarie Schimmel, *Mystical Dimensions of Islam* (Chapel Hill: University of North Carolina Press, 1975), 108.

11. Bourdieu, *Language and Symbolic Power*, 92, 93.

12. See Bourdieu, *Language and Symbolic Power*, 166, on linguistic capital and integration.

13. See William E. Shepard, "Muḥammad Sa'īd al-'Ashmāwī and the Application of the Shari'ah in Egypt," *International Journal of Middle East Studies* 28 (1996), 39–58, at 49.

14. See Lefebvre, *The Production of Space*, 50–51, on differential and absolute space.

15. The text was available in English in 1674, and much earlier in Latin. Muḥammad Ibn 'Abd al-Malik Ibn Ṭufayl, *Ḥayy Ibn Yaqẓān: A Philosophical Tale*, trans. with intro. and notes by Lenn Evan Goodman (Los Angeles: gee tee bee, 1983).

16. *Nabia Abbott, "A Ninth-Century Fragment of the 'Thousand Nights'*: A New Light on the Early History of the Arabian Nights," *Journal of Near Eastern Studies* 8 (1949), 129–64; reprinted in Ulrich Marzolph, *The Arabian Nights: A Reader*, 21–82.

17. Bourdieu, *Language and Symbolic Power*, 73.

18. Bourdieu, *Language and Symbolic Power*, 79.

19. The term was and is currently used to attack Shī'īs. It means "rejectionists" of the successive appointments of the "Rightly Guided Caliphs" after the Prophet, and the counter belief in the unequivocal designation of 'Alī by the Prophet as the next ruler and imam.

20. See Louis Massignon,*The Passion of al Ḥāllāj Mystic and Martyr of Islam*, trans. Herbert Mason (Princeton, NJ: Princeton University Press, 1982), 3:190.

21. There are more conciliatory positions in the case of Ibn Taymiyyah. Ḥudhayfa, as Massignon notices (3:190), established it under 'Uthman; so did Ḥasan al-Basrī under "autocratic Umayyad viceroys," Ibn Ḥanbal under the Mu'tazilite power, Tustarī, and al-Ḥallāj (3:191) for other reasons, too.

22. Massignon, *The Passion of al Ḥāllāj*, 3:191.

23. Massignon, *The Passion of al Ḥāllāj*, 3:191.

24. Massignon, *The Passion of al Ḥāllāj*, 3:192.

25. 'Alā' al-Aswānī, *'Īmārat Ya'qūbiyān* (2004; English translation: *The Yacoubian Building*, by 'Alā' al-Aswāny; trans. Humphre Davies. New York: Harper Perennial, 2006).

26. Lefebvre, *The Production of Space*, 52.

27. Ibn Khaldun, *The Muqaddimah: An Introduction to History* (1967; Princeton, NJ: Princeton University Press, 2005), 131.

28. See Bourdieu, *Language and Symbolic Power*, 39.

29. Bourdieu, *Language and Symbolic Power*, 73.

30. Lefebvre, *The Production of Space*, 57–58.

31. Lefebvre, *The Production of Space*, 54.

32. Lefebvre, *The Production of Space*, 55.

33. This emphasis on a specific number of texts is only partly true. The Brothers rely on their leaders, but, ever since the notorious training regimes of the 1980s, other radicalized Islamist groups in the Arab-Afghan line have been influenced first and foremost by Muḥammad Ibn 'Abd al-Wahhāb, Ibn Taymiyyah, and aspects of the teachings of Ibn Ḥanbal.

34. Patrick D. Gaffney argues for "the predilection for the more obscure stories" so that preachers can "propose original readings of their meaning," which may apply to

a noncontroversial, less focused and challenging sermon. See "Magic, Mirage, and the Politics of Narration," *Religion and Literature* 20, no. 1: 111–135, at 112.

35. Lefebvre, *The Production of Space*, 23.

36. Lefebvre, *The Production of Space*.

CHAPTER FOUR

Mass Culture Narratives

Mass culture narratives is a term that can be used to describe narratives that take the general public as their subject matter. Although there is a strong and dynamic narrative in Arabic tradition which is usually labeled popular, its resurrection in published texts has raised it, through Western mediation, to the status of canonicity. The history of *A Thousand and One Nights* (*The Arabian Nights*) is a case in point. The term mass culture narratives applies specifically to writings that locate their antecedent authority in this popular repository of tales and its insertion into contemporary writings that bid farewell to the Western model that has paradoxically both enriched and confined the novelistic tradition in Arabic literature. Whether in agreement and rapprochement or in opposition and conflict with its antecedent authority, this literature demonstrates a partial separation from the European model. While Maḥfūẓ has been and continues to be the most influential writer in effecting the primacy of this model and its application to Arabic literary production, his writings from the 1970s onward also demonstrate an anxiety of influence, as they fall under the impact of his juniors, specifically ʿAbd al-Ḥakīm Qāsim and Jamāl al-Ghīṭānī. Both bring to the attention of their masters the rich source that mass culture and the availability of history and religious traditions can provide for skillful narrativity. More responsive to Islamic fervor, collective memory, and the political and social plight of the masses, these writers are less prone to middle-class narratives or allegorical constructions. Their contribution is not an isolated effort; in other Arab states there are also narratives of recent history, rural life, and myths that still survive in people's lives and attitudes. In Syria, for example, Ḥaydar Ḥaydar writes his *Walīmah li-a'shāb al-baḥr* (1983; *A Banquet for Seaweed*); Algerian authors have already brought something new, barely related to European middle-class narratives; and the Iraqi writer, ʿAbd al-Khāliq al-Rikābī, resorts to rural myths in order to construct talismanic narratives that capture distant echoes from an ancient tradition. In these texts there is more attention to the central role of religion with regard to structures of feeling. In the following readings, two texts are studied because of their use of mass culture narrative as the basin wherein religious sentiment seethes and develops. Moreover, in these narratives there is a deliberate swerve from those that characterize the *nahḍah* in terms of priority. Instead of selfhood versus or in relation to the West, there is now an engagement with nationhood, its various representations and channels, including the nation-state. The conflict now is between mass culture and the ideological nation-state apparatus. This same conflict and juxtaposition on the level of language and its symbolic power echo a material reality whereby the nation-state has shown itself as touching only the superstructure, its apparatuses, but not the life of people. Popular narrative emerges from this neglected space, fresh, rich, and resourceful enough to forge a compelling presence among readers and recipients. The contestation takes place discursively and on the street where the terms of negotiation or opposition and conflict are enacted.

ʿAbd al-Ḥakīm Qāsim: *The Seven Days of Man*

ʿAbd al-Ḥakīm Qāsim's *Ayyām al-insān al-sab'ah* (1969; *The Seven Days of Man*)[1] is a pioneering narrative that depicts the Sufi experience of a group of villagers yearning for Divine blessing through the intercessions of a Sufi saint, Sayyid Aḥmad al-Badawī. His shrine in Ṭanṭā becomes a catalyst that brings together a number of narrative threads and events through the eyes and experiences of a young boy, ʿAbd al-ʿAzīz, the son of ʿAbd al-Karīm, the chief and leader of the Sufi group. The shrine functions as more than Henri Lefebvre's representational spaces, for it not only enlists everyday experience but also touches hearts and minds. Although Lefebvre's space "embraces the loci of passion, of action and of lived situations,"[2] the shrine reaches psychological depths and entails the assemblage of an accumulated tradition. It emerges as a catalyst for feelings, traditions, yearnings, and aspirations. It operates as the locus and magnet toward which every heart's aspiration and longings are directed. The shrine becomes, as never before in Arabic narrative, the dynamic force that imparts meaning and resonance to an experience that may otherwise sound placid and dull. Although usually enacted and built to meet the demands of a vision or to honor a saint who has sojourned or died there, shrines carry an enormous cultural, social, and economic value. To the village, town, or city, it is a major source of income, too. The question of which is first, the shrine or the city, will remain problematic for shrines lead to the growth of places into towns and cities. Playing the role of the recipient, the shrine welcomes supplications, intercessions, pleas, sighs, groans, canticles, and songs. Its answers are already there in the entreaties and beliefs of the mass audience. Faith implies this reciprocity. Nobody, including Najīb Maḥfūẓ, can avoid this sincere engagement with common sentiments and feelings. Indeed, as late as 1982, Maḥfūẓ makes use of Sayyid al-Badawī and his *mūlid* (*mawlid*: birthday celebration) in the above-mentioned *Layālī Alf Laylah* where the celebrated Sufi al-Warrāq is introduced instead.[3] Maḥfūẓ's awareness of Qāsim's pioneering text also manifests itself in his creation of Qindīl in *Riḥlat Ibn Faṭ ṭūmah* (*The Journey of Ibn Fattoumah*), for the child protagonist is modeled after Qāsim's child, 'Abd al-ʿAzīz, who, bearing in mind this novel's emphasis on the journey to the Sayyid Badawī shrine in Ṭanṭā, himself begins to entertain a persistent craving for travel. Maḥfūẓ's Qindīl is no less driven by this desire.[4] The Sufi experience that occupies the center of Maḥfūẓ's narratives of the 1970s and the 1980s also makes up the entire rural matrix of Qāsim's narrative of 1969. The fusion of the rural with the urban, of Sufi devotion with human desires, also takes place around and in relation to the shrine. The dome evolves as a panoptic lighthouse supervising everything, but without enforcing itself or invading the privacy of anyone. Every movement, motion, journey, procession, and supplication, the preparation of biscuits and bread, the amulets and entreaties for fertility and health, everything is directed toward the dome. If there is any transaction in this exchange, it is based on a different understanding of reciprocity. The saint may offer blessings, but there is no binding arrangement like the ones that distinguish gift exchange. The architectural supremacy of the dome is unchallenged despite the increasing questions that arise in 'Abd al-'Azīz's soul, much to the disappointment of his father, Ḥājj 'Abd al-Karīm, and his companions.

Qāsim does not allow his narrative to unfold as unproblematic panorama only showing villagers traveling to attend the *mūlid* in Ṭanṭā. 'Abd al-Azīz is the conflicted soul who represents the long-lived *nahḍah* legacy: a division between an awareness of science and responsiveness to urban allurements, enchantments, and desires on the one hand, and a communal spirit of faith and peaceful togetherness on the other. He carries inside him the simmering tension and doubt that has been the bane of urban novelists, the inheritance of *nahḍah* aspirations, and, on the artistic level, the perpetual Western model of narrative. He has Maḥfūẓ's Kamāl 'Abd al-Jawād's doubts and the frustrations of Yaḥyā Ḥaqqī's Ismā'īl in *Qindīl Umm Hāshim* (*The Lamp of Umm Hāshim*).

Qāsim allows 'Abd al-Azīz, a child coming of age, enough space to observe, survey, and experience, and then to express his frustrations. The turn or the shift from the *nahḍah* legacy to another paradigm of urbanism versus Sufism, or of rural pride and sense of independence and honor versus the violence exercised by the police state is what distinguishes Qāsim's protagonist from the heroes of the bourgeois epic.

Like the remnants of the *nahḍah* aspirations, Qāsim's child resists the urge to be swept away by the powerful human procession. "The crowd would be like the Day of Resurrection, a monstrous body stretching out through the city, flexing its huge muscles and extending its trunk to shove it at last into the Shrine of the Sultan [the saint]" (p. 237). The phrasing is still indebted to *nahḍah* doubts and suspicions regarding the common public, especially peasants. Nevertheless behind this uncouth reference to monstrosity there lies recognition of a peasantry which will be soon capable of enforcing its presence on the street as users of public space. The human procession loses its individual identity; and the focus of the urban novel on individuals gives way to a communal bond that brings to mind Frantz Fanon's early reminders of the collective spirit, something that escapes the attention of the Westernized elite as it returns with its ideals of individualism and free enterprise as being the only facts that distinguish the spirit of the age. No, through the eyes of the disenchanted youth, the reader watches "people [who] were pressed so close together that they seemed to be one mass of flesh with thousands of heads as they surrounded the brass grill that enclosed the tomb. They were a single body full of all strange temptations that assailed mankind, temptations Abdel-Aziz's awakened senses picked up" (p. 239). The growing child is well aware of desire and temptation as human instincts, and his awareness is duly ignited by the power of city life, as manifested by women in particular. "Down beneath the surface, temptations and unspeakable desires that could not be controlled writhed like worms, moving, groping, and clinging and then drowning in ambiguity" (p. 239). In other words, more than one institution works on his formation: the *nahḍah* through the city school, hereditary values, Sufism, and the powerful presence of the village in the city as a compelling declaration of faith.

He realizes, too, that human will and determination can drown these desires. The usual divide between the countryside and city that has long sustained the bourgeois epic quivers and snaps under this pressure. What we get instead is a different outlook, one that resists subscription to the traditional view of the country-city dichotomy. Although we are given a number of perspectives, impressions, and notions that deride villagers (pp. 205–6), there is nevertheless a more comprehensive perspective that finds in this particular occasion, the procession towards the shrine and the early preparations for the visit that precede it, enough evidence of a basic communion that holds both together. "The blood from the brown body of the countryside poured in an unending flow into this radiant heart. The eye of the believer could see it from thousands of leagues away, with all those lights" (p. 238). 'Abd al-ʿAzīz has already surmised that the "city was a tree with its roots in the countryside" (p. 172), but at this stage in his life, as an adolescent responsive to human sexual impulses, he strives to explain the connection in complementary rather than organic terms, as social contracts rather than filiatory or genetic connections. "The countryside was covered in darkness and longed for a brightly lit night" (p. 238). In contrast to *nahḍah* representations of shrines as perceived sites of anti-*nahḍah* superstition, the shrine summons all the power of faith which was thereafter to be unfortunately confused with fundamentalism as being incompatible with democracy.[5] This yearning is no casual matter; it is mandatory, especially as the shrine is the panopticon that draws the human river toward its destiny. In this instance, usually everything else dwindles to a minimal presence and another consensus is forced that competes strongly with state political power for some time, at least during the celebration. Indeed, the referential space of Lefebvre works here to demonstrate homogeneity of faith against a political or social one as envisioned through rules and codes by the impersonal pseudo-subject which has no name but which virtually stands for the state.[6] Impersonalizing this reciprocity and fusing it with his own sexual excursions in the dark corners of the city, he comes to a conclusion that will establish the connection in terms of possible fruition through biological intercourse: the "countryside had clasped thousands of arms around the city and embraced it. It had breathed its breath in a long kiss into its lungs" (p. 242). Religion as Sufi practice, a popular faith, becomes a magnetic pole that at this moment absorbs divides and leaves bewildered souls with a faint cry of resistance that cannot materialize into an act of rejection. When the young protagonist thinks of his individuality, as being separate from the crowd, he "summon[s] all the resolve a human will possessed to separate himself from the crowd and say 'No.' " He realizes that the only consequence of his efforts is futility and uselessness (p. 241). Trying to understand the reason behind his inability to deal with his dilemma in spite of the "stubborn, persistent question in his mind," he asks himself whether it is merely his father's "brown eyes, soaring with longing" that stir in him the "yearning to see the Sultan's shrine" (p. 238). He tries to conceive of this driving power in some way other than through his own father's faith, for "What mechanical heart, what unbelievably powerful machine could generate this entire splendor and light on the face of the towering mosque?" (p. 238). However, no matter how he tries to rationalize this entire flow of humanity, there is a fact that remains in place, supreme and unchallenged: "He was carried along by that single moving will created by thousands of bodies walking towards the shrine" (p. 238).

The reader may well point to this adolescent boy's response, a blend of resistance and acquiescence, as being yet another retrieval of a *nahḍah*-based inner conflict that many intellectuals have gone through, a struggle against tradition as sustained through family and community. But Qāsim is not concerned here with intellectual insight. To be sure, he lends his vision to the boy, 'Abd al-ʿAzīz, but he never allows him to pose as representative of some intellectualized outcome. It is only the city that exerts an influence on him, one that continually competes with his father's faith, which is always presented in pleasant, peaceful, and soothing terms. The issue has a double bind. There is first this usual dichotomy between the rural and the encroaching urban; but there is on a narrative level another problematic that relates to the form of writing. Does Qāsim as yet decide to leave behind the old epic structure or does he implicate his protagonist in the dilemma before trying further options in his *Al-Mahdī*? Does he try to show the protagonist's undecidedness on purpose? We are let into the mind of the protagonist to look at his dilemma in very simplistic terms: should he be himself and leave behind the village and the Sufi circle? Or should he continue living out this duality? In Lukács's terms, a protagonist in this vein "realizes this duality: he accommodates himself to society by resigning himself to accept its life forms, and by locking inside himself and keeping entirely to himself the interiority which can only be realized inside the soul."[7] We are speaking here then of a narrative of disillusionment, of incongruity between one's interiority versus the exteriority of the world. But opposite the direction of narratives read by Lukács, this novel has its exterior other: it actually questions and doubts the community of "feeling among simple human beings closely bound to nature,"[8] which is Tolstoy's authentic and hoped-for world. His quarrel is with this nature, which his *nahḍah* legacy has already doubted, questioned, and denied. In the last pages of the narrative, he is drawn to the coffeehouse, where the radio imposes no control on the audience, who are playing cards, arguing, and shouting at each other, but keeping track of the news nevertheless. They argue politics, especially international affairs, and hardly listen to each other. "They talked about politics, cooperatives, feudalism, oppression, Kennedy, and Khrushchev" (p. 322). Hajjah Showk, who was once the vivacious and pleasant lady, now looks around the place, and mourns "the good old days, the affectionate words . . . the glances filled with longing, the radiant cheeks. Those days were gone" (p. 328). The new dawn brings with it more secular politics, and the new generations are obviously involved in what is going on, but they are such "boisterous, exasperated men" that they cannot restrain themselves and argue "slowly and deliberately" (p. 322). The protagonist is torn now between the familiar things around him, things that make writers like Tolstoy yearn for a pleasant union with nature, and the din of present-day life, with its new consciousness and also its lack of tempered discourse. Surveying the scene at home, and "the houses in the village, the homely, squat minaret of the main mosque, and the distant dome over the tomb of his grandfather's wife in the village cemetery" (p. 327), he realizes that "he had no desire to return to the house and bury his joy in that room of suffering on the roof" (p. 335). In iconic and pictorial details a boundary is drawn between the sacred and the secular: the minaret, with its connotations of faith and pleasant life, and the coffeehouse. He chooses instead the coffeehouse, "the small room," the "little parcel of boisterous life buried beneath the silence of the village" (p. 336). Rather than questioning the choice, he finds himself assimilated into that atmosphere where he "felt the same bitterness, anger, and pain" (p. 338). The noise recalls the noise of 1967, where there is excitement and rhetoric with no action. The moment of hesitation is done with, and the adult accepts the outside world, a decision that means also his ultimate departure from his father's legacy, a legacy that he has not fully comprehended.

The protagonist cannot fathom and make use of his father's appropriation of city life in times of need and necessity. In the city, the father acts in a manner that draws 'Abd al-ʿAzīz's attention to the need to change discourse and intention in order to match urban expectations and ways of life. In view of such adaptability and openness the father can never be a fundamentalist.[9] Observing one of these urban scenes through the boy's discerning lenses, we as readers are made aware of the father's "pleasant conversation," his "specialty" that makes his "friendly words like a cushion on which a woman could lean back and relax" (p. 172). Thus, the woman responds with reciprocity, and "would no longer be so tense nor would she attempt to hide the cleavage between her heavy, white breasts" (p. 172). Certainly women here have a role of their own, as they engage in a life of supply and demand, the village and the city, without letting themselves be carried away by rigid exchange. Reciprocity works nicely and pleasantly, and manifests a community that resists being swept away by an encroaching regime of political control. Even her subsequent "mischievous and flirtatious" smile signifies this pleasant reciprocity, which the father appreciates (p. 174). In other words, we read a growing child's report on the things he has seen, noticed, and surveyed before being subjected to a subsequent mature analysis. Thus, upon noticing his father's careful but mellifluous conversation with the landlady, he comes to the conclusion that his own volubility is hereditary. In that he may well be mistaken (as in many other surmises), but this is how the narrator reads his response: "Ḥajj Karīm was a mighty horseman, and she was his pampered mare. The fire that raged in Abd al-'Aziz's breast had not fallen out of the sky" (p. 190). In the city, his father spoke in terms different from "the way he spoke to the women in the village. He had the twisted dialect of the townsfolk" (p. 190).

Nahḍah and post-*nahḍah* intellectuals typically acknowledge a village-city dichotomy, which is also a divide for them. Every journey toward the city is an ascent, an engagement with sophistication, challenge, and hazardous encounters. Not so in Qāsim's narrative. In 'Abd al-Azīz's mind, there is to be sure a problematic struggle, but he is given enough scope to consider other responses. The adaptability of the pleasant popular Sufi, Ḥājj Karīm, humanizes the role of the shrine as the meeting ground where peasants and city dwellers gather together. Every other divide fades and disappears. Indeed, even 'Abd al-Azīz's disgust at many scenes he witnesses is replaced by a counterunderstanding that brings him back to his own village: "he clung to his love for these people. They were always there, looking at everything with simplicity and love" (p. 275). Whenever the city encroaches on his sensibility, like the voice that "split the darkness like a crack of a whip, . . . stern and direct," calling on him to halt, he realizes his need for that bond with the village that makes him feel stronger: "He wanted to run away and rejoin the huge body that was convulsing the city with its thousands of heavy steps" (p. 243). If there is a *nahḍah* sentiment lurking in his soul, there is also some ambivalence whenever he has to make straightforward choices. The protagonist may adhere to remnants of the *nahḍah* spirit but, through the growing protagonist's eyes and voice, the narrative gives due attention to the masses, their rituals, devotions, and enormous and compelling presence. Never before in fiction have they appeared in such an overwhelming manner. Indeed, Qāsim establishes anew the institutions that produce this narrative: faith, symbolized and perpetuated by the shrine, is the dynamic power that the protagonist simultaneously acknowledges and resists, like any *nahḍah* remnant. Here narrative bridges function as structural devices that balance the strong distancing sense of estrangement that spasmodically invades his soul.

The absence of the West is the other distinguishable aspect that problematizes the village-city dichotomy in *nahḍah* or post-*nahḍah* writings, and thus deepens Qāsim's reciprocal exchange in terms of feelings, dialects, interests, and, significantly, faith as the dynamic cultural motive. There is no "other" in this novel's terrain where the shrine presides like the heart that enlivens all, for the "blood from the brown body of the countryside poured in an unending flow into this radiant heart" (p. 238). The flow is neither disparaged nor commended; it is simply there as a fact that has to find its own narrative. The latter unfolds in parallel with the preparation for the journey, the *mūlid*, followed by the return home. "From every village people were going to the moulid [*sic*]. Little paths led along the edges of the plots and the fields like veins in a leaf" (p. 147). The language of narrative has to carry the rural stamp; hence the preparation of loaves, lime-yellow shawls, baskets, and "bundles of provisions" before swarming into the city (p. 147). Although for a short time the symbolic power of the shrine summons all, and shows in unequivocal terms that the power lies there, we know also that the rest of the year passes under the state's full control of the whole city, encroaching over towns and villages, dissolving their power through their dependency and need on the economic level, and their ultimate subordination to state apparatuses.

The narrative focuses more on the protagonist's own dilemma, his agonized soul placed at the intersections of the country and city, faith and doubt, desire and resignation, the motivating force that rationalizes the journey beyond its unconditional motion in time and space toward the *moulid* (*mūlid*) and the shrine. But this traumatic moment in 'Abd al-'Azīz's growth cannot assume its full significance without its local and cultural background, the faith that his father, Ḥājj Karīm, has nourished and sustained through the qualities of sheer pleasantness and generosity that lead him to end up bankrupt and totally penniless. Although the pensive mood of his final weeks escapes the attention of his son, the other members of the Sufi brotherhood seem to realize his financial situation as he continues to host the gathering, guests, and anyone in need, as if he were the wealthiest person in the village. There may also be other reasons behind the way he avoids looking his son, 'Abd al-'Azīz, in the eye, an attitude shared by the Sufi brothers. "Their truncated smiles passed over him too" (p. 221). Held together by a strong bond, a feeling more powerful than a blood tie, they respond to each other with smiles and laughter. "They were all connected by electric wires, and he was a section of insulation" (p. 221). His effort to break the ice, to invade the circle, might come to fruition if he were to leave his own ego behind and allow his soul to soar like theirs; becoming one in "the grinding movement [that] crushed everything and swept it away" (p. 221). Only through a rite of passage, one that involved annihilation of the ego, would he be able to go beyond his belated desire to "take his father by the arms, stop him for a moment and ask him: what does this [avoidance] mean?" (p. 221). The young protagonist, like other symbolic remnants of *nahḍah* institutions, cannot escape the constraints and limits with which he has been living, especially as part of his city schooling. He is unable to question his ego and move beyond it toward ordinary people, the providers of mass culture whom the *nahḍah* institutions, including his secondary school, have left behind. Still enveloped by this ego and engulfed by walls of separation, he fails to internalize the scenes of rapture and elation among his father's group. Watching the dervishes during the celebrations of the *mūlid*, he responds with a repugnance that betrays his estrangement from "the wanderers, those mangy tomcats who roamed through the countryside with their beards, long hair, and shining eyes" (p. 224). The men whom his father welcomes with love and generosity only arouse his sarcasm and disgust. "Their laughter was as piercing as daggers, and their faces were as strange as the clothes they wore" (p. 224).

Does this mean that Qāsim is trying to situate this narrative of childhood, maturity, and disillusionment in the form of a bildungsroman that is no less a Western technique than precedents composed by his predecessors, including Tawfīq al-Ḥakīm, Ṭāḥā Ḥusayn, Laṭīfah al-Zayyāt, and especially Sayyid Quṭb's *Child from the Village*? Does he echo some earlier (auto) biographies (*siyars*) in Arabic, including Abū Ḥāmid al-Ghazālī's (d. 1111) autobiographical sketch of his journey through doubt and skepticism, before embracing the Sufi path? We know as readers that Qāsim's protagonist, 'Abd al-'Azīz, will appear again in his later writings, in the same way that al-Ḥakīm's Muḥsin was used as the protagonist in his own veiled autobiographies. The amount of internalization involved in Qāsim's narrative is an important factor, not overlooking the childhood experience whereby the father's chest plays a role, since childhood and maturity work together to complement an experience that avoids the principles of linearity through series of short shots, scripts, dialogues, recitations, and rituals. Nothing stands still in a Sufi experience of ecstasy, supplication, and greeting; the chest itself, though static and concrete, becomes no less symbolic of imaginary details, flights of fancy, and cravings for travel. Inside the chest is the whole repertoire of Sufi literature known and cherished by the common folk: for example, *The Tokens of His Blessings*, al-Buṣīrī's *Mantle Ode*, *The Intercession of the Saints*, and *The Deeds of the Religious* (p. 31). More important are the images that linger in the child's mind: "Misty images burst into the mind, images of men not like other men, stirring in the four corners of the inhabited world. Nails were hammered into hands and feet, and backs were lashed with whips" (p. 33). But there are no stronger images that are able to convert this impressionable child into another dervish. Aware of the miraculous lives of these saints and realizing that "there was something in these men, something that remained above the torture and did not bleed" (p. 33), Qāsim's child tries to understand and sympathize with these men as he watches his father, with "the tears [that] rose in Ḥājj Karīm's eyes [while] 'Abd al-Aziz tried with all his heart to capture the fabulous secret—the dark, coarse bread, the bitter salt, the turbid water, the tattered shreds, the eyes like strange birds, alighting nowhere. Men not like other men" (p. 33). And yet the experiences narrated in Sufi narratives of saintly experience cannot affect the boy, not merely because he is too spoiled to identify with them but rather because his frame of mind moves in a different direction. The impressions left in his mind involve creatures that are vague and unreal. To him, these saints may have legs, but they must be "like pointers moving over a map covering huge distances in an instant; their hands were not like other hands, but like markers on the wayside or draining destinies" (p. 33).

But there is a rural background to all this, something that makes the chest a mixed tradition of hagiography, history, and adventure. Whenever adventure is involved, the child's attention is captured. In every gathering there are readings, recitations, mention of miracles (pp. 32–44), and *dhikr* rituals. What balances these events and kindles his yearning for travel is the tangibility of *al-Hilāliyyah*, the biography and heroism of Abū Zayd al-Hilālī. This tangibility "mingled with his soul" (p. 122), as he follows Aḥmad al-Badawī's reading of the narrative to the rest of the company at his father's Sufi gatherings. Only the preparation for the journey to Ṭanṭa, the "way to the Sultan" Sayyid al-Badawī and his shrine, is able to dissipate this sense of tangibility or dislodge it from his memory. Toward this very destination his father's "longing brown eyes cut across the dull green expanse. His full brown face was beaming with contentment" (p. 123). Caught between two possible tracks, one the Hilālī adventure and the other the journey toward the saint, he needs visualization more than flights of the imagination. Thus he "stood up like a man who was a thousand years old," declaring a need to travel (p. 160). Limited by his taste for the concrete, he can only see two roads, the railroad track and, parallel to it, the line of telephone poles (p. 160). The desire inside him is powerful, due in part perhaps to an incomplete grounding and in part because travel implies a journey away from home. Besides that, the boy may have wanted to disconnect himself from the towering presence of his father: "But he had to travel. Nothing but a long journey could quench this strange burning thirst" (p. 160). Perhaps 'Abd al-Azīz is destined to stay that way, tortured by conflicting desires that offer both the Sufi path and the outside world, desires that show no signs of abating. Through these choices we, as readers, can see the growing complexity of an outlook that goes beyond the dichotomous patterns that had once to a certain extent bedeviled urban narratives and poetry, whereby village and city, peasants and urban dwellers, came to be seen in paradigmatic frameworks outside their normal cultural milieu.

The emerging narrative tries to engage responses and practices as they are, unmediated by intellectualized premises. On the other hand, these are often reminiscent of Maḥfūẓ's distrust of preachers, a tendency that has been one of the dominating aspects of the proclaimed scientism of the *nahḍah*. But coming through the eyes of a child, they are supposed to be rather innocent. For instance, the boy becomes angry at both sites and practices, and yet he still remains open to different sentiments that show an appreciation of certain aspects of village life. Thus, he dislikes the preacher for his castigation of others, absolute trust in his own judgments, and susceptibility to anger while yelling "at the top of his voice terrifying things about the fire of hell, liars, thieves, and fornicators" (p. 25). The boy "had never liked that preacher at all: He liked his donkey much better, a small white she-ass" (p. 25). He also dislikes the fake Sufi shaykhs, such as the one whom the Iraqi's old mother harbors at her place for months. He keeps repeating to the wretched woman that her son is under "a spell, written on flakes of bran, and that the bran . . . had been scattered to the four corners of the earth" (p. 27). He stays in her house and has been fed pastry and honey "for breakfast" and "meat and a cooked dish for lunch" (p. 27). Ḥājj Karīm is the only one who can dump out this fake shaykh's incense and drive him out of the village (p. 28). No less appalling to the boy is the shaykh of the order, "a small god, graceful, tranquil, and serene, toying monotonously with the beads of a rosary and reclining on a mattress," while "spitting in the mouths of children and stroking their foreheads." As a grown-up, 'Abd al-'Azīz comments angrily: "What a farce!" (p. 224). While Qāsim clearly subscribes to the sharp, sarcastic critique leveled at fake shaykhs with their superstitions and unwholesome practices, he is no less wedded to his ideological commitment to combat practices that have long been responsible for the spread of backwardness and regression.

A number of thematic and structural patterns help in constructing a narrative that engages seriously with popular Sufism within spatial, temporal, and transcendental parameters. There is first 'Abd al-'Azīz's coming of age and increasing interest in sexual encounters. There are also the conflicting images of the city, with its pleasures and dangers, its availability, and its resort to state coercion or brutality. There are also its women. All these factors are also considered from other perspectives. The emerging frame that is to encapsulate them all is the shrine on the occasion of the saint's *mūlid* that gives meaning to time and space and takes form through prayers, benedictions, invocations, and supplications. The boy's experience in sexual encounters is not initiated under the spell of the city; it has already started with Samīrah in the village. Even so, under the impact of the new power he is no longer as keen, for "she did not have the flare of the Tanta girls nor did she affect him in the same way" (p. 198). That Ṭanṭa experience takes place as part of a reaction against his father's group, their way of eating, and so on (pp. 226–28).

Although 'Abd al-Azīz does not undergo a well-defined conflict involving doubt and faith, there is nevertheless a struggle that sets him apart from his *nahḍah* predecessors, one that involves a divided self, preferring city life without a full acceptance of its potential brutality: "he loved its noise, its cleanliness, and its girls. He loved the cinema and books" (p. 182). Each of these preferences is reflected in his character, but, upon facing "the harshness of the city," he "turned a blind eye to it" without being able to banish the idea from his mind. The city enforces itself on the whole habitat: "Suppose this city were one day to turn him into a policeman with a country face, a stick, a mouth of curses in the language of city folk . . . what a terrifying thought!" (p. 183). The image evolves after seeing "those policemen, country faces spewing out anger on crowds of country folk" (p. 183). This force of "informers and policemen . . . with their sticks and the butts of their rifles" (p. 251), which hunts down a vagabond, must detract from this love he nurtures for the city, but his anger cannot last in the presence of other distractions. In contrast with the *nahḍah* celebration of the state, there is now a realistic picture of a situation in which brutality affects village folk, including his own father. However, this same brutality is matched by a counterimage of a bewildered being confronting a popular fervor embodied in the thousands of bodies moving toward the shrine (p. 186). Looking at the perplexed police (p. 235), he identifies at times with their feelings of shock and bewilderment as they watch so many people whom he himself wishes to exclude from humanity and lump together as a monstrosity: "How was it possible to control this monster that spread over the ground and twisted its flesh through the streets like a worm" (p. 235). The image rehearses a *nahḍah* fear of the masses and points to the way in which it wishes to celebrate an ideal elitist state. But the "crowd would be like the Day of Resurrection, a monstrous body stretching out through the city, flexing its huge muscles and extending its trunk to shove it at last into the shrine of the Sultan" (p. 237). His distrust of the masses is equaled only by a similar one of the police force, which is merely "a human machine set to strike fear in the hearts of the peasants who kept pouring out of the station" (p. 179).

The implications that are behind this depiction of peasantry and police force are worth investigating. Despite the emphasis on the bond between the two, there is now a dichotomy that eludes an organic unity. To cope with this issue we need to go back to Lefebvre's *Production of Space*. The police force at the station manipulates the only space that may be termed "abstract," that is, one that is to be set up as the "space of power."[10] Ironically it is here that the seeds of conflict and difference are laid. The child's impressions tell us as much. The street that leads to the shrine is no longer the monopoly of the police force, for there the throbbing body of the masses moves on, unhindered by any competing power, no matter how brutal it may be. Until there will be further confiscation from nature through a series of transpositions, the street will remain in the hands of peasants whose motivating power is faith in the shrine.

The narrator is clearly showing this discomforting image of conflicting forces as a way of illustrating 'Abd al-'Azīz's ambiguous struggle. The conflict is presented as an "inner crisis," something he would like to drown "by yielding to it [the city] and giving himself wholly over to it" (p. 183). The city itself gives people identity, and he himself is afraid of being turned into a policeman just like the ones he is describing. The "aching pain that lay hidden in him like a cancer" (p. 183) reminds one of a trend in the 1960s among existentialist intellectuals who had experienced an infantile leftism and then become increasingly disappointed at the increasing brutality of the state. The perplexity that haunts them and shapes their writings can no longer accommodate the expectations and hopes of the *nahḍah*. This ultimate disappointment can offer no other anchor of comfort. Even when watching his father moving warily toward the heavily guarded gate of the shrine, 'Abd al-'Azīz notices how sad and powerless he is in the face of "the harassment and the pain" awaiting him there; he looks "like a Magian about to walk on fire" (p. 183).

His father's resignation has a purpose: to endure in order to reach the shrine. Faced with that, 'Abd al-'Azīz can adopt a conciliatory attitude, but that cannot allow him to tolerate the utter awkwardness and powerlessness of the group in the face of unwarranted brutality. Qāsim offers us no alternative to this unacceptable submission. All we learn about is the protagonist's disgust at the idea of any kind of "unison with the group of men" for being so afraid, "perplexed and obviously ashamed" (p. 184), leading to a total rejection on his part. The shame that he feels at their weakness in the face of the city's brutality only increases his sense of estrangement, in spite of his recognition of their being "his parents and his kin, his heart and his eyes" (p. 181). As if repeating the Victorian Pip in Dickens's *Great Expectations*, he is no less lured by the city and its locations of both wealth and beauty. Pip displays the same feelings of repugnance toward his benefactor, the convict of the earlier graveyard scene, a repugnance that emanates only from an illusion of fashionable expectations fostered by a deranged, jilted lady in an urban space where young women seem alluring and intriguing. In Qāsim's novel, instead of the solidarity espoused by Frantz Fanon with regard to rural life—its sociability and togetherness as opposed to Westernized alienation and estrangement—the boy wishes the village community to be something other than what it is now: "cleaner, and bolder, not like this—a poor, ignorant, and frightened" mass (p. 181). Worse still is his admission that, though boasting at school of his roots as a peasant, "inside he was angry and resentful" (p. 181). This snobbishness, unwarranted insofar as his upbringing and material status are depicted within the narrative, is noticed by his father and the group of Sufi devotees. When he is reluctant to join their group meetings during meals and recitations, their furtive looks gradually wear him down (pp. 181, 184, 186). While faith connects them to his father (p. 186) and draws them to the shrine "like flecks of iron drawn towards the pole of a magnet," the boy feels that he is "made of a different metal" (p. 186).

The only occasion when this snobbishness dissolves is during moments of sexual excitement, a state which, in terms of the binding faith that holds the group together, signals a divide, one that is both sharp and demanding. Such snobbishness and sexual intrigues are not in keeping with the Sufi way of thinking, even though the young protagonist tries to justify his interests as being atavistic, inherited genetically from his father (p. 190). When on one occasion the group is reciting *al-Fatiḥah*, the *Opening* of the Qur'ān, 'Abd al-'Azīz follows the sound of tinkling that attracts his attention to "the provocative sounds" of women's laughter as "it trail[s] off in the darkness" (p. 228).

Thus far, there is nothing in this narrative to demand its designation as "post-Maḥfūẓian." It still functions within Maḥfūẓian parameters of propriety before the boy glimpses "the hem of the dress of a Tanta girl he knew glowing in a splinter of light in the dark stairwell across the courtyard" (p. 228). The sight of the hem, the trail, the stairwell, and the splinter of light all evolve metonymically as a threshold for a radical shift, a break with the sacred contract that has kept Maḥfūẓ and his *nahḍah* predecessors within the ethics of "Victorian" propriety. Now the young protagonist goes beyond this limit to succumb to passion:

> She stood in the corner breathing heavily, and the sound of her breath pulled him towards her. He had his arms out in front of him like the antennae of an insect, and his hands pumped into the rough wall. He pressed his body against the softness of her flesh as she leaned against the wall. He thrust his lips onto her open mouth, and his teeth grated against hers. Her lips, two small cushions, soft and fiery, danced in his mouth like serpents. He rubbed his face against hers. Their lips were polluted with saliva. (p. 228)

While going beyond limits, such descriptions of sex are still not free of taboos and prohibitions; words such as "polluted" and "serpents" express an unconscious reluctance to go beyond prohibitions and warnings. 'Abd al-Azīz, for and through whom the narrator speaks, is still caught in his internal conflict, involving a personal urge to carve out a life of his own which is opposed to his sense of dependency and social solidarity. Qāsim's novel sets the ground for further excursions in folk practices and Sufi orders, but also problematizes the agonies and struggles of young generations who have tasted some of the promises implicit in the *nahḍah* without seeing an overall improvement in their social life and state services. The state may provide free education and health care, not to mention transportation, but its apparatus is rigid in its resort to coercion and brutality. "A social transformation, to be truly revolutionary in character," argues Lefebvre, "must manifest a creative capacity in its effects on daily life, on language and space."[11] Written after 1967, the novel is obviously critical of a state apparatus that knows force and cares less for the improvement of social life.

The "real subject,"[12] the state political power, takes over, and cafés will spread the monopoly of the state, its gradual secularization of the society, which the police and the train clerks have already manifested in action. The question that is worth asking then should be: does the narrative lay the blame of ensuing troubles and complications on the rising conflict between the minaret and the coffeehouse, the community of the faithful and the products of secular education that are the fruitful production of the *nahḍah*? The narrative gives us glimpses of what the state offers, especially in public education, health care, transportation, and other services. It also lets us see uncouth state apparatuses and brutal exercise of force. It is not engaged as yet in the sophisticated problems that beset the postcapitalist societies. We are left with a sense, however, that there is a need to broach these issues before it is too late. Indeed, Lefebvre's warning that so long "as everyday life remains in thrall to abstract space" (state political power) and "so long as the only improvements to occur are technical improvements" and so long "as the only connection between work spaces, leisure spaces and living spaces is supplied by the agencies of political power and by their mechanisms of control," so long "must the project of 'changing life' remain no more than a political rallying-cry to be taken up or abandoned according to the mood of the moment."[13]

Coming from the countryside, the army and police are still not free of their own miserable backgrounds. The recurrent image of brutality may reflect aspects of Qāsim's experience in prison, but its overall presence in the novel certainly depicts the state in an unfavorable light. The Sufi order, through the protagonist's eyes, possesses simplicity, faith, and practices regarded as miracles in a village of limited resources. Through the eyes of a child coming of age, a division between two ways of life is portrayed, between country and city, society and state. The author is uncertain in respect to the secular choice, yet he is also afraid of the rise of a politicized Islam beyond the resignation of the dervishes. The latter are not to his liking after all, but he cannot overlook their enormous disinterestedness. His protagonist will appear in his *Al-Mahdī*, a pious soul, but without the enthusiasm and zeal of the rest, one whose meditations estrange him from the Brothers without associating him closely with the Sufis. The latter are still as devoted as ever to the Divine, but they are not detached from other concerns, including holding governmental jobs. The Brothers are in control of the street and the masses, not the state, and the protagonist does not show signs of happiness at what he observes. What remains in one's mind, however, is the shrine that functions like a magnet, regardless of where the reader stands. The state is soon to spread its presence through cafés that will gradually threaten Sufi gatherings and meetings of communion, as in the last pages of the narrative, but the Shrine remains as the minaret that calls every now and then on people to come over, especially in times of crisis and war. Its symbolic presence presiding over practices and languages sums up the villagers' lives as though the "seven days" were those of Genesis.

The Politics/Poetics of Contemporary Islamic Popular Narrative: The Case of Najīb Maḥfūẓ's *The Epic of the Ḥarāfīsh*

Arab authors since 1967 are less inclined to focus on the phenomena of a rising bourgeoisie, social climbing, and state functionaries. The defeat of that year revealed serious fissures not only between the claims of the state and realities on the ground, but also between the masses and the regimes in question. Hence 1967 becomes pivotal to any analysis of a subsequent burgeoning of ideas, attitudes, and concerns. Writers were forced to rethink priorities.[14] Even Maḥfūẓ's early unease about the role of the novel as a bourgeois epic is no longer enough. The rupture is deep and thorough, and requires an examination that goes back to its roots. History is no longer a record of events, and the careers of rulers and leaders are not enough. There must be a return to people, their culture and actual life, at least since the gradual fragmentation of the Abbasid Empire into small states and dynasties and its complete collapse in 1258. Luckily, there survive contemporaneous records and writings concerning Egypt (1200–1600) that escaped destruction. The Mamluk period in particular bequeathed a significant historical legacy, involving thorough and detailed accounts of the lives of urban centers, especially Cairo, that serve to displace or at least to complement Western narrative styles, preoccupations, and concerns. In making use of such a historical perspective, 'Abd al-Ḥakīm Qāsim (d. 1990), Maḥfūẓ (d. 2006), and Jamāl al-Ghīṭānī (b. 1945) were not alone. 'Abd al-Khāliq al-Rikābī and Salīm K. Maṭar in Iraq, Mubārak Rabī' and Ben Salīm Ḥimmīsh in Morocco, Ibrāhim al-Kūnī (b. 1948) in Libya, and Ṭāhir Waṭṭār (b. 1936) in Algeria were no less involved. Furthermore, history as a mirror of a fragmented past has also attracted the attention of scholar-novelists like Raḍwā 'Āshūr, or novelist-critics like Salwā Bakr.

Mixing Genres or Facing a Traumatic Choice

In a discerning and sharp critique of Maḥfūẓ's output, especially the *Ḥarāfīsh*, J. M. Coetzee writes that this work, one that perhaps takes its lead from the works of a younger generation of writers like Jamāl al-Ghīṭānī,[15] signals an enterprising narrative effort to establish prose fiction on "classical and folk antecedents, distancing it from the conventions of Western realism it had earlier embraced." He finds in Maḥfūẓ's later works, *Layālī Alf Laylah* (*The Thousand Nights*, 1982; English translation: *Arabian Nights and Days*) and the *Journey of Ibn Fattouma* (1983), a definite return to "traditional forms." Coetzee is not far from the truth. There is indeed "a clue," based on Maḥfūẓ's increasing disillusionment with both the bourgeoisie and the nation-state and his attachment to his childhood years in the Gamaliyya quarter of old Cairo where a medley of classes, a few mansions, and a large number of modest dwellings coexist. Furthermore this series of works certainly demonstrates a lingering interest in the world of the Cairo trilogy (1956–57), though it has more of the environment created by *Awlād Ḥāratinā* (*Children of Gebelawi*), a work that first appeared in serialized form in *al-Ahrām* (1959) before being published as a book (unauthorized) in Beirut (1967). *The Epic of the Ḥarāfish* shares with the earlier work a number of characteristics: it is allegorical and concerned with generational succession that culminates not in a man of science who can put an end to the clans and gangsters who correspond to Nāṣir's officers, but rather in an epic figure who proves so loyal to the founder's legacy that a kind of Mahdī-like return is suggested through the proclamation of the conclusion of the Great Shaykh's seclusion.

Secular criticism has a point in its negative comments on Maḥfūẓ's break with his old sacred contract with the bourgeoisie and nation-state. While this criticism is right in suggesting a loss of contact "with the classes really at the center of social struggle in contemporary Egypt,"[16] there is nevertheless a problem in that it continues a tradition of overlooking the role and power of religion, something that has been relegated to the margins of political and ideological discourse. Maḥfūẓ here shows a radical shift, away from urban and secular politics toward popular sentiment and religious fervor as embraced by not only the poor but also a growing middle-class readership. As if to avenge themselves for all the empty rhetoric, sham promises, and lost ideals characteristic of the brutal opportunism of new models of nation-state functionaries, these large readerships switch to religion, embrace it with unconditional fervor, and then listen to eloquent preachers with admiration and love. Some preachers such as the handsome 'Umar Khālid have become TV stars, satellite prodigies, listened to by young generations of women who were previously the enthusiastic fans of the late Syrian poet Nizār Qabbānī (d. April 30, 1998).

Islamic Space: The Mosque, the Mansion, and the Alley

Considering Maḥfūẓ's *Ḥarāfish* in the context of ideological space, we can perhaps view it as part of a shift in his narrative art, from bourgeois politics to mass culture. His narratives before the 1970s describe protagonists operating in relation to an urban space, and their ups and downs are evaluated by others in terms of social mobility and static space. Nobody can escape the imperatives and demands of time and space. In such works religious space is minimal despite the fact that Maḥfūẓ's *hārah* (or district) rarely ignores the implications of an Islamic design of urban space. The design of Maḥfūẓ's novels prior to the 1970s is state-bound. His protagonists are part of the managerial class, scribes and police, who are part of the sociopolitical forces with a vested interest in this enterprise. The space gradually loses its naturalness to evolve into one manufactured and appropriated, not as its early artisans envision it, but as run now by the new owners. This space is gradually emptied of its users to fit into another category, that of the "abstract space," in Lefebvre's terms.[17] Indeed, users are rarely allowed enough freedom to exercise their rights. Since the 1970s, however, his narratives show a specific manipulation of space so as to fit into allegorical or popular narratives that are devoid of sophisticated urban narrativity. In these narratives there is always a prefatory note of a meditative tone that tends to situate the forthcoming narrative in a worldview with specific Islamic concerns that also have a universal validity and value. In *Riḥlat Ibn Faṭṭūmah* (1983; *The Journey of Ibn Fattouma*), as well as in *Layālī*, Maḥfūẓ avoids immediate urban concerns even though scattered details in the narrative make it clear that his religious discourse is functioning between mosque, *takiyyah* (monastery), and alley—between home and dome. The memory of the protagonist's (Qindīl) homeland in *The Journey* is a site of well-preserved reminiscences in his travelogue:

> So long as I live I shall passionately love the effusions of the perfume vendors; the minarets and the domes; the radiant face of a pretty girl illuminating the lane; the mules of the privileged and the feet of the barefooted; the songs of the deranged and the melodies of the rebab; the prancing steeds and the lablab trees; the cooing of pigeons and the plaintive call of doves. (p. 2)

While the ghost narrative in Maḥfūẓ's *Journey* is the fourteenth-century travel account of the Moroccan Ibn Baṭṭūṭa (d. 1377), these reminiscences deliberately antiquate Qindīl's own narrative, giving it an aura of old times. The mosque is brought home in the figure of the protagonist's master and mentor, Shaykh Maghagha al-Gibeili, who has provoked Qindīl's curiosity for foreign lands because "you will not come across any thing really new in the lands of Islam" (p. 5). Teaching him at home, the shaykh manages to achieve some transference of the mosque to domestic space that will soon culminate in a marriage contract between the shaykh and Qindīl's mother. There also develops a further divide, one that not only sets foreign lands apart but also defines the lands of Islam as actually distant from Islamic faith. The lands of Islam, contends the shaykh, "are close in circumstance, inclination, and ritual, all of them far distant from the spirit of true Islam" (p. 5). This is certainly a spatial divide, but it is also a highly volatile ideological one that questions locale, space, and practitioners as being involved in hypocrisy and a disregard for Islamic religiosity. Space therefore is rife with anxieties, excitements, tensions, and seeds of diversity and difference. Space and human agency are the sites of an interplay which the travelogue tries to cope with.

Maḥfūẓ is no less preoccupied with visionary or theological interests in his *Layālī Alf Laylah* (1982), for the sultan's decision and decree are expected just after the dawn prayer. After three years of hope and fear, "death and expectation," these "stories had come to an end . . . so what fate was lying in wait" for Scheherazade? The stories operate as "white magic," says the sultan, as they "open up worlds that invite reflection" (pp. 1–2). Starting where the original *Arabian Nights* ends, Maḥfūẓ deliberately uses reversal strategies to accommodate his new experimentation with visionaries, statesmen, and theologians.

In the *Ḥarāfish*, he is more focused, perhaps under the sway of a powerful anxiety of authorship, as the result of which the father has recognized the genius of his ephebes and is fully aware of the need to surpass them while still presiding over the general literary scene as the undisputed master. The same delicate divide between life and death, joy and sadness, prefaces the *Ḥarāfīsh* in anticipation of Shaykh 'Afra's customary walk to perform his dawn prayers at the Ḥusayn Mosque. "In the passionate dark of dawn, on the path between death and life, within the view of the watchful stars and within earshot of the beautiful, obscure anthems, a voice told of the trials and joys promised to our alley" (p. 1).

The three narratives which demonstrate Maḥfūẓ's new alignment with the Arabic-Islamic narrative tradition have one thing in common: an intertextualizing process with subtext and narrative strategy that makes use of traditional *malāhim wa-siyar* (loosely, epics and biographies), the *Thousand and One Nights*, and the *Journey of Ibn Baṭṭūṭa*. These texts also have a number of things in common: first, they are little concerned with psychological depth and character analysis; second, they are episodic, focusing on events, characters, and impressions; third, they rely on sequentiality as indicative of mortality and temporality; fourth, they are not afraid to take account of the extraordinary, the uncanny, and the wonderful; fifth, faith and trust in God is the central focus of their belief system, superseding and subsuming everything else; sixth, they provide a broad scope for social integration and sporadic diversions; seventh, they subscribe to a historiographic endeavor that views life as a testing ground, a lesson, and a trial for the faithful. Whether it is a travelogue or a tale of Scheherazade, the storyteller, narrator, or scribe (in the case of Ibn Baṭṭūṭa) endeavors to assert that the material is worth recording in order to ensure its availability to succeeding generations. Eighth, there are formulas that are shared with the *khabar* (report, anecdote) tradition, including the recognized Islamic categories of salutation and supplication that are part and parcel of the Islamic tradition.

Published soon after *Zaynī Barakāt*, Maḥfūẓ's narrative seems to demonstrate a more than passing interest in (or even a continuation of) his earlier Sufi protagonists following on from *Awlād Ḥāratina* (1959, *Children of Gebelawi*). Anxiety of authorship, the repression perhaps of a feeling that the father figure should have been courageous enough to engage with the Islamic fervor, may sound far-fetched for a writer who has been recognized as the actual founder of mature Arabic fiction. In contrast with his firm belief in science and progress but at the same time in due recognition of a feeling of piety that keeps on emerging as a side current in his narratives, Maḥfūẓ now attempts to engage Islamic fervor indirectly through texts and traditions. The cautious critic of social classes and opportunists may perhaps find in Qāsim's *Seven Days* and *Zaynī Barakāt* an experiment that is worth emulating, not only in order to sustain his urbanity but also to promote an independence from Western modes of writing. Realizing that the growth of Islamism during the Sādāt era is not exactly what he is looking for as a replacement for the secular nation-state, he expresses in these texts a preference for Sufi religiosity.

Like his prototype, the Moroccan traveler Ibn Baṭṭūṭa, the eponymous hero of this novel, Ibn Fattouma, otherwise known as Qindīl, examines political systems, ways of behavior, and lifestyles. He can still enjoy travel and also return with a reformist understanding that was once the primary concern of *nahḍah* intellectuals. His author has to have reconsidered al-Ṭahṭāwī's experiences in Europe, Aḥmad Fāris al-Shidyāq's (d. 1887) perspectives, and Tawfīq al-Ḥakīm's critique, all with a new focus that considers the way that Islam is practiced in his "homeland" as a glaring deviation from the path. Even the meeting with the Muslim family and their father, the shaykh, is intended to promote the idea of *ijtihād* (free reasoning or thinking). Everywhere Ibn Fattouma's experiences are primarily a critique of his own homeland; his prototype is not a reformist, nor is he interested in any details other than those that demonstrate the respect that should be allotted to Islam and his own strong unflinching faith. At least this is what the scribe's record of Ibn Baṭṭūṭa's narrative indicates. So is Maḥfūẓ's narrative intended to be a parody of Shams al-Dīn Ibn Baṭṭūṭa (d. 1377)? The novel is in the first place a fable, and yet it is also an allegorical journey that completely departs from Ibn Baṭṭūṭa's travelogue. There are similarities in the protagonist's series of marriages and comments on beliefs, but the narrative is as detached from reality as befits allegory, a genre that may include criticism but which connotes no harsh judgments.

Layālī Alf Laylah (*Arabian Nights and Days*) collapses a number of tales, starting where the *Arabian Nights* concludes, with celebrations of Scheherazade's success, and condenses motifs and events from the original to suggest a growing Islamic dynamic against tyranny and misuse of religion. The Shahrayar of the original ends up as a wanderer in Maḥfūẓ's novelistic text. Even though there are popular uprisings and confrontations with a fractured political system, there is nevertheless, and as always in Maḥfūẓ's novels, a belief in a few positive and robust individuals who continue to maintain justice and order. But the *qalandari* of *Layālī*, who appears again as Qindīl in *The Journey of Ibn Fattouma*, is simply a variation on the *ḥarfūsh* of his 1977 narrative. While it can, with some reluctance, be qualified as an epic narrative (as some critics have suggested),[18] the *Ḥarāfīsh* is in fact closer to the Arabic popular saga (*siyar*) literature than to strictly Western generic structures. Its various protagonists are thugs, visionaries, and *qalandars*, the *qalandar* being a wanderer, mystic, and brigand. The Sufi shaykh Aḥmad al-Ghazālī (d. 1126) describes an ideal Sufi lover as one who incurs blame as proof of his total surrender and devotion to the Divine beatitude; he depicts the Sufi as "A *qalandar*-like man needed with torn robe / so that he can pass over like a brigand and without fear."[19] 'Abdullah or 'Ubayd al-Ḥarfūsh (d. 1399) was at a later date to repeat something similar: "We *ḥarāfīsh* take no pleasure in dwellings . . . We are content with a morsel and rags in a deserted mosque."[20] Although the *ḥarāfīsh* may be destitute, they are still the common people who have long been omitted from the pages of Arabic fiction, as Maḥfūẓ himself explains in a letter to his English translator, Catherine Cobham (August 7, 1991).[21]

In view of Maḥfūẓ's explanation there are two aspects to this issue: the first relates to the historical background of the word since the appearance of the *ḥarāfīsh* in medieval Cairo; the second involves the process of structuring an epic concerning the common people. Quite apart from the historical record that shows the *ḥarāfīsh* as being organized urban poor, with a sultan of their own who might well serve with the sultan's troops in times of war, there is the aforementioned shaykh, 'Ubayd al-Ḥarfūsh (d. 801/1399), whose group of dervishes adopted begging as a kind of Sufi practice or *ṭarīqah*. Ibn Ḥajar reports seeing him in 801/1399: "his clothing was like that of the *ḥarāfīsh* and so was his speech."[22] He was so popular among these groups that al-Sakhāwī's account of him shows considerable discomfort at his views and manners: "there emerged from him immoderate [obscene] words in the manner of the *ḥarāfīsh* in Egypt, leading to heresy (*zandaqah*), therefore let us ask God to grant him pardon."[23] The *ḥarāfīsh*, the organized segments of the common people, thus have a lengthy history in urban centers. They are the *'āmmah* (common people) of Baghdad during the Amīn-Ma'mūn war over the caliphate; but they also constitute the *futuwwah* of the Caliph al-Nāṣir (1180–1225) and his grandson al-Mustanṣīr (1226–1242). Under the leadership of their sultan the *ḥarāfīsh* also operated as substitutes for the sultan and his entourage—an ironic but meaningful exchange of roles, as seen, for example, during the reign of Sultan Barqūq (in 791/1389) when he refused to go and fight rebels from among his own emirs. As noted in Ibn Sasrā's *Chronicle*, "the judges and notables intervened and the judges suggested, 'Let the *sultān al-ḥarāfīsh* go forth with them [with other emirs] so that their oath may be fulfilled.' And so the sultān of the *ḥarāfīsh* went forth with them."[24] The role of these organized groups was recorded in Egyptian chronicles, as noted by William Brinner.[25]

Even so, Maḥfūẓ's *Epic of the Ḥarāfīsh* is unique, a quality that stems from its subtle narrative that engages with Islamic fervor, digests it, and superimposes on it a Maḥfūẓian perspective consisting of a politics of contained rebelliousness that stops short of an open armed revolt. Furthermore it reveals a poetics that subtly but forcefully forwards its own narrative politics. Here both politics and poetics encounter good source material, not only in order to legitimize their drive but also to make it sound like part of an anecdotal record that has wide acceptance among readers, including intellectuals. Going back in the history of urban centers, and divesting space of its immediate sociopolitical force, the author is capable of touching sensitive chords in his audiences. Space is regained by its actual users regardless of their marginality and poverty. This is perhaps the first thematic pattern that holds an enormous appeal to readers. The other implies Maḥfūẓ's distrust of power, for there is a changing power relation depending on people's dispositions. While recognizing forces of production, and the mode and the relations of production, Maḥfūẓ knows also that there is no actual engagement with history despite the seeming subordination to its legacy in the educational system. History is used piecemeal to fit into an ideology, where there is virtually total neglect of social fringes and margins. As the sphere of production and exercise of will and power, space becomes the center of his attention in this narrative, but it is so insofar as it is given life by its users. While urban space has these vagabonds and their like, they are also the ones who give it language and meaning. They are the initiators of another revolution, the one that comes by itself after the failure of a state and the consequent tedium that paralyzes the social order. No matter how oblique and indirect this narrative may sound, its conclusion declares with Lefebvre that a "revolution that does not produce a new space has not realized its full potential."[26]

Source Material

Source material is not presented as cumbersome paraphernalia; rather it is introduced as being part of a traditional folklore that could well be missed by less discerning readers, but whose penetration into the reader's consciousness is as certain as the reception of popular tradition. Narrative here consists of a popular anecdotal record of ten tales that focus on the lives and careers of ten characters whose origins as *ḥarāfīsh* are maintained in spite of their very different aspirations, failures, and successes. In comparison to the petit bourgeois leaders of national revolutions, one may find in Maḥfūẓ's narrative traces of correspondence between the rise, fall, and rebirth of tradition.

The term *ḥarāfīsh* (pl.; sing. *ḥarfūsh*) was more popular in Mamluk Egypt than in other parts of the Arab East. As an underground popular movement, it was commonly taken to mean vagabonds and beggars. Although I argue differently, it is necessary to consult those records that discuss them. W. M. Brinner's research into the etymology of the term and its varied translations as vagabond has yielded some results. It may be true that writers of the Mamluk period used the term as "a derogatory epithet" for greed, vulgarity, and evil (Brinner p. 194), and yet there is also some reason to believe that this discourse partakes in the classical tradition that looks at all connotations of poverty as signs of lowliness. Taqī al-Dīn al-Maqrīzī, quoted by Brinner, writes in 736/1326 of the exorbitant prices of grain in famine years and how some stores "were attacked and plundered by the rabble [*sūqa*] of ḥarāfīsh."[27] Brinner notices with regard to the events of 742/1341 that the term "seems to be equated with the *'āmmah* (common people)."[28] Yet evidence shows this group to be people with national and religious feelings, and thus Ibn Wāṣil (d. 697/1298) notes that "the Franks suffered greatly at the hands of the *ḥarāfīsh* of the Muslims who would seize some of them and kill them."[29] No less important is the fact that in 661/1263 there was on record some recognition of them as a powerful segment in the social fabric. In the Frankish invasion of 1217, for example, they were participants in the defense of Muslim lands; their very presence, so well established in the minds of some Mamluk sultans, had already encouraged the latter to emulate the Caliph al-Nāṣir (577–620/1181–1223) in organizing the youth into groups of *fityān* who were used as his spearhead against the many encroachments on a weakened caliphate. According to Ibn Iyās in the *Badā'i'* chronicle of 661/1263: "the Sultan ordered that all the *ḥarāfīsh* be assembled; there were about 2,000 of them. He divided them up among the emirs, taking some of them for himself and assigning a number of others to his son, al-Malik al-Sa'īd, and still more to the viceroy, Emir Bīlīk. For each of them he ordered a *ratl* of bread and a half *ratl* of meat every day and commanded that from then on they should not beg from the people."[30] Their organization and significant presence within the society were certainly behind this gesture of recognition. In other words, the association of the *ḥarāfīsh* with vagabondage as being necessarily derogatory needs to be reconsidered in such a context; their capacity to petition for some of their leaders is a further impetus to such reconsideration. Although not building on the case as a means of demolishing this myth of rejectionist epithets for the *ḥarāfīsh*, Brinner does refer to other sources in order to document their political power. Ibn Baṭṭūṭa reports how the *ḥarāfīsh* came to the rescue of Emir Qushtamur, who was so kind to them that they requested that al-Malīk al-Nāṣir in 727/1326 release him. They "took up position below the Citadel and shouted as with a single tongue: 'Ho, thou ill-starred limper fetch him out!' so [al-Malīk al-Nāṣir] released him from his place of confinement. He imprisoned him a second time, but the orphans made a similar scene, and he set him free again."[31] The linkage here between orphanage, social need, poverty, and also national identity and power is significant. The other side involves the association with Sufi orders, especially the *qalandariyyah*. In the year 801/1399, Ibn Ḥajar reports that he saw the Sufi *qalandar* and Shaykh 'Abd Allāh (Shaykh Shuʿayb al-Ḥurayfūsh, d. 801/1398–1399), who was perhaps so called because he lived among them. Ibn Ḥajar writes: "his clothing was like that of the *ḥarāfīsh* and so was his speech."[32] According to Ibn Ḥajar, the Sufi shaykh was revered by them, and his sermons and tales were also very popular.[33] No less important is the fact that his association with the *ḥarāfīsh* earned him critical remarks from certain jurists and historians. Al-Sakhāwī noted: "there emerged from him immoderate words in the manner of the *ḥarāfīsh* in Egypt, leading to heresy, therefore, let us ask God to grant him pardon."[34]

This last comment is no less important to our reconsideration of Maḥfūẓ's use of source material. It certainly draws attention to the consistent line of demarcation that Maḥfūẓ draws between institutionalized religion and the Islam of the street on the one hand, and between dominant Sunni discourse and Sufi and other practices and schools of faith on the other. This remark sets the Sunni institution apart as being supreme and unchallenged in comparison to the poor practitioners of Sufism, not to mention the Khārijīs and Shī'īs whom Maḥfūẓ specifies in *Layālī Alf Laylah* as dissenters, always to be blamed by the state for its own troubles and corruption. In summing up his impressions of thirteenth- through fifteenth-century records, Brinner reaches the following conclusions which are pertinent to this reading. There is first the impression that the "*ḥarāfīsh* were an organized group of urban poor found in Cairo and Damascus." Second, they "lived from begging . . . and were to be found in the streets and around the mosques in considerable numbers." Third, they were "an unruly element, given to violent action and clashes with authority and sometimes engaged in public demonstrations to influence sultan and viceroy." Fourth, their "dress was distinctive, and they held ideas considered heretical by orthodox Sunni writers." In sum, writers use the term as "an epithet of opprobrium," though the use is inconsistent.[35] Furthermore, their existence and role were so widely acknowledged that authority had to assign them a function. Ibn Iyās notes in 922/1516 that their shaykh also had a symbolic role. Conflated with the guilds, it seems that the *ḥarāfīsh* were a body of working or unemployed classes who influenced the street and politics in general. When the Mamluk sultan made preparations for his campaign against the invading Ottoman Turks, a "large company of builders, carpenters, and blacksmiths" gathered who "accompanied the sultan, as was the ancient custom when sultans went on campaigns." He adds: "the chief shaykh called the sultān al-*ḥarāfīsh*—with his troops, banner, and drums—accompanied him and preceded the cavalcade of the sultan when he entered Damascus and Aleppo."[36]

This historical evidence concerning the existence of organized labor and unions, and the inclusion of the unemployed in this movement, was perhaps present in Maḥfūẓ's mind in his depiction of clan chiefs. Indeed his clan chiefs are the ones who are held accountable for any wrong or disorder, regardless of the means of achieving stability and order. Thus, when sultan al-Malik al-Ashraf Barsbāy (1422–1438) received complaints from his agent regarding efforts to distribute alms among them, only to end up thrown down from his horse by the crowd, the sultan held their shaykh responsible. He "was angry at this and summoned the 'sultan of the vagabonds' and the shaykh of the organization of beggars (*shaykh al-ṭawā'if*), and obligated them to prevent professional beggars from begging in the streets and force them to find employment."[37]

Apart from this correspondence between historical annals and narrative reenactment in Maḥfūẓ's epic, it can be noted that Ibn Taghrī Birdī also makes mention of a prominent shaykh *al-ḥarāfīsh* who was once in charge of a band of street performers, namely Muhammad Ibn 'Alī or Ibn al-Fa'lātī (d. 870/1465) or *al-fawwāl* (omen reader). Although he later gave himself over to learning and became a recognized Shāf'īte jurist, al-Fa'lātī was descended from a family that adopted omen reading, astrology, geomancy, and storytelling as a profession. A last word on the etymology of the term, one that may serve to release it from its negative connotations, would reposition it in Sufi discourse in correspondence with the *qalandar* of Aḥmad al-Ghazālī (d. 1126). And yet the specific characterization of the protagonist in Maḥfūẓ's epic may descend from 'Ubayd al-Ḥarfūsh or al-Ḥurayfīsh (d. 801/1399).[38] He speaks in terms that should align him with the pious leaders of the *ḥarāfīsh* in Maḥfūẓ's epic. The revered saint speaks as follows:

We *ḥarāfīsh* take no pleasure in dwellings.
We do not act hypocritically, nor bear witness in words of falsehood.
We are content with a morsel and rags in a deserted mosque.
Whose deeds are such as these, his sins are forgiven.[39]

The piety and resignation depicted in these verses were not condoned by al-Sakhāwī or similar jurists and theologians, and their implications as a critique of wealth and worldliness did not fit well with the greed of the dominant *'ulamā'* and their alliance with power.

Reading Maḥfūẓ's epic against these parameters and terms of definition, it is not difficult to see that he must have been well aware of these historical sources that treat the group as an organized community which was disinterestedly led. It emerges as a societal byproduct, one whose impact in urban centers, especially in times of war and instability, needed to be taken into account. Society is clearly divided between rich and poor, between the powerful and powerless. But the powerless have nothing at stake, and are thus in a position to voice their protest. Although there is always a changeable politics of power relations, the shaykh of the group commands respect for certain qualities that distinguish him from the rest. Along with disinterestedness, his piety and care for the community of the dispossessed help to portray him as a heroic character, a popular hero who, unlike the protagonists of the bourgeois novel, suffers no eclipse.

An Epic or an Anecdotal Narrative

It is by no means presumptuous to suggest that Maḥfūẓ's narrative signals a new stage in his writing, not only in the minimal attention that is paid to the middle class that has been his primary concern for a long time, but also in a conspicuous shift to the repertoire of anecdotal literature that works through saga cycles, paying scant attention to psychological dimensions. Moreover, there is more than one reason for his reluctance to describe this narrative of his as epic. The narrative has indeed the characteristics of a saga, but it also reflects the anecdotal quality of the *khabar* tradition. If there are obstacles to surmount, the protagonist has to cope with them physically or through moral or religious obligations. For a pious soul, temptations have to be overcome, but for the greedy Jalal there is no end to the process of acquisition or search for immortality. For the heroic 'Āshūr, the quest combines physical prowess in the service of God and an endless struggle against temptation.

In order to construct 'Āshūr as a folk hero, a person who will have an impact on society, Maḥfūẓ finds it necessary not only to bring him down to earth so as to fit into a common tradition in urban suburbs, but also to involve him in seemingly wayward interests. Three significant events are meant to achieve this effect on the narrative level. All three find justifications in tradition, but they are nevertheless debatable: first, his decision to get married to the barmaid Fullah; second, his ultimate justification for taking over the deserted mansion of the al-Bannan family after a devastating plague; and last, his decision to initiate a process of "eliminating the thugs and bullies" (p. 57).

While these events motivate the narrative, establish the character as a legendary folk hero, and create an ancestry that was once a cherished principle among the *fityān* of old, they also open up the Islamic context for more debates that reflect on the problems of the nation-state, the rising bourgeoisie, and the issue of theology and utopia as a central divide. In the first instance, 'Āshūr is aware of Fullah's powerful allure; indeed the temptation is so overwhelming that it threatens to dislodge Shaykh 'Afra's teachings from his heart. "All he had learned from Shaykh 'Afra was crushed under the donkey's hooves as he drove along, his back molten in the heat" (p. 29). The carter speaks to his donkey of his total infatuation: "Your master's finished" (p. 29).

When informing his first wife, Zainab, that it is "God's will" that he get married to the barmaid (p. 31), her answer is uncompromising: "Why do you make a mockery of God's name? Why don't you admit it's the devil? Do you think you can palm me off with that?" (p. 31). This decision of his also upsets his relations with others, and serious questions are raised against his integrity. Fullah is infamous as the bewitching bartender, a woman over whom even his three sons fight in order to win her admiration and love. Still the narrative needs to problematize the issue in a folkloric narrative pattern where nothing is impossible and gossip accounts for little. On the other hand, Maḥfūẓ is aware that the same folk tradition has modes that can find sanction in Islamic theology. Nobody accuses 'Āshūr of being unfair to his first wife, Zainab, and in any case there exist affinities and origins that bring him and the barmaid together. Like him, Fullah is an orphan: "One of the things that made her exquisite in his eyes was his discovery that she, like him, had never known her mother or father" (p. 32). That confession sets them on a path together that will confront social norms and enable them to exert greater efforts to compensate for this lack. This narrative benefits as much from this process as do the narratives of prophets. This dimension also plays on the unconscious, and it is not hard to envisage a charismatic character as emerging from such chaos.

The rhetoric involved in the strong temptation to reside in the deserted mansion is intended not only to test his will and confront him with authority and its representative shaykhs who function as its spokesmen and legitimizers, but also to place him on an ever changing wheel of fortune. It is a test of both him and his community of *ḥarāfīsh*. A careful juxtaposition of him and his ruffians on the one hand, and the state and its functionaries on the other, may polarize the narrative but still enables him to grow as a charismatic hero, the guru whom his group needs. The polarization between the guru and the state is important, not only because it will test the legitimacy of the state apparatus, its ideological base and official language, but also the counter language of the street, its religious dynamic and capacity to stand up to power. The contestation is enormous and it involves the writer in the most narrative venture he has ever undertaken. Under the guise of a folk narrative of past times, he resurrects Mamluk history in terms of contemporary religious fervor. Both space and discourse are significantly drawn with dexterity and focus to enforce the fringes of the society as they were once in a bygone period. Maḥfūẓ's narrative restructures annals in such a way as to uncover the interest that informs and shapes the voice of their authors. His recapitulation amounts to a revisionist reading that examines the illnesses of a social and political order that strives hard to sustain its own claim to truth, a claim that necessarily implies depriving others of any voice. At best, it resorts to a discourse of disparagement based on class and status distinctions. Al-Sakhāwī's above-mentioned indictment of 'Ubayd al-Ḥurayfīsh may also have been in Maḥfūẓ's mind.

This process of recapitulation allows Maḥfūẓ a number of narrative engagements. He involves himself in the dominant category in Arabic historiography: the *khabar* (report or anecdote), that cuts across a number of genres and finds an appropriate place in the tradition of annalistic writing. This enables him to skip some types of material, focus on others, and provide a semblance of truth. This also fits well with the narrative's subdivision into tales that focus on successors, like traditional dynastic narratives. It thus turns into a saga, but minus the detailed description of urban life and household affairs. The outcome is a narrative that resembles history without being so; it may show some of its major components, but not its focus on courts and rulers. The poetics of prose here directs history in a different direction. No longer the domain of rulers, it is removed from the custody of elite historians or highbrow intellectuals and allowed to deal with the very ruffians and scamps whom history often relegates to a very insignificant margin. While space here is recovered by the underprivileged in specific circumstances, the narrative offers us a chance to see through the nature of power vacuum. Manipulated by the ruffians as the actual users, space enforces a different discourse, one that reminds authority of their existence and linguistic presence which has suffered devaluation under the monopoly of the old order.[40]

Maḥfūẓ's saga of clans and *ḥarāfīsh* chiefs thus releases history from its predominant elitism. It resurrects a folk tradition which literary modernism has long since lost. But he is careful to make sure that this shift in focus and attention is not too closely identified with history. There is, for example, a greater dependence on dialogue as a way of overcoming the obvious shortcomings of annals in that regard and compensating for any lack of psychological depth and absence of rounded characters. Here dialogues are used as a means of summing up conflicts or preparing for still more. Hence Darwish tries to recruit 'Āshūr and use him as his accomplice in burglary and theft. He tells 'Āshūr that his physical appearance, strength, and energy will be of little help. "No one will trust you all the same. The clan chiefs will see you as a rival and the merchants as a bandit and a thug" (p. 7). Such a short-lived company, we are told, "had taught him ['Āshūr] more about the realities of the world than twenty years spent under the wing of the good shaykh 'Afra" (p. 11). The remark skips the psychological dimension and delves omnisciently into the inner self of the would-be folk hero so as to portray him as a divided individual between two worlds: the wicked and the good. Between the two is a gray area where temptation lurks in different guises. Comparing his wife Zainab to Fullah, the barmaid, he is well aware of the strong pull that beauty can have on him. His physical strength and his kind Shaykh 'Afra's early teaching and pious training are unable to dislodge the enormous grip that Fullah has on his heart. That very infatuation places him firmly in this gray area, the in-between space of indecision, fear, and worry.

In addition to annals there is also hagiography. 'Āshūr is an orphan, like Fullah, found by Shaykh 'Afra. There is a suggestion that, through his individual piety, good use of strength, attachment to the poor, teaching of Fullah, and his escape from plague as a result of another migration away from a vile city of corruption, 'Āshūr is in fact retracing the footsteps of the Prophet. When listening to early reports of the plague, he concludes: "Then it must be the wrath of God!" (p. 33). The plague can reach anywhere regardless of mansion or wealth; the advice to avoid crowded places at such times may be useful for people with homes, attendants of cafés, bars, and hashish dens, but how can it be applied to the *ḥarāfīsh*? "[T]hey lived their lives in the street. At nights the *ḥarāfīsh* congregated under the archway and in derelict buildings" (p. 34). Once again, the social aspect of this direct reference to the *ḥarāfīsh* community serves to corroborate the close resemblance between 'Āshūr's planned migration to the wilderness and the Prophet's migration to Yathrib or Madīnah (622 CE). When 'Āshūr tells Fullah the "journey's over," he hastily adds, "The journey's just begun" (p. 39). The *ḥarāfīsh* community consists of would-be believers, and it is there that his actual initiation into the celestial starts; the journey into the self aims to test his ability to control his desires and to embark on his destined course before commencing his concealment at the peak of his career. "He slept part of the day and stayed up all night. He thought so long and deeply that he had a strange presentiment he would soon hear voices and see figures from the spirit world" (p. 40). Maḥfūẓ's inclination to draw subtle comparisons between the Prophet's migration and ʿĀshūr's journey into the wilderness of selfhood is revealed in several ways: ʿĀshūr, for example, "was about to be reborn" (p. 41). Against the background of this initiation into the unforeseen, he knows too that the "notables, the *ḥarāfīsh*, Darwish, all revolve around a twisted axis, bent on mastering its awkward secret" (p. 41). On another level, the fact that the *ḥarāfīsh* are homeless and dispossessed aligns them with workers who, in Marxist thought at least, have nothing to lose other than their shackles. The plague threatens the virtual owners of power who are also, in Kateb Yacine's *Nedjma*, the ones who "had banished the Prophet" (p. 157). In other words, sustaining these analogies in keeping with his basic beliefs and formative readings, Maḥfūẓ devises more than one narrative strategy to allow his recapitulations a powerful grip on readers.

Perhaps with ʿUbayd al-Ḥurayfūsh's visionary experiences in mind, Maḥfūẓ inserts a streak of Sufism into ʿĀshūr, too, not only through incessant references to the monastery, its mysterious voices and closed door, but also through the deeper sorrow "tearing his heart from its moorings," to such an extent that "tears" are "flowing down his cheeks" (p. 44). The sorrow needed to fulfill the innermost yearnings of the soul has to emerge as a consequence of temptations that are no less challenging than the persuasions of the Meccans who hoped to bring Muhammad back through the offer of riches. The monastery has already been retained within the narrative as the symbol of the mysterious call for detachment from the city of vileness; it also functions as the celestial beatitude, culminating in the divine and far removed from the ego self. On both historical and contemporaneous levels, its Persian hymns serve to remind the reader of the surging fervor of the Iranian Islamic revolution in the late 1970s. The monastery in context has the actual and symbolic power of a shrine, but its mysterious hymns and secrecy endow it with extra power that heralds change and transformation. It has the promise of bliss and certitude. Its hymns endow it with poetry and assign to it an epic dimension beyond the confinements of the realistic novel.

Against this promise and bliss stand the temptations. The deserted Bannan house is no less a temptation. "Temptation stole over him like sleep over a weary man. He resolved to find a way out of the crisis and arrived at a new formulation. 'Money is forbidden when it is spent on forbidden things,' he announced" (p. 47). Such faulty essays in logic accumulate in direct correspondence to the various snares that mirror those to which state legislators and jurists regularly resort; they can all too easily grow into laws with which caliphs and rulers entrust to jurists the task of enhancing their rule and ensuring continuity. With the passing of time, such formulations will emerge in manuals and compendia. Even ʿĀshūr is now under the pressure of time: "With the passing of time their scruples eased, and ʿĀshūr and his family took up residence in the Bannan house" (p. 47), a mansion that is now deserted following the owner's death in the plague. But there is also a positive aspect to his endeavor, in that he uses wealth to support the poor who "raised him to the ranks of saints," not only as someone who has survived the plague (and thus ʿĀshūr the Survivor, p. 48), but also because his efforts are aimed at raising the conditions of the poor. However, the government that usually arrives late at scenes of devastation is now aroused from its deep slumber and is eager to regain control of whatever is deserted, list it as its own property, and punish any trespassers and transgressors. From a narrative viewpoint, this belated interference serves not only to move the action beyond the stage in which the hero is subject to temptation and to reclaim the affection of the poor, but also to illustrate the polarization of the conflict between the state apparatus and the masses. Thus we read, "One morning the giant figure of Āshūr al-Nagi appeared in their midst in handcuffs, his head bowed" (p. 53), as the shaykhs of the district fully enjoy the privileges resulting from their alignment with the government and wealthy classes.

Maḥfūẓ's resort to this incident of imprisonment and subsequent release is of some significance, in that it serves "to create a legendary figure of him, braver and more heroic than before" (p. 57). As the government is automatically considered suspect, his indictment by the state and its clerics only succeeds in intensifying the public's affection for him. ʿĀshūr therefore emerges from the experience to be claimed by everyone as their leader. "He's the new chief," says Darwish resentfully, "and he didn't even have to fight for it" (p. 57). In summary fashion the omniscient narrator takes over the annalists' role to record that, just as the *ḥarāfīsh* "expected, he set about his duties in an entirely different manner from his predecessors. He returned to his trade as a carter and lived in the basement room of his earlier days" (p. 57). With the history of the *ḥarāfīsh* in mind, Maḥfūẓ models his clan chief on the sultans of the *ḥarāfīsh*: "He obliged all his followers to work for a living, thus eliminating the thugs and bullies" (p. 57). Rather than distracting him from his piety, the fact that he is clan chief, *sultan al-ḥarāfīsh*, only intensifies his spiritual leanings. " ʿĀshūr would sit in the monastery-square late into the night, transported by the sacred melodies. Spreading his hands in front of him he would pray, 'O god, preserve and increase my strength so that I can use it to protect your faithful servants'" (p. 57).

Another aspect of this work that is significant to this study is the author's use of dreams and visions. Although a folk hero needs more action than speech or visionary experience, folk traditions, especially those that reflect Sufism and *ḥarāfīsh* lore of sainthood, cherish these features as part of their frame of reference, their religious base that distrusts state functionaries and clerics. 'Āshūr's vision of Shaykh 'Afra is a Sufi phenomenon, a manifestation of the Divine will that comes only to the blessed in chosen moments; it is that same experience that has led him into the wilderness to escape the plague. The Saved, as he is called thereafter, is now the savior, the guru, the hero. Without this Sufi interlude there would be no growth that would bring him closer to the populace. His nocturnal sojourn near the monastery (*takiyyah*) releases his mind from earthly concerns and puts him in touch with the melodious Persian hymns; and with piety now deeply rooted in his heart, temptations no longer work. Hence his disappearance comes as a surprise and a shock. Maḥfūẓ here plays on the familiar chord of the mysterious disappearances of many religious leaders and intellectuals who may have been killed by the state, but he is also reviving narratives of prophets who have temporary absences or embark on heavenly journeys. We are informed that the wealthy and state clerics are happy that he is no longer there: "Only a miracle could deliver them from the tyrant's authority, from his eternal youth, his iron will!" (p. 61). The mood of the poor, however, is very different as they recall "the giant figure going about the neighborhood, restraining the powerful, protecting the rights of humble breadwinners, and creating an atmosphere of faith and piety" (p. 63).

Two things about 'Āshūr's legacy need to be underlined. His career and life reveal certain hallmarks and ambiguities that are sometimes misread in the process of accommodating the needs, whims, desires, and aspirations of his successors. His marriage to Fullah and residence in the Bannan house, for example, can be exploited as deviations from a career of piety and probity. On the other hand, his entire career as a pious person, who uses his power to serve the poor and the needy and curb injustice, can be reborn in a son like Shams al-Deen. Among clerics even shaykhs can emerge who are devoted to God, not Mammon, such as Shaykh Ḥusayn Quffa in Shams al-Deen's times (p. 73). Thus Shams is made to voice this delicate reading of his father's legacy: "There was no shame in weakness if you overcame it," he tells himself. "What was the point of strength if not to subdue these impulses of frailty?" (p. 83). But he is also aware that his own successors may use 'Āshūr's career differently. " 'The time will come' he said disparagingly, 'when we attribute all our weak impulses to the great 'Āshūr' " (p. 83). When such passages are read through the lenses of the 1970s, a time when Egyptians could still remember Nāṣir and his early ideals, Maḥfūẓ sounds as if he were apologizing for Nāṣir. His narrative manages to accommodate different interpretations depending on institutions and their representation.

Before reading Maḥfūẓ's narrative both against the backdrop of the historical record and as a critique of the nation-state since 1952, it is important to interpret Shams al-Deen's last surmise in terms of desire, conflict, and a dramatization of rise and fall in the dynastic order. However, a word of caution is in order. Maḥfūẓ does not have absolute faith in Ibn Khaldūn's paradigms of rise and dissolution; instead he regards corruption in terms of human frailty, a latent impulse to court fleshly and physical desires, and looks on it as being as old in human history as Adam and Eve's surrender to temptations. All desires reveal a quest for power, but power itself may well tempt the human soul to further corruption. Unless curbed by a strong piety that acts as a bulwark against the tides of temptation, power soon becomes synonymous with corruption. On the other hand, Maḥfūẓ believes that a craving for power, whatever its motivations and manifestations, generates an ideology that deliberately reconstructs the past, its icons and markers, in order to match its new paradigms of control. History is therefore ransacked in order to support a position, not to question or destabilize a system. A regime involving new concepts is constructed out of the heap of history, its fragments and landmarks alike, and the emerging ideology never shies away from this reconstruction; quite the contrary, it is defended and upheld as evidence of a new spirit that evolves in response to the demands of the age. The construct is cherished in propagandist literature as a creative remolding of a past by the custodians of tradition. Maḥfūẓ's Shams al-Deen looks upon 'Āshūr and his legacy in the same way as these custodians look upon past history and tradition. The fluctuating career of 'Āshūr's successors is portrayed in such a way as to recall examples of not only regime change, but also power relations in general that can be summarized under the binary divide of corruption and goodness.

There is even so an echo of Ibn Khaldūn in Maḥfūẓ's use of Sulayman as the third generation in the dynasty of the Nājīs, or the Survivors (called so after 'Āshūr's miraculous survival). Although still defending 'Āshūr's legacy, Sulayman's marriage to Saniyya, the daughter of the notable al-Samari, brings him into the middle of an "enchanting paradise" that exists "in a tumbled corner of the alley" where the *ḥarāfīsh* survive (p. 105). This alliance with the wealthy is probably intended to symbolize the union between the free officers and their descendants of the Egyptian revolution of 1952 on the one hand and the moneyed classes on the other, that being a union that illustrates the petty bourgeois's craving for the good life. Hence Sulayman is represented as changing from an 'Āshūr-like goodness and restraint to a vulgar product of luxury and comfort. "The giant's appearance changed completely: he wore a cloak and turban and used a light carriage for his outings, forgot his principles, and drank to the point of depravity, he put on so much weight that his face swelled like the dome of a mosque and his jowl hung down like a snake-charmer's pouch" (p. 108). Apart from the transposition of religious referents from their context as central to an Islamic space onto the personal outlook of a reprobate, there is a deliberate shift in language to a secular one that empties religious symbols of their connotations and value. Strongly corresponding to Ibn Khaldūn's theory of successive generations in a dynastic order, Sulayman's "conscience had relaxed; his greedy body had abandoned itself to temptation and abuses of the flesh" (p. 109). The seed of corruption will poison the rest of the line; the further it spreads, the greater the estrangement not only from the populace, the *ḥarāfīsh*, but also from 'Āshūr's covenant. The *ḥarāfīsh* will look upon the past with nostalgia, but scrutinize the present in terms of divine punishment. The sense of despair creates its own system of faith as a way of annulling a terrible reality: "the *ḥarāfīsh* regretted the passing of the old Naji covenant, and considered what had befallen Sulayman and his sons as punishment for his waywardness and treachery" (p. 118). In other words, a corpus of sacred critique crafts its frame of reference from the failures of deviant successors in order to account for their fall in terms of divine wisdom and justice. This surmise is not totally absent from the comments with which Ibn Khaldūn concludes his analysis of the principles of rise and fall.

On the other hand the close parallel that is drawn between clan and national regime cannot escape one's attention. The weakened regime resorts to alliances that only survive at the expense of the impoverished nation (p. 120); it is therefore bound to renounce every ideal cherished by its first leaders. Bikr, Sulayman's son, will openly denounce the whole legacy: "To hell with Āshūr al-Naji and his false mystique! To hell with the crazy dervishes and their incessant singing!" (p. 124). With this open denunciation, the regime or the clan has nothing on which to rely. It is now so divorced from the people that it becomes a burden, a nuisance, and a disgusting implement of coercion and falsehood. People on the other hand are driven to despair, for Maḥfūẓ's *ḥarāfīsh* "thought of it [the new period of degeneration] as a new phase in the tragedy which was slowly grinding them down" (p. 143). With this proclamation, the estrangement from the people is complete. In Fanon's terms, "masses begin to sulk as they turn away from this nation in which they have been given no place and begin to lose interest in it."[41] As the proclamation denies both legacy and the symbolic space of communion, everything else ceases "to be the symbols of the nation," becoming instead "empty shells."[42] The religious dynamic is intertwined with the social and the political, and the society will eventually search for change. In this narrative, the emphasis is laid on the dynasty which can stand for the precarious nation-state, its regimes and institutions. Only through return to the roots, a return through a "moving consciousness of the whole of the people," to regain "dignity to all citizens," says Fanon, can such societies survive the damage done to their national feelings and lifestyles.[43] "The national government, if it wants to be national, ought to govern by the people and for the people, for the outcast and by the outcasts."[44]

Amid this confusion and corruption, Maḥfūẓ suggests, there are always instances of grace; indeed, the apparently inexorable process of degeneration is interrupted with the character of Qurra who sees something "sacred" in the inner sufferings of the human soul (p. 194). But, as usual with these exceptional cases, they are short-lived and serve as all too brief reminders of the possible rebirth of an ideal that has been abandoned for so long. Qurra dreams of such a rebirth, embodied perhaps in the newborn baby whom he has enamored with the melodies of monastic anthems that once touched 'Āshūr and made out of him "a vessel for sacred dreams and not a victim of destructive passions" (p. 200).

The monastic reverberations, the melodious tones, echo Maḥfūẓ's incessant thematic concern with Sufism, a strand in his writing whereby riddles, murmurs, and solitude combine to compose a rubric of piety which has never left Maḥfūẓ's religious subtext. Even when the hard-tested Samaha returns to the quarter to find his sons scattered, some of them murdered by their brother and others lapsing into utter corruption, there is only a faint whiff of piety involved, and Maḥfūẓ is careful not to overstate it within his genealogy of clans, communities, and *ḥarāfish*. Aware that his focus on the nation-state and its regimes might be diverted, he allows his historical survey to take control, showing the reader how corruption gets the better of Wahid, Samaha's son who is behind the death of Aziz's father, Qurra. Maḥfūẓ comments in summary fashion on the end of the Naji reign as follows: "No one grieved for the Nājī's reign, now that their sweet dreams had come to nothing at the hands of Wahid" (p. 228).

This interruption in dynastic genealogy seems to imply that Maḥfūẓ is planning to accept the rise and fall paradigm, thus making Wahid's reign the death knell for a dynasty. The clan and its clientele can be easily exchanged for any other ruling dynasty. However, this apparent correspondence would only serve to empty the narrative of a complexity that is badly needed for it to evolve beyond history. Now the police state is involved, not because of the termination of a pact between it and the clan chiefs, but largely because there is yet again a powerful temptation to fight for an attractive female and to take her away from her husband and other competitors. Like the newly empowered nation-state apparatus with its vulgar dreams of power, luxury, and survival, Maḥfūẓ's officer in the novel is no less drawn to both charm and wealth. Temporary alliances with other powers require the reconstruction of nation-state tactics. The police inspector respects the pact and tells Nuh, who is now the clan chief, that he "is the brave knight and protector of the alley, the embodiment of chivalry and honor, the hands and eyes of the police in his domain . . . that's how the Ministry of Interior regards you" (p. 254). Maḥfūẓ decides to provoke a confrontation, the kind of which historical records of the Mamluk periods as well as those of the Caliph al-Nāṣir's reign in Baghdad offer plentiful examples. Such records tell us that there were times when the caliph or sultan chastised clan chiefs for a lack of control or some unruly conduct or behavior. In this narrative the confrontation focuses on a serious matter: Zahira's body is the battleground that involves a number of contenders, including her husband Muhammad Anwar, the clan chief Nuh, `Aziz al-Naji who is now a wealthy notable, and the police inspector. Maḥfūẓ exploits this rivalry among the men to enhance the role of women who have only figured thus far as catalysts for attraction, homely settlement, and domestic comfort or nuisance; but to do so, the narrative has to depart from both the records of historical annals and Maḥfūẓ's usual paradigms of women, who are either devout, well-meaning prostitutes or shrewish domineering wives. This narrative is in need of a woman who can speak of herself as belonging to the Naji dynasty and who, with her "God-given beauty and intelligence," can operate as a "clan chief in a woman's skin" (p. 268).

No less significant in our analysis of Maḥfūẓ's efforts to make sure that his narrative does not entirely fall within the paradigm of rise and fall is his emphasis in this particular episode on reminders, comments, and recollections. The reiterated comment of the common folk is to the effect that the Najis have died a long time ago and their legacy no longer survives. Only through repetition can narrative forego its dynastic cycles. If there are still Najis, then they are just part of a system, a divine order, where they have no significant role other than being foils or reasons for other happenings: "the *ḥarāfīsh* said that the Nājī family had become like actors in a tragedy—a warning and deterrent to others—as a punishment for their betrayal of their mighty ancestor, the blessed miracle worker" (p. 272).

The emergence of yet another Naji, Jalal, did not mean a great deal as long as he "was uninterested in the state of the *ḥarāfīsh* or the Naji covenant, not due to egotism or weakness in the face of life's temptations," as the narrator puts it, "but because he despised their concerns and found their problems trivial" (p. 293). His *Citadel* and accumulation of wealth only manage to recall similar monuments that rulers are bent on erecting in order to perpetuate their name and reputation. Jalal's search for immortality, even when it involves "an everlasting pact with the devil" (p. 301) cannot be understood outside the context of its direct correspondence with the well-known preoccupation of rulers regarding monuments, reputation, immortality, and a desire to preserve their dynasty through a line of many male children. Although repeating the old mythical desire for immortality well known ever since Gilgamesh, the invocation of such a craving is new to Maḥfūẓ's corpus and its occurrence in this work needs to be seen as another subtle critique of the nation-state and the whole caliphal order. Jalal's citadel repeats Beckford's Fonthill, the whims of Vathek, and the bygone Babylonian and Egyptian structures, signifying a total estrangement from the ancient legacy. It signals a severance of the covenant of the miracle maker, surrender to Satan previously unheard of in the history of the nation-state. Jalal's achievements and actions turn him into an alien figure, no less alienated than the rulers whom Fanon describes as the ultimate failures of a postcolonial rule that is incapable of moving beyond its dependency complex and mimicry.[45] Jalal "was an alien presence among the people of the alley, like the minaret placed among other buildings: strong, beautiful, sterile, and incomprehensible" (p. 311). The seemingly innocent analogy with the minaret among buildings works within a matrix of similar references, where one dynasty member's cheek is compared to a mosque dome and another is associated with monastic reverberations. The dome, the minaret, the citadel, the mosque, and the monastery are iconic spaces that hold symbolic power and operate strongly in the organic structure of an orderly Muslim society. They suffer slippage and undergo change in meaning and association whenever there is something out of joint, something that turns the society upside down. The confusion attending this mixed use of icons, symbols, and functional spaces foreshadows disaster or drastic change.

But these divides corroborate the juxtapositions and parallels that Maḥfūẓ has incorporated into earlier parts of the narrative. Even if we assume that 'Āshūr, now the ancestor, is to return in mysterious circumstances to command renewed respect and control through physical power and competence, this signals yet another atavistic repetition of a cycle that is by no means alien to the fictional worlds of Maḥfūẓ and his generation, especially Tawfīq al-Ḥakīm. What is new is the fact that Maḥfūẓ brings into the tenth tale three elements that involve him in Mamluk history without jeopardizing his narrative of the downtrodden, their troubles and aspirations. There is first his depiction of popular rebellion, whereby the *ḥarāfīsh* emerge as a powerful body when there is a leader. This happened many times in history as a way of protesting against sultans or supporting their rule. The *ḥarāfīsh*, the overwhelming majority of the populace, "had suddenly joined forces and prevailed over the wielders of clubs and long sticks" (p. 402). Not only this, but Maḥfūẓ is so taken by the idea of this rebellious force that he allows his narrator to contradict the usual media assumption that chaos will always be the result of such situations: "contrary to expectations, chaos did not follow" (p. 403). Second, there is his emphasis on historical facts that attribute to some *ḥarāfīsh* leaders a careful indoctrination of the rest so that they will have their sons trained "in the virtues of the clan to maintain their power and prevent it ever falling into the hands of hooligans or soldiers of fortune" (p. 404). Records show that they would command them to "earn their living by a trade or a job" (p. 404).[46] Even the shaykhs support such an exercise of authority, and both types of decree effectively involve the populace in social and political life. Third, there is an important conclusion woven into the narrative, one that has only a single similarity in Maḥfūẓ's output, namely the fusion of the monastic into public life. The "shadowy figure of a dervish" that emerges from the monastery for the first time leans over toward 'Āshūr in order to tell him to prepare for jubilation; the "Great Sheikh will come out of his seclusion. He will walk down the alley, bestowing his light and give each young man a bamboo club and a mulberry fruit" (p. 406). It is not too far-fetched to suggest that Maḥfūẓ is celebrating the Mahdī tradition here, the appearance of the savior imam who will fill the universe with justice and love after so much oppression. This advent means that the efforts exerted by 'Āshūr and his people and those who "seize boldly with the innocence of children and the ambition of angels" (p. 406) will now come to fruition and maturation. The period of occultation, absence, or invisibility has to come to an end, and the Mahdī-like figure may be equated with the 'Āshūr of old, the infant found on the road who has to disappear without a trace or sign except for the murmuring of the dervishes in the *takiyya* where he used to spend nights near the wall. People keep looking for him outside, but nobody suspects that the inside may be his abode of seclusion. The *takiyya* evolves like a self that struggles to escape the walls of its ego in order to achieve Divine beatitude. The narrative depicts the struggle which 'Āshūr has been enduring, and the journey he has to undergo to become the shaykh of the *takiyya*, not the chief of a clan. The text is yet another quest of the same kind as we encounter in Maḥfūẓ's *Journey of Ibn Fattouma* (1983).

Historical evidence suggests that the leader of the *ḥarāfīsh* is not merely a *futuwwah*, but also a well-recognized figure among the *'āmmah* (common people) whose capacity to lead is tested by his own groups as well as by the state. This leads inevitably to a consideration of the relation of the epic genre to common people, and from a number of perspectives. The urban novel, the bourgeois epic, that has occupied Maḥfūẓ for so long has a number of narratives of the bildungsroman type, novels of education and growth that demonstrate the possibility of rising in a society despite humble origins. But we also know that Victorian English and French novelists regularly made use of benefactors and coincidental wills and letters in depicting such achievements.

However, whereas the European novel rarely shows the common people as a source of power and political participation,[47] Arab-Islamic history by contrast is rich in descriptions of such involvements in association with Islamic precepts of equality and justice. The common people can produce leaders, but there is no suggestion that they can ever aspire to rise to the position of caliph. Even so, they may become shaykhs, as the conclusion to Maḥfūẓ's epic illustrates. On the other hand, his shaykh, who decides to end his seclusion and engage the *ʿāmmah* after both the advent of the right successor who is loyal to the first covenant and the need to bring about total justice, is more than a Sufi Pole (*quṭb*). Each *quṭb* acts like a mentor to his devotees or disciples, occasionally investing them with a cloak (*khirqah*) corresponding to the green garment or belt of the Sayyids (as descendants of Imam ʿAlī). The last of the dynasty, ʿĀshūr, is a habitual listener to the monastic hymns of the *takiyya*, an involvement that explains a larger role as keeper of the forefathers' covenant and herald of a new age of order, equality, and justice.

In terms of genres then we need to explore the general characteristics of the epic and their applicability to Arabic traditional *malāḥim* as well as to the Greek and medieval European forms. "Authentic epic" is said to be "a record of man's noblest achievements," whether in unsettled communities as befitting an oral tradition or civic life as suitable to the written form.[48] Within such a context the evolution of the category of hero also implies an ability to demonstrate reliability, religious observance, and a feeling of responsibility toward others as an encapsulation of "the spirit of a nation."[49] In this effort, the hero should always master his own passions for the sake of this national spirit. While the epic develops as a process of adjustments "between the hero's capacities and limitations," there is at the same time recognition of his limitations as well as an aspiration to transcend them. The epic therefore exceeds the limits of high mimetic art, since the hero cannot move beyond his own natural environment.[50] Physical prowess is central to the heroic endeavor, but there must also be some form of "divine authorization" which will expand the scope of conflict beyond a limited space in order to suggest "a cosmic power struggle."[51]

Obviously, many of these characteristics pertain to Maḥfūẓ's *Ḥarāfish*, but there are a few other details that make his work more analogous to the Arabic popular sagas (*siyar*) and to *shīʿī* hagiographic literature. The occultation, in the form of ʿĀshūr's mysterious departure, does not fit seamlessly with the Greek or European tradition, but it does fit well into a vigorous Fatimid belief in a Mahdī (the divinely guided) as being the expected imam and leader. On the other hand, ʿĀshūr's Qur'ānic grounding and his history as an orphan with mysterious origins also remind us of the effort by modern historians to explain the poet Abu al-Ṭayyib al-Mutanabbī's claim to be a prophet (the literal meaning of the name Mutanabbī). Although there is no indication of eloquence within such a community of vagabonds and poor people, there is certainly enough piety to make 'Āshūr refrain from any such monstrous claims and temptations. On the other hand, Shaykh 'Afra's upbringing of the child 'Āshūr guarantees that he will fulfill a religious role involving piety and commitment to the service of God. Reminiscent of the Prophet's career as an orphan, 'Āshūr's life is more intimately entangled in the life of an alley, and yet it is a career and life that unfold through action and belief, turning him into a folk hero despite the antagonisms of thugs and the wealthy. In other words, Maḥfūẓ cannot move beyond his career as a writer who is essentially the product of a *nahḍah* mixed secularism and Islamism in confrontation with European modernity, a process that is perhaps accommodatable within the parameters of Mahdism and reason. The nation-state is discarded, and a new formation spills out of the *takiyyah* as if to echo the simmering Iranian revolution that developed between 1973 and 1979 under the leadership of Imam al-Khomeinī (the shah was deposed on January 16, 1979). The incessant melodies of the Persian hymns only intensify the need for this kind of correspondence. Within the context of the kind of religious thought that Maḥfūẓ is here espousing, the appearance of the shaykh heralds the end of the period of occultation, whereby it is now possible to "walk down the alley bestowing his light and give each young man a bamboo club and a mulberry fruit." Greek and European models of the epic seem to recede.

We should recall at this juncture that Maḥfūẓ's farewell to the Shahrayars of the nation-state occurs in *Layalī Alf Laylah* (1982), while his allegorical critique of the notion of homeland occurs in *Riḥlat Ibn Fattoumah* (1983). However, his 1977 narrative, *The Epic of the Ḥarāfīsh*, heralds a peaceful revolution, one that will of necessity lapse, just like national revolutions, into expressions of disappointment and criticism. This work reveals other narrative qualities, in that it reworks two paradigmatic structures in Ibn Khaldūn's thought: first, the gradual fragmentation and collapse of dynasties due to affluence and the concomitant disintegration of solidarity; second, a wish for the return of an expected Mahdī, a radical shift at the end of an epoch that merits epic treatment in an Arab-Islamic context.[52]

Maḥfūẓ's *Ḥarāfīsh* will appear more significant within the context of his entire career if we look at it in terms of the major themes of his novels and their stylistic shifts in time. According to Roger Allen, Maḥfūẓ intimated to him that, if there is one book he would like to be remembered by, it is this *Ḥarāfīsh*. While the intimation indicates a serious commitment on the author's part to the art and message of the book, it certainly also draws our attention to the fact that this 1977 narrative shares with his earlier works a number of common themes and structural patterns that consolidate its essential Islamic frame of reference. It adopts from his novels of the 1960s a marginal Sufi presence, but rather than relegating it to the periphery of societal and political concerns, it now places it squarely in the center. The monastery and mosque anthems and prayers frame the narrative in an audio discursivity that inevitably draws our attention to the deliberate use of competitive discourses. These anthems and the call to prayer are at the back of the protagonist's mind every time he encounters a problem. In the graveyard scene where he is pressed to make a choice between loyalty to Shaykh 'Afra's son (something that would imply his complicity in theft and robbery and total rejection of his pact), 'Āshūr confronts a choice without being in any way wordy; rather the retort is terse and sharp, duly complemented by his physical prowess. In this scene not only is his will tested, but his entire future career and mission are determined. The other testing ground is the bar, for it is there that he realizes that his three sons cannot become upholders of a covenant. It is there, too, that he himself realizes that he is no longer immune to human desires. Both realizations demand a decision on his part. His marriage to Fullah will only increase the temptations to come, but it will also lead to his confirmation of the continuity of a covenant symbolized by the birth of his son by Fullah, Shams al-Dīn. With this balance in mind, the trial emerges as an effective test for his future career and that of the covenant. The third testing ground is the Bannan house. Without its implications and the expressed disapproval of state authorities, there would be no consolidation of the powerful emotive link with the *ḥarāfish*. Only through a series of battlegrounds can 'Āshūr effectively overcome his frailties and strengthen his Sufi leanings. Listening to anthems may purify his soul, but trials impart power to his will. By centering his Sufi character in action, Maḥfūẓ shifts the distribution of power and restores to the poor what is their due. With that, he can justly claim that he is no longer following the assumptions and ethos of the Victorian middle-class novel.

Through 'Āshūr's rebirth—reincarnation in an ultimate 'Āshūr at the end of the long narrative—Maḥfūẓ centralizes his protagonist's covenant not only through a transposition of the most popular paradigm in Arabic modernism—the regeneration myth which was once the most acclaimed premise among poets and ideologues—but also and most importantly through a regeneration of a covenant in the form of the Mahdī paradigm whereby the shaykh puts an end to his seclusion and proclaims an era of peace and justice. Unlike the disillusionment of the young disciples of Shaykh Abū al-Su'ūd in Jamāl al-Ghīṭānī's novel *Al-Zaynī Barakāt*, there is here a positive restoration of a peaceful ethos that blends with Maḥfūẓ's sense of moderation. For in Maḥfūẓ's writings no one would expect the Mahdī to return brandishing his sword.

Other issues that connect this narrative to Maḥfūẓ's oeuvre, but with a transposition that suits his paradigm shift, are the role of women, the divides of poverty and wealth, and the different faces of religion. Maḥfūẓ's women in the *Ḥarāfish* stand only as foils for the protagonist; even Zahrah is no more than a powerful and charming lady closely involved in 'Āshūr's legacy that is much in need of resurrection. In the absence of men, she is willing to take responsibility but, since she is bent on fighting society with its own tools and tactics, she fails the trial and the test.

'Āshūr's legacy itself invites interpretations as disparate and conflictual as people's interests; every descendant will perceive it from an angle that is not necessarily faithful to the original. Some justify their greed for wealth by emphasizing 'Āshūr's use of the Bannan house; others with more interest in women of questionable behavior use his marriage to Fullah as the yardstick to measure their own choice and behavior; still others regard him as a pious ascetic *ḥarfūsh*. In a word, Maḥfūẓ here produces a work of multiple possible interpretations that obliquely reflects on idealistic ideologies. Its resort to Mamluk history is nothing less than an oblique questioning of an age that is bound to witness change after years of aspiration, achievement, and failure that constitute the legacy of the nation-state. In narrative writing, the change is already there, but it emerges through representations of conquest, occupation, and a contrarian religious fervor. On occasions, and as Lefebvre's differential space begets conflicts and transformations that keep history on the move,[53] there is also the possibility of anger and protest amounting to armed struggle, as the next chapter demonstrates.

Notes

1. 'Abd al-Ḥakīm Qāsim, *Ayyām al-insān al-sab'ah* (1969; English translation: *The Seven Days of Man*, trans. Joseph Norment Bell, Cairo: GEBO, 1989).
2. Henri Lefebvre, *The Production of Space*, (Oxford : Basil Blackwell, 1991) 42.
3. Najīb Maḥfūẓ, *Layālī Alf Laylah* (1982; English translation: *Arabian Nights and Days*, New York: Anchor Books, 1995), 159–61 ; and *The Seven Days of Man*, 147.
4. Qāsim, *The Seven Days of Man*, 160.
5. See Habermas, *The Inclusion of the Other*, ed. Ciaran and Pablo De Greiff (Cambridge, MA: MIT Press, 1998), 224.
6. Lefebvre, *The Production of Space*, 51.
7. Georg Lukács, *The Theory of the Novel* (London: Merlin Press, 1978), 136.
8. Lukács, *The Theory of the Novel*, 145–46.
9. See Habermas, *The Inclusion of the Other*, 224.

10. Lefebvre, *The Production of Space*, 51.
11. Lefebvre, *The Production of Space*, 54.
12. See Lefebvre, *The Production of Space*, 51.
13. Lefebvre, *The Production of Space*, 59–60.
14. See also, though from an entirely surveylike documentation of the impact of 1967, Shukrī ʿAzīz Māḍī, *In'ikās hazīmat ḥazīrān 'alā al-riwāyah al-'Arabiyah* (Beirut: MADN, 1978).
15. J. M. Coetzee, "Fabulous Fabulist," *The New York Review of Books* 41:15 (September 22, 1994).
16. Coetzee mentioned critics, specifically, Elias Khouri.
17. Lefebvre, *The Production of Space*, 48–49.
18. See Catherine Cobham, "Enchanted to a Stone—Heroes and Leaders in *The Ḥarāfīsh* by Najīb Maḥfūẓ," *Middle Eastern Literatures* 9:2 (2006), 123–35, at 126.
19. Cited in Julian Baldick, *Mystical Islam: An Introduction to Sufism* (New York: New York University Press, 1989), 66.
20. See William Brinner, "The Significance of the Ḥarāfīsh and Their 'Sultan' " *Journal of the Economic and Social History of the Orient* 6:2 (1963), 190–215, at 210.
21. See Cobham, "Enchanted to a Stone," 124.
22. See Brinner, "The Significance of the Ḥarāfīsh and Their 'Sultan'," 199.
23. Brinner, "The Significance of the Ḥarāfīsh and Their 'Sultan'," 199.
24. Brinner, "The Significance of the Ḥarāfīsh and Their 'Sultan'," 202.
25. Brinner, "The Significance of the Ḥarāfīsh and Their 'Sultan'," 195–97, 198.
26. Lefebvre, *The Production of Space*, 54.
27. Brinner, "The Significance of the Ḥarāfīsh and Their 'Sultan'," 195; Maqrīzī, *Sulūk*, II: 396.
28. Maqrīzī, *Sulūk*, II: 576.
29. Quoted in Brinner, "The Significance of the Ḥarāfīsh and Their 'Sultan'," 196, n. 1.
30. Cited from Ibn Iyās, 1:103, in Brinner, "The Significance of the Ḥarāfīsh and Their 'Sultan'," 196, and n. 3.
31. Quoted in Brinner, "The Significance of the Ḥarāfīsh and Their 'Sultan'," 197.
32. Cited in Brinner, "The Significance of the Ḥarāfīsh and Their 'Sultan'," 199, from Ibn Hajar, *Inbā' al-Ghumr*.
33. Shaykh 'Abd Allāh (Shaykh Shuʿayb) al-Ḥurayfūsh, *Rawḍ al-fā'iq fī al-Mawā'ḍ wal-al-raqā'iq* (*The Splendid Garden of Sermons and Edifying Tales*). Cairo: Muṣṭafā al-Bābī al-Ḥalabī, 1949).
34. Cited in Brinner, "The Significance of the Ḥarāfīsh and Their 'Sultan'," 199; al-Sakhāwī, *al-Daw' al-Iāmi'*, V:20.
35. Brinner, "The Significance of the Ḥarāfīsh and Their 'Sultan'," 201.
36. Cited in Brinner, "The Significance of the Ḥarāfīsh and Their 'Sultan'," from Ibn Iyās, *The Ottoman Conquest of Egypt*, trans. W. Salmon.
37. Cited in Brinner, "The Significance of the Ḥarāfīsh and Their 'Sultan'," from Ibn Taghrī Birdī, *Nujūm*, VI:763.
38. See Brinner's account based on Ibn Tagrī Birdī, Popper's translation, *History of Egypt*, VII:210 n.
39. Cited in ibid., from Sakhāwī, *Al-Tibr al-Masbūk*, 349.

40. See Pierre Bourdieu on this point, *Language and Symbolic Power*, (Cambridge, MA: Harvard University Press, 1991) 46–47.

41. Frantz Fanon, *The Wretched of the Earth*, (New York: Grove Press, 1963) 169.

42. Fanon, *The Wretched of the Earth*, 204.

43. Fanon, *The Wretched of the Earth*, 205.

44. Fanon, *The Wretched of the Earth*, 205.

45. See Fanon, *The Wretched of the Earth*, 205.

46. On historical records, see Brinner, "The Significance of the Ḥarāfish and Their 'Sultan'," 195–200.

47. Exceptions are very few, such as Dickens's *A Tale of Two Cities*, where there is a different perspective. The novel documents one moment, which is associated with Robespierre, when "a public sphere was no longer the educated strata" but the uneducated "people." See Jürgen Habermas, *The Structural Transformation of the Public Sphere*, trans. Thomas Burger (Cambridge, MA: MIT Press, 1991), xviii.

48. See H. L. Tracy, "The Epic Tradition," *The Classical Journal* 42:2 (1946), 78–81, at 78.

49. Tracy, "The Epic Tradition," 79.

50. For a review of C. M. Bowla and Frye, see Thomas Greene, "The Norms of Epic," *Comparative Literature* 13:3 (1961), 193–207.

51. Greene, "The Name of Epic," 200.

52. See 'Abd al-Raḥmān Ibn Khaldūn, *The Muqaddimah*, trans. Franz Rosenthal (Princeton, NJ: Princeton University Press, 2005), 165, 166, 258.

53. Lefebvre, *The Production of Space*, 52.

CHAPTER FIVE

In the Aftermath of Failures: The Reliance on Popular Religious Politics

The Global, the National, and Islamic Faith in Jamāl al-Ghīṭānī's *Zaynī Barakāt*

A number of issues connected with Jamāl al-Ghīṭānī's narrative *Al-Zaynī Barakāt* (1970–1971), are worthy of investigation.[1] The novel is a compelling narrative of the Mamluk era, especially the decades leading to the collapse of a dynasty in the wake of the Ottoman invasion. The conquest of Egypt in 1517 put an end to the Mamluk dynasty that had ruled the country for 267 years, a period that is usually divided between the Baḥrī dynasty (1250–1390), which settled on the Nile island where they had their barracks, fortresses, and palaces, and the Burjī one (1382–1517), which took its name from the towers of the Cairo citadel. The entire period was very complex; indeed, it remains so even for historians. While this powerful dynasty displayed ruthlessness toward others and indeed toward opposing factions within its own ranks, it also had significant achievements, not only in architecture, the arts, and Islamic sciences, but also in its role as protector of Egypt from foreign attack, especially the Mongols. While historians have assayed a number of methods in their attempts to cope with such complexity, novelists may actually prove to be more successful, not only in keeping up with the historical data but also in explaining this complexity in more synthetic ways that can be plausibly narrated through juxtapositions, reportage, textual inclusion or exclusion, and multiple perspectives. In the case of al-Ghīṭānī's narrative the result directs the reader's attention to a historical period while at the same time invoking a present period characterized by no less authoritarianism and police surveillance, factional competition, corruption under the veneer of righteousness, opportunism, and total disarray in matters of administration. Al-Ghīṭānī's reconstruction is carried out within a neohistoricist perspective, with a focalization that summons facts and details to produce a full image of unity in disintegration, or control within chaos, but goes beyond that so as to enable the reader to see through the emerging troubles of the nation-state, its double-standard discourse, preoccupation with survival, and, hence, its relentless assault on religious institutions.

The Egyptian historian and chronicler Ibn Iyās and a ficitious Venetian traveler, Visconti, are brought into the narrative, not only to substantiate its historicity and authenticity, but also to dissuade the reader from minute comparisons with the present. The double technique of direction and distancing, historicity and critiquing of the present, works well in a narrative that has a lot to say, especially in a period that had recently witnessed the death of national leader Jamāl 'Abd al-Nāṣir (1970), a presidency that had witnessed a period of powerful nationalism and support for the poor, but also one marked by repressive measures and crackdowns on not only leftist groups and movements but also on the Muslim Brotherhood in 1965–1966. The Sādāt regime that followed proved no less devastating, as the free economic policy that opened the country to multinational corporations (*infitāḥ*) and the peace treaty with Israel did not coexist well with a state run economy and certainly did not garner the approval of the left, which suffered a new crackdown that allowed some state maneuvering with the Muslim Brotherhood. The latter made full use of their relative freedom without losing sight of their ideological goals to liberate occupied Palestine and establish Islamic rule, or at least to become more active participants in state building. Such a historical context is not drawn so sharply in this novel, but its presence in the reader's mind is bound to lead to a process whereby a compelling and pleasant narrative such as this inevitably leads to comparisons.

The power that this narrative possesses is both stylistic and historical. The style is marked by its flowing ease, readability, and anecdotal quality. Each character is preserved as a rounded personality, a site of conflicting emotions and passions. The police chief Zakariyyah, for example, can be kind and even passionate whenever his own child, Yāsīn, is involved, and yet he is cruel, ruthless, and calculating when such traits are needed. No less complicated is the market inspector, the title character of the novel, who is more of a politician, a manipulator who is always being spoken about but who rarely speaks in his own voice. His power engulfs the street, and his presence is hinted at in the responses of others. The deliberate minimalization of al-Zaynī's own speech requires a greater focus on his actions, something that surges up every now and then despite the many setbacks which he faces. The polyphonic quality of the book enables this interplay between silence and power, speech and politics. People who crowd the street or the mosque find themselves the victims of other people's actions; they are the recipients of messages, orders, and commands. But even when acted on as mobs and rabble, their numbness, subjection, and paralysis under manipulation helps to explain the ease with which the city and dynasty fell to the Ottoman conquest. The outcome testifies to what Frantz Fanon stipulates in relation to regimes that ignore or humiliate people under the camouflage of fighting the enemy.[2]

The historical mode is no less conspicuous in this narrative. We can sense the presence of an authority concealed behind names and tableaus; but these names also provide the narrative with multiple perspectives that create and project their own space through images of great resonance. Whether the text talks about mosques, pulpits, streets, processions, dungeons, prisons, cafés, spacious palaces, residences, or places that efface their presence through self-denial, these multiple perspectives act as human agents, replete with their own specific connotations. Even when each character makes use of a number of masks, including al-Zaynī Barakāt, the market inspector, who takes incognito strolls, and Zakariyyah Ibn Rāḍī, the chief spy who behaves in a similar fashion, these sites and actions depict the nation-state or city-state as a space rife with intrigue, competition, alliances, factions, and conflict, all of them fostering moods of curiosity, resignation, love, and pain. These activities are representations of space as characterized by Lefebvre: they conceptualize space and afford it voices that emanate from ideology and knowledge. These activities create a volatile space, "tied to the relations of production and to the 'order' which those relations impose, and hence to knowledge, to signs, to codes, and to 'frontal' relations."[3] Everywhere there exists one or more of these elements that help to produce a text that teems with noises and troubles, very much like the fortunes of each of the major characters: the market inspector, al-Zaynī Barakāt Ibn Mūsā; the chief spy, Zakariyyah Ibn Rāḍī, the Sufi shaykh, Abū al-Su'ūd, and his disciple Sa'īd al-Juhaynī, or even his antagonistic analogue, the pseudo-shaykh and actual spy, Shaykh 'Amr. Around these principal characters there hover many others who take the roles of narrative foils, to substantiate a detail, strengthen an impression, enforce an image, or simply to enliven the narrative tableau and make it more readable. Processions, proclamations, and announcements only add to the voice of authority and give it a presence even when its producers are physically not there. Once in a while the central authority intrudes openly, but its presence is usually made possible through the mediation of others through a system in which street and even private property are kept under state control. The more covert its dealings and the more absent its voices in a narrative that keeps state power mysteriously present but with no specific language of its own, the greater becomes the ever-mounting fear of a further extension of its proliferation and control. But by concentrating on this aspect we may be in danger of ridding the narrative of its Islamism as a dynamic force with many perspectives and voices as it confronts or works with authority. But within the domain of confrontation between absence and presence, two camps emerge that negotiate with or defy each other. In the space between, the two opportunists and parasites are to be found whose presence only testifies to a deracinated space controlled and ordered solely by power. Here Henri Lefebvre's "will above" operates as an overwhelming force whose "exploitation and domination" and "protection and—inseparably—regression" employs its strategy of "dissociations and separations" that keeps power relations in ferment while ensuring hegemony.[4]

While the sultan should understandably be visibly present, as historians of Islamic history have it, in this narrative the sultan's voice only reaches the reader through others. From time to time the market inspector may issue proclamations or decrees in the sultan's name, and yet the power of this narrative does not reside in these scattered references to the sultan and his favors and whims, but rather in the prevalence of a mysterious force of surveillance that is felt under the surface camouflage of security, law, and order. Indeed, this force pervades the society as a whole, its networks, guilds, mosques, and streets. Every symbolic space is made to appear appealing and acceptable, but at the same time it provokes anxiety, mystery, and fear. The passage that appears in Visconti's report is even more telling and powerful for being cited in the Venetian traveler's account, while its temporal referentiality, the last years of the Mamluk Sultan al-Nāṣir's reign, focuses attention on structural problems inherent in both nationalism and the nation-state: a rigorous drive toward rebirth, a tendency to invoke all means of legitimacy and co-opt or control every faction, and a desire to displace religion as faith or conversely to claim it as its own. In this particular instance, whenever the conflict becomes more intense and pivotal, the chief spy spreads a new claim that religious people have no knowledge of state politics. From Zakariyya Ibn Rāḍī's dispersed rumors and communiqués we learn that "the shaykh [Abū al-Su'ūd] was a man of God, a blessed saint, but what were shaykhs doing in matters of state? What were hermits doing concerning themselves with affairs of this world? If they were to preoccupy themselves with concerns over dinars, they would be deviating from the right path" (p. 226).

Even so, the shaykhs in this narrative are no ordinary power; since they are not united and the state has its particular ways of dividing, dismantling, implanting, and coercing, even to the point of murdering some, it manages to survive as the only force possessed of legitimate and coercive processes. In making the latter choice various modes of governance emerge, including subtle maneuvers supported by material gifts and achievements and imposing a regime characterized by sheer terror. Visconti's account is meant to convey a sense of bewilderment, especially since it concretizes space and describes Cairo, not in terms of streets and squares, but rather as a blindfolded human. The ultimate evocations of nationalism and sincerity command respect and even affection, but the inclination to overrule others is bound to breed dislike and opposition. Hence the Venetian's image of Cairo combines submission and potential revolt. "I haven't seen anything like it in any country," he writes. "People love a specific person; everybody says good things about him and praises him. But at the same time there is a hidden undercurrent, an imperceptible feeling permeating people and even inanimate objects." This undercurrent, he adds, is "a fear of Zaynī, something that does not show on anyone's face but which can be felt. This has really puzzled and confused me" (p. 168). Historical accounts speak of Zaynī Barakāt in glorious terms, though there is always a mention of his "ingenious methods of entrenchment," which "rendered him untouchable."[5] They also speak of his occasional punishments by the Sultan who was usually forced by the public to reinstate him.

This kind of hegemonic authority, so pervasive and so seemingly acceptable, transcends one person's sway; it penetrates social space and saps the foundations of resistance. While the narrator, even Visconti for that matter, distances himself from the scene, his other accounts place this hegemony into a context that manages to convey a further possibility of rupture. In Lefebvre's words, "state-imposed normality makes transgression inevitable."[6] Moreover, transgression is not a random phenomenon, though at the outset it may seem so. It soon gathers momentum, bringing sentiments and positions into uniformity. "These forces," he argues, "are still capable of rattling the lid of the cauldron of the state and its space, for differences can never be totally quieted" (p. 23).

Although this narrative cannot correspond exactly to the pattern of a binary divide as long as there exists another space that harbors an enormous body of parasites, it nevertheless navigates between two poles. The state and its competing factions are represented by the authorities of the intelligence service, while the economy and its legislative power have traditionally been represented by the figure of the market inspector, the *muḥtasib*. Around the two hover espionage and surveillance networks, permitting exploitation and enormous taxation that are legitimized through a compulsory endorsement demanded from a religious authority. After feigning self-denial and an unwillingness to be a market inspector, al-Zaynī Barakāt makes his reluctance to serve so widely known that many Sufis, shaykhs, and young Azharites concur with the public that such self-denial is unheard of and must be a sign of good will and a readiness to enforce the word of God against mismanagement, injustice, and exploitation.

The narrative uses such moments of discovery, recognition, and action to accelerate its own dramatic effect, but its basic drama focuses more on a continuing dynamic, the Islamic one. That does not imply belonging to an institution (despite the existence of such an institution like the Azhar University and Mosque and their many young disciples who are also penetrated by a network of spies), nor does it emerge from the official religious apparatus and its appointees—imams and shaykhs—who internalize and disseminate its orders through sermons and speeches. Instead this Islamic dynamic is foretold using all the insight of a talented author whose familiarity with the relevant historical accounts enables him to detect close similarities between past and present. The Mamluk dynasty possessed an empire of a kind, with a center and hierarchy; but it was afraid of religious authority that considered any subordination to the state and sovereign to be a pagan practice. While the state at the time strove to win over as many opportunists as possible, the historian Taqī al-Dīn al-Maqrīzī tells us about many shaykhs who were shunned and ridiculed for their subordination and opportunism. No wonder then that a different kind of religious authority developed, one that was upheld by public recognition and given form and stature by public affection and respect.

The author of *Al-Zaynī Barakāt* enables this form of authority to emerge gradually in response to rumors concerning the market inspector, al-Zaynī Barakāt, and his announced reluctance to assume a post that requires a full commitment to justice, rumors that preoccupy the public sphere for some time. At this nexus, the shaykh's authority takes form, as he calls on al-Zaynī Barakāt to come to his place and perhaps instructs him in the requirements of such an economic-religious post. The shaykh thus emerges as a power to be reckoned with; to invoke a comparison with President Nāṣir's times, this kind of authority had not yet come into the open. Najīb Maḥfūẓ depicted the Sufi presence in the 1960s and 1970s as being pious, God-fearing, respectable, and widely recognized, but it was only allowed to exist in the shadow of a bureaucracy that, in Lefebvre's terms, occupied abstract space. The Sufis appeared as an alien force, apolitical and reluctant to be involved in any power struggle, not least because their discourse is one of ambiguity, riddles, and open-ended answers. Maḥfūẓ himself had discovered faith as the only outlet. With the suicide of secular thought and its too optimistic immersion in the Western model of modernity and its freakish notion of the nation-state, a political vacuum had developed that demanded the identification of substitutes.

As one of the primary texts in a paradigmatic shift in Arabic fiction, this narrative does not engage with a secular-religious binary, the early legacy of the *nahḍah* as modeled on the European divide. Like Qāsim before him, the author engages with this in order to undermine it first before engaging a historical frame where contingency has been holding and where the binary is one of degree in religious or nonreligious commitment. It presents the issue as one of interpretation where religion holds sway and where remembrance of God can forestall greed and vileness. Interest and self-survival operate within this frame of thought, not outside it.[7] The state had already destroyed all centers of opposition, whether religious or secular, and was left in the hands of the bureaucracy, presided over by the intelligence service, and the hierarchy of the national bourgeoisie. In the words of the Azharite rebel Saʿīd al-Juhaynī: "This is an age whose Imam is Zaynī, whose Shaykh is Zakariyya, whose custodians are the spies, and whose confidential secretary is ʿAmr Ibn al-Adawi" (p. 180). This transposition and transference of terms, icons, and symbols from one sphere to another accelerates tension and demonstrates volatile contestation that is bound to bring about an explosive situation.

While these words refer to a Mamluk-era register in which chancery terms and positions have a particular prominence, they also allude to the growth of bureaucracy in modern Egypt, a symptom, no doubt, of a growing sense of frustration that may well engender an alienation from such a state of affairs. Nevertheless within the novel itself such impositions and restrictive practices lead people to develop levels of annoyance, a movement of social protest that begins to occupy every space, whether it be actual and lived or imaginary. Thus even the relatively quiescent Shaykh Manṣūr has to conclude in despair that "no intercession for people is to be hoped for; . . . even if our beloved Prophet were to come back and try to fill the earth with justice and peace instead of the injustice and oppression with which it is now filled" (p. 176). Nothing, it seems, can stop corruption and coercion. In a deliberate move aimed at linking the lingering Fatimid faith with mainstream Sunnism, the novelist empowers two voices so they can speak of al-Mahdī and the Prophet as the ultimate source of succor for the needy and dispossessed. The sense that even these two voices, even with all their authority and guidance among the principal Islamic sects, cannot maintain a system of justice serves as a summation of a pervasive sense of frustration. Worse still is the implication that this frustration can be a prelude to the success of foreign invasions. On the other hand, frustration gives way to distrust of long-held beliefs that oppression and corruption cannot last for long. As Manṣūr notes: "O, Saʿīd. I have given up hope for the long-awaited Mahdī. If he were to rise and come from the Kaaba, brandishing his golden sword, Zakariyya would confront him, ban him from entering the country, arrest him, and throw him in the Magshara Prison, that being the only reality in the world" (pp. 176–77). That "only reality" makes itself felt through a sustained effort that is exercised by the state apparatus to drive fear into people's hearts lest they end up in that reality. As long as the prison becomes a trope for physical annihilation, torture, sheer fear, and mysterious occurrences, it is a space that will manage to alienate and paralyze everything else.

Like any space with disproportionate power, the prison needs its other. Without some alternative space, competitive and defiant, it loses its effect. Whence the function of Shaykh Abū al-Su'ūd's residence, with its austerity, solitude, and ensemble of dervishes and Sufis. Only such a space can present a counternarrative, one that provides comfort and certitude. Thus it is in Kūm al-Jāriḥ where the shaykh resides that Sa'īd and other disciples derive some comfort: "Shaykh Abū al-Su'ūd, the good, pious, noble, generous, and learned scholar who has traveled all over the world" (p. 19). Countering this space there is the "citadel on the mountain" where the administration resides and the representative of evil, the chief spy, Zakariyyah Ibn Rāḍī, "impaled next to the Gate of al-Wazir" (p. 19). The shaykh is not devoted to material reality: "From time to time I need to be by myself, and for that purpose I have dug this cellar. I have done so in order that I can use it to rest my body whenever my soul feels perplexed and let down by time" (p. 107). But once he learns that the market inspector has gone so far as to claim the support of religious circles, the shaykh decides differently, namely "to abandon solitude and take action." Maḥfūẓ's shaykhs can never assume such a role. However, when Abū al-Su'ūd hears what al-Zaynī has been doing, "raising prices and arresting people," claiming throughout that he has been following "the thrust of the teachings of my master and Imam, Shaykh Abū al-Su'ūd al-Jarini" (p. 204), reports reach the chief spy to the effect that the shaykh has upbraided al-Zaynī: "You dog, why are you attributing the things you say to me?" The scene ends with al-Zaynī being beaten by dervishes "until he almost expired," then dispatched in irons to Amir Allan and Viceroy Emir Tuman (p. 208).

Yet the increasing presence of this Islamic dynamic is not self-renewing, nor indeed does it intensify. It needs to be seen more in the wider context of an Islamic façade, one that includes fawning and pretentious, but good-hearted people like Shaykh Rīḥān with his limited knowledge of Islamic law, who relishes any support or sign of attention from amirs and administrators, claims to belong to the elite, and is very fastidious about his worldly appearance. Contrary to this representative of religion are the "Azhar students from lower grades in Qur'ānic schools" who are specifically trailed by the chief spy's network because they may "support dissension and sedition and instigate the rabble against their masters," to quote the chief spy's report to the international conference on counteracting revolution (p. 130). While people like Shaykh Rīḥān are no more than toys to be played with, these potential troublemakers receive special attention through a network of pseudo-shaykhs, former students, and their like who are recruited as the result of duress, need, intimidation, or other conditions. Their job is not limited to reporting, but also includes fomenting trouble "to find out those who stray," as the same report duly notes (p. 130). Some may advance in rank and receive a state promotion allowing them to act as preachers and imams for Friday prayers, a position that allows them to repeat what both the market inspector and chief spy wish to have proclaimed. Thus as part of the open conflict between the two sides on the limits of each one's responsibility and privilege, the chief spy states that the lamps which the inspector installs in the streets should be removed. Preachers now repeat a long section, one part of which declares: "The Noble Messenger has enjoined us to lower our eyes so that we may not see the nakedness of people" (p. 96). It adds: "God has created night and day: dark for night and light for day; God has created night as a cover and shield; do we then remove the cover?" (p. 96). These speeches and sermons used to operate in former times, just as they do nowadays, as powerful communications media that can change public opinion or prepare for a reign of terror. The extract just quoted plays well on the use and misuse of the Qur'ān whenever an interested group intends to pursue a specific goal and win over the minds and sympathies of the common public. "This is heresy," the sermon goes on, "which we do not accept. It is deviation from the law, and we reject it" (p. 97).

This sermon is not merely a piece of narrative that motivates dramatic action, but also a source that is steeped in those essentialist perspectives that consider Islam as static, not dynamic, dormant and unchanging in the face of the spirit of the age. The "pastism" of the sermon, its essentialist reading of a dormant past, stands for the fixed orthodoxies of creeds that had already been challenging the innovative reformist ideas of Shaykh Muḥammad 'Abdū and his followers, along with similarly enlightened shaykhs in Iraq, Syria, Lebanon, and North Africa.[8] This sermon is thus not simply a piece of religious discourse with a specific purpose or intent. The very fact that it emanates from a pulpit in a mosque that, in this case, has been chosen by the state through its co-opted shaykhs does not make it binding on the community. As long as the state is not regarded as the representative of a nation, there is a possibility of dissension and rift. Even so this deliberate use of specific space conveys an authority of its own. Even when it is not necessarily overwhelming enough to displace other competing discourses, there is nevertheless enough persuasion through association with religious authorities to provoke dissent, disapproval, and anger. Manipulating the pulpit and speaking for the state, the sermon imposes an official discourse that can challenge and undermine other practices and discourses, as Pierre Bourdieu argues in *Language and Symbolic Power*.[9]

The other context within which the potential of the Islamic dynamic is enhanced relates to political polarization: a process whereby a bureaucracy produces abstract space, in Lefebvre's terms, and a people led by professional guilds participate in the production of the Islamic dynamic in public places, streets, squares, poor areas, schools, factories, and the like.[10] The narrative is enriched by this dynamic since it establishes interaction and active production of various positions, dispositions, and attitudes that emerge from volatile sites of power. And yet power also functions in proportion to the challenges posed. Bureaucracy of this type, for example, has no specific mission or belief system other than self-interest—what the chief spy describes as an allegiance to authority, no matter what its color or nationality. Had it been vigilant enough, argues the chief spy, it would not have lost power.

The application for such logic certainly creates a distinct rupture with the concepts of nationality or belief. An avowed reliance on God is a legitimizing process, and hence any resort to ruthlessness is always prefaced with an invocation of the deity. According to the chief spy in the report noted earlier, the goal of the spy is "to please God Almighty, then the Sultan, then the State" (p. 192). On such scale God is only included for convenience, something to be freely manipulated. In this way narrative gives holders of power a voice in order to reveal their way of thinking, their manipulation of other people, and their ultimate protection of their own interests.

This kind of attitude is qualified by another premise that is invoked to explain the continuity of bureaucracy as the newly emerging producer of power relations in concert with a center. This center may change, but not the apparatus, and thus its power will rely on the perceived need for it, that being the impetus to its promotion and nurturing. According to the chief spy's report: "we say that as long as someone has been able to seize power from the person sitting on the throne and to sit on that very same throne that could only indicate the weakness on the part of the former. How could he establish justice if he couldn't protect himself?" (p. 193). In other words, the chief spy refuses to take responsibility or accountability for failure, but levels the blame at the throne itself.

These premises and strategies, including a penetration into religious orders, form the background and incentive for the rise of militancy in an otherwise quiet religious order. The author obviously elaborates most of the loose threads in such a way as to lead to a legitimating narrative process, one that justifies action and uncovers certain bureaucratic mechanisms that can be claimed as abstract space, a space that is "a locus and milieu of all kinds of power," in the words of Lefebvre.[11] While the birth of this powerful bureaucracy in Jamāl al-Ghīṭānī's narrative fits Lefebvre's thesis well, it also explains the ultimate militancy that will command its own "differential space," a place that seethes with dissidence and opposition in comparison with the seemingly nonviolent, but menacing, abstract space with its homogenizing tactics and premises.[12]

Jamāl al-Ghīṭānī's narrative allows for such interpretations even though it is located in a chaotic nation-state, one that relies on a power center rather than on well-sustained institutionalized structures. The power of the narrative derives not only from its claim to historicity, its documentary record—both authentic and fake—and its multiple perspectives in line with annals and surveys of heralds and rumors in Mamluk Cairo, but also from the gradual transformation of the Islamic dynamic from an ordinary practice of piety to a state of perplexity, before finally achieving the status of action. Thus, in keeping with historical records,[13] and in preparation for his appointment as market inspector, al-Zaynī Barakāt has already bribed the sultan. To forge relations with the public, he needs to establish further connections that will enable him to wield yet more power, whether real or imaginary, power that will encompass the totality of social life. He is searching for a monopoly that will make him the only rival power to be reckoned with, all that in spite of the existence of other competing powers in the same abstract space where the intelligence service pervades every section of the social order, modes of production, and every potential group, guild, or economic and political center. To achieve such a goal, he has to spread the rumor that he is reluctant to accept a job that needs full authority in order to exercise control over corruption and injustice. The rumors are effective, and as a result religious orders swallow the bait and entreat him to accept. For the pious shaykh, this is the trap which leads to his state of perplexity. But once the dissimulation is uncovered, the young disciple Shaykh Saʿīd has to admit his folly, an admission that demands public action in the sense of openly opposing al-Zaynī when the latter delivers a sermon as a way of propagating his views. It is only at this stage, when many disciples are reporting al-Zaynī's transgressions, his accumulation of wealth, and his use of unfair revenue collection to keep the sultan pleased with his performance, that the shaykh realizes how badly tricked and deceived he has been.

Now the media becomes yet another aspect of this abstract space. It can be manipulated by the powerful in control of this space but, even if the opposition suffers heavy losses, the space of political power can still be threatened by a competing differential one which Lefebvre depicts as one of conflict and protest.[14] Although intended as a symbolic space, a pulpit where the word of the preacher is derived from God's power, this abstract space can still face contestation. Within a dynamic of Islamic thought that moves beyond a unitary homogeneous discourse, abstract space becomes an arena for opposition. In Lefebvre's words there is a need for a struggle which "prevents abstract space from taking over the whole planet and papering over all differences."[15] Shaykh Sa'īd's reaction to al-Zaynī's sermon, as he shouts out his protests, is no minor act. Here is how the narrator reports it: "What is there left for him to care about? This is an age whose Imam is Zaynī, whose Shaykh is Zakariyyah, whose custodians are spies, and whose confidential secretary is `Amr Ibn al-Adawi" (p. 180). This internalization which delves into the mind of the young shaykh at a time when his beloved, the young Samah, Shaykh Rīḥān's daughter, has already been deliberately married off to a wealthy amir brings together a number of motives to justify the new line of rebellion. We should bear in mind that these combined motivations are to operate in Arabic fiction as leitmotifs in the years to come, as in *The Yacoubian Building*, for example, with regard to the protagonist Ṭāḥā. This kind of rebellion may amount to nothing less than open opposition to authority: "Let him end this premature old age, recover the youth of his life, remove the sharp blade from the tongue. 'Liar!' " Al- Zaynī was taken by surprise, "and the hand froze in mid-air on the pulpit" (p. 180). This rebelliousness is deliberately placed into another context, one of martyrdom, which is in keeping with history as well as with a narrative that has been gradually developing a montage of Fatimid sentiments in conjunction with the prevalent mood of Sufi devotion. Both work together, and their resurgence indicates the breakup of official religion, with its pseudo-shaykhs like Shaykh Rīḥān and state-appointed preachers whose role is to proclaim whatever the state apparatus, and especially the intelligence service, chooses to pass on to them (pp. 96–97, 169). Thus Shaykh Sa'īd decides to undertake the mission originally set by the example of the Prophet's grandson, Imam al-Ḥusayn Ibn 'Alī (d. October 10, 680), whose martyrdom is the example for Shī'īs in their redemptive suffering and ultimate resistance to injustice and corruption. Here history is reconstructed in order to cater to a fighting mood. One can see here the correspondence between this process of internalization in the novel and the resurgence of Islam in Iran, Lebanon, and other areas. Shaykh Sa'īd internalizes the historical event, thereby strengthening his morale so that he can fight back: "If they were to slaughter his son right in front of his very eyes, if they withheld water from him, if they took the severed head and toyed with the lips, it wouldn't matter. Al-Ḥusayn has prior claim to the honour of bearing torture" (p. 180). Although the intelligence service will not allow him the chance to let this identification materialize, this defiance is a step toward two further developments in the narrative formation of the Islamic dynamic: the global context of the struggle that anticipates the chief spy's conference; and the open battle with the Ottomans.

This broadening of narrative borders to include the interest of the nation-state in pacts of survival is not merely a technical device to polarize the narrative action. It is basically focused on the challenge posed by the nation-state, a challenge that has no limits and is ready to accommodate other means, regional and global, so as to replace home-bought legitimacy with a more regional and global one. The narrative also operates within a particular context, in that Egyptian nationalism was wider and more powerful before the June 1967 defeat and the subsequent admission of failure.[16] It had gained Arab and third world recognition, but, as was the case with many other nation-states, the price paid for this process was high, as it actually proved to weigh heavily on civil society. The blame leveled at Ṣalāh Naṣīr (1920–1982), who served as head of the intelligence service, was thus not a random occurrence; the powerful and tight control of Zakariyyah Ibn Rāḍī in the novel recalls the same image.[17]

What makes the narrative effective for such a broad readership is perhaps this blurring of distance (in terms of both time and space), a place where past and present exchange roles. This very ambivalence gives the narrative an uncertainty that does not detract from its allusive power. The tendency to mix more than one narrative genre—the anecdote, the chronicle, the report, and narrative vignettes as sermons and Sufi meditations, within a single narrative corpus, borrows from historical writing its claim to authenticity. But at the same time it debates that claim by inserting fictitious historicized records. On the other hand, the method also uses fiction in order to produce a pseudo-history. Both interact and attest to what Hayden White describes as "the fantasy that *real* events are properly represented when they can be shown to display the formal coherency of a story."[18] The intelligence service accounts of Mamluk times are often fictitious, and as fictitious are love stories and their like. Only Zaynī Barakāt has a lot of the historical character in his delineation and production. The historical figure has this complexity and ingenuity which baffled the sultans and appealed to the common people.

But why does this polarization between the coercive state and Sufi orders exist? Although the narrative does not incline toward a single Islamic stance, its focus is on corruption as a disease that pervades any social order with conflicting interests. By contrast Sufis are disinterested intellectuals who can be likened to what late-nineteenth-century European theorists tried to depict: the kind of exemplary intellectuals that Julian Benda was desperately searching for in his *The Treason of the Intellectuals* (*La trahison des clercs*). In the religious camp others can be found, but the state can reach them through their weaknesses. In this novel other religious groups are given portraits that are in stark opposition to Sufis: they are innately corrupt, corrupted, or infiltrated. The best figures to be found among such groups are shaykhs like Rīḥān, who have a very thin veneer of scholarship and knowledge of Islamic law, a disposition to worldliness and pretentiousness, and a nonactive role in life. Against this background, it is only the Sufis who appear as a disinterested group. Infiltrators, like the ones who report on Shaykh Abū al-Su'ūd's treatment of the market inspector, can do so without problems, since Sufis do not care for worldly gifts nor are they afraid of any power except the Divine; they can be taken as devotees who follow the shaykh or the mentor. Hence Abū al-Su'ūd is able to wield power, especially at a time when the search for support in confronting social evil is enormous. Even the government's subtle communiqué intended to dissuade the shaykh from continuing his political involvement has to acknowledge the shaykh's piety in order to be acceptable to the public. On the other hand, there are no rival groups apart perhaps from a few emirs and their subordinates, and they can be easily monitored by services, the intelligence agency, and the market inspectorship. Perhaps this narrative offers through these groups and conflicts, along with their positions and interests, a neat example of both literary production as a careful and deliberate combination of historical detail with fiction to reflect on the contemporary scene, and a case study for the production of space, its languages, and agents. In his letter to al-Zaynī, the chief spy argues that Egypt is divided into four classes: the sultan and leading emirs; the lesser emirs and the Mamluks; their sons and "men of the turban" (or shaykhs), along with merchants, artisans, and members of guilds; and last, the common people (p. 130). Each class has its own particular spies, and they are all infiltrated, surveyed, and kept under control. Here knowledge operates as the primary agency in an abstract space that is produced and monopolized in order to ensure its survival and that of the sovereign or his replacement. With this description of a thorough and pervasive mechanism, executed in narrative terms through correspondence, heralds, reports, and chats or discussions, there is little room left for any kind of dynamic resistance, other than through the Sufi orders. We should recall here that ardent Islamists such as Sayyid Quṭb (executed 1966) always combine Sufism with organized Islamism when it comes to dealing with contemporary struggles against the French colonization of Algeria, Italian occupation of Libya, and British occupation of Sudan.

Al-Ghīṭānī's choice in this regard is pertinent, as it leaves the abstract space open to change of a more differentiated kind, or to a dynamic one with even greater potential for transformation.[19] Indeed, the novel's cogency derives from this play on the transfer of space through the role of agency. Though space itself may become an agent, functioning like any other, other agents also participate in the process. Space here implies endless change. Yet the historian al-Maqrīzī, in his topographical and socioeconomic record of Cairo in the Mamluk period, provides us with the names of a good number of shaykhs who stood up to corruption and coercion and criticized sultans or functionaries openly while shunning those who sold themselves to the state.

The power of al-Ghīṭānī's narrative also lies in its capacity to anticipate and foreshadow both the Islamic dynamic and the lobbying of nation-states so that they can adapt to the global order through servile subscription to its agenda. As usual with survivalists, life is measured in Prufrock's spoonfuls. The novel's Cairo conference, called for by the chief spy and indeed the latter's report to the participants, anticipates the 1984 meeting of Arab interior ministers with a view to coordinating efforts in the exchange of information, defectors, dissidents, and other suspicious groups. As narrated in the novel, the conference goes well beyond that, anticipating global coordination as commanded and supervised by the most powerful forces.

The conference and its concerns, as spelled out in the chief spy's address, should alert us to the linguistic dimension involved. While homogenizing discourse and establishing an official language through heralds and sermons, both the chief spy and the market inspector are shown to be the creators and manipulators of this discourse. This "official language," to use Bourdieu's words, "is bound up with the state, both in its genesis and in its social uses."[20] Through heralds, sermons, speeches, and communiqués, its producers fit this discourse into a hierarchical system presided over by the chief spy and the market inspector. These producers can be cliques, preachers, teachers, public administrators, and other functionaries, all of whom participate in the creation of a uniform discourse. While this language, in Bourdieu's analysis, "concurs with the demands of bureaucratic predictability and calculability," it functions through such "functionaries and clients" in the figures of preachers and pseudo-shaykhs who are part of an apparatus with its particular duties and assignments.[21] Yet this discourse can also operate on situations and people that it has already learned about and studied, as the encounter between the chief spy and the young Azharite Shaykh Sa'īd clearly shows (p. 232).

As for the Sufis, they remain an enigma. Thus the chief spy has to try different means to understand how they relate to each other, whether in communication or action. The historical focus of the narrative is so sharp that it draws attention to the religious groupings of the present day, such as the Brothers in Egypt and the Da'wah (mission) in Iraq, which have proved imperceptible to normal security methods. Official discourse tries to root itself firmly in a land and culture, and its goals are already established and fixed, regardless of who is head of state. The narrator therefore lets the Islamic dynamic work in its own subtle way, perhaps in secrecy, in order to provoke officials into monopolizing its entire means, reveal itself and suffer the consequences, especially in times of radical confrontation. Whenever a report has to take over some narrative space, the narrative steps outside chronology, but it returns to that logic in order to impose some coherence on a historical framework within a Mamluk period where space is numb, blindfolded, supine, and ostensibly available to actors. Time itself undergoes suspension, but within a dialectic of opposition and conflict, not only between the two official sources of effective power but also between those sources and other centers inside or outside the official domain. Even the Sufi source of power relations is held in suspense, between acceptance of rumors or claims to decency and sacrifice and open rejection of or opposition to the misuse of power.

Al-Ghīṭānī may well have the future era in mind. Soon after the 1967 defeat, any enthusiastic reception for a nationalist discourse which propaganda had managed to debase and empty of meaning vanished; the defeat itself had showed its hollowness and lack of substance. Instead of providing a critique that might point toward some kind of revisionist outlook, manipulative official discourse leveled the blame at the Soviet Union, and, by implication, the national left. The intelligence service began once again to crack down on the left. Meanwhile Islamists enjoyed the same period as one of revival, a process that reached its peak during the Sādāt era, leading to open conflict with Sādāt's peace accords with Israel and his economic open-door policy involving the introduction of a free-market economy.

Al-Ghīṭānī does not go into these details, and only engages with matters of a contemporaneous nature through implication and subtle suggestion. There are valid artistic reasons as to why the emphasis on state discourse is significantly spread throughout the narrative. Through interrogations, reports, heralds, announcements, correspondences, and addresses like the one submitted to the international conference on spying, this official discourse makes its Arab, non-Arab, and transnational concerns known. The same focus entails an opposite dynamic, one that develops and gradually pervades the whole social order. The Sufi discourse and its wished-for militancy as predicted in the narrative has no specific partisan attitude: it is against local corruption as much as it is against Ottomans as invaders, an attitude that bewilders the intelligence service and its functionaries. Conversely, the security office considers the option of siding immediately with the invaders to be completely logical and in complete conformity with its reasoning, in that, according to such logic, anyone who displaces the other is legitimate enough to rule. The author builds on historical records in this instance, as Zaynī Barakāt continued his inspectorship under the Ottomans. Thus, an Islamic discourse grows within a national one, that in itself being an approach which the founder of the Muslim Brotherhood, Ḥasan al-Bannā (d. 1949), made quite clear in his early lecture, Between Yesterday and Today.[22]

It is interesting to read the novel against the backdrop of some of these tracts in order to understand the formation of religious discourse and both its potency in times of confrontation and weakness in times of stability and ease. When Ḥasan al-Bannā wrote his tracts (the 1930s), it was an era of great international polarization. It forced intellectuals, whether secular or Islamist, to revisit various positions, compromises, attitudes, and ideological stands. Ḥasan al-Bannā felt the need to channel Shaykh Muḥammad 'Abdū's discourse in a new direction, not in line with Western ideologies, but more focused on creating an Islamic way that would not be tethered to the compromise which his shaykhs were compelled to accept as part of an endorsement of the establishment of a nation-state, something that had been fought for jointly by all social forces. It was a time when he aspired to put an end to the duplication of the European model as being unsuitable for the '*ummah* (Islamic nation). More significant to this discussion was his recognition of Egyptian nationalism as a legitimate struggle for independence. In other words, the joining of forces was still acceptable on the basis of this rapprochement between nationalism and Islamism. He was more critical of capitalism and its ideologies and of Marxism. Both positions would continue to inform Sayyid Quṭb's subsequent role in the ideological formation of the Muslim Brotherhood. It was in the same tract, however, that Ḥasan al-Bannā made it clear that there would be an Islamic '*ummah* project, with due recognition given to learning, education, and women's rights. Throughout he was less sympathetic to the habitual reliance on the ancestral past despite its presence in his justification for using and exploiting European science. He was clear, however, on issues that have a direct bearing on the organization of the Muslim Brotherhood and on the need for a degree of independence from the nation-state. By placing this emphasis on organization, appeal to the masses, and a possible rift with the nation-state and its apparatus, Ḥasan al-Bannā was setting the scene for an Islamic dynamic that would correspond with the facts on the ground. Even his urgent tone when asking the Muslim Brothers to take note of what was being communicated in the tract was not random. He was already aware that he was under surveillance, and in danger of imprisonment or assassination. He specifically noted such possibilities and implied even more. The nation-state and its intellectual elite were both depicted as an alien or antagonistic entity, opportunist or, at best insofar as the national bourgeoisie was concerned, of a different caliber and interest. A leader like Sayyid Quṭb was ready to go a step further and was later to be publicly executed by the nation-state. In fictional literature, this kind of historical background compels writers to make one of two choices: either to depict this kind of closed route for Islamists—assassination or execution, which would involve a mere duplication in writing of state action—or else to carve out a different path, not too far removed from the facts, which would derive its power from popular Islam and its representative spaces and symbolic sites, including the al-Azhar Mosque, with its history as a Fatimid establishment and the center of formal Islamic training in scholarship and Qur'ānic studies, and the shrine of al-Sayyidah Zainab, in the heart of ancient Cairo. These sites are able to accommodate all Islamic platforms, attitudes, rituals, interpretations, and their like, and can also serve as a site where the state apparatus can test its authority, gather information, and plan its propaganda and media wars. Especially when popular religion burgeons through Sufi orders, there is no written confrontation with the nation-state. In such a context censorship will require the use of narrative strategies so that more can be said through ellipsis and indirection. Omission thereby becomes addition, and the Islamic dynamic gains power through this very confrontation with the nation-state apparatus, before being compelled to change direction in order to challenge invasions, attacks, and their like. The Israeli War and other attacks like the 1956 Anglo-French-Israeli aggression may have been in the mind of a writer like al-Ghīṭānī who sees the present through the lenses of a past historical record, especially the Mamluk period during the Ottoman invasion. The Islamic dynamic derives its power from a confrontation with anti-Islamic discourse, with its acknowledged markers, frames of reference, and capacity to sustain a nation-state. It works in the same manner, but with additional power, as the discourse of the nation-state is bound to make use of aspects of the same Islamic referentiality so as to appeal to the masses and seek their approval. In a nexus of contamination, the competing Islamic discourse gains in urgency and immediacy, especially whenever the nation-state's secular rhetoric reveals its own weaknesses and empty rhetoric, as happened in 1967. The progress of the Islamic dimension had begun, and nationalist discourse lost the battle, along with many liberal formations and arguments that had made up the intellectual treasury of a national bourgeoisie that had held the leadership role for several decades.

ʿAbd al-Ḥakīm Qāsim's *Al-Mahdī*

Modeled on the Muslim Brotherhood leader Ḥasan al-Bannā (assassinated in 1947), Brother Sa'īd in 'Abd al-Ḥakīm Qāsim's novella *Al-Mahdī* (1977) may well represent the charismatic leadership which will have great potential in years to come. Brother Sa'īd's articles, writings, manuals, personal charisma, and organizational expertise make him the Brotherhood's model of leadership. This is the type of leader who is to replace traditional clergy among Sunni movements. It is not the same model for Shīʿī populations, which still need a clerically recognized leader, despite the fact that both Ḥasan Naṣrallah and the less charismatic or sharp-minded Muqtadā al-Ṣadr did not emerge from among the established hierarchy. Naṣrallah, as the successor to ʿAbbās al-Mūsawī, derives his legitimacy from his party as an antioccupation force. Lebanese Shīʿīs were willing to offer this legitimacy to such an excellent speaker, well-versed young scholar, and unrelenting fighter and political maneuverist. In Iraq Muqtadā al-Ṣadr has relied on his lineage, family name, and the political vacuum to rally disenfranchised youth behind him. Still, the model Qāsim proffers falls into the tradition of both Ḥasan al-Bannā and Sayyid Quṭb. The powerful youth organization is not a random happening, in that ever since the 1930s nationalist education had included this semimilitarization of youth as part of its program of physical fitness. The German experience was very much in the minds of educators, especially in those regions where education adopted this policy in the face of the growing challenge of Zionist terrorist groups in Palestine throughout the 1930s and 1940s. Qāsim defines this role on the ideological, organizational, and state-within-state levels. The ideological dimension focuses on debates that aim to confound contending religious positions. The argument that Brother Talʿat has with the Sufi, ʿAli Effendi, is a case in point. According to Talʿat, Ali's piety, veneration for saints, and pious discourse is an example of paganism. Talʿat's opinion is central to the Brotherhood's distrust of visitations, veneration for saints, and shrines. The Brotherhood upholds the fourteenth-century theologian Ibn Taymiyyah's line of attack on such practices, including visits to tombs and shrines, as being alien to Islam. His pronouncements were issued during a period of regression, when popular beliefs were the consequence of a sense of disappointment at the general condition of Muslim lands after the fall of Baghdad (1258) and the repeated loss of Jerusalem to the invading Mongols and Franks (as the "Crusaders" were termed in Arabic annals). But Ibn Taymiyyah's polemics had a topicality of their own which later reformists such as Muḥammad Ibn ʿAbd al-Wahhāb took literally in the course of launching their own fundamentalist discourse of Islamic reform.

In this novel Qāsim is well aware of the burgeoning Afghan nexus, and describes Brother Sa'īd as "having connections with the Islamic state of Pakistan" (p. 41) where, in collaboration with Saudi Arabia and the American Central Intelligence Agency, cells began to prepare so that the Afghan Taliban could fight against the Communist government and the presence of the Soviets. His other attributes serve as an index and agenda of the activities of the Brotherhood: he writes, edits a paper, makes speeches, moves briskly from one meeting to another (p. 13), supervises ceremonies and militaristic processions (p. 32), and meets state representatives where he can draw attention to his requests for help in the mission that is extending services to people. Processions, Qāsim intimates, are admired by the public (p. 32); so are the organizations or youth militias whose members are "all strong, slim, and good-looking, with powerful shoulders and necks, each with the mark of frequent prayer on his forehead and a Brotherhood Book in his hand" (p. 31). When looked at in their totality, these activities and rituals may well represent what Althusser terms otherwise as the ideological state apparatus. Though still in the preliminary stage of growth, this group has already manipulated public space, taken over this space from the weakened state, enforced its will on others, and used methods of containment that will prove intimidating to the shaky state apparatus. With the exception of Sufis, the public is thrilled by the organization and performance; in the process it loses the will to debate or challenge the intimidating pressure of the Brothers. They are able to replace the state's poor performance, its bureaucracy, estrangement from the public, and the selfishness of its figures. In the same narrative the mayor represents the nation-state. Secular-minded, he mocks Qur'ānic recitations, distrusts processions, and from the very start is suspicious of such carnival ceremonies as the so-called conversion of Master `Awadullah, the Copt umbrella maker. More often than not he is drunk, tired of responsibilities, and focused exclusively on his appetites, not least of which is his intemperate sexual longing for the young maid Fatima. And yet he can make very valid comments about this process of indoctrination and conversion, something that is no more than a mouse falling from "the rafters" (p. 26). "They will toy with him until the blood runs out of his nose," says the mayor, "or dress him up like a boy scout and march him bare-kneed through the town, shouting, 'Allahu akbar' " (p. 27). While Brother Talʿat, a member of the village Brotherhood leadership, considers the care offered to the Copt as being no more than kindness to the "People of the Book, intended to incline their hearts to Islam" (p. 26), the mayor comes to see the sequence of events in the procession as a trap or, in the opinion of the Sufi Shaykh Sayid al-Hasari, as an act of coercion.

`Ali the Sufi feels pangs of remorse for allowing the Brotherhood to take care of the Copt. His mentor, Shaykh Sayid, feels that the whole process is coercive; believing that the entire scene is nothing more than intimidation, inhuman, irreligious, and cruel. "This big commotion makes hearts heavy and blinds perception. No man can see any good in it at all" (p. 49), Shaykh Sayid al-Hasari murmurs, and then continues, "This spectacle denies the wisdom" of the Book, "and their vehemence has the savor of coercion" (p. 49). He goes on to explain what he means by coercion: "I see coercion when your brother greets you in a voice louder than is needed for you to hear him, so as to test your intentions toward him. I see it when someone invites a guest to shame him, in order to prevent him from refusing" (p. 49). Framing these views neatly within a power relational dialectic where action derives its potency from positionality and site, he adds, "I see it when a wrongdoer overdoes his apologies, to shame the man he has wronged out of showing his pain" (p. 49). Sufis, we learn, tried to hold their usual meeting "around a long, low, narrow table upon which some small lamps had been placed" (p. 48). They tried to recite their supplications solemnly despite the loudspeakers broadcasting "Brother Sa'īd's speech" (p. 48). The scene outside is viewed as nothing more than a noisy Day of Judgment. As Shaykh Sayid al-Hasari observes, "this looks like Resurrection Day," a spectacle that is supposed to take the place of evening prayers without an actual promise of love and sympathy (p. 48). The Sufi discourse that has been growing in narrative as a belated recognition of the need to speak up in more than ideological voice functions on more than one level. While its impact and efficacy is limited to its Sufi space, its symbolic presence provides competition to the formalized language of the brothers. On the other hand, Sufi simplicity and litany divest and liberate discourse from codifications and formalizations that are superimposed once by the state through education and by the brothers through the control of the street.

Sufi misgivings are founded on a concern with the nature of human piety: "God's servant finds his path to godliness through a Lord that he knows, with whom he is content, and whom he loves" (p. 50). To a limited degree Sufi discourse can operate as a corrective or balance to the resolute practices of the Brotherhood and its hold on the street, a sphere it has won from secular forces.

The young brother's advocacy of Brotherhood doctrines as opposed to those of the Sufis in particular should not be regarded lightly. In his influential piece "Ideology and Ideological State Apparatuses" (1970), Louis Althusser makes use of the term "ideology." State apparatus is as repressive in its formation as it is inclusive of the administration and its modes of implementation, like the army, police, courts, and prisons. In Qāsim's *Al-Mahdī* all these entities are almost absent, except for the mayor as administrator. What remains, however, is a void, and it is soon taken over by another power which is no less dominant and authoritarian, as Tal'at's responses to the Sufi `Ali clearly demonstrate. Indeed, the Brotherhood takes over the ideological base which, in Althusser's theorization, usually consists of religious components, education, family, organizations, media channels, and culture in general. Everything, from processions to scenes of conversion, is now under their control, and this newly institutionalized space incorporates the street, which is no longer seen as an independent subject.

The nongovernmental body becomes even more so, especially in the absence of a strong competing system. Talʿat is even ready to speak on behalf of God against Sufi piety and practice, whereas Brother Saʿid is so charismatic as to secure hegemony through his presence, charm, and eloquence. Through this combination of intimidation, confrontation, and charming and disarming eloquence, the public is implicated and interpellated, duly transformed into subjects who are in a state of total "subjection to the subject." This process is normally achieved through ideology, and both Talʿat and Saʿid make use of a mechanism that was once the monopoly of the ideological state apparatuses.[23] The process manages to illustrate the shift in power politics that occurred during the Sādāt era in Egypt with its crackdown on the left and Nāṣirītes.

During this period the Brotherhood was given a larger margin of freedom. It was able to use it to such an extent that it was capable of assassinating President Sādāt because of his signing of the Camp David accords with Israel. In such times the state was as dysfunctional as the mayor in the novella. Isolating himself so as to avoid being visited or asked to view the spectacle, he hears loudspeakers reverberating "dreadfully": "What did those people want? The man had converted to Islam. What did they want now? They were convulsing the whole town; it was a convulsion that he rejected, that drove him to silence; it denied and excluded all reason and wisdom; it was a pitiless scourge, this mass rush into the abyss" (p. 52). The interior monologue which is further accelerated by his drunkenness also signifies the paralysis of a state that has lost contact with its people. Other powers know the rules of the game and play by them, regardless of how much convulsion, instability, or fear they may cause. Indeed, this is their deliberate way of exercising power, not only to consolidate their emotive links to the masses, but also to secure their own leadership roles. Althusser's theory of incorporation whereby subjects accept their subjection by the subject resonates here. Hegemony, as described by Gramsci in his *Prison Notebooks*, can find no better illustration. The public is so excited and enthralled by the procession, spectacle, and general jubilation that nobody is aware of the dying person who is supposed to be the reason and excuse for all the demonstrations and religious fervor. The state is no less terrified than the mayor. "What inferno . . . what terrible plague, huge massacre or catastrophic earthquake is needed to make those people stop and look around them, to contemplate in silence what terror had wrought" (p. 60). Instead of attempting to intervene, the mayor "stood up, frightened, and looked out through the window blind" (p. 61). Rather than moving him to act, the Copt's "feverish face and froth-stained mouth" increases his sense of paralysis. The mayor is overwhelmed by fear of a similar spectacle, whereby he would be placed on the back of a donkey and paraded through the streets "with a loudspeaker shrieking out my shame" (p. 61). The very thought makes him both cry and guffaw (p. 61).

The three positions (the Brotherhood's full control, the Sufis as outsiders, and the state) provide a good summary of the political scene in the 1970s when streets were monopolized by the Brotherhood. In other Arab countries, nation-states were still forging a nationalist program which would soon collide with Islamic ideologies, leading to terrible wars and losses, like the Iraq-Iran War. Both sides proved to be losers. Nationalist discourse found itself entangled in contradictions, pitfalls, and failures because it had been appropriated by state politicians to fit into their agenda. Thus it was not unable to prevent the invasion of Kuwait, for example, nor could it later halt the participation of Arab states in the American-led coalition in 1991 under the banner of the UN. While participation in the wars prompted by the New World Order has stigmatized that order ever since and signaled its aggressive posture, the nation-state has been evolving as an antagonist who is viewed with suspicion and hatred.

Which Door to an Enclave? Najīb Maḥfūẓ's *al-Liṣṣ wa al-Kilāb: The Thief and the Dogs*

Published in Arabic in 1961, *The Thief and the Dogs* is more allegorical than might be initially indicated by its story of imprisonment, release, and police hunt.[24] Maḥfūẓ wrote it after some years of silence during which he felt the need to adjust to the new order following the Egyptian revolution of 1952, Egypt's valiant struggle against imperial aggression in 1956, and its subsequent leading role in third worldism and Arab nationalism. Yet this significant forward progress in world and Arab politics also weighed heavily on Egypt's national life. Many steps were taken to improve the economy, establish equality, enable the peasantry and the lower classes to achieve a better livelihood, and put an end to economic exploitation and forms of social oppression.[25] Like the pattern of many nation-states that were emerging from colonial rule, Egypt was soon aspiring to become a strong nation-state, but not in terms of institutionalized democracy. The quest was not a usual one, especially in light of 'Abd al-Nāṣir's valiant pan-Arabism—his vision of a unified Arab nation stretching from the Gulf to the ocean, as his slogans explicitly declare. On the relics of a colonial system the state set out to construct another model of "democratic centralization," involving no more than the banning of all political organizations and their fusion into the Arab Socialist Union, an entity presided over and led by the president. Some intellectuals may well have participated in the creation of this new political grouping. While there were certainly achievements in many fields, including culture, there was also an expanding bureaucracy that forcefully established itself as the center of power. All ideals of revolutionary thought were converted into hollow slogans, while political activists, Communists, and members of the Muslim Brotherhood began to suffer long terms of imprisonment, torture, and execution.

The Thief and the Dogs takes the form of a detective novel in order to cope with the causes for such disillusionment, the sense of betrayal, and the converse rise of the petit bourgeois bureaucrat as the opportunistic beneficiary in a corrupt state. Maḥfūẓ's focus is on the increasing isolation of the system, its estrangement from people, and its mechanical response to challenge. Although the disillusioned young protagonist, Sa'id Mahran, is blinded by anger and betrayal, there is still a common ground that links him to the populace and makes him a hero in their eyes. His mistakes have an allegorical significance. Maḥfūẓ's own moderate predisposition directs the course of the narrative on the basis of his innate distrust of violence as a solution to moral issues. Every act of violence is another trap leading to still further mistakes. The teacher and ideologue Ra'uf Ilwān has now become the primary beneficiary in an abstract space that allows bureaucracy to exercise its power and make gains on the ruins of petit bourgeois ideals during eras of social and political mobility.[26] The choice is not one that can be welcomed by the betrayed and disillusioned Sa'id Mahran, who regards his earlier initiation into an ideology of Robin Hood justice as an ongoing enterprise, justified and accelerated by betrayals from among his own family and friends. Unable to grasp the pragmatic side of life and angered by a whole corrupt system, his choice is suicidal. The little light that might be able to lead him out of this impasse comes from an unofficial spot: in this work, Sufism. Sufi orders fit into a popular paradigm, where there is a differential sphere free from total state monopoly. Through Sa'id Mahran's stream of consciousness, we have access to two powers with unequal bearing on a basically disenfranchised, dispossessed, underprivileged character: on the one hand, the revolutionary petit bourgeoisie with an infantile leftism that under the new social-and-political will soon turn into an opportunistic bureaucracy, and on the other, the Sufi order which remains unchanged and unconcerned with the outside world and its rewards or retributions. As Sa'id Mahran emerges from prison with an embittered sense of distrust, he takes infantilism to its extreme, through his notion of a Robin Hood self-legitimizing order, and faces further rejection from the world he believes in, represented by his daughter, Sana. Only Shaykh 'Ali al-Junaydi remains as he is, the same serene face and smiling eyes, unconcerned with Sa'id

Mahran's worldly complaints and disappointments which thereby emerge as merely selfish concerns occasioned by a compelling attachment to this world that is devoid of love for God. This is what Shaykh 'Ali al-Junaydi no doubt intends with his riddle-like responses. On his first visit to the shaykh, this is what Sa'id Mahran has to say:

"I thought that if God had granted you long life, I would find your door open."
"And the door of Heaven? How have you found that?"
"But there is nowhere on earth for me to go. And my own daughter has rejected me."
"How like you she is!"
"In what way, Master?"
"You seek a roof, not an answer." (pp. 165–66)

Maḥfūẓ's shaykhs at this stage of his writing career are not political activists. Their pronouncements veer away from a mundane abstract space already marred and corrupted by the intrigues and concerns of the nation-state bureaucracy and its newly moneyed classes, the very ones who will soon suffer fatigue and ennui. In *Al-Shahhādh* (*The Beggar*), the physician tells the wealthy lawyer 'Umar, "You've got a bourgeois disease" (p. 10), and continues, "You're a successful and wealthy man. You've virtually forgotten how to walk. You eat the best food, drink good wine, and have overburdened yourself with work to the point of exhaustion. . . . Anxiety about the future of your work and your functional situation has got the better of you" (p. 10).

The presence of Sufis in this narrative is nevertheless significant. Although Maḥfūẓ is never inclined himself toward active Sufism, the presence of Sufis serves to offset the limiting grip of bureaucracy and materialism, the two devastating aspects of the inexperienced nation-state. Even as late as 1982 in *Layālī alf Laylah*, his Sufi shaykh, 'Abdullah al-Balkhi, advises Sindbad to follow these steps if ever thinking of the devout path:

Know . . . that you will not attain the ranks of the devout until you pass through six obstacles. The first of these is that you should close the door of comfort and open that of hardship. The second is that you should close the door of renown and open that of insignificance. The third is that you should close the door of rest and open that of exertion. The fourth is that you should close the door of sleep and open that of wakefulness. The fifth is that you should close the door of riches and open that of poverty. The sixth is that you should close the door of hope and open the door of readiness for death.[27]

These exhortations echo the earlier statements and Sufi intimations that Shaykh 'Alī al-Junaydī gives to Sa'id Mahran in *The Thief and the Dogs*. The latter has left the prison, but he still carries it inside him; not only in the physical sense, which has kept him away from contact with society for years, but also as the prison of the self which is still burdened by a sense of betrayal and a consequent desire for revenge. Sa'id Mahran's quest is not merely a search for refuge; it is rather a search to justify difference and anger. Hence Shaykh 'Alī al-Junaydī repeats that Sa'id is not in search of salvation. Even the love that the prostitute Nur offers is wasted, since he is incapable of understanding and cherishing such affection as a way of balancing his own emotional aridity. It is only at the end of the road that Sa'id Mahran has come to recognize Nur's love. At this final stage when redemption sounds possible, he comes to see the end of the road. He is hunted down by police dogs and the state, both of which are brought to bear on him by his teacher, the ideologue Ra'uf 'Ilwān. Now 'Ilwān is no longer the ideologue, but has become a beneficiary of a system, "the way of the world" (p. 176), as he calls it.

Shaykh 'Ali al-Junaydi knows that Sa'id Mahran is still residing in the prison of the self, which now harbors a bitter sense of betrayal and revenge: "You seek the walls, not the heart," he says, and then adds, "You have not come from jail" (p. 164). It is because of this jail that Sa'id Mahran turns into an arid land unable to retain love, even for his daughter, whose rejection of him repeats his own rejectionist mode: "How like you she is!" (p. 165). In Maḥfūẓ's universe Mahran has not found the door of heaven (p. 165); such a self will always remain shut up in its prison: "You seek a roof, not an answer" (p. 166). The doors to salvation that Maḥfūẓ opens here are as limited as the ones that were available in Egypt at the time (the 1960s). The door of the old ideologue and present-day opportunist no longer welcomes revolutionary ideals. Now family structure also partakes of the same malaise and ends up in disarray under the pressures of economic need and social demands, just like the nation-state itself. The door of heaven is beyond the reach of the remnants of the disciples of the *nahḍah*. Maḥfūẓ's novel as basically ironic demonstrates Mahran's search for meaning, a soul that strives to find its essence through a series of tests that are more interior than their exterior manifestations. The Sufi shaykh draws his attention to this search which he has not fathomed or fulfilled yet. Hence, this novel by Maḥfūẓ speaks for a generation that has put its trust wrongly in a world outside itself, a world of claims, promises, and ideas, a world that is bereft of poetry. The novel in this sense fits in what Georg Lukács says: "The novel is the epic of a world that has been abandoned by God."[28]

Maḥfūẓ's Sufis make no commitments beyond those common to their practice. When Sa'id Mahran asks for refuge in the house, the Shaykh obliquely denies ownership of any place or property. The meaning of a "house" refers to God's property and ownership of all: "The Owner of the house welcomes you . . . as He welcomes every creature and everything" (p. 167). There is no possibility of redemption unless Saʿid goes back to a celestial moment in childhood when it was possible for him to be on the same Sufi path as his father. The shaykh gives him a chance to start all over, to purge his imprisoned self from the mundane, and set out on a different path: "Take a copy of the Qur'ān and read" (p. 167), and then, "Wash yourself now and read" (p. 168). Repeated three times soon after, the "wash and read" phrase is the pivotal narrative catalyst, the dividing line between the old self, moving blindly from one prison to another, and the new one that finds itself at a crossroads. To make the initiation anew, he is asked again: "Wash and read the verses: 'Say to them: If you love God, then follow me and God will love you' and 'I have chosen thee for Myself' " (p. 168). This is the path to love; but it can also blend into human love. Sa'id Mahran cannot discern the difference between heavenly love and human passion. Every mention of love degenerates into associations of defeat, betrayal, and loss. To the shaykh, no love will make its way to Sa'id Mahran's heart unless he embarks on a renunciation of the ego; for it is only then that forgetfulness of the past can take over and the Sufi path commence; only then that he can resume his father's path, for, as the shaykh had observed to Sa'id Mahran's father, his heart as a child "is as spotless as yours" (p. 230).

The shaykh is able to discern the sheer impossibility of Sa'id Mahran's recovery and redemption and the reality of his lingering amid walls of pride in a world which is no less given to vanity. Afraid of being captured at the shaykh's house, Saʿid asks for protection: "Please protect me" (p. 268). The shaykh is aware that Saʿid is too estranged from the Sufi path to understand that trust in God annihilates every other concern; as the shaykh intimates: "Trusting God means entrusting one's lodging to God alone" (p. 268).

Maḥfūẓ's Sufis do not offer active commitment to life; at this stage in his career their narrative role is primarily to offset the dealings of bureaucracy. The shaykhs have no connection with institutionalized religion, which, to them, signifies another prison with walls and fortifications. The author depicts his Sufis as the only available example that can reveal the negativity of the other side: the nation-state, its bureaucracy, and the increasingly corrupt society. Maḥfūẓ is as yet unconcerned with the role of the masses, a topic that belongs in another agenda such as the one which the Muslim Brotherhood upholds and propagates among the underprivileged, professionals, workers, peasants, and students. These groups will later appear in the Epic of the Riff-Raff (*Al-Ḥarāfish*), but in the 1960s the author is focusing on a polarized scene, where a rebel is unable to channel his anger into an organized response. The search for Islam has not yet commenced, and the dialogue with the self has not initiated the path toward salvation which other narratives explore, as is argued in the next chapter.

Notes

1. Jamāl al-Ghīṭanī, *Al-Zaynī Barakāt* (Damascus: Ministry of Culture, 1974); English translation, *Zaynī Barakāt*, trans. Farouk Abdel Wahab Mustafa (1988; Cairo: American University in Cairo Press, 2004).

2. Frantz, Fanon, *The Wretched of the Earth* (New York: Grove Press, 1963), 169.

3. As cited in Andrew Merrifield, "Place and Space: A Lefebvrian Reconciliation," *Transactions of the Institute of British Geographers* N. S. 18:4 (1993), 516–31, at 524.

4. See Henri Lefebvre, *The Production of Space* (Oxford: Basil Blackwell, 1991), 366; see also Merrifield, "Place and Space," 526.

5. For a summary of this career, see Carl F. Petry, *Protectors or Praetorians? The Last Mamluk Sultans and Egypt's Waning as a Great Power* (Albany: State University of New York Press, 1994), 144–47, at 145.

6. See Lefebvre, *The Production of Space*, 23.

7. On this binary in European thought, the reader can consult the writings of Taylor, Warner, and Gourgourise.

8. As a spectrum of different responses to tradition, reform, Islam, and Europe, see John J. Donohue and John L. Esposito, eds., *Islam in Transition: Muslim Perspectives* (New York: Oxford University Press, 1982).

9. Pierre Bourdieu, *Language and Symbolic Power* (Cambridge, MA: Harvard University Press, 1991), 45.

10. Lefebvre, *The Production of Space*, 23.

11. Lefebvre, *The Production of Space*, 51.

12. Lefebvre, *The Production of Space*, 52.

13. See Petry's summary of Ibn Iyās's account of Zaynī, his canniness, availability, cruelty, ingenuity, and caution, *Protectors or Praetorians?*, 145–47.

14. Lefebvre, *The Production of Space*, 52.

15. Lefebvre, *The Production of Space*, 55.

16. See S. A. Morrison, "Arab Nationalism and Islam," *Middle East Journal* 2 (1948), 147–59; John S. Badeau, "A Role in Search of a Hero: A Brief Study of the Egyptian Revolution," *Middle East Journal* 10 (1955), 373–84; and Gamal Abdel Nasser, "The Egyptian Revolution," *Foreign Affairs* 33 (January 1955), 199–211.

17. See Samaḥ Idrīs, Al-Muthaqqaf al-ʿArabī wa-al-ṣulṭān: baḥth fiī riwāyāt al-tajribah al-Nāṣiriyah (Bayrūt: DĀr al-Ādāb, 1992).

18. See Hayden White, "The Value of Narrativity in the Representation of Reality," *Critical Inquiry* 7:1 (1980), 5–27, at 8.

19. For more on space, see Lefebvre, *The Production of Space*, 34, 55.

20. See Bourdieu, *Language and Symbolic Power*, 45.

21. Bourdieu, *Language and Symbolic Power*, 48.

22. See Ḥasan al-Bannā, *Five Tracts of Hasan al-Banna (1906–1949)*, trans. Charles Wendell (Berkeley: University of California Press), 29–30.

23. For Louis Althusser, see "Ideology and Ideological State Apparatuses," extract in *A Critical and Cultural Theory Reader*, eds. Antony Easthope and Kate McGowan (Toronto: University of Toronto Press, 2002), 50–58.

24. Najīb Maḥfūẓ, *al-Liṣṣ wa al-Kilāb.* English translation: *The Thief and the Dogs*, New York: Anchor, 2000.

25. Badeau, "A Role in Search of a Hero," 381–83.

26. On the application of the term "abstract space," see Lefebvre, *The Production of Space*, 48–51. On the adaptation and appropriation by the petit bourgeoisie of higher formal language and practices, see Bourdieu, *Language and Symbolic Power*, 83–85.

27. Najīb Maḥfūẓ, *Arabian Nights and Days*, trans. Denys Johnson-Davies (New York: Anchor 1995), 219.

28. Georg Lukács, *The Theory of the Novel* (London: Merlin Press, 1978), 88.

CHAPTER SIX

The Search for Islam

Despite the temporary resurgence of Islamic topics in writings of the 1930s, there is no serious engagement with Islam outside the imperatives and demands of modernity and economic transformation. On the other hand, the interest in autobiography, like Ṭāhā Ḥusayn's *Al-Ayyām* (1929; *Days*) is not totally divorced from the impact of Goethe's *Werther*, the translation of which by al-Zayyāt appeared in Arabic in 1920, along with an introduction by Ṭāhā Ḥusayn. The search for Islam has not died, but it has proceeded down a thorny path of binary choices, all centered on the paradigmatic juxtaposition of modernity and tradition. Tawfīq al-Ḥakīm's *Bird of the East*, to give just one example, cannot be viewed outside this paradigm; even the protagonist's veneration for the lady saint is no more than a justification of his cultural dependency. French culture takes over the narrative space and shows him as a culturally destitute dilettante with no anchor or faith other than some childhood veneration for the Prophet's granddaughter, whose gradual disappearance from his memory is considered a reason for his worldly failures in love. The Egyptian writer Salwā Bakr tries to reach this same collective memory in her novella *Maqām 'Aṭiyyah* (*The Shrine of Atia*). The protagonist is a journalist who is about to publish a full story of the shrine before she is forced to disappear. Her husband, the archaeologist ʿAli Faheem, is much keener on the kind of facts that can shatter myths and beliefs and reveal those institutions and people who manipulate the whole subject of this narrative, the shrine, along with all the rumors and superstitions. His search is not a search for Islam, but for the truth behind popular faith, its presence and manipulation by different powers; it is thus connected with an intellectual effort aimed at coming to terms with the popular understanding of Islam and the consequent estrangement from the nation-state. It is only in Najīb Maḥfūẓ's *The Journey of Ibn Faṭṭouma* (*Riḥlat Ibn Fattūmah*, 1983)[1] that we find an allegorical search for Islam as a system.

Among institutions and states Islam is receding, but it remains alive among people and jurists who argue against countereffort to fundamentalize it. This chapter offers a reading of these narratives along lines of discussion which argue that Arab intellectuals have yet to come up with a satisfactory narrative quest beyond the dichotomous patterning of modernity and tradition, or the people and nation-state apparatus.

Tawfīq al-Ḥakīm's *Bird of the East* and the Door to Faith

Tawfīq al-Ḥakīm's *'Uṣfūr min al-Sharq* (*A Bird of the East*)[2] can be compared to a number of novels that appeared around its date of publication in Arabic (1937). The Iraqi Dhū al-Nūn Ayyūb's *Duktūr Ibrāhīm* appeared in 1936 and was published in full in 1938, whereas Yaḥyā Ḥaqqī's short stories were already popular before the appearance of his novel, *The Lamp of Umm Hāshim* (1944). While there was a lingering distrust of institutionalized and organized religion and the clergy, there was also in the 1930s a noticeable attention to Islamic topics that coincided with the rise of the Muslim Brotherhood,[3] and also with the notorious British management of sectarianism and sectarian divides that were soon to be lumped together within the framework of worldwide ideological and confrontational conflicts. People were more concerned with life, personal salvation, and a religious identity that could offer another place of refuge that was otherwise unavailable in a mundane reality of poverty, depression, and death. The three attitudes noticeable in Arabic literature at the time were: first, a distrust of traditional religious ideas and the clergy; second, an alternative search for ancient non-Islamic roots; and finally, a wider resort to popular religion with all its concrete representational spaces in shrines, tombs, and visitations. At a later period, especially in the 1960s, in conjunction with an increasing disappointment at the nation-state, the door to Sufism seemed the most welcome access to heaven, affording the devotee enough release to allow the soul to be somewhat free from the shackles of bureaucracy with all its obligatory demands.

This was not the case with the door for al-Ḥakīm's Muḥsin as represented in the 1930s. In times of disappointment and emotional setback, his patron, Imam 'Alī's daughter, the granddaughter of the Prophet Muḥammad, Lady Zainab, comes back to his mind, filling it with a sense of comfort, serenity, and certitude:

> One day as he was eating his meager lunch with at least spiritual satisfaction and with a satisfied smile on his face, the dark recesses of his soul were suddenly illuminated as he remembered his boyish happiness when he used to sit daily near the mausoleum of the Lady Zainab with his book, eating black sprouts. (p. 135)

Recollection here is working as both a catalyst for his present resignation to the vicissitudes of fortune and love, and an endorsement of a modest lifestyle that befits his status as a student or dilettante with Bohemian aspirations. In this trajectory between past and present, food is no ordinary matter. The "meager lunch" and the black bean sprouts represent a symbolic shift away from the fashionable restaurants where he has to go to accommodate and nurture a love affair with Suzy Dupont (p. 61). It is also symbolic in another sense: the associations of the meager lunch and sprouts are symbols of a sense of ease and satisfaction that he feels in Cairo, and especially in the district around the shrine of his patron, since it does not confront him with serious obstacles. It is far different at the fashionable restaurants, where he may come across Monsieur Silvain and Monsieur de Féraudy (p. 110), not to mention Suzy's friend Henri. Henri's presence turns everything upside down, for it is clear to Muḥsin, al-Ḥakīm's alter ego, that he—Muḥsin—is only there in a purely temporary role, an alternative prop as provider for Suzy's emotional needs until things resume their normal pace and rhythm between her and her lover (pp. 110–13). Within the body of a text that builds on concretized detail to give expression to changing states of feeling, these connotations of food go even further. The meager meal brings him closer to exiles, workers, and the rest who eke out a living in modest lodgings. Suzy takes him to a hotel and also shows him her working environment at the cinema; her daily routine thus becomes his—her ticket window, the cinema, the restaurant, and the hotel. Moreover, his adherence to this Suzy trajectory brings more than ordinary fulfillment; the entire brief episode brings him the greatest possible bliss. It is so paradisiacal that it fills his life with secular intimations of love, rejoicing, singing, and an endless store of wit, anecdote, love poetry, and a broad Western referentiality that confirms itself through a Greek heritage that aligns him with a vigorously Eurocentric cultural tradition (p. 95). If the Persian poet Omar al-Khayyam is mentioned, it is only to compensate for disappointment and desolation. To be deprived of Suzy means a loss of heaven: "She had given him the keys to heaven on earth. She had offered him ambrosia to taste and had placed her lips beside his on the brim of that crystal cup filled with the water of some earthly Kawthar!" (p. 118). The Islamic reference to heavenly water lapses into an earthly one where Islam recedes into the background. In other words, the paradisiacal water is forsaken in an unequal exchange, one in which he, the supplicant, offers a gift which is not entirely his to offer. It is conferred on an earthly subject who is simultaneously transfigured into a heavenly presence deserving his supplication: "She was staying in that night . . . , but how could he get to her when her door was closed, and no prayer or offering would penetrate or open it" (p. 119). The analogy grows into a larger trope to accommodate this transaction, for, in his frustration and loneliness, he compares her to heavenly bodies:

> Muhsin looked out at the sky he could see through the window of this room and reflected that, distant as the galaxies were, he could at least see them and even speak to them. Whereas she who was only a few feet away from him was further away than the stars. (p. 119)

The love affair is a culmination of a series of reorientations that redirect him toward a Eurocentric tradition, produced and predicated on his own otherness, a tradition that has already claimed its compelling hold on his mind and practice. As part of his French apprenticeship, "he had read a hundred works, from the ancient Greeks to Voltaire. He had reviewed the disordered events of history, ranging from the crises of the last century to the post-war *coups d'état*" (p. 89). The schizophrenic split experienced by the early Arab intellectual visitors to Europe in their navigation between a meager knowledge and grounding in their own culture on the one hand and a compelling European presence on the other makes such choices difficult. As decisions are taken under the strains of duress and bewilderment, each choice has a catastrophic aspect. The split builds on an either-or dichotomy, a compelling sense of lack, and a depressing mood of antagonism toward one's family, society, and history. Years after experiencing this very same dilemma, the Egyptian writer Yaḥyā Ḥaqqī recognized the need to be well engaged with one's own culture and not to belittle it out of negligence. Criticizing al-Ḥakīm, he reminisces:

> It is foolish to attempt to write off one's part, one's heritage, in a blind attempt to imitate the West, for this course of action can, in the long run, lead nowhere. In Egypt there used to be people who believed that heritage was something to which lip-service should be paid, and that heritage was only for museums. Tawfiq El-Hakim [sic]once explained his play *People of the Cave* to me in such terms, insisting that we did not owe a living to our heritage. Instead, he said, we should kiss its hand, and lead it firmly back to the place from whence it came.[4]

By universalizing his own love experience and subsequent preference for Europe, the Arab intellectual tries to disclaim responsibility, ending, in

Sartrean terms, in bad faith. Through a disengagement from one's self and the availability of free choice, the *nahḍah* intellectual holds others and circumstances responsible for whatever he enjoys or suffers. "This was a fever which swept through every head, and his was no different from all the others around him" (p. 89). Even Muḥsin's own discourse partakes of a daily French discourse of food and drink. "One bubble among many filled with thoughts and events and popping up as though from a saucepan full of boiling wine" (p. 89). Such a total reorientation is bound to displace the long-claimed beliefs of boyhood. The faith which the author tries to recover in the very act of the book's dedication, "To my patron saint Sayyidah Zainab" (p. 1), has long since gone: "In his present life Muḥsin simply had no place for the saintly Lady in her beautiful white robe" (p. 89), not because he is reluctant to do so, but because he is unable to retain that faith. "His soul had dried up and disappeared just like a planet disappearing under the white-hot heat of the sun" (p. 89). All references in this novel to spheres and planets assume this earthly aspect as they displace an older treasury of pleasant faith, undisturbed by the "frightening fact" to which the Russian émigré Ivan's talk awakens him. Throughout these years, "He had not had a single warm thought about the Lady Zainab" (p. 88). While her presence in his mind connotes serenity and communal life, her departure signals an unbearable sterility.

> [I]f Muhsin had ever felt for an instant that he was absolutely alone, that heaven did not exist, or that it was a desolate and sterile place devoid of the sublime things with whose lives his was connected, he couldn't have endured life for a single day, even if he could have had the whole earth to himself forever, but also had to be alone. (p. 88)

Al-Ḥakīm's faith is limited to this popular tradition rooted in Egyptian culture since Fatimid times. In the novel, the narrative voice is aware of a whole popular faith system with its representational and symbolic icons, shrines, and practices. It blends with a Sufi tradition of striving and consequent spontaneous entry into heaven's gateways. As is the case in Maḥfūẓ's *The Thief and the Dogs* (1961), al-Junaidī's door is always open and the shaykh is always awake, both being qualities of the Divine presence. Al-Ḥakīm builds his recollection of and supplication to Lady Zainab on a different scale of reciprocity. Maḥfūẓ's shaykh answers Mahran in terms that tend to untie the restraining cords of selfishness, arrogance, and anger that work as shackles on Mahran's soul, ensuring thereby his imprisonment inside the walls of life. In al-Ḥakīm's case, his alter ego, Muḥsin, measures success and failure in terms of divine acceptance or rejection. Muḥsin is ready to criticize the self, repent, or even change course, since each fault implies the Lady's disapproval and abandonment of him. "Muḥsin always placed heavy responsibilities on her. If he took a false step, his patron saint would be the one who had abandoned him" (p. 88). For an intellectual who has the potential to become closely involved in French cultural life, this kind of belief may seem unjustifiable to a non-Arab or non-Egyptian reader from the same generation. But the traditional faith is always there, even among ardent Marxists. Although they may try to explain it as an emotive link with the masses, its virtual presence as a cultural force may not be so noticeable. This is no hoary tradition or ancient affiliation that goes against the spirit of the age, but something with a strong historical background, identifying the speaker with Islam in its spiritual side, the nonorthodox (formal Sunni) orientation. The speaker is aligned with the victimized family of the Prophet, its ordeals and suffering as a result of the ascendancy of traditional Arab tribal values (vs. principles of Islamic non-Arab solidarity) soon after the death of the fourth caliph, ʿAlī (d. January 24, 661). But this type of identification process could not continue for long in Arab narrative traditions, especially under the impact of secular ideologies or even the rise of the Muslim Brotherhood. Its presence in al-Ḥakīm's *Bird*, however, signifies the unease which early Arab *nahḍah* intellectuals felt and experienced regarding the application of Islam and the simultaneous adherence to European modes of life. Thus his conduct is based on hesitation and latent fear rather than firm belief. Arab intellectuals, whose influence on native readership is powerful, also implanted the seeds of irresolution in the developing Arab intelligentsia. Thus, like Muḥsin, they perhaps end up asking for her intercessions: "whenever he placed his hopes in something, he always turned humbly to her so that she might stand at his side and combine her profoundly reverent voice with his in supplication to God" (p. 88).

In Muḥsin's life his orientation in belief is no casual matter. But, instead of letting the reader come across it through a number of narrative details, the author makes us read Muḥsin's own survey of this grounding that stays with him despite subsequent fluctuations as a result of the encroachment of different cultures and ideas, and his unresolved willingness to ignore this Muslim saint and her early impact on his mind (p. 88). His relationship with the Muslim saint is not as clear-cut and smooth as his uneasy recollections prompted by the Russian exile's critique of secular ideologies might initially suggest. There is clearly a divided self that is trapped in a neurotic nexus of likes and dislikes that are equally a reflection of a scrambled agenda and confused positions. Is it true that Muḥsin is sincerely committed to his popular faith? If he is, then why is he so forgetful when entangled in a love affair? Does he feel cheated or betrayed? After this failure, why does he decide to move to the building where the Russian exile lives? Does the Russian exile stand for an inevitable refuge, of the same kind as the Lady Zainab's shrine once was for him? Is the new location simply another place of exile?

In an extended passage Muḥsin sums up his life and career trajectory as follows: "The Lady Zainab mosque was the place where he spent the day when he was in school" (p. 88). Furthermore, "Muḥsin used to imagine that Lady Zainab personally turned the pages of his school books, that she instilled forbearance in him or strengthened his will as the case might be, and that she dried the tears of this first love with her own pure delicate fingertips" (p. 88). For this reason, there is no sense of loneliness or vulnerability, for he is "strong with the strength of a man who believes that he has a friendly advisor in heaven" (p. 88). In terms of the role of education in *nahḍah*-period writings in general, it needs to be borne in mind that the teacher-instructor-patron is the symbolic figure for knowledge and trust. Although some narratives are critical of the early *madrasah* teaching, the veneration shown to education falls within a larger Islamic context of respect and appreciation for knowledge. When collapsing the saint and educator or advisor into a single entity, the protagonist subscribes to a tradition that usually associates education with early schooling in the mosque or, after the twelfth century, in separate schools and centers which could be either public or private. This should not deter us, however, from reading al-Ḥakīm's protagonist and his dilemma as representative of a serious crisis, one that involves a cultural shock only because of the Ottoman legacy of coercion and exploitation, and a concomitant societal political degeneration resulting from devastating wars and invasions. Self-blame emerges as a distinctive aspect of these narrative encounters, which reveal a rupture that cannot be viewed in isolation from colonialism and the ways in which it debases a native culture and valorizes a metropolitan one. Self-blame invokes scars and wounds rather than any rigorous engagement with one's responsibility. In the protagonist's meditations, his mistakes or setbacks are seen as indications of the saint's annoyance with him. She is as intact and steadfast as a divine power and yet his own life is pictured as one of a whole series of ups and downs that can only achieve success by measuring up to the standards of the saint. Since he is vulnerable to emotional setbacks, he has to reassess his life: "he had surely forgotten his heavenly protector. . . . Had he felt her hand on his shoulder, Suzy would not have frightened him into taking such halting steps" (p. 89).

Muḥsin's reclamation of his lost faith seems more like a narrative contrivance, a way of compensating for an emotional lack. The woman saint, as the divine and holy representation, is summoned to counterbalance the secular Suzy Dupont and, ultimately, to outweigh the latter's shake-up of his life. In allegorical terms, the saint is his own local culture standing in opposition to

Suzy as the trope for Europe. His otherness remains the most distinguishable aspect of his stay in Paris despite his simulation of Bohemian artists and Parisian dilettantes. On the other hand, the saint is recalled to remedy the situation in which he finds himself driven by Ivan's incisive criticism of materialism (pp. 68–69, 88). This strong critique also caters to Muḥsin's predisposition to romanticized love, with all its secrecy, courtesy, and refinement. No wonder Muḥsin is appalled by the sight of people kissing each other in the street: "A young Parisian couple was embracing behind him. They were openly kissing each other in the Parisian way, oblivious to anyone who might be watching" (p. 41). While the narrative has already justified the couple's behavior as a "Parisian way," Muḥsin is "shocked to see emotions paraded in the streets and on the boulevards. He did not approve of vulgar exhibition of the soul's most noble treasures, which ought to be jealously preserved in the heart like pearls in a jewel-box" (pp. 41–42).

Sensitivity to delicate feelings may attest to the Andalusian scholar Ibn Ḥazīm's conditions for true love; secrecy is viewed as another term for guarding not only one's intimate passion, but also the integrity of the woman with whom one is in love. But the whole attitude also reveals an earlier spiritual love for the saint who is occasionally represented in terms of grandeur and splendor; her idealized image is the one that in a comparative framework is able to reveal the mundane nature of his experiences. Women are a commodity in the view of upholders of institutionalized religion, such as the lecherous cleric and the "foppish old shaykh with his rich robe, his henna-reddened hair, and the made-up eyes that fastened on the offering box as well as on the expensive rugs and great chandeliers inside the mosque [shrine]" (p. 135). These are figures of whom the protagonist makes fun, but his own saint demands a purity of soul and thought which he applies to his own ideas about human love.

In the narrative, the line of demarcation between ascetic sainthood and an institutionalization of splendor and wealth becomes more conspicuous when Suzy Dupont is no longer available to excite his interest in fashionable restaurants. Hence he asks: "Why do people think God's house needs to be furnished with Persian rugs? And that the Lady Zainab needs offerings, chandeliers and candles—as though she could not sleep in the dark?" (p. 136). Such questions are only possible now, in Paris, after an unrequited love affair. At this sequential narrative turn the splendor of the church is touched on, something he has never criticized before. "And in the church," he asks, "why that silver censor, the symbols, and the signs—for what?" (p. 136). "With the passage of time," he concludes, "people forget the original and essential and merely remember the secondary and superficial," then continues, "In both religion and art sincerity requires a reduction to bare essentials" (p. 136). Such levels of discrimination and differentiation enable him to regain faith in his early apprenticeship and overcome his prior disappointment. His religion becomes broad enough to accommodate music and thus to find an antidote for his painful experience: "Yes! With some assistance from music he would be able to overcome his continuing withdrawal from that earthly love that had so rubbed his nose in the mud" (p. 137).

The key words regarding this changed state of mind are music, earthly love, and humiliation, something that he now phrases as the passion that "rubbed his nose in the mud." These words can be read as central to his idea of faith as affiliation, a disposition that gains strength in time and in accordance with the intimacy involved in early apprenticeship. There is an atavistic aspect to these feelings: his tendency to sit waiting in the café in front of the Odeon cinema, facing the ticket collector, is exactly like his uncle Selim when he is waiting for the woman with whom he is in love. Music operates in a manner similar to the affection that he feels for the Lady Saint. Such lofty attachment is able to dislodge any other Parisian fashion. It is only humiliation that drives him to music and provokes his return to an artistic disposition, one that is in line with an early association between great pain and great art and in tune with de Musset's sentence on the pedestal of his statue where there is the equation between pain and art. "Even here they know that!" he exclaims (p. 4). As I have argued in *Arabic Poetry: Trajectories of Modernity and Tradition*,[5] this exchange with the dead poet, along with all its intercultural potential, should not be overlooked. It introduces him to the Parisian experience, initiates his acculturation, and prepares him for even more painful occasions. This exchange does not rely on dichotomous poles, but it does recognize a geographical separation that will gradually assume the dimensions of an ideological estrangement due to colonial and imperial incursions. At first we hear him say: "After all East and West are really only two sides of a single coin that in itself is whole" (p. 168), but soon afterward he comes to recognize a "civilizational" rift which he vaguely addresses every now and then but nevertheless critiques in his conclusive remarks as one of separation: "If these two civilizations could once be united into such a total civilization, man would see the dawn of true peace" (p. 168).

While he denies the existence of a spiritual East, at least as imagined by his departing friend Ivan, the protagonist's faith in the saint evolves as no more than a trope for much-needed serenity, affection, certainty, and assurance. Otherwise, the East as he sees it is no longer the same: "Eastern heroes have died even in Eastern hearts" (p. 167). Moreover, "Asceticism in the east is also gone" (p. 166), while the clergy are as materialistically involved in life as any others: "Today men of religion there are also interested in buying cars, getting raises in pay, and reddening their cheeks with high living" (p. 166). But rather than a critique of religion as faith, these final summations provide a scathing criticism of modernity as an unrestrained and indiscriminating application of European ways. "In the East today, even the fine and beautiful clothes that were worn for centuries have given way to a curious mixture of European clothes that makes one laugh" (p. 166); "Public primary schools, the right to vote, Parliament, and all other European ideas have become firm principles in today's East" (p. 166); "Easterners hold to these ideas as though they were basic religious principles. It would be easy to convince an Easterner that his religion was corrupt, but it wouldn't be easy to convince him that heavy industry was a devilish scheme leading humanity to ruin" (p. 166); in conclusion, "it would be easy to downgrade the message of the Prophets, but impossible to do the same to the message of modern material power" (p. 167).

All these formulations attest to the author's disillusioned vision of modernity, especially its materialistic manifestations and impact on traditional societies. His Islam is instead a diluted faith of mixed "Prophets" whose messages of love converge in an epitomic shrine in Cairo that stands for his symbolic need for certitude and comfort. This symbolic space, with its sublimity and grandeur, retains traditional ways of life and thereby counterbalances the advent of industrial change. The overall picture that it presents runs counter to organized Islam, the practices of schools of law, and definitely against the obligatory discourse of the Muslim Brotherhood. It is perhaps more in tune with the popular practice of religion that we associate broadly with Sufism as it has been made available to the mass audience during both the precolonial and colonial periods.

However, the narrative has to remain open-ended, since the author and his alter ego are not indoctrinated in religious thought. They are more concerned with a two-sided Europe, the cultural and imperial. The cultural can be approached and cherished, but the materialistic aspect is to be shunned or criticized, while the imperial is to be denounced outright. Pervading the cultural trajectory is a romantic ideal that is as enchanting as Suzy's kiss which transforms him into a happy soul (p. 102). The romantically idealized woman is like any other, but for the dilettante's eye that elevates her to a level of divinity that demands to be worshipped and cherished. In order for his narrative to come full circle—from its threshold at de Musset's statue, where agony and art merge and interact, to his disenchanted vision after the failure of love—the author and his protagonist end up with still more questions and uncertainties that only underscore the absence of belief and the need for a continuing search for Islam. The whole discourse remains rife with uncertainties and search with no obvious understanding of the social and political requirements for improvement as befitting postindependence states. Language, like the formal and official discourse which these narratives help forge, lacks depth and sounds pragmatically geared toward mundane preoccupations. The inner depth of the society is put aside, and with it a legacy of cultural richness. The opening dedication is a virtual act of recognition, not an initiation in faith.

The Shrine of 'Atia: A Novella by Salwā Bakr

The title of *Maqām 'Aṭiyyah* (1992; *The Shrine of 'Atia: A Novella*) by the Egyptian woman Salwā Bakr (b. 1949) plays on the word *'aṭiyyah* or gift,[6] and when connected to *maqām* or shrine as in the title, the meaning of the word takes on a mystic connotation, suggesting another quest for Islam that takes shape in a narrative trope of archaeological debate and excavation activity, deterred or hindered by a number of forces representing the nation-state: smugglers of relics and traditional clergy. Thus the word 'Aṭiyyah, which is the proper name of the lady whose shrine becomes a contested space, no longer retains any secular function, as the meaning of the word indicates. Instead it is transposed to the sacred domain where the woman saint grows in stature and repute amid reports, gossip, rumors, and discussions that focus on her, and not on the reasons behind the controversy. Through the story of the lady, the reader is led along the Sufi path or *ṭarīqah*, which builds on the repetition of liturgical Qur'ānic incantations or remembrance of God. This path initiates its followers into both remembrance and repentance; it is only through the latter that the self can pass through a number of *maqāmāt* (stations) that involve self-denial, mortification of mundane desires, and a constant aspiration toward the Beloved One. That final state is only achievable through a series of ecstatic states, *aḥwāl*, that usually (but not easily) culminate in *fanā'* (oblivion), as the soul's lower attributes are annihilated and a *baqā'* (survival of the "celestial" self) is achieved. The soul is dying to its basic human attributes in order to pass into another state that may be incomprehensible to the outside world but is as clear as crystal in Sufi ecstasies. Contemplation of human beauty and, indeed, mediums of enchantment in nature and life may stimulate such contemplation and inspire pronouncements and actions that may cause trouble, hubbub, incomprehension, and bewilderment among non-Sufis.

While this novella makes no strong claim to present 'Aṭiyyah as a *walī* (friend of God), there is still a constant reference to her presence as an encompassing maternal ideal, offering love, affection, and support to all. She is there to answer the call of the needy, their supplications for succor, and their intercessions in matters of human exchange. Her breast-feeding of the newborn and her general availability make her an embodiment of a deistic omniscience, but within a human form. This very humanity is deliberately brought into focus within the narrative through multiple voices that speak of ʿAṭiyyah, her history, life, and sainthood as represented by the present celebrated shrine.

The whole story of the enactment and construction of the shrine must tell us a lot, not only about the appearance of saints or fakes and pretenders during times of crisis, including wars, drought, famine, plague, and political upheavals or sectarian violence. Many shrines get enacted and born under such circumstances, and intellectuals early in the twentieth century were reluctant to give these credit. In fact they looked on these as superstitious practices or tricks played by interested people or groups on the credulous and the native. Dhū al-Nūn Ayyūb makes fun of this phenomenon in his novel *Duktūr Ibrāhīm*, and Yaḥyā Ḥaqqī thought of this as no more than subordination to superstition. But the birth of this shrine is another example of the production of space, for there are actual forces and powers that have also some interest in this birth. There are others who also make use of it toward other purposes. While still falling within Lefebvre's representational space, it also has the complexity of abstract space depending on manipulators. Even relatives and family have their interests despite the inner objection of the Communist son to this phenomenon.

The rumor that the land in Cairo where the shrine is located covers a significant excavation site triggers media interest in the shrine, one that soon involves further rumors, conflicting positions and perspectives, and a description of the neighborhood where the lady has lived and displayed her loving accessibility to people. Information on this subject and indeed the narrative itself survives as the result of an ongoing journalistic report. 'Izzat Yūsuf, a correspondent for the *Ṣabāḥ* (morning) paper is commissioned to cover the topic that she has introduced to her editor, thereby provoking a climate of discussion and controversy even before publication, the end result of which is that publication is withheld. The editor advises her to forget it, but her husband, the archaeologist 'Ali Faheem, is run over on the way home. He has already told his friends that he has been followed and may be killed soon, a premonition that is also in the journalist's mind. She decides to disappear and leave a number of versions of her unpublished report at the door of houses of a number of people. The report, now as a narrative, is addressed to "Whom it may concern." It becomes the concern of all who feel that there is something going on that needs a better explanation than what has already been made public. In other words, a public sphere is created by default to involve the public in a case that has not as yet drawn enough attention due to public negligence, state coercion, and corrupt apparatus.

While the disappearance of the journalist implies a conspiracy against any press release respecting the shrine, the news in the *Ṣabāḥ* daily that there will be a report on the matter succeeds in raising many comments focusing on Lady Atiyyah and her human and saintly attributes before and after her death. Each voice with its narrative space sustains a perspective that reveals its own interests, background, and disposition toward a title character that is simultaneously ordinary and out of the ordinary. Even when one voice disapproves of the Lady's common touch (pp. 164–66), there is also counterrecognition of a generous Lady whose house is always open to all and whose prodigality is unlimited (p. 164). On the other hand, the theory of the Lady's daughter is deeply rooted in a human interpretation of a mother with exceptional gifts, for she is "a political woman" (p. 153), one who "was a strong personality capable of asserting herself with the greatest of ease" (p. 154). At the same time she was ready to lie in order to secure a benefit for the people for whom she was interceding (p. 155). She treats people as part of her family to ensure their survival and good behavior, even when there is still a possibility that thieves may pull some ruse or trick on her (p. 157).

Breast-feeding evokes motherhood, an omniscient maternity that enables her to supervise a universe of offspring who may not have control over the state, but who are forced by this fact to listen to her words of blame and rebuke "like a failed student in front of his teacher" (p. 149). In line with a sense of national commitment that is part of her overall disposition, she scolds a senior officer, one among her breast-fed family of offspring, for failing to live up to the challenge of 1967: "The people said that it was a step forward, but you turned the whole thing upside down. You've ruined it, and now you're sitting happily on the ruins" (p. 150). The critique is directed at an individual, but its wider applicability turns it into a critique of a nation-state that must be punished for its ruinous inadequacies.

In other words, perspectives may vary, but they still depict a character of exceptional qualities, including a benevolent disposition and warm heartedness. Only through such a maternal image can criticism assume a national connotation. Her presence as *umm* (mother) fuses into national tropes that have been sustaining nation-state rhetoric for a long time. The mother is able to expose the betrayal of the nation, *'ummah*. The image of the *umm* needs some explanation here. The neighbor describes her as the "foster mother" to a large number of children, including some high-ranking people in the army and the government (p. 148). She scolds one of them, an officer, for the 1967 defeat: "You've ruined it, and now you're sitting happily on the ruins" (p. 150). The lover is disconcerted by the rumor that the department of antiquities would embark on excavation there, and his question is no less pertinent: has the department covered all other antiquities and sites of excavation? Who is going to benefit from these excavations which might lead to more plunder of national treasures? (p. 161). With strong doubts that the nation-state is merely engaged in further destruction and excavation that will end up in "museums of the whole world," he finds in the whole hubbub "some reason by which you will gain and through which you will ravage the earth" (p. 161). While these reflections accelerate the feelings of love for the mother, the earth, the land, the nation, and the named woman as a symbol for all, the narrative adds more speculations that situate these in a historical frame that tries to bridge an Egyptian continuity between ancient Egypt and the present one. The university student finds a connection through birthplace between herself and Akhenaton: "I have discovered they came from the same district in which the teachings of Akhenaton thrived and flourished, the area from which emanated every idea inviting the sacrifice of self to the love of the One Creator, the Origin of Existence" (p. 168). The sanctifying discourse creates an absolute space for a Divine presence with a number of manifestations that culminate at this point in a Lady who is the Mother of all,[7] and hence the embodiment of a nation. In this discourse the author elaborates on the link between the great Egyptian king, some other successors, and such Sufi shaykhs as Dhū al-Nūn al-Miṣrrī and al-Niffarī. The link means a continuity which shows up again in the Lady (p. 169). The significance of this speculation lies in its effort to bring together lines of thought that delineate a continuous history, with no interruption, between Islam as Sufism, Egyptian nationalism, and the dominating concept of *'ummah*. As 1967 shows a setback, a regression, it has to be blotted out of this history to sustain this continuity. The Lady has to scold officers and rebuke them for the failure which has to be mentally and morally denied, banished outside this line of achievement, sacrifice, and continuity. Islam is recovered as a Sufi strain, while Nāṣir's nationalism is put aside for the time being. But as literary production cannot vie, in its new effort, with the official discourse as consolidated through the media, it has to carve and forge its line of thought carefully, as the archaeologist ʿAli Faheem argues. Being the only one who has already paid for his thought, his speculations and ideas deserve more attention as the most credible, and hence incurring reprisal. His words, he argues, cannot appear in the media, because whatever appears should be part of the state propaganda. "Everything that is said about the freedom of the press and the freedom of expression is a big lie" (p. 171). He himself is "no longer able to bear the superabundance of lying and falsehood that has come to affect everything" (p. 172). He also thinks that the area of the shrine is the richest archaeological site in the country, but it is so rich as to entail a rewriting of history, and hence it will lead to more misfortunes to Egyptians under so many corrupt regimes. While this excavation needs a colossal effort and great integrity, commitment, and loyalty to the nation, the present government cannot handle it, and this may lead to a "new series of those classic imperialist wars" (p. 174). A postscript to his letter also mentions that "the existence of the shrine . . . in this place is no mere coincidence" (p. 175).

In other words, the shrine is produced and enacted here for a purpose to forestall any thoughts respecting excavation and hence rewriting of history. There are people whose interest in the area lies behind the enactment of the shrine. While discrediting the nation-state and its formal discourse, the narrative enforces its presence as a literary production that vies for space through multiple voices. This multiplicity grants it richness, diversity, and plurality; it also maneuvers a place for itself through difference. Debate or the production of debate can fragment formal discourse, undermine its seeming unity, and penetrate therefore its holes and fragments. On the other hand, the sanctifying rhetoric that gathers momentum through other perspectives testifies to an ongoing cult of sainthood. The Lady's physical death only increases this stature and prompts people to readdress her life as a series of exceptional and miraculous gifts that testify to her sainthood. The reports on her funeral amount to a testimonial to her sacred attributes which align her with other saints and entitle her to have a shrine. No matter how parodic of its predecessors, with its use of the cult and the emergence of shrines in times of havoc, instability, and frustration, the narrative manipulates these to drive home its sharp critique of the nation-state. On the other hand, its emphasis on her friendship "with all and sundry, and down-and-outs and low-class types" (p. 164) consolidates the other attributes of her populist presence and elevates her to a different stature in times of nostalgia for the ideal past of justice and solidarity. Through this language she is able not only to adhere to "the symbolic negation of hierarchy,"[8] but primarily to act on her spontaneous affection and innocent disposition toward others. The character is freed from the constraints of social gradation and distinction that have reinvaded the Egyptian society since the rise of bureaucracy and the advent of the market economy during the Sādāt era. The sacral discourse can reach a wider audience and can also elude scrutiny and censorship, especially around the mid-1980s, the time of its publication. Thus, the "consoler," the "condoler," the "sorrowful," the "remover of cares," and the "merry," as the lover calls her (pp. 160–61), evolves as the Divine Beatitude, with basic attributes that Sufis aspire to correspond with through self-annihilation and abnegation. With this transposition of attributes and terms, and regardless of the ironic substructure that directs attention to the spread of the Sufi phenomenon in literary production, especially in Egypt, space is sacralized and its overflow in the street is ensured. Now, the common public, which forms the majority of visitors to the shrine and the recipients and proliferators of the sainthood cult, can interact with a literary product that provides a perspective on the cult, addresses the corruption and weaknesses of the nation-state, criticizes those in charge, and also raises questions regarding the whole issue of excavation, antiquities, interests, double dealings, and strategies of intimidation to silence potential critics.

Although "signs taken for wonders" that assign her a sacred role and identity sound exceptional to a non-Arab or Egyptian audience, these are usual among rural populations where people read signs into specific phenomena, especially if they are well-disposed toward the person in question. Her woman neighbor recalls how "the dough from her hand would yield a lot" (p. 151). On the other hand, people like Shaykh Saʿīd suggest that the Lady has already received signs and premonitions to prepare for her physical departure from this world (pp. 144–45). Her son is no less overwhelmed by signs that show her life and death as bearing witness to something exceptional; upon seeing the grave open, he joins the gravedigger in spotting a "strange golden thing which in shape and form looked most like a lotus flower, with a single long leg extending into the earth" (p. 134). Yet, when the gravedigger tries to move it, it makes a sound "like the flapping of the wings of a small bird, after which it vanished completely" (p. 134). Another testimony comes from a university student specializing in ancient Egyptian history. A participant in the funeral, he is surprised to notice the bier starting "to get lighter and slip from our hands, getting ever lighter and darting off to the mosque at great speed" (p. 166). The student regards her as a Sufi whose soul has already passed through self-annihilation and is now in a state of longing for the Divine, as the ancient Egyptian tradition has it (p. 167). Even the Lady's lover, a Copt, who has been living his infatuation, feels the pangs of her departure, realizing that his unexplainable trip and fall is a signal of the event (p. 160). He continues in a poetic vein to sing of their infatuation and her overwhelmingly charming presence that will survive her physical death. The narrator obviously wishes to accumulate this anecdotal repertoire as part of a neohagiographic inventory. Its presence can be as questionable or acceptable as any analogous set of ancient reports, but in the text it is used to testify to Islam on the street, a summary of beliefs and superstitions that continue to operate on a political unconscious that is also being manipulated by both state and archaeological opportunists. On the other hand, to cover these areas in literary production, but without the early *nahḍah* vituperative critique, has the potential of bridging the gap with the masses and hence engaging with Islam on the street.

The author accumulates these testimonies as reported by the woman journalist. She and her husband, ʿAli Faheem, are secular minded, for the archaeologist knows that the whole situation reflects a mood of regression and failure and that the social order is corrupt: "I am no longer able to bear the superabundance of lying and falsehood that has come to affect everything and which envelops everything in our life from the tips of our toes to the tops of our heads" (p. 172). Furthermore, he regards the state as living in a dire state of indebtedness that transforms everything into patterns of life that negate identity. His critique includes such things as morals, dress, food, buildings, and architecture. It is "a state of deterioration" (p. 174), he says, one that cannot and should not lead to the unearthing of the shrine, which would mean "the removal of the whole of the Greater Cemetery and the neighboring districts" (p. 174). His objection emanates from the inability of the state and its apparatus to carry out such a project that could well require excavations involving "foreigners" in both research and operations (p. 175). He goes so far as to predict that the projected excavations "might well break out a new series of those classic imperialist wars familiar since the early years of the last century" (p. 175). According to the archaeologist, this project to excavate and uncover what is hidden involves an imperialist plan aimed at exploiting the weakened state to rewrite the nation, disfigure it, and erase its culture. Joining with popular faith, the secular voice now looks upon the looming threat as an anti-Islamic plot.

The author does not seem to subscribe to this view, but she still allows her voices to speak out against manipulation of faith and belief. The journalist's reliance on multiple voices and the archaeologist's predictions alert readers to the underlying narrative order. The archaeologist is the only one who has already had to pay the price for rejecting excavation projects, while the journalist is forced to disappear in order to save her life and ensure the investigation is publicized. Like the writer, they are implicated in what is prohibited and taboo. What makes this narrative significant for the Islamic dynamic is both the incongruity of the sainthood phenomenon and the materialistic and opportunist tendencies followed by the modern nation-state. While that state may be interested in excavations, companies and groups come to monopolize the opportunity, putting aside the interests of the poor and lower classes. The narrative leaves it to the reader to come to a decision on the matter, but the archaeologist's perspective also shows that, whenever corruption is rampant, sainthood grows at a phenomenal pace. Underprivileged publics rely on popular religion for comfort and support, and no one else proffers a different solution. The poor find their Islam in sainthood, while "dark" forces have another target. In between the two poles we come across prospective students who have purely scientific interests, and yet the narrative chooses to associate sainthood with cultural dynamics in Egypt that go back to Fatimid times. As a youngster the Lady herself used to sing national songs but, annoyed by the disastrous June 1967 defeat, she switched to women's political and social activities. In other words, sainthood emerges free from superstitious connotations and fuses well into a national discourse and practice of commitment that places Lady 'Aṭiyyah among a long list of Sufis and shaykhs who have significantly contributed to an Islamic dynamic of revolt.

Najīb Maḥfūẓ, *The Journey of Ibn Fattouma*

As an allegorical journey, a quest for the unknown and perennial certitude, *The Journey of Ibn Fattouma* culminates Najīb Maḥfūẓ's engagement with modernity and Islam.[9] The journey sums up a life of perplexity that never finds enough comfort and certainty in modernity and the programs of various institutionalized or politicized Islams. It covers a number of stations, which in this case are not Sufi ones but intellectual encounters with political systems that range between absolute authoritarianism and democracy. Each one is assessed. Systems that claim Islam as their religion serve as the background, but the final conclusion to these assessments is open ended, for the protagonist leaves us papers that contain the journey itself, a narrative reconstruction of a critique which the author has had in mind but has not been able to express in his more realistic narratives. The allegorical journey thus signifies a desire to give vent to frustration. The search ends nowhere, and the protagonist keeps to himself whatever knowledge he may have gained. What we are left with consists of blank pages that are waiting for inscription. The written ones provide us with little while the questions that remain in the readers' minds regarding the land of bliss and the idealized prospects resonate with the same promise and the resultant yearning which religious texts leave in the minds of believers.

In a reconsideration of his life and career, Najīb Maḥfūẓ's protagonist in *Riḥlat Ibn Faṭṭūmah* (*The Journey of Ibn Fattouma*), Qindīl, or Ibn Fattouma as his brothers call him, leaves no doubt that he is a wanderer who seeks certainty and faith, or what he calls "stations for the perplexed soul." This soul is none other than his own, and it "traverses" these stations one after the other, "taking signs and hints from things, groping about in the sea of darkness, clinging stubbornly to a hope that smilingly and mysteriously renews itself" (p. 1). This soul clings to an elusive hope which is based on a realistic vision of the present Islamic world as an arena of conflict and misuse where "every action, fine or base, is initiated in the name of God the Merciful, the Compassionate" (p. 1). Like his other novels of the 1970s, Najīb Maḥfūẓ's *Journey* is certainly about what the Lebanese thinker Munaḥ al-Ṣulḥ in his speeches and articles used to call "*'urūbat al-nukhbah wa-Islām al-jamāhīr*," or "the Arabism of the elite and Islam of the masses." The question that irritates

Qindīl and prompts his odyssey is the one that he addresses to his master-teacher, Shaykh Maghagha al-Gibeli: "if Islam is as you say it is, why are the streets packed with poor and ignorant people?" (p. 4). The answer he receives may be seen as a foreshadowing of the growing Islamic fervor, but beyond this fervor "Islam today skulks in the mosques and doesn't go beyond them to the outside world" (p. 4). In this narrative, Qindīl concludes: "then it is Satan who is controlling us, not the Revolution" (p. 4). Targeting the nation-state as the product of modernity, this narrative considers recession in faith as the outcome of negligence, mimicry, and lip service to religion. Against such a backdrop of paganism and unbelief, the journey becomes a search for something other than novelty. All lands "are close in circumstance, inclination, and ritual, all of them far distant from the spirit of true Islam" (p. 5). If there is nothing new in Islamic lands, then one is forced to investigate heathen lands that aspire at least to worldly perfection, a place where there is "no compulsion" to adopt their beliefs (p. 6). It is only after trying to pry open the "closed secret" of the Jabal lands that a human soul may rest: "like any closed secret it drew me to its edge," Qindīl explains, "and plunged me into its darkness. My imagination was fired" (p. 6). Imagination can give direction to a quest, but its motivating source is a sense of betrayal and consequent disillusionment: "I have been betrayed by religion, betrayed by my mother, betrayed by Halima. God's curse be upon this adulterated land" (p. 13). These words sum up his disappointment at the third chamberlain's decision to take his fiancée, Halima, as his own wife, and at his mother's acquiescence to a marriage proposal. Najīb Maḥfūẓ does not wish to construct a narrative of the soul without rooting it deep in material rationales; true to his own grounding and upbringing in *nahḍ ah* values, he has to substantiate a spiritual journey, an allegorical travelogue, by reference to realistic detail. Indeed, even Qindīl's travels have a material purpose, that of a *nahḍah* reformist: "I want to learn and then return to my ailing homeland with a remedy to heal her" (p. 15). In other words, the author is as keen as ever on providing another text to cover the ground which is left untouched in his other works, that is, the place of Islam in the Islamic regions and lands. To work this out through an allegorical narrative that can reach the common reader and hence participate in critiquing both the formal discourse of institutionalized Islam and the official one of the nation-state perhaps stands behind the desperate effort to "heal" the ailing homeland.

Here the protagonist is repeating what *nahḍah* intellectuals have long been claiming or doing. The same applies to Islamists who emphasize reform, but within an essentialist perspective that claims close observance to the dicta of the Qur'ān and *Sunnah*. Najīb Maḥfūẓ is not keen on either, for his protagonist is driven to embark upon this quest in order to find out more about pure faith in its form as a deep sense of piety and religiosity that excludes selfishness and bigotry. Qindīl's visit to other lands increases his sense of disappointment at his own homeland; the words that keep recurring as his comments on experiences or in response to questions or interventions from others fall broadly within an Islamist critique that rejects current applications of Islam and raises doubts about their viability. The conclusions that he reaches after his experiences and observations further Najīb Maḥfūẓ's early disappointments at the corruption of the state apparatus, the falsity of principles, and sham national proclamations. "Our religion is wonderful . . . but our life is pagan" (p. 41). Observing the *Mashriq* (East) and its landlords as absolute governors of people's destiny, he draws a comparison with the situation in the land of Islam, concluding that in "any event, our own erring, in the land of Revelation, is more shocking than that of the rest of mankind" (p. 27). In another land the president is elected by the elite on condition that he does not deviate from the path that they set for him. Najīb Maḥfūẓ allows Qindīl to pass through lands as political systems, ranging from ones run by absolute rulers to elected presidents. The latter system "reminded me of the system of the caliphate in the land of Islam," he contends, "but it also reminded me of the tragic events of our gory history" (p. 124). But what disturbs him more in the land of Aman, which he visits after *Mashriq* and *Haira*, is their heathenism. They worship the earth as the "creator and supplier of . . . needs" (p. 125), a point which he cannot swallow despite his approval of the natives' view that this forestalls illusions and superstitions. His approval of one side and disapproval of the other is only a pretext for a critique of his own homeland: "what saddened me even more was the state to which Islam in any country had sunk, for the Caliph is no less despotic than the ruler of Aman." He adds: "He [the Caliph] practices his forms of corruption blatantly, while the religion itself is beset with superstitions and trivialities. As for the people, they are rewarded by ignorance, poverty, and disease" (p. 125).

As travelogue, this narrative cannot fashion its sequentiality and moral justifications on the basis of observations; there also need to be trying circumstances to test both body and soul. To grow into a quest, the narrative has to let the protagonist pass through trials that will test his early idealist grounding at the hands of his shaykh, now his stepfather. Hence both temptation and a counteradvocacy of hard work have to be played out as well. It is not enough to traverse lands and experience their novelty and difference; there has to be some agony involved so as to elevate his wanderlust beyond mere curiosity: "the eternal desire for travel ripened in the flame of continued pain" (p. 15), he concludes early on when making the decision to travel following the model of the renowned Moroccan traveler Ibn Baṭṭūṭa (d. 1368 or 1377).

His search for knowledge is coupled with a strong belief in hard work: "He who believes in work will not know poverty" (p. 19). Thus far in his career there is no clue to justify this maxim. There is, however, a tendency to admit personal weaknesses, an attitude that is needed for the quest to commence. Thus, after observing the nakedness of everyone in Mashriq, for instance, he concludes in surprise: "What land is this that hurls a young man like me into the flames of temptation!" (p. 23). Although he tries to abide by the tenets of Islam and stay with Arousa, as his wife from Mashriq, he finds himself facing other complications like the war on Mashriq, which ends with many people being captured as war prisoners, including Arousa herself. The Land of Haira turns out to be as cruel as anywhere else; idealism is far-fetched, and disillusionment only intensifies his comparison with his own homeland. Indeed it is his homeland that provides him with a negative experience, negative application of principles, and deliberate confusion between ethics and practice. Seeing how many heads are paraded in the Land of Haira, he concludes that these should be considered "martyrs to justice and liberty, a deduction that he bases on what usually occurs in the land of divine Revelation" (p. 58). The whole experience has already established its own negative foil, namely his own homeland where Islam is proclaimed but not practiced. This then is the narrative's recurrent leitmotif, and its recurrence is so pervasive that it becomes a subtext that is quite different from Ibn Baṭṭūṭa's travelogue. The latter depicts China, for example, as a land of paganism: "The people of China are infidels," he says in preparation for his account of his experience there. Although appreciating ethics of hard work, security, exactitude in business and commerce, observance of every foreigner, and availability of different goods and fabrics, there is in Ibn Baṭṭūṭa's account a refrain suggesting segregation despite the presence of a well-respected Muslim community, as the narrative duly notes.

For Qindīl in Maḥfūẓ's work every moment is an occasion worth comparing to his homeland. Visiting the "sage" of Haira, for example, someone who holds enormous power in his hands, Qindīl allows us to listen as he celebrates the ruler as "Our Majesty," for he "is the god, and he is the source of all wisdom and good" (p. 60). In other words, the sage is no more than a puppet in the hands of the sovereign; the sage and the elite have no actual role other than serving power. "We talk to the elite in terms that will strengthen the power, control, and growth that is in their souls," the sage says (p. 61), and goes on to criticize the practice of Islam in Qindīl's lands, focusing on those who "exploit" the Qur'ān for their own ends (p. 62). Thus far the author is presenting Qindīl as nothing more than a mirror for a critique of his homeland, and Maḥfūẓ makes use of him to say things that he has been struggling with for a long time, ever since he grew tired of the national bourgeoisie with its double standards and sham politics. When the shaykh of a small Muslim community in the Land of Halba shows a more cultivated practice of Islam (i.e., communication among men and women, education, etc.), Qindīl is there as an interlocutor to set out some correctives to the claims of certain fundamentalists: "and were . . . [the Prophet] to be resurrected . . . would he not reject the whole of your Islam?" (p. 86). Qindīl has to agree, asserting that his journey is driven by a desire for learning: "to see my homeland from afar . . . in the light of other lands that I might perhaps be able to say something of benefit to it" (ibid.). The course of the *nahḍah* or the encounter with Europe now evolves as a journey within neighboring lands where different political systems are explored and Islam as practiced or claimed is criticized.

What both interlocution and response attempt to do is to provide an authorial pretext for criticizing the understanding and practice of Islam. While the political system in Qindīl's homeland is scrutinized and criticized through the lenses of analogy and comparison, the understanding of Islam is critiqued differently. A wider context of family gatherings is needed in order to transform a polemic of debate and refutation into an assemblage of voices. Shaykh Hamada of the Muslim community in Halba, for example, is only one among many. He invites Qindīl to have dinner with his family, where all gather and communicate freely: "Even glasses of wine were served," to Qindīl's surprise. But the shaykh reminds him of the jurist Abū Ḥanīfa's rule in this matter: "We drink according to the weather and traditions," the shaykh explains, "but we do not become drunk" (p. 90). Women "talked with a bold and spontaneous frankness just like men." While Samia, the shaykh's daughter, compares the situation of women in some lands with their life during the Prophet's times when women were respected and recognized, she concludes, "Islam is wilting away at your hands and you are just standing back and contemplating" (p. 91). She acts as an authorial voice that criticizes practices that are only conducive to the interests of certain ruling groups that impose their authority and a reign of absolutism as a way of preempting criticism and forestalling the call for equality and justice. Only through *ijtihād* (independent judgment) can Islam cope with life and reality: "the difference between our Islam and yours," she tells Qindīl, "is that ours has not closed the door of independent judgment, and Islam without independent judgment means Islam without reason" (p. 103). This is not the only voice that underscores the author's intention to describe another version of Islam. In the land of Halba, Samia's father, Shaykh al-Sabki, asserts, "Your homeland is the land of Islam, and what do you find there? A tyrannical ruler who rules to please himself, so where is the moral basis? Men of religion bring religion into subjection in order to serve the ruler, so where is the moral basis? And a people think only of the morsel to fill their stomachs, so where is the moral basis?" (p.107).

It is not difficult to observe that this travelogue offers an occasion to speak truth to power. Voices provide a variety of perspectives with which to intensify a sense of inadequacy in the lands of Islam due to malpractice by rulers, authorities, and privileged groups. Like the late-nineteenth-century reformists, Maḥfūẓ lays the blame not on Islam and its message, but on rulers and communities. The travelogue evolves as a spiritual quest whose stations of aspiration are designed through experience and movement to prepare the soul for another mission that sets it apart from contemporary authority and privileged groups. Maḥfūẓ's travelogue is a spiritual quest, but its plain critique minimizes its narrative potential as a confessional experience worth recording. The record of these stations (pp. 19, 32, 148) is meant to be open ended, for closure works against independent judgment and ongoing assessment. In its final version, this record is less than a Sufi quest, but more than an ordinary travel account. Lack of any actual trying circumstances minimizes even the protagonist's prison experience and the dispersion and loss of his family among warring factions.

Obviously in this work the author is bent on saying things that he cannot say in a polemical discourse that would serve to uncover corruption, misrule, and abuse of Islam under the pretension of practicing it. The narrative quest remains thin and pallid, for Maḥfūẓ is more experienced in realistic representations, and allegory is not his strongest point, especially when Islam is his subject. When seen in relation to other narrative accounts in search of a meaningful religious experience, it is more allegorical than al-Ḥakīm's *Bird* and less engaged in nation-state politics than Bakr's *Shrine of 'Atia*. Even so it is a powerful illustration of Maḥfūẓ's concern with the future of Islam in its domains, regions where political corruption and fundamentalist interpretations harm Islam as both faith and culture. Through allegory, parody, and an accessible discourse, literary production as such attempts to start another round with the reading public whereby it can reach and influence the street, especially the masses that have been left to state media and the manipulation of the powerful institutions.

These three writers all experiment with narrative forms; tropes, allegories, parody, and travelogue are invoked to cope with situations that elude realistic representation. Like poets who approximate narrative reconstructions in their Sufi poetics, these writers in their stylistic experimentation convey a certain unease whenever approaching faith. Their strategies vary between a search for similitude and strangeness. Poets, on the other hand, have other ways of engaging with this issue. The need for representation becomes minimal in comparison with other poetic strategies that are not necessarily opposed to the demands of modernity and may have a limited influence on the street, though their hold on the educated segment cannot be minimized, something that is explored in the next chapter.

Notes

1. Najīb Maḥfūẓ, *The Journey of Ibn Fattouma*, trans. Denys Johnson-Davies (New York: Anchor 993).

2. Tawfīq al-Ḥakīm, *'Uṣfūr min al-Sharq*. 1973; English translation: *A Bird of the East*; trans. R. Bayly Winder, (Beirut: Khayats, 1966).

3. See in particular, Christina Phelps Harris, *Nationalism and Revolution in Egypt: The Role of the Muslim Brotherhood* (Stanford, CA: Mouton, 1964), 13–15. See also Charles Smith, "The 'Crisis of Orientalism': The Shift of Egyptian Intellectuals to Islamic Subjects in the 1930s," *International Journal of Middle East Studies* 4 (1973), 382–410.

4. Mona Anis, "Thus Spoke Yehia Haqqi," *Al-Ahram Weekly* (weekly.ahram.org.eg/2004/688/bo7.htm).

5. Muhsin al-Musawi, *Arabic Poetry: Trajectories of Modernity and Tradition* (London: Routledge, 2006).

6. Salwā Bakr, *Maqām 'Aṭiyyah*. 1992; English translation: *The Shrine of Atia: A Novella*, trans. Denys Johnson-Davies, (Cairo: American University in Cairo Press, 1997).

7. On the absolute space of religion, see Henri Lefebvre, *The Production of Space*, (Oxford: Basil Blackwell, 1991), 163.

8. See Pierre, Bourdieu, *Language and Symbolic Power* (Cambridge, MA: Harvard University Press, 1991), 68.

9. Najīb Maḥfūẓ, *Riḥlat Ibn Faṭṭūmah*. 1983; English translation: *The Journey of Ibn Fattouma*, trans. Denys Johnson-Davies, (New York: Anchor 1993).

CHAPTER SEVEN

The Bifurcated Poetic: Islam as Poetry

Is it possible to speak of modern Arabic poetry in terms of religious resurgence? Doesn't this sound paradoxical since, despite poetry's occasional mimetic excursions, it is rarely seen as a representational art because "lucidity founders in metaphor," as Camus argues?[1] Modern poetry is evocative and suggestive, and thrives on its allusiveness, parallelism, and metaphorical interweaving. In Michel Foucault's words, the poet's function is "allegorical . . . beneath the language of signs and beneath the interplay of their precisely delineated distinctions, he strains his ears to catch that 'other language,' the language, without words or discourse, of resemblance. The poet brings similitude to the signs that speak it, whereas the madman loads all signs with a resemblance that ultimately erases them."[2] Its occasional incantations, benedictions, and outbursts of faith remain different from occasional poetry that celebrates faith or commemorates the birth of the Prophet and the death of his family. As a product of modernity, it signifies a divorce from rules of versification that have been accepted as the distinctive aspects of classical and neoclassical versification. The literary production of the *nahḍah* overwhelmingly subscribes to a secular spirit that centers on man, not on the divine. Single poems by Aḥmad Shawqī (d. 1932), for example, and a large number of other neoclassicists who have survived the onset of modernity make up only a small portion of a literary production that has been in a process of development for a long time. In the 1950s there was even a rebellious spirit that rewrote the Qur'ānic story of Nūḥ (Noah), aligning the poet's voice with Noah's son who rejects God's command communicated through his father's supplication to desert his homeland which is endangered by a God-ordained deluge. Adūnīs's rewriting in "The New Noah" (1957) depicts Noah as a rebel who rejects commands: "If time rolls back to the beginning and water immerses the face of life again, if the universe trembles and God hastens to use me: 'Noah, save the living!' I will not heed his words."[3] Years later, the Egyptian poet Amal Dunqul (d. 1983) lets the son argue in defiance of those who speak for leaving lands under occupation, neocolonialization, or dire political and social circumstances such as are found in the Arab world and Egypt of the 1960s. In a sarcastic tone, he allows the son to muse on those who desert their homelands: "Blessed are those who ate her bread in goodly times / And turned their backs on her in adversity."[4] Another Egyptian poet, Ḥasan Ṭilib, published his collection *Ayat Jīm* (1992) as a contrafaction to Qur'ānic *āyāt* or chapters. The third letter in the Arabic alphabet serves as a title for the whole collection because of its exclusion from any prefatory Qur'ānic verse. The reading may not sound anti-Qur'ānic, for poets readdress Qur'ānic verses as a subtext whereby to combat manipulation and misreading by corrupt rulers and institutions who ransack tradition in order to justify rapprochement with colonial powers and invaders. Against this trend, there is nevertheless a countertendency aimed at reconstructing historical or canonical texts so as to fit into a religion of the oppressed. *Ayat Jīm* imitates Qur'ānic versification, and it is listed as the fifth sura or division in the collection. Its title is "The letter Jīm wounds," but it is not followed by the usual refrain in recitations that asks for God's protection from Satan the accursed; instead it asks for the "people's protection against the evil Sultan."[5] The whole spirit of the 1950s and 1960s is one of protest that finds in secular ideology and modernity viable subjects for the expression of anger. In other words, though secularist writings of social and political protest may show this irreligious spirit, they still need traditional and canonical texts in order to indulge in mimicry, emulation, contrafaction, reconstruction, irony, travesty, and pastiche. Poetry is by no means unfamiliar with a whole climate of ideas where these devices and literary modes evolve as the manifestations and markers of postmodernity. In 1994, when Ṭilib's collection was exhibited at the state-run Cairo Book Fair, the Azhar forced its withdrawal from the bookstalls.[6]

Despite this tendency, one can still detect a certain subtle engagement with sites of piety, where both the Sufi lexicon and lives of Sufis become pivotal to a bifurcated poetics, one involving the use of verbal simulation and contrafactional activity that cannot claim genuine piety. It is a poetics of rupture that makes no claim to harmony in thought or form. Language is a site of deviation, dubious interaction, and contestation. Although not strictly religious, this reliance on a Sufi lexicon and poetic matrix expands the frontiers of poetry itself and brings religious texts closer to literature. This tendency is certainly as limited in its impact as modern Arabic poetry itself; it fails to reach a mass audience. Its referents and shared codes target the more educated public with whom it has already established its emotive links.

No modern Arab poets can claim an extensive and deliberate use of Sufi figures and lexicon more than the contemporary Syrian-Lebanese poet ʿAlī Aḥmad Saʿīd (Adūnīs) and the Iraqi poet ʿAbd al-Wahhāb al-Bayātī (d. 1999). The latter's Sufi poems are not many in number, but there is nevertheless a Sufi strain to his poetry that seriously challenges his own disclaimer to the effect that his Sufism is simply a name for a visionary poetics. In a personal conversation, he once told me that al-Sayyid Abū Khawlah, as he used to call my late brother, the Iraqi intellectual and thinker ʿAzīz al-Sayyid Jāsim (executed in 1991), had assessed his poetry through the lenses of Sufism, something that the poet disputed. That remark came as a comment on al-Sayyid Jāsim's book *Al-Taṣawwuf wa-al-Iltizām fi Shi'r 'Abd al-Wahhāb al-Bayātī* (*Sufism and Engagement in 'Abd al-Wahhāb al-Bayātī's Poetry*). Even so, al-Bayātī's lexicon certainly shows Sufi influences which also manage to convey a deep and, at times, excessive concentration on Sufi interpretations of love, especially Iblīs's (Satan's) love for the Lord. In Satan's disobedience of God's commands, Sufis find evidence of a lover's total infatuation and madness, a feeling that accepts none other than the object of love, namely the Lord. The delicate poetic manner adopted by al-Bayātī is worth considering, not only because of his subtle manipulation of Sufi lexicon and vision, but also because of a neutralizing strategy that relies heavily on his sociopolitical register, a register that draws attention away from the focus of his Sufi poems and their pivotal "satanic" love. In this context al-Bayātī's poetry becomes Sufi by default, since he assumes the position as a modernist whose aspirations for an earthly paradise have not materialized. The Sufi lexicon serves a negotiating function whereby Sufi perplexity finds a suspended abode. The poems that deserve analysis in this context are: "Reading from the Book of al-Tawasin by al-Hallaj" ("Qirā'ah fī kitāb al-Ṭawāsīn by al-Ḥallāj," in *Shiraz's Moon*, 1975); "Variations on the Suffering of Farid al-Din al-Attar" ("Maqāṭi' min 'Adhābāt Farīd al-Dīn al-'Aṭṭār," in *The Kingdom of Grain*, 1979); "I Am Born and Burn in My Love" (*Shiraz's Moon*, 1975); and " 'Ā'isha's Mad Lover" (in *Love Poems at the Seven Gates of the World*, 1971).[7] These poems are no less capable of reaching the reading public than the narratives we have been discussing earlier in this study. They also convey the unease of Arab intellectuals with respect to a fervor demanding communication through shared codes that are not always the ones cherished by modernity and its predicament and consequences.

A review of the poems from the collections of 1971 and 1975 may serve to introduce his Sufi poetics. These provide an overview of his conceptualizations of love as it evolves in Sufi writings, especially Sufi recapitulations of the great Arab *ghazal* (love poetry) tradition as manipulated and enriched by both Ibn al-ʿArabī (d. 1240) and Ibn al-Fāriḍ (d. 1235). Al-Bayātī's poetic career and itinerary may not transcend certain Sufi positions, the ones needed to overcome one's human limitations; thus the personas he invokes rarely reach total abnegation of the ego-self. In " ʻĀ'isha's Mad Lover," the quester is still in the process of search, the perusal of the "real of reality," or, as the speaker-persona phrases it, "the meaning of meaning."[8] Like his fellow Sufis at that stage of perplexity, he must display an enormous and gnawing endurance: "suffering exile in the in-between" (pp. 90–91). Endurance does not yet achieve ultimate self-abnegation and has to pass through a phase of sacrifice, as was the case with al-Ḥallāj (ex. 922) and the martyrs of love:

For the new language of the upcoming tribe,
For the poem's idol (panegyrics)
I follow my death, carrying my head to the caliph
On a plate . . . (pp. 90–91).[9]

The love experience is one of trial, since the Sufi dimension removes it from its human limits of ecstasy and consummation and places it in a site of endurance from which no one ever returns to tell us more than what we can obtain from verbal constructions of visionary experience. Leaning on the Persian Sufi lexicon but also drawing on al-Hallāj, the speaker summons the Sufi vocabulary of light, rose, and vows from the inside (*sawād*) of the heart, not from the organ (*fu'ād*) itself. This poetics finds its objective correlatives in well-known *ghazal* idioms:

Spring passed and then returned, but I am still at the gate of the arches
Praying for its flowering branch, to the light
carrying my vows to the capital of the caliphate (pp. 82–83).

Identifying with Ibn al-ʿArabī, the speaker subtly passes through a visionary experience, the like of which is reported in the latter's *al-Futūhāt al-Makkiyyah* (The Meccan Conquests / Revelations). In these visions transfiguration takes place, whereby the Meccan shrine becomes the spatial catalyst for this transfiguration. ʻĀ'isha is no longer a mere female:

I saw
ʻĀ'isha in her funeral shroud enriching the black stone

and when I called her, she fell to the ground ashes, and I
also fell.
The wind scattered us
And inscribed our names side by side as the tombs (pp. 84–85).

This blending of Islamic and pagan myths is witness to another oneness which is vaguely reminiscent of the Sufi annihilation in the Divine. In the poem, "I Am Born and Burn in My Love" (pp. 196–97), the love vision works differently. The birth of Lara in the speaker's memory is no less visionary than any other Sufi experience; it possesses all the terms and conditions of Sufi illumination, more even than the epiphany that shines upon one once the moment is congenial enough. The Sufi illumination builds on other moments that take place only after a journey of trial and endurance. Exile is part of the journey; so is the unattainability or departure of the lover/beloved. Lara becomes the embodiment of this lover, the ever present/absent lover for whom the speaker searches. In this site, embodiments or transfigurations keep the speaker suspended, always "on fire," as is the case with the Sufis who are in the ongoing journey toward the Divine lover/beloved.

Lara wakes up in my memory
A tartar cat, lying in wait, stretching, yearning
scratching my feverish face, depriving me of sleep.
I see her in the bottom hell of the polar cities
hanging on with her tresses,
Suspending me like a hare upon the wall
Fettered in my trail of tears (pp. 296–97).

In his poem, "Maqāṭiʿ min ʿAdhābāt Farīd al-Dīn al-ʿAṭṭār" ("Variations on the Suffering of Farid al-Din al-ʿAttar"), al-Bayātī is even more meticulous in his application of a Sufi lexicon and images. Sufi traditions afford him space to navigate and construct a poem that borrows from stock images of wine poetry in both the Arabic and Persian traditions. Drunkenness, a wine pourer (*sāqī*), mirror, light, waking, remembrance (*dhikr*), and identity exchange are now fused into al-Bayātī's register. In a double-bind removal of an earlier language that is socially laden, in the 1970s there was a shift in al-Bayātī's poetry to this lexicon where luminous Sufis like al-Ḥallāj, al-Niffarī (d. 965), and Ibn al-ʿArabī pervade his poetic lexicon. The al-ʿAṭṭār of this poem may be any of these figures or a Sufi poet like Saʿdī of Shīrāz, someone who is also collapsed with Abū Nuwās. The outcome needs to be regarded as a factor that enriches poetic language through a process which Adūnīs had already begun following his realization of the ultimate deadlock of modernity, its abundance of secular details and uncertain promises.

There is one reservation concerning the poet's dabbling in Sufism, namely that the Sufi lexicon weighs heavily on a poetic that has no more substance than an unresolved love experience. While that may be so within the Sufi tradition, there is also a rejoicing voice to be heard that excludes the exilic agency of the modern secular poet. In Sufi visions of annihilation into the Divine a release from the boundaries of the ego is the desirable outcome, but al-Bayātī's mask of the victimized poet cannot sustain for long such a celebratory and joyful moment of rapture. Even so, the mask can present a passing moment of such ecstasy: "See how I prostrate in the shrine drunk / A guest of the queen of this night that is haunted by the spirit of wine" (pp. 248–49). Al-Bayātī may allow the Sufi lexicon to crowd the poem, but he cannot offer more than a fleeting love experience, and even then it is usually suspended somewhere between an elevated Sufi ecstasy and a rapturous navigation of a secular poet:

> He was first to call to drunkenness, saying: "I am wine, you are the cup bearer. If only you could become me, O my beloved." He pawns his sacred cloth for wine and weeps, mad with love (p. 249).

The poet's persona draws on the Persian poet Sa'dī of Shīrāz and Ibn al-'Arabī to capture the ecstatic moment of oneness:

> My heart is covered with dust from traveling to you—from you. So serve me wine and tuck me in a bed, at the foot of the wine. . . . Under the seven celestial spheres, and with ardent kisses, light a blaze in the flesh of earth. To me you were a mirror, I have become the mirror, I undress you and I see my nakedness. In my drunkenness and waking (sobriety) I search for you, as long as the cupbearer's goblets speak without a tongue (pp. 248–49).

His very sources betray his dilemma. As a well-read intellectual he may well have an accumulated knowledge of Sufi literature, and yet his linkage to Sufism is very different from that of Adūnīs. The latter revels in a kind of cosmopolitan foray where fusion takes place between discourses or poetics, from surrealists to Sufis, from Apollinaire to Eliot, and from Abū Tammām (d. 846) to Abū Nuwās. His mirrors are not necessarily polished Sufi ones, unblemished and free of any egotistical manifestations. They function in conjunction with a theater or playground, a place where everyone may have fair play, albeit under the masterly leadership of the puppeteer.

Al-Bayātī's major source on Sufism, and on Ibn al-ʿArabī in particular, may be Henry Corbin's study *Creative Imagination in the Sufism of Ibn Arabi*.[10] On the other hand, the work of al-Ḥallāj was also accessible through early translations in Louis Massignon's monumental study.[11] But al-Bayātī's poem rests on Ibn al-'Arabī's celebration of the "positive attributes" of the Divine which are behind our "love of God," as Corbin explains. In the introduction to *The Interpreter of Ardent Desire*, Ibn al-'Arabī adds, "It is He who in every beloved being is manifested to the gaze of each lover . . . and none other than He is adored, for it is impossible to adore a being conceiving the Godhead in that being."[12]

Ibn al-'Arabī's introductory note explains the relation between the concrete form that "makes Him visible"[13] and the Divine Beatitude. Corbin explains that Ibn al-'Arabī sees two sides of this divine love: God's desire to manifest Himself in His creatures, "to be recreated for them in them" as God "epiphanized in beings and yearning to return to himself."[14] Yet God in the creature also "sighs toward Himself, since He is the source and origin which yearned precisely for this determinate form, for His own anthropomorphosis."[15] Al-Bayātī's interest in this Godly-human intersection is brought forth in his depiction of the poet as the voice in charge, the giver of words, and the sufferer who atones for human miseries.

Ibn al-'Arabī's reference to nostalgic poetics as a variation on the yearning of the loving creature for "the vision of divine beauty" which keeps on appearing in new forms affords some leeway to al-Bayātī, and he is fully prepared to build on it, not necessarily to reach a Sufi state, but definitely to achieve what can be retained in poetry: the exchange between the physical and the visionary. Corbin explains Ibn al-'Arabī's poetics as follows: it is the same "infinite desire to which Abū Yazīd al-Bisṭāmī (d. 874) alludes: 'I have drunk the portion of love, goblet after goblet. It is not exhausted and my thirst has not been slaked.'"[16] Al-Bayātī rephrases this encounter as one between the cupbearer, the speaker, and the wine: "As long as the cupbearer's goblets speak without tongue."[17] In other words, the entanglement in each other is irrevocable, joining "the being of the Lord and the being of his vassal of love into a unity which an essential *passion* splits into two terms, each yearning for the other, the Creator and the creature in their bipolarity."[18]

Although more attuned to the wine lexicon and its richly endowed poetic in both the Arabic and Persian traditions, al-Bayātī chooses to focus on Ibn al-'Arabī's solution to human love predicaments and his elaborate discussion gives plenty of scope to the idea of divine manifestation in beauty. In Corbin's words, "Beauty, Love, Sadness" come together as the "primordial triad,"[19] as in al-Suhrawardī's (d. 1191) prologue of "Mu'nis al-'Ushshāq."[20] There is legitimate justification for the sigh that recurs within the poetic tradition and, by implication, in al-Bayātī's agonized cry: "Why do we depart when we have already arrived? Why do we die before gathering flowers?" as the persona cries in "Variations."[21] Al-Bayātī construes the encounter in the same polished mirror of Sufi thought, usually applied by many and highlighted in Ibn al-'Arabī's idea of love. In his *al-Futūḥāt al-Makkiyyah II*, Ibn al-'Arabī says:

> And if you love a being for his beauty, you love none other than God, for He is the beautiful being. Thus in all its aspects the object of love is God alone. Moreover, since God knows Himself and it came to know the world ["by knowing Himself"]; He produced it *as extra* of His image. Thus the world is for Him a mirror in which He sees His own image, and that is why God loves only Himself, so that if He declares: God will love you (II:29), it is in reality Himself that He loves.[22]

In "Variations" al-Bayātī says: "For me you were a mirror, I have become the mirror," a phrase that he repeats thrice.[23] This repetition binds the encounter together, enriches it with wine symbolism, and integrates it with a more secular register that was a distinctive feature of his earlier poetry. In this mirror imposition, the secular integrates well with the divine without losing its textual density as a sample from the Sufi lexicon.

In al-Bayātī's "Variations," as well as his poems in *The Kingdom of Grain*, physical desire or passion disappears. His concept of love is in line with Ibn al-'Arabī's concept of "divine love," the love which operates as both love of the Creator for the creature in which He images Himself, and love of that creature for his Creator, as a yearning to return to its origins. In other words, the Hidden God yearns for its source. Spiritual love survives as a quest for the Beloved for whom he has been the image.[24] Ibn al-'Arabī argues that "the most perfect of mystic lovers are those who love God simultaneously *for* himself and *for* themselves, because this capacity reveals in them the unification of their twofold natures."[25] Al-Bayātī feels quite at home here since:

> I undress you and see my nakedness, and I search for you in my nakedness and my waking (sobriety) (*Love, Death, and Exile*, pp. 248–49).

Then he adds in terms of yearning,

> Be me, oh my love, pawing your sacred cloth, weeping, mad with love (*Love, Death, and Exile*, pp. 254–55).

This journey, return, and yearning are all captured by the poem in terms of wine poetics: "I, because of excessive traveling to you and from you, I wonder about you in my drunkenness and waking (sobriety)" (pp. 254–55).

In his poem on al-Ḥallāj, the love complex is even more challenging. Titled "A Reading in the Book of Tawāsīn by al-Hallaj," the poem invites comparison with al-Ḥallāj's own work, its trajectory of faith and trial and its Sufi stations and states, before culminating in a plea for understanding Iblīs's justifications of disobedience. Sinful in arrogance and defiance, Iblīs or Satan admits the accusation but finds justification in his overwhelming love for God which he refuses to allow anyone else to share. The Sufi trajectory in al-Ḥallāj's poem should also be present in the reader's mind in order to examine and test al-Bayātī's reading, its textual and intellectual implications, and its ultimate placement within the poet's Sufi production. Al-Ḥallāj uses the Qur'ānic tradition which is clearly established in the title that he gives to his quest. "The Ant" (sura 27) begins with the alphabetical symbols Ṭā'/Sīn, which also set the tone for the sura in which emphasis is laid on God's signs that imply "a guidance and good tidings unto the believers," as opposed to nonbelievers, for whom "an evil chastisement awaits" and who "will be the greatest losers in the Hereafter" (27:1–5). The signs include Moses's fire where he hears God's endowment of him with miracles like those conferred on Solomon. In other suras, like "The Poets" (26), the threshold includes "Ṣād/Sīn" and "Mīm"; and "The Story" (28) has also the same. Moses's story is also found there, as is Noah's. The emphasis on faith and reward for the faithful contrasts with warnings to unbelievers and oppressors. Al-Ḥallāj uses "Ṣād" and "Sīn" to elaborate on the Prophet's luminous light, his unswerving gaze at God, as the column of light that entails purification of the heart. The "Mīm" letter in the suras mentioned before attests to this specific relevance to Muḥammad. It is this luminosity that brings him so close to God, "the distance of the two shots of the bow," as noted in the sura "By the Star, and Its Waning" (2:27). Sufi interpretation, especially in al-Ḥallāj's "Ṭawāsīn," highlights this closeness and unswerving focus on the Divine as the best expression of perfect love, the one usually sought by Sufis who aspire to the status of the silkworm or the burned moth. Poets like Sa'dī of Shīrāz also focus on this theme. Sa'dī writes, "O bird of morning, learn from the moth about love, burned (by fire): he gave up his soul without a cry."[26] The moth is not satisfied with the offers of the candle, its light or heat, but "flies headlong into it," annihilating itself, careless of everything else, including his peers who are awaiting news of his experience. Now burned, the moth is the "one who has seen," rejoicing in "the one whom he saw," as Louis Massignon explains.[27] The same can be said concerning the Prophet in his unswerving devotion, as the sura "By the Star, in Its Waning" says (2:27). All this is meant to prepare for the primary focus of "Ṭawāsīn," that is, the implications of Satan's love. His pride, reasoning, and claim to defer to God's decree (*iḥtijāj bi-al-qadar*) rest on a rejection of anything that may detract from his love, compete with it, or take him away from his absorption. Satan is unlike Muḥammad, who "threw his glance neither to the right nor to the left, his mind's eye did not become less keen and did not violate (i.e. the sacred enclosure)." According to Massignon's reading, "There had been no monotheist . . . comparable to Satan among the inhabitants of heaven."[28] Yet, Satan's sin is his fear of turning into a "scorned lover," a fear that leads to his damnation. Using the Sufi Baqlī's commentary, Massignon writes, "His attempt to leave (his origins toward his end) was thwarted by the fixity of his moorings. Satan was caught between the fire enflaming his own masonry and the divine light of his predestination."[29] As a "martyr of love," Iblīs is bound to be considered differently in Sufi texts, a point which attracts the attention of the poets of modernity. In their rebelliousness, bewilderment at the terrible human sense of oppression and brutality, and disappointment at the outcome of modernity's promises of welfare and progress under the guidance of human reason, poets find this Iblīs worthy of identification. In al-Ḥallāj's book, Satan or Iblīs argues:

I am one of those who
love, and those who love are cursed. And
say I have gone down; have fallen; ah, I
who has drawn knowledge of the book of light—O all-powerful:
how it befell? Why it befell—? O, how to
face what I have to face?
You made me of fire, and him of clay; and
we two are mutually opposite; can the
opposite be reconciled?
In obedience and in serving You I am the
most ancient, in partaking of Your love I am the most acknowledged; in
knowing I am the wisest, and in time
I am the most
enduring.[30]

Al-Bayātī's Iblīs hides behind many images and words that rely on the poet's social-political register. The register diverts the reader's attention from the presence of Iblīs and the problems involving his violation of God's decree. Iblīs becomes a poetic mask to problematize choice and predestination. The poet, as the maimed spokesman for the tribe, finds himself or herself no less humbled and damned than Iblīs. Thus, al-Bayātī's mask cries:

> This is the edge of the fake witnesses, the age of obelisks of castrated Bedouin kings (*Love, Death, and Exile*, pp. 168–69).

On the other hand, there is the kingdom of poetry where a wider metaphorical space allows the poet to see and argue the case of the poor and underprivileged: "I bring my face close to the nation of poetry; I see thousands of rejected, desperate people behind the stony walls" (*Love, Death, and Exile*, pp. 168–169). The mask also functions as the poet's persona while identifying with Iblīs of the book of *Ṭawāsīn*. In al-Bayātī's poetry, Iblīs is complaining as a forlorn lover, deprived of rights and privileges:

> I bring my face close to the great mason. I fall in the trap made of words. A wall is built around me, it rises and rises: books and commandments coil around me like ropes. I shout, terrified, at the base of the wall. Why, my Lord am I exiled in this kingdom?" (*Love, Death, and Exile*, pp. 168–169).

In al-Ḥallāj's *Ṭawāsīn*, Iblīs is as exiled and damned:

Iblīs refused [to prostrate before Adam], for
he was blinded by
his observation.
And, at last, when he had
come to naught; his expectations ended; he said:
'I am better than he,' and forever
remained in
state of detachment, unsuccessful; was lost in
the dust, and forced
suffering from end to end.[31]

Al-Bayātī's Iblīs speaks of a trap of words, for he understands al-Ḥallāj's figure to be one ensnared by the command to prostrate himself, something that he is bound to debate. Hence, both the poet and the damned Iblīs are the victims of reason and a fate with which their pride refuses to accommodate. Al-Ḥallāj's Iblīs is made to recognize where he errs:

> If I have erred in my words, then leave me not; for You are all-knowing all-hearing. And had You willed prostration, I would have prostrated. And no one else is among the travelers on the path who knows better than I; I know and understand.[32]

Al-Bayātī's mask is no less than al-Ḥallāj's fallen angel, for he also admits that his love is just as irreplaceable; he also acknowledges his recognition of a trial in which he is the loser and martyr, knowing full well in advance that he is destined to lose:

> Why, then, my Lord, you did not raise your clement hand? (*Love, Death, and Exile*).

This question, however, is asked out of love and due recognition, just as al-Ḥallāj's Iblīs does:

O my creator!
So this is
ordained for me? You made me not to prostrate by Your
will, and you are all-powerful, most high.[33]

But al-Bayātī's mask takes preordination a step further by questioning an overwhelming injustice:

From beneath the obelisks of the tyrants of this world
From beneath the ashes of the centuries
From behind the bars,
I cry in the night of the continents,
I give my love as an offering
To the wild beast waiting at all doors (*Love, Death, and Exile*, pp. 170–71).

While the drive in al-Ḥallāj's poem purports to convey pride in love and delight in showing it, the focus in al-Bayātī's poem is on sacrifice through love as the ultimate destiny of poets in an unjust world. This love is transferred to the poor who are no less destined to suffer. As creative minds, both the poet and al-Ḥallāj share one destiny and enjoy an intellectual companionship beyond time:

> In the flower beds and in the forests of the childhood of my love, al-Hallaj was my companion on all voyages, we shared bread and wrote poetry about the visions of the hungry, abandoned poor, in the kingdom of the great mason, about the secret of the rebellion of this man burning with desire for the light his head bowed before the tyrant (*Love, Death, and Exile*, 172–73).

Exposed to the secular politics of modernity and enraptured by al-Ḥallāj's dialogic poetics that allows enough space for the inclusion of Satan's rejoinders, al-Bayātī's poet openly critiques the "great mason," leaving it to the reader to apply the term (which is repeated twice) (pts. 1, 9). The poet uses love and martyrdom as focal points in al-Ḥallāj's exposition of Satan's stubborn stance as lover, but he gives the reader enough discretion to debate rebellious sentiments and the politics of despair:

Why, my Lord, did you not raise your clement hand in the face of the evil coming from all the doors?
Why are the words exiled? Why does love become suffering?
The silence a torture in this exile and

The words
Life buoys
For those drowned by this wave
Full of the anarchy of things? (*Love, Death, and Exile*, pp. 174–75).

As al-Bayātī's title indicates, al-Ḥallāj's *Ṭawāsīn* is intended as the subtext, but its overall design and dialogic presence situate it more in Sufi modernity as a paradoxical combination of warring factions. Al-Ḥallāj himself shows a lot of unease in justifying and critiquing Satan's impulsive response. The most eloquent of mystics remained silent on the subject of Satan, and the sages lacked the strength to utter what they had learned about him. In Massignon's interpretation, to Ḥallāj's contemporaries, like Shīblī and Jīlī, Satan "is more informed than they about worship, he is closer than they to the Being; he is zealous in devotion to Him; he has kept more to his vow than they. He has drawn nearer than they to the Beloved."[34] Thus, while allowing Satan to justify his irrevocable love for God as unlimited and unsurpassed devotion, he criticizes his "detachment, as he has not reached the end / as there was no beginning."[35] His status is an "inversion of his essence, which is burnt by the / fire of his unbending / zeal; and is brightened by the light of his / detachment" (p. 91). Al-Bayātī deviates yet further, and collapses al-Ḥallāj's Iblīs into the author, resolving the poem in a conclusive metaphor of committed and sacrificial love. To be sure, this basic thematic pattern is also central to al-Ḥallāj's *Ṭawāsīn*, but al-Bayātī frames it anew and places the symbolic power of the Sufi image of the fluttering moth in human terms. People hover around al-Ḥallāj, and by extension around the poet as companion and around the fire, in anticipation and expectation. The self-annihilation involved in the second journey of the fluttering moth around the lamp or the candle is to fulfill the desire to reach perfect ecstasy through total annihilation. The burned moth is "the one who has seen," but who is unconcerned about passing satisfaction and secondhand accounts.[36] In al-Bayātī's poem, the persona recognizes the fact of martyrdom; this perfect love, self-annihilation in yearning for Oneness, is reached by al-Ḥallāj, but not by Iblīs, nor by the poet for that matter:

All the poor gathered around al-Hallaj.
Around the fire
In this night haunted by the fever of something
which might or might not come from behind the walls (*Love, Death, and Exile*, pp. 174–75).

Both the burned moth and al-Ḥallāj have enjoyed the moment of grace. They have seen what Moses can only see through a medium, a fire, or a mountain. The poet may conjecture and envision, but he has not seen what the other two have already seen, leaving us in distraction and perplexity as befits modernity and its discontents.

What Might or Might Not Come

The implications of "which might or might not come" may well come forth through the Sufi trope of the moth around the candle. Hovering and fluttering around the flame and heat, the moth is delighted to observe and relate the experience to its awaiting peers. In *Ṭawāsīn*, al-Ḥallāj says:

> The candle moth hangs around the light of the candle all night and in different forms returns with the morning sun, in the morning; and then relates what happened, how it happened; and in what happened lies joy, his only happiness; for his breast contains the hope to meet perfection.[37]

The impossible return signifies ultimate self-annihilation, whereas waiting is synonymous with anxiety and suspense in anticipation of what "might or might not come." This waiting takes another form in al-Bayātī's poetry, especially in his poems of the 1970s. The thing, person, or figure "which might or might not come" operates as a creative impulse that is no different from the Sufi "Creative Feminine" as discussed by Henry Corbin.[38] In Jalāluddīn Rūmī's words, as cited by Corbin:

> Woman is a beam of the Divine Light. She is not the being whom sensual desire takes as its object. She is Creator, it should be said. She is not a Creature.[39]

Al-Bayātī takes Christian and extreme Shī'ī dicta much further, being unconcerned with the Virgin Mother or Glorious Fāṭima, the Prophet's daughter. Instead his focus is on the construction of the image that eludes him and leaves him always distracted and perplexed. The creative feminine may operate as an abstraction, something that takes shape only in relation to the speaker's experience and his accumulated repertoire of poetic imagery. In "I Shall Reveal My Love for You to the Wind and the Trees" (*The Kingdom of Grain*, 1979), the speaker or persona addresses the lonely and forlorn self as it recollects a past of yearning and desire: "You crouch alone now in your room. Memories wash over you. Such is life: the body of a woman sighing beneath you, eyes closed, as black snow falls on her cheeks. She cries in silence" (*Love, Death, and Exile*, pp. 256–57). The speaker knows how sad his image may sound and thus continues, "The sadness of the Spanish night and the snow of the Russian forests penetrate your heart" (pp. 260–61). He is no more than "[a] man . . . now burning alone in his room" (pp. 260–61). As a poet, all he is capable of is "[p]raying for the naked dazed people from shore to shore" (pp. 260–61). As for the woman who is to receive this confession of love as it appears in the title, she has no physical existence, but she may be in the process of becoming, not only in order to balance the stark life of the poet, but also to culminate the creative process which takes place under a glimmer that "might or might not come":

O woman who will be
I shall reveal my love for you to the wind and the trees
And I shall rewrite your history on the blank map. (pp. 262–63)

Al-Bayātī's Sufi exilic poetics does not necessarily reach the Islam of the common people; indeed it may fail to establish those emotive links that are needed in the first place in order to build on shared codes. This surmise may apply to the Arab modernist tradition before the pivotal break with the politics of the *nahḍah* in 1967 and the aftermath of the 1968 birth of a new avant-garde consciousness through the surging alliance between students and workers all over the capitalist world. There is, nevertheless, another dimension to the politics and poetics of protest. Especially when al-Bayātī's poetics of protest are located and well entrenched in the context of Sufi pieties, it can speak to the common public as shareholders in a predicament which is not of their making. In an alliance that holds the dispossessed together there is room for a poetics of repair, one that displaces the *nahḍah*'s maxims of assurance and certainty. Harking back to an ancient tradition and echoing forlorn predecessors, the poetic persona forges more links with a public that wants to look to tradition as a resource and repertoire in times of global challenge.

Notes

1. Albert Camus, *The Myth of Sisyphus* (Harmondsworth: Penguin, 1942), 25.
2. Michel Foucault, *The Order of Things: An Archaeology of the Human Sciences* (New York: Vintage Books, 1973), 50.
3. John M. Asfour, *When the Words Burn: An Anthology of Modern Arabic Poetry, 1945–1987* (Dunvegan, Ontario: Cormorant, 1988).
4. Amal Dunqul, "A Special Interview with Noah's Son," trans. Fatma Moussa-Mahmud, "Changing Techniques in Modern Arabic Poetry," in *Tradition and Modernity in Arabic Language and Literature* (Richmond, UK: Curzon, 1996), 61–74, at 73–74.
5. Dunqul, 74.
6. Dunqul, 72.
7. References are to ʿAbd al-Wahhāb al-Bayātī, *Abdul Wahab Al-Bayāti: Love, Death, and Exile*, trans. Bassam K. Frangieh (Washington, DC: Georgetown University Press, 1990).

8. Āl-Bayāti, *Abdul Wahāb Al-Bayāti: Love, Death, and Exile*, 92–94. Further references are incorporated within the text.
9. Translations are slightly amended.
10. Henry Corbin, *Creative Imagination in the Sufism of Ibn Arabī* (originally in French, 1958). His other works on Ibn ʿArabī and Suhrawardī were also available in Arabic, 1941, 1945, 1951, and 1956.
11. Louis Massignon, *The Passion of al-Ḥallāj: Mystic and Martyr of Islam*, trans. Herbert Masson (Princeton, NJ: Princeton University Press, 1982).
12. Corbin, *Creative Imagination in the Sufism of Ibn Arabī*, 146.
13. Corbin, *Creative Imagination in the Sufism of Ibn Arabī*, 146.
14. Corbin, *Creative Imagination in the Sufism of Ibn Arabī*,147.
15. Corbin, *Creative Imagination in the Sufism of Ibn Arabī*, 147.
16. Corbin, *Creative Imagination in the Sufism of Ibn Arabī*, 148.
17. Al-Bayātī, *Abdul Wahab Al-Bayāti: Love, Death, and Exile*, 249.
18. Corbin, *Creative Imagination in the Sufism of Ibn Arabī*, 148.
19. Corbin, *Creative Imagination in the Sufism of Ibn Arabī*, 330.
20. Corbin, *Creative Imagination in the Sufism of Ibn Arabī*, 330, n. 21.
21. Al-Bayātī, *Abdul Wahab Al-Bayāti: Love, Death, and Exile*, 254–55.
22. Corbin, *Creative Imagination in the Sufism of Ibn Arabī*, ref. 330, n. 22, to Ibn ʿArabī, 326:9.
23. Al-Bayātī, *Abdul Wahab Al-Bayāti: Love, Death, and Exile*, 248–49.
24. Corbin, *Creative Imagination in the Sufism of Ibn Arabī*, 149.
25. Corbin's paraphrase, *Creative Imagination in the Sufism of Ibn Arabī*, 150.
26. Massignon, *The Passion of al-Ḥallāj*, 3:290, n. 70.
27. Massignon, *The Passion of al-Ḥallāj*, 3:290.
28. Massignon, *The Passion of al-Ḥallāj*, 3:309.
29. Massignon, *The Passion of al-Ḥallāj*, 3:314.
30. Gilani Kamran, trans., *Anā al-Haqq Reconsidered: With a translation of Kitab al-Ṭawasin* (Lahore: Maqsh-e-Awwal Kitab Ghar), 89–90.
31. Kamran, *Anā al-Haqq Reconsidered*, 91–92.
32. Kamran, *Anā al-Haqq Reconsidered*, 90.
33. Kamran, *Anā al-Haqq Reconsidered*, 96.
34. See Massignon, *The Passion of al-Ḥallāj*, 3:315, and n. 286.
35. Kamran, *Anā al-Haqq*, 91.
36. See Massignon, *The Passion of al-Ḥallāj* 290.
37. Kamran, *Anā al-Haqq*, 11:61.
38. Corbin, *Creative Imagination in the Sufism of Ibn Arabī*, 175.
39. Corbin, *Creative Imagination in the Sufism of Ibn Arabī*, 160.

Conclusion

Since the advent of *nahḍah* discourse, words such as science, development, evolution, progress, happiness, freedom, and the spirit of the age have been catchphrases for the Arab elite, but they no longer enjoy the same status and dominance as they once did. In their stead there has arisen a mounting discourse which first simmered latently among the *'ulamā'* (the learned shaykhs and theologians) and their disciples before eventually expressing itself publicly in terms of disappointment, frustration, and anger, not only against the devastating failures of the nation-state, with all its bureaucracy and opportunism, but also in response to a neocon-led backlash against Islam collapsed into a single entity along with fundamentalism and terrorism. This counterdiscourse has taken shape in the fight against colonial military and administrative power, and has drawn further legitimacy through a sustained questioning of the attitude of compromise long upheld by the disciples of Shaykh Muḥammad ʿAbdu (d. 1905) in particular, with their keen interest in striking a balance between Islamic civilization and culture on the one hand and the gifts of European enlightenment on the other. Such a discourse of compromise was further misused by the Arab elite in the period preceding June 1967. It no longer fares well in the face of an aggressive anti-Islamic discourse that has taken the "clash of civilizations" as a given, a globalized version of Kipling's geographical binary of the incompatible East/West. The noncompromising Islamic discourse, such as the one fostered by the founder of the Muslim Brotherhood in Egypt, Ḥasan al-Bannā, for example, does not totally refuse an engagement with the achievements of civilizations and cultures, but it has nevertheless opted for a clear-cut Islamic application that meets what it conceives to be the needs and demands of an Islamic nation.

The strength of the *nahḍah* discourse among the elite was originally founded on its critique of an Ottoman legacy that in the minds of some was associated with backwardness, an idea that was opposed and even resisted by Turkish nationalists. This confusion was responsible for the anxieties that accompanied the *nahḍah*, its advocates' compelling desire for change, and their distance from the street, which was usually conceived as being a common public that needed to be controlled and disciplined. Textbooks, educational inculcation, and media avenues have all been invoked as ways of using an official or semiofficial language of codification and legitimation to exert a tight grip on the educated public. The literary language itself is involved in this effort to bring common people under the control of this system.[1] To codify Arabic within the new compromise between the revivalist tendencies of classical Arabic and the impulse toward European modernity, lexicons were compiled and efforts were made to codify education through programs that made use of European systems. No wonder then that the graduates of the colleges of higher education in Egypt and Iraq were the forerunners of the modernist trend in poetry; in departments of English, Palgrave's *Golden Treasury* of English poetry was not only the most celebrated text, but also the most influential in leading to the engagement with modernist poetics.[2]

Even when preparing for important projects such as Arabic-English lexicons, Ismāʿīl Maẓhar, like other *nahḍah* intellectuals, explains three things that may bring this discussion to a conclusion: There is first the fact that language, and Arabic in particular, is the receptacle of national spirit; it is its "natural register which reflects its progressive movement towards perfection."[3] It has an organic life.[4] If it wanes during a particular era, that may not indicate failure, but merely a temporary decline. Hence the value of dictionaries and lexicons in maintaining the linguistic heritage and preparing for revival. He adds that he never resorts to colloquial Arabic, dialects, or vernaculars, but is more attuned to the emerging contact with Europe in order to revive words and phrases that were once dead but may now assimilate the emerging language of science or retrieve the old register as a way of coping with the new. This effort and rationale are aspects of the *nahḍah* spirit, but there is little concern with the common public, which is referred to simply as a potential recipient of care.

The estrangement of this *nahḍah* discourse from the masses relegates the religion of the street to the background. Among these elites there is a definite tendency toward secularism, a trend that is far removed from any kind of vacillation between the European model of progress and Islamic theology and

Sufism. The Iraqi Maḥmūd Aḥmad al-Sayyid shows no qualms concerning religion, and his advocacy of Darwinism highlights a struggle for survival that places fierce demands on the individual and society. Faith in science and doubts concerning traditional explanations of life and human genealogy are a central theme in Maḥfūẓ's *Trilogy*, between Aḥmad 'Abd al-Jawād and his son Kamāl. The Iraqi Marxist Dhū al-Nūn Ayyūb makes fun of religion as practiced by pretentious shaykhs and fake saints like the protagonist's father in *Duktūr Ibrāhīm*.[5] One can say that these works fit well in the growing secular discourse which has its roots not only in translations from other cultures, but also in Islamic rationalist philosophy since the tenth century. Ṭāhā Ḥusayn's *Fī al-Shi'r al-Jāhilī* (1926; *On Pre-Islamic Poetry*) and 'Alī 'Abd al-Rāziq's *Al-Islām wa 'Uṣūl al-Ḥukm* (1925; *Islam and the Foundations of Rule*) were isolated neither from Islamic rationalist thought nor from an early engagement with mainstream European culture in the second half of the nineteenth century. The genuine and relentless effort to study, question, and revoke Islamic thought took place in monographs that never saw the light of day because of their open discussion of tradition on human bases and making use of human, not divine, criteria. Such was the renowned Iraqi poet Ma'rūf al-Ruṣāfī's *Al-Shakhṣiyyah al-Muḥammadiyyah* (*The Muhammadan Character*), which was censored by the Iraqi Academy (Scientific Society) in the 1940s.

Islamist discourse, as distinguished from "Islamic discourse," is to receive different treatments at a later stage, for in Maḥfūẓ's *Arabian Nights and Days* it implies service to man, not God; in Qāsim's *Al-Mahdī* it denotes coercion, since, according to the Sufi shaykh, yelling and raising one's voice are ways of enforcing an opinion which involves intimidation and misuse of power. Both authors provide a different version of Islamic discourse, one that is pleasant, compassionate, and full of love, a preference in which Sufism is the dominant factor. In al-Aswāny's treatment, Islamist discourse, as a fighting mode, means persuasion coupled with manipulation of the angry masses in order to confront reactionary regimes that support imperial and neocolonial encroachments on Muslim lands. In all these works language is a space for contestation.

In its many layers and shades, the entire discursive effort invokes a European legacy, especially in the depiction of ideas, positions, and types. Whether in rapprochement, subservience, or opposition, the contending platforms that emerge develop in relation to European, and later American, referentiality. A thin grounding in tradition or an unlimited fascination with the European model lead to a transposition of systems of thought. New values and expressions displace cultural specificities, not only in relation to the Arab homoerotic lexicon that has lately been the subject of attention, but also in literary terminology, philosophy, philology, nationhood, and religion. Especially in the context of a superimposed colonial legacy and the consequent failures of national revolutions and their nation-state apparatuses to create a cohesive body politic, unlimited borrowing and the wholesale application of different systems of thought that have nothing to do with the demands of the spirit of the age have led to serious misconstructions. If a wholesale application of European and American sexual politics has led to the understanding of Arab homoeroticism as being a deviation from heterosexual norms and thus as a "symptom of societal and economic degeneration . . . denoting failed national aspirations as well as dysfunctional Arab masculinity,"[6] then similar conceptualizations of nationhood, structures of feeling, and individual and communal roles have suffered no less damage. Systems of education heavily influenced by Western-educated graduates who have returned to their homelands with meager knowledge of their culture have led to the internalization of concepts and attitudes that fit very well into inclinations and practices of the petit bourgeoisie and thus seem totally anomalous in comparison to the mainstream societal and religious attitudes that feed Islam on the street.

In literary production, under the impact of the discourse of the *nahḍah*, Islam rarely appears as a dynamic force, a powerful cultural drive to determine trends and directions. Indeed literary production until the 1970s was oblivious to the Islamic component. If it ever appeared, it was confused with an outworn tradition of superstition, ritual, and visitation, such as those that make up the dichotomous and paradigmatic poles in *The Lamp of Umm Hāshim* by the Egyptian Yaḥyā Ḥaqqī, discussed earlier. Between the sciences he learned in Britain and the traditional patterns of life and belief, Isma`il decides in the end to align himself with tradition as a corpus of outworn practices and beliefs that appeal to the masses; he will treat their serious problems through make-believe rather than actual treatment and cure.

While this paradigm of literary production confuses religion with popular faith, the other tendency mocks the clergy. The well-known Egyptian writer Ibrāhīm 'Abd al-Qādir al-Māzinī's (d. 1949) story, "How I Became a Demon of the Jinn" may be a good example.[7] The narrator overcomes his fears at night while walking through a graveyard, only to find out that the sound of footsteps that have frightened him are those of an old shaykh on his way to the Imām al-Shāfi'ī mosque. The narrator decides to frighten the shaykh; every now and then he hides and reappears, until the shaykh is gripped by fear to the extent that he begins to confuse some verses from the Qur'ān with others, their beginnings with their ends. In the mosque he tells his audience the story of the devil that can only be warded off through recitation of the Qur'ānic Kursī (Throne) verse. Upon setting his eye on the protagonist in the mosque, the shaykh points to him in fear and perplexity, about to identify him as the devil he has seen. Indeed, writers' surrogates operate as such in a large corpus of literary production in the first half of the century. There are many other narratives in this same humorous vein, such as "Grace" by the Iraqi Ja'far al-Khalīlī (d. 1984),[8] and *Duktūr Ibrāhīm* (Ibrāhīm the Doctor) by Dhū al-Nūn Ayyūb (d. 1988).

This mockery is unlike the intentional critiques that choose to rewrite scriptural narratives anew, divesting them of the omniscient divine presence that determines the directions of each destiny. Tawfīq al-Ḥakīm's drama *Ahl al-Kahf* (The Cave Sleepers) is free of the divine lesson that the Moroccan writer Driss Chraibi depicts as corresponding to the Prophet Muḥammad's state of mind when flooded with revelations and scriptural narratives. Chraibi's work appeared in French in 1995, whereas al-Ḥakīm's play appeared in 1933. Chraibi's text is neither a new biography of the Prophet nor a secular narrative. It is obviously a narrative of a combined representational and poetic nature, aimed at making the profile of the Prophet accessible to the French readership and the Muslim community there. It is neither a heavily detailed biographical sketch hampered by faithfulness to historical records nor a poetic recreation of biographical data. It has both those qualities, but its significance lies somewhere else: its French habitus, and the émigré's search for rapprochement with a tradition that is under attack as Europe witnesses a new upsurge of dichotomies and polarizations as part of a deliberate global-imperial onslaught. But this comparison between Chraibi's *Muḥammad* and al-Ḥakim's *Sleepers* is worth pursuing for a more specific reason. *Muḥammad* appeared in good time, anticipating an era of confusion that deliberately provoked cultural clashes; it therefore fits into the cultural nexus of the global system while contesting its dominant power politics. Al-Ḥakim's play, on the other hand, was motivated by a different impulse, namely the incentive of modernity, with its freedom from divine obligations. In spite of al-Ḥakim's balanced navigation of ideas between East and West, it nevertheless functions in allegiance with European modernity.

The surging Islamic fervor, especially with respect to its political manifestations that have interested different international powers and regional regimes, is not a spontaneous growth, the result of an unaccountable emergence. Apart from the well-known reasons—mechanisms employed by global powers to exploit, use, misuse, and redirect the phenomenon—there are also more substantial and dynamic factors, founded on dissatisfaction and frustration with the nation-state before and after its perceived mandatory role in the region. While historians, strategists, and political scientists have been involved in studying the phenomenon for different reasons and from various perspectives, literary production has been considerably less preoccupied. It has only recently begun to take the entire issue more seriously, a position that evolves from politically and ideologically oriented imperatives rather than from faith in Islam and tradition as actual components of the individual's identity and life. The shift toward religion has become so noticeable as to enlist many Islamists and Islamic thinkers in discussions of literary and cultural works that were once the monopoly of secularists. Indeed we need to remember that the prolific and influential Egyptian Shaykh ʿAbd al-Ḥamīd Kishk only provided a scathing critique of Maḥfūẓ's *Awlād Ḥāratinā* (1959) in 1990, accusing Maḥfūẓ of communist views expressed at a time when the Communist fervor in Egypt and the Arab world was at its height. Writing his critique in book form,[9] he went over Maḥfūẓ's literary production and focused in particular on this controversial novel, something he could only do in the 1990s when Islamic discourse had the power to debate secular politics openly.

The religious fervor was not necessarily prompted as a reaction to secular ideology or neoconservative onslaughts on Islam. Many Communists switched to religion in their search for certitude. In *Women on a Journey between Baghdad and London*, for example, the Iraqi Haifa Zangana depicts Kāẓim as a communist leader whose disillusionment with his party drives him to religion. "He's searching for an identity now that he's lost the beliefs which he's held all his life," as his wife argues.[10] However, neo-Marxists choose to interpret this turn to religion in a different way, explaining it as one way of consolidating their connection with the masses. Only through a good grasp of religion and tradition and a faith in one's culture can modern Arab intellectuals retain any emotive links that will keep them abreast of public preoccupations and needs. While it is possible to detect an opportunist endeavor in recent literary production, driven and formed by the logic of supply and demand, there is at the same time a belated faith that may come to influence, enhance, and equip the literary market with new tools and visions. Arab writers are no longer in the vanguard of social and political movements, and they need to assess their role, critique it, and envision it anew in order to cope with Islam on the street.

Notes

1. For more on this issue, see Pierre Bourdieu, *Language and Symbolic Power* (Cambridge, MA: Harvard University Press, 1991), 60–61.

2. See Muhsin al-Musawi, *Arabic Poetry: Trajectories of Modernity and Tradition* (London: Routledge, 2006); J. Brugman, *An Introduction to the History of Modern Arabic Literature in Egypt* (Leiden: Brill, 1984), 98–99.

3. Ismā'īl Maẓhar, "Introduction," *Qāmūs al-Nahḍah* (Al-Nahḍah Dictionary; Cairo: Maktabat al-Nahḍah al-Miṣriyyah, The Egyptian Renaissance Bookshop, n.d.).

4. As central to the mission of education, expressed by Georges Davy and building on Humboldt and Durkheim, this view of education and language was in the minds of most Arab intellectuals in the first half of the century. See Bourdieu, *Language and Symbolic Power*, 49.

5. Ayyūb, *Duktūr Ibrāhīm* (1938; first part, "The Pillar of Babylon," 1936).

6. See Hannadi al-Samman's review and encapsulation of such attitudes in "Out of the Closet: Representation of Homosexuals and Lesbians in Modern Arabic Literature," *Journal of Arabic Literature* 39:2 (2008), 258–98, at 259.

7. Ibrāhīm 'Abd al-Qādir al-Māzinī, "How I Became a Demon of the Jinn," in *Modern Arabic Fiction Anthology*, ed. Salma K. Jayyusi (New York: Columbia University Press, 2005), 99–103.

8. Al-Māzinī, "How I Became a Demon of the Jinn, " 92–96.

9. See Fauzi M. Najjar, "Islamic Fundamentalism and the Intellectuals: The Case of Naguib Mahfouz," *British Journal of Middle Eastern Studies* 25:1 (1998): 139–68; for this discussion, 145–46.

10. Haifa Zangana, *Women on a Journey between Baghdad and London*, trans. Judy Cumberbatch (Austin: Center for Middle Eastern Studies at the University of Texas at Austin, 2007), 166.

Works Cited

Abbot, Nadia. "A New Fragment of the 'Thousand Nights': A New Light on the Early History of the Arabian Nights," *Journal of Near Eastern Studies* 8 (1949): 129–64. Reprinted in Ulrich Marzolph, *The Arabian Nights: A Reader*, pp. 21–82.

Abdel Nasser, Gamal. "The Egyptian Revolution," *Foreign Affairs* 33 (January 1955), 199–211.

Althusser, Louis. "Ideology and Ideological State Apparatuses," extract in *A Critical and Cultural Theory Reader*, ed. Antony Easthope and Kate McGowan. Toronto: University of Toronto Press, 2002: 50–58.

Altoma, S. J. "Westernization and Islam in Modern Arabic Fiction," *Yearbook of Comparative and General Literature* 20 (1971): 81–88.

Anis, Mona. "Thus Spoke Yehia Haqqi," *Al-Ahram Weekly* (weekly.ahram.org.eg/2004/688/bo7.htm).

Asfour, John M. *When the Words Burn: An Anthology of Modern Arabic Poetry, 1945–1987*. Dunvegan, Ontario: Cormorant, 1988.

'Aslī, Bassām. *'Abd al-Ḥamīd Bin Bādīs*. Beirut: Dār al-Nafā'is, 1986.

Al-Aswānī, 'Alā'. *'Imārat Ya'qūbiyān*. 2004; English translation: *The Yacoubian Building*, by 'Alā' al-Aswāny, trans. Humphrey Davies. New York: Harper Perennial, 2006.

Amīn, Aḥmad. *Fayḍ al-Khāṭir*. 1942 Cairo: Lajnat al-ta'lif wa-al-tarjamah wa-al-nashr, 1942–44; reprint Maktahat al-Nahḍah al-Miṣriyyah, 1965.

Ayyūb, Dhū al-Nūn. *Duktūr Ibrāhīm*. 1938; first part, "The Pillar of Babylon," 1936. Baghdad: Wizārat al-thaqāfah, 1973.

Badawī, M. M. "Islam in Modern Egyptian Literature," in *Modern Arabic Literature and the West*. London: Ithaca Press, 1985.

Badeau, John S. "A Role in Search of a Hero: A Brief Study of the Egyptian Revolution," *Middle East Journal* 9/10 (1955): 373–84.

Bakr, Salwā. *Maqām 'Aṭiyyah*. 1992; English translation: *The Shrine of 'Atia: A Novella*, trans. Denys Johnson-Davies. Cairo: American University in Cairo Press, 1997.

Baldick, Julian. *Mystical Islam: An Introduction to Sufism*. New York: New York University Press, 1989.

Al-Bannā, Ḥasan. *Five Tracts of Hasan al-Banna (1906–1949)*, trans. Charles Wendell. Berkeley: University of California Press, 1978.

Al-Bayātī, ʿAbd al-Wahhāb. *Abdul Wahab Al-Bayāti: Love, Death, and Exile*, trans. Bassam K. Frangieh. Washington, DC: Georgetown University Press, 1990.

Bourdieu, Pierre. *Language and Symbolic Power*, trans. Gino Raymond and Matthew Adamson; ed. and intro. John B. Thompson. Cambridge, MA: Harvard University Press, 1991.

Brinner, William. "The Significance of the Ḥarāfīsh and Their 'Sultan' " *Journal of the Economic and Social History of the Orient* 6:2 (1963): 190–215.

Brugman, J. *An Introduction to the History of Modern Arabic Literature in Egypt*. Leiden: Brill, 1984.

Cacchia, Pierre. *An Overview of Modern Arabic Literature*. Edinburgh: Edinburgh University Press, 1990.

Camus, Albert. *The Myth of Sisyphus*. Harmondsworth: Penguin, 1942.

Cobham, Catherine. "Enchanted to a Stone—Heroes and Leaders in *The Ḥarāfīsh* by Najīb Maḥfūẓ," *Middle Eastern Literatures* 9:2 (2006): 123–35.

Coetzee, J. M. "Fabulous Fabulist," *New York Review of Books* 41:15 (September 22, 1994).

Corbin, Henry. *Creative Imagination in the Sufism of Ibn Arabi* (originally in French, 1958). Trans. Ralph Manheim. Princeton, NJ: Princeton University Press, 1969.

Currie, Mark. "Jean-Paul Sartre, Albert Camus and Existentialism," in *The Continuum Encyclopedia of Modern Criticism and Theory*, ed. Julian Wolfreys et al. New York: Continuum, 2002.

Dawwārah, Fu'ād. *Najīb Maḥfūẓ*. Cairo: GEBO, 1989.

Donohue, John, and John Esposito, eds. *Islam in Transition: Muslim Perspectives*. New York: Oxford University Press, 1982.

Dunqul, Amal. "A Special Interview with Noah's Son," trans. Fatma Moussa-Mahmud, "Changing Techniques in Modern Arabic Poetry," in *Tradition and Modernity in Arabic Language and Literature*. Richmond, UK: Curzon, 1996: 61–74.

Easthope, Antony, and Kate McGowan, ed. *A Critical and Cultural Theory Reader*. Toronto: University of Toronto Press, 2002.

Fanon, Frantz. *The Wretched of the Earth*, trans. Constance Farrington. New York: Grove Press, 1963.

Foucault, Michel. *Discipline and Punish: A Critical Cultural Reader*, ed. Antony Easthope and Kate McGowan. Toronto: University of Toronto Press, 2002: 81–984.

Foucault, Michel. *The Order of Things: Archaeology of the Human Sciences*. New York: Vintage Books, 1973.

Gaffney, Patrick D. "Magic, Mirage, and the Politics of Narration," *Religion and Literature* 20:1: 111–35 .

Al-Ghīṭanī, Jamāl. *Al-Zaynī Barakāt*. Damascus: Ministry of Culture, 1974. English translation: *Zaynī Barakāt*, trans. Farouk Abdel Wahab Mustafa. 1988; Cairo: American University in Cairo Press, 2004.

Greene, Thomas. "The Norms of Epic," *Comparative Literature* 13:3 (1961): 193–207.

Grunebaum, G. E. Von. "The Spirit of Islam as Shown in Its Literature," *Studia Islamica* no. 1 (1953): 101–19.

Habermas, Jürgen. *The Inclusion of the Other*, ed. Ciaran De Greiff and Pablo De Greiff. Cambridge, MA: MIT Press, 1998.

Habermas, Jürgen. *Religion and Rationality*, ed. Eduardo Mendiete. Cambridge, MA: MIT Press, 2002.

Al-Ḥakīm, Tawfiq. *'Uṣfūr min al-Sharq*. 1938; English translation: *A Bird of the East*, trans. R. Bayly Winder. Beirut: Khayats, 1966.

Ḥaqqī, Yaḥyā. *Qindīl Umm Hāshim*. 1944; English translation: *The Lamp of Umm Hāshim*. Cairo: American University in Cairo Press, 2004. It also appeared as *The Saint's Lamp and Other Stories*. Trans. M. M. Basawi, Leiden: Brill, 1973.

Harris, Christina Phelps. *Nationalism and Revolution in Egypt: The Role of the Muslim Brotherhood*. Stanford, CA: Mouton, 1964.

Al-Ḥirz, Ṣabā (pseudonym). *Al-Ākharūn*. Beirut: Al-Sāqī, 2006.

Hitti, Philip K. *Cities of Arab Islam*. Minneapolis: University of Minnesota Press, 1973.

Ḥusayn, Ṭāḥā. *Al-Ayyām*. (vols. 1, 2, 1929; vol. 3, 1973; English translation: *The Days*). Trans. E. H. Paxton, Hilary Wayment, and Kenneth Cragg. Cairo: American University of Cairo Press, 1997.

Ḥusayn, Ṭāḥā. *Al-Mu'aththabūn fī al-arḍ*. 1947; English translation: *The Sufferers*. Cairo: American University in Cairo Press, 1993.

Ḥusayn, Ṭāḥā. *Qādat al-fikr*. Cairo: Al-Hilāl, 1925.

Ibn Khaldūn, 'Abd al-Raḥmān. *The Muqaddimah*, trans. Franz Rosenthal. Princeton, NJ: Princeton University Press, 2005.

Ibn Ṭufayl, Muḥammad Ibn 'Abd al-Malik. *Ḥayy Ibn Yaqẓān: A Philosophical Tale*, trans. intro. and notes by Lenn Evan Goodman. Los Angeles: gee tee bee, 1983.

Idrīs, Samāḥ. *Al-Muthaqqaf al-'Arabī wa-al-ṣulṭān: baḥth fī riwāyāt al-tajribah al-Nāṣiriyah*. Bayrūt: Dār al-Ādāb, 1992.

Idrīs, Yūsuf. *The Language of Pain*, trans. Nawal Nagib. Cairo: GEBO, 1990.

'Izz al-Dīn, Yūsuf. *Al-Riwāyah fī al-'Irāq*. Cairo: Ma'had al-Buḥūth wa-al-Dirāsāt al-Adabiyyah, 1973.

Al-Jabartī 'Abd al-Raḥmān. *Al-Jabartī's Chronicle of the First Seven Months of the French Occupation of Egypt*, trans. S. Moreh. Leiden: Brill, 1975.

Kamran, Gilani, trans. *Ana al-Haqq Reconsidered: With a Translation of Kitab al-Tawasin*. Lahare: Maqsh-e-Awwal Kitab Ghar, 1977.

Khaldi Boutheina. "Going Public: Mayy Ziyādah and Her Literary Salon in a Comparative Context," unpublished doctoral dissertation. Indiana University, Bloomington, 2008.

Khūrī, Ilyās. *Riḥlat Ghandī al-Ṣaghīr*. 1989; English translation: *The Journey of Little Ghandi*. Minneapolis: University of Minnesota Press, 1994.

Lane, Edward W. *An Account of the Manners and of the Customs of the Egyptians*. Cairo: American University Press in Cairo, 2003.

Lefebvre, Henri. *The Production of Space*. Oxford: Basil Blackwell, 1991.

Le Gassick, Trevor. "The Path of Islam in Modern Arabic Fiction," *Religion and Literature* 20:1 (1988): 97–109.

Lukács, Georg. *The Theory of the Novel*. London: Merlin Press, 1978.

Macherey, Pierre. *A Theory of Literary Production*, trans. Geoffrey Wall. London: Routledge, 1978.

Māḍī, Shukrī. *'Azīz. In'ikās hazīmat ḥazīrān 'alā al-riwāyah al-'Arabiyah*. Beirut: MADN, 1978.

Maḥfūẓ, Najīb. *Al-Liṣṣ wa al-Kilāb*. English translation: *The Thief and the Dogs*. New York: Anchor, 2000.

Maḥfūẓ, Najīb. *Arabian Nights and Days*, trans. Denys Johnson-Davies. New York: Anchor, 1995.

Maḥfuẓ, Najīb. *Mahhamat al-Ḥarāfīsh* (1977). English translation: The Ḥarāfish. Trans. Catherine Cobham. New York: Anchor Books, 1995.

Maḥfūẓ, Najīb. *Riḥlat Ibn Faṭṭūmah*. 1983; English translation: *The Journey of Ibn Fattouma*, trans. Denys Johnson-Davies. New York: Anchor, 1993.

Massignon, Louis. *The Passion of al-Ḥallāj: Mystic and Martyr of Islam*, trans. Herbert Masson. Princeton, NJ: Princeton University Press, 1982.

Maẓhar, Ismā'īl. "Introduction," in *Qāmūs al-Nahḍah* (Al-Nahḍah Dictionary). Cairo: Maktabat al-Nahḍah al-Miṣriyyah, The Egyptian Renaissance Bookshop, n.d.

Al-Māzinī, Ibrāhīm 'Abd al-Qādir. "How I Became a Demon of the Jinn," in *Modern Arabic Fiction Anthology*, ed. Salma K. Jayyusi. New York: Columbia University Press, 2005, 99–103.

Al-Māzinī, Ibrāhim 'Abd al-Qādir. *Ibrāhim al-Kātib*. 1931; English translation: *Ibrāhīm the Writer*, trans. Magdi Wahba. Cairo: GEBO, 1976.

Merrifield, Andrew. "Place and Space: A Lefebvrian Reconciliation," *Transactions of the Institute of British Geographers* N. S. 18:4 (1993): 516–31.

Morrison, S. A. "Arab Nationalism and Islam," *Middle East Journal* 2 (1948): 147–59.

Mūsā, Salāma. *The Education of Salāma Mūsā*, trans. L. O. Schuman. Leiden: Brill, 1961.

Al-Musawi, Muhsin. *Arabic Poetry: Trajectories of Modernity and Tradition*. London: Routledge, 2006.

Al-Mūsawī, Muḥsin. *Al-Istshrāq fī al-fikr al-'Arabī* (Orientalism in Arab Thought). Beirut: MADN, 1993.

Al-Musawi, Muhsin. *The Postcolonial Arabic Novel*. Leiden: Brill, 2003.

Al-Musawi, Muhsin. *Reading Iraq*. London: I.B. Tauris, 2006.

Al-Musawi, Muhsin J. *Scheherazade in England*. Washington, DC: Three Continents Press, 1981.

Najjar, Fauzi M. "Islamic Fundamentalism and the Intellectuals: The Case of Naguib Mahfouz," *British Journal of Middle Eastern Studies* 25:1 (1998): 139–68.

Petry, Carl F. *Protectors or Praetorians? The Last Mamluk Sultans and Egypt's Waning as a Great Power*. Albany: State University of New York Press, 1994.

Qāsim, 'Abd al-Ḥakīm. *Ayyām al-insān al-sab'ah*. 1969; English translation: *The Seven Days of Man*, trans. Joseph Norment Bell. Cairo: GEBO, 1989.

Quṭb, Sayyid. *Child from the Village*. Tran. and ed. John Calvert and William Shepard. Syracuse, NY: Syracuse University Press, 2004.

Ricouer, Paul. *The Critique of Religion and the Language of Faith*, trans. R. Bradley DeFord. New York: Union Theological Seminary, 1971.

Said, Edward. *Reflections on Exile*. Cambridge, MA: Harvard University Press, 2000.

Sāliḥl, Ṭayyib. *The Wedding of Zein*, trans. Denys Johnson-Davies. Portsmouth, NH: Heinemann, 1968.

Al-Samman, Hannadi. "Out of the Closet: Representation of Homosexuals and Lesbians in Modern Arabic Literature," *Journal of Arabic Literature* 39:2 (2008): 258–98.

Al-Sayyid, Maḥmūd Aḥmad. *Jalāl wa Khālid*. 1928; *Al 'māl al-Kāmila*. Baghdad: Wizārat al-thaqāfah, 1978.

Schimmel, Annmarie. *Mystical Dimensions of Islam*. Chapel Hill: University of North Carolina Press, 1975.

Sharabi, Hisham. "Islam and Modernization in the Arab World," in *Modernization of the Arab World*, ed. J. H. Thompson and Robert D. Reischauer. Princeton, NJ: D. Van Nostrand, 1966.

Sharārah, 'Abd al-Laṭīf. *Ma'ārik Adabiyyah*. Beirut: Dār al-'lm lil-Malāyīn, 1984.

Al-Sharqāwī, 'Abd al-Raḥmān. *Muḥammad Rasūl al-Ḥuriyyah* (Muḥammad the Messenger of Freedom). Cairo: 'Alam al-Kutub, 1962.

Al Sharqāwī 'Abd al Raḥman. Ibn *Taymiyyah: Al Faqīh al Mu 'adhdhab Ibn Taymiyyah: The Suffering Jurist*. Cairo: Dār al-Mawqif al-'Arabī, 1983.

Sheppard, William E. "Muḥammad Sa'īd al-'Ashmāwī and the Application of the Shari'ah in Egypt," *International Journal of Middle East Studies*, 28 (1996): 39–58.

Shinnāwī, Kāmil. *Alladhīna Aḥsabbū Mayy wa Ubīrīt Jamīlah* (Those Who Loved Mayy and the Opera of Jamīlah). Cairo: Dār al-Ma'ārif, 1972.

Smith, Charles. "The 'Crisis of Orientalism': The Shift of Egyptian Intellectuals to Islamic Subjects in the 1930s," *International Journal of Middle East Studies* 4 (1973): 382–410.

Soage, Ana Belén. "Shaykh Yūsuf al-Qaradawi: Portrait of a Leading Islamic Cleric," *MERIA* 12:1 (2008): 1–26.

Al-Ṭahṭāwī, Rifā'ah Rāfi'. *Takhlīṣ al-ibrīz fi talkhīṣ Barīẓ*. English translation: *Imam in Paris: An Account of a Stay in France by an Egyptian Cleric, 1826–31*. London: Al-Saqi, 2004.

Thompson, John B. Editor's Introduction, in *Language and Symbolic Power*, by Pierre Bourdieu. Trans. Matthew Adamson. Cambridge, MA: Harvard University Press, 1991.

Tracy, H. L. "The Epic Tradition," *The Classical Journal* 42:2 (1946): 78–81.

White, Hayden. "The Value of Narrativity in the Representation of Reality," *Critical Inquiry* 7:1 (1980): 5–27.

Zangana, Haifa. *Women on a Journey between Baghdad and London*, trans. Judy Cumberbatch. Austin: Center for Middle Eastern Studies at the University of Texas at Austin, 2007.

Index

About the Author

Muhsin J. Al-Musawi is professor of Arabic and comparative studies at Columbia University. He has taught at the American University of Sharjah and taught at a number of Universities in North Africa and the Middle East. He has published many books in English and Arabic, including *Scheherazade in England*; *Anglo-Orient*; *The Postcolonial Arabic Novel*; *Arabic Poetry: Trajectories of Modernity and Tradition*; *Reading Iraq: Culture and Power in Conflict*; and *Islam on the Street: The Islamic Dynamic in Literary Production*, as well as four novels. He is the editor of the *Journal of Arabic Literature* and the recipient of many awards, including the prestigious Owais Award in literary criticism.